Interpreting Bone Lesions and Pathology for Forensic Practice

Interpreting Bone Lesions and Pathology for Forensic Practice

Lucie Biehler-Gomez

Cristina Cattaneo

ELSEVIER

ACADEMIC PRESS

An imprint of Elsevier

Academic Press is an imprint of Elsevier
125 London Wall, London EC2Y 5AS, United Kingdom
525 B Street, Suite 1650, San Diego, CA 92101, United States
50 Hampshire Street, 5th Floor, Cambridge, MA 02139, United States
The Boulevard, Langford Lane, Kidlington, Oxford OX5 1GB, United Kingdom

British Library Cataloguing-in-Publication Data
A catalogue record for this book is available from the British Library

Library of Congress Cataloging-in-Publication Data
A catalog record for this book is available from the Library of Congress

ISBN: 978-0-323-85162-6

For Information on all Academic Press publications
visit our website at https://www.elsevier.com/books-and-journals

Publisher: Stacy Masucci
Acquisitions Editor: Elizabeth Brown
Editorial Project Manager: Mariana L. Kuhl
Production Project Manager: Maria Bernard
Cover Designer: Miles Hitchen

Typeset by MPS Limited, Chennai, India

CONTENTS

ABOUT THE AUTHORS

Lucie Biehler-Gomez, PhD, is postdoctoral research fellow in bioarchaeology and forensic anthropology at the Laboratory of Forensic Anthropology and Odontology (LABANOF), University of Milan, Italy. She obtained her BSc at the Université Lumière Lyon 2 (France) in 2014 finishing her degree with a year abroad at the University of California Davis, CA, United States, her MSc in 2016 at the Faculty of Medicine, Université de Lorraine Nancy, France and in 2020 her PhD at the Università degli studi di Milano (Italy). Her research emphasis is on the recognition and diagnosis of bone disease, in particular based on the modern and documented CAL Milano Cemetery Skeletal Collection of LABANOF. She wrote several chapters, published over 15 research articles in international journals and is currently a Reviewer for the journal Forensic Science International. In 2020, she was awarded the L'Oréal-UNESCO *For Women in Science* Fellowship (Italian edition).

Cristina Cattaneo, BSc MA, MD, PhD, forensic pathologist and anthropologist, is currently Full Professor of Legal Medicine at the Faculty of Medicine and Professor of Anthropology for the Faculties of Sciences and Humanities of the Università degli Studi di Milano, Italy and Director of LABANOF, Laboratorio di Antropologia e Odontologia Forense and of CAL (Collezione Antropologica Labanof). She is a forensic expert for various courts in Italy and occasionally in Europe, President of Forensic Anthropology Society of Europe (FASE), member of the Swiss Disaster Victim Identification (DVI) team and co-Editor-in-Chief for the journal Forensic Science International. She has been actively involved with the Italian Ministry of Internal Affairs in the creation of a national database for unidentified human remains and has since 2014 been the medicolegal coordinator for the Governmental Office of the Commissioner for Missing Persons for the identification of dead migrants. She also coordinates the medicolegal activities on victims of abuse, maltreatment, torture, and on unaccompanied minors in Milano.

ABOUT THE CONTRIBUTORS

Annalisa Cappella, PhD, is a biologist and forensic anthropologist with a PhD in Morphological Sciences, and Adjunct Professor in Human Anatomy at the University of Milan, Italy. She works at LABANOF on identification, injury analysis, and histology. She is a Fulbright Scholar with research on the identification of dead migrants. She participated as anthropologist in the medical forensic activities in Melilli (SR) on the victims of the April 18th, 2015 shipwreck.

Danilo De Angelis, DDS, PhD, forensic odontologist at LABANOF (Laboratory of Forensic Anthropology and Odontology of the University of Milan), graduated in Dentistry and obtained his PhD in Legal Medicine. First researcher, he is now Associate Professor of Legal Medicine at the University of Milan. He teaches Legal Medicine and Forensic Odontology in various undergraduate and postgraduate courses. In addition to teaching, he deals with research and consultancy, especially in the field of personal identification (both corpses and living), age estimation, bite marks, and other issues related to odontology and malpractice and liability within dentistry. Author and coauthor of many scientific articles and book chapters, he is a speaker at international forensic science conferences. He is also Assistant Editor for the journal Forensic Science International.

Domenico Di Candia, PhD, is a Forensic Toxicologist of the Section of Legal Medicine of Milan. Since 2003, his research has been focused on the detection and dosage of substances of toxicological interest of cadaveric origin or collected from the crime scene. Recently, he has extended his research interests to toxicology on dry bone. He teaches a Forensic Toxicology course at the School of Specialization in Legal Medicine of the University of Milan.

Daniele Maria Gibelli, MD, PhD, is a physician with specialization in Legal Medicine and PhD in Morphological Sciences. Since 2014 he has been a researcher in Human Anatomy in the Department of Biomedical Sciences for Health – University of Milan, Italy. Since

2020 he is an associate professor in Human Anatomy. His areas of expertise include 3D surface acquisition (laser scanner and stereophotogrammetry) and 3D image elaboration for documentation and analysis of faces and osteological and dental material, 3D segmentation from CT-scan and NMR, the validation of novel techniques for 3D acquisition and assessment of their reliability in the analysis of facial anatomy. The specific topics include the study of facial morphology in acquired and genetic pathologies, of facial mimicry in healthy subjects and patients affected by facial nerve palsy, the analysis of anatomical variants of the cranium (with applications to otolaryngology, odontology, maxillofacial and aesthetic surgery, neurology, anthropology), the assessment of skeletal morphology for the diagnosis of sex, age estimation, diagnosis of ancestry, and the research in the field of anatomical individuality. Moreover, he deals with history of anatomy and the practice of anatomical dissection. He is author of more than 120 articles published on peer-reviewed impacted journals.

Gaia Giordano, MS, is a molecular biologist and research intern at the LABANOF. Bachelor (2017) and Master (2020) theses were carried out at the LABANOF, performing paleopathological and toxicological studies. Her recent research focuses on toxicological analyses on alternative matrices, mostly human bones. She has coauthored several articles.

Emanuela Maderna, PhD, obtained her degree in Biological Science in 2002 at the Università degli Studi di Milano. From 2007 to 2012, she was a trainee in Clinical Pathology at the Università degli Studi del Piemonte Orientale "Amedeo Avogadro" Facoltà di Medicina e Chirurgia. Since 2003, she is a Senior Researcher at the laboratory of Neuropathology, Division of Neurology and Neuropathology "Carlo Besta" Neurological Institute, Milan, Italy. Her main activities include research assistant and diagnostic activities in neurodegenerative disease and brain tumors. She possesses expertise skills in histological and immunohistochemical analysis of human tissues and biochemical analysis of biological fluid (ELISA, chemiluminescence and Western Blot), light microscopy, and electron microscopy.

Mirko Mattia, MA, archaeologist and PhD fellow of the University of Milan, deals with skeletal recovery methodologies and the anthropological study of ancient Italian populations. He actively collaborates in the MiAntropo (diachronic study of the ancient Milanese people from Roman times to the present day) and Ca' Granda (recovery and analysis of the skeletal population of the most important hospital in Milan) projects.

Debora Mazzarelli, BSc, is a forensic anthropologist with a background in the field of cultural heritage; she works at LABANOF and deals in particular with unidentified bodies, in particular migrants. She is an expert in identification techniques, archaeology, and trace analysis on bone, as well as an expert for courts in forensic anthropology. She participated in the forensic medical activities in Melilli (SR) on the victims of the shipwreck of April 18th, 2015 and in the identification of the victims of the Lampedusa disaster in October 2013. She is currently coordinating the anthropological activities on the victims of Italian shipwrecks at LABANOF with funding from the Isacchi Samaia Foundation. For LABANOF, she especially coordinates the anthropological activities on domestic unidentified bodies of the city of Milano.

Carmelo Messina, MD, Assistant Professor of Radiology at the University of Milan, works as full radiologist at the Department of Diagnostic and Interventional Radiology, IRCCS Orthopedic Institute Galeazzi, Milan. His clinical and research activity is dedicated to the imaging of musculoskeletal system, with a focus on bone injuries and metabolic bone diseases.

Pasquale Poppa, PhD, has been working at LABANOF since 2002 and deals with forensic anthropological methodologies for the inspection, survey, and geoarchaelogical excavation of human remains in criminal and archaeological contexts. His research interests include forensic taphonomy and personal identification of the living and the dead. He actively collaborates in the MiAntropo, Ca' Granda, and mass disaster projects of LABANOF.

Davide Porta, BSc, is a biologist and the technical manager of LABANOF (Laboratory of Forensic Anthropology and Odontology), Department of Biomedical Sciences for Health, University of Milan, Italy as well as a technical consultant for the Public Prosecutor at various Courts of Northern Italy on the subject of personal identification. His fields of study include fingerprinting methods, facial reconstruction, and the study of bone lesions. He is a lecturer of forensic anthropology in the Master of Bioarchaeology, Paleopathology, and Forensic Anthropology, organized by the Universities of Pisa, Bologna, and Milan. He also collaborates in the preparation of museum exhibitions for archaeological and historical sections.

Francesco Sardanelli, MD, PhD, is a full professor of Radiology and director of the Postgraduate School in Radiodiagnostics at the Università degli Studi di Milano, chief of the Unit of Radiology at the Research Hospital Policlinico San Donato. His main interests are evidence-based radiology, breast and cardiovascular imaging.

FOREWORD

As a forensic anthropologist for 23 years at the Central Identification Laboratory (CIL) in Hawaii, the world's largest skeletal identification laboratory, it should come as no surprise that I am an avid reader of forensics, especially as it relates to the human skeleton. My personal journey from novice to board-certified forensic anthropologist has been one of excitement, travel and adventure, enthusiasm, and an evolution in my thinking, skills, and expertise as a scientist.

I vividly recall my undergraduate years spent numbering and cataloging historical artifacts in the archeology laboratory in the Wren Building at The College of William and Mary in Virginia. Even more vivid was the first time I saw a human skeleton laid out anatomically on one of the examination tables. That was my first look inside the human body and an event that would forever change my world. Purely by accident, I had found my passion and stepped through a door into a world of scientific exploration and forensics that I could never turn away from.

One of my earliest memories as an aspiring anthropologist was analyzing few skeletons at William and Mary and a feeling of self-confidence that I somehow knew more about physical anthropology than I actually did. I drew this inaccurate conclusion based on the fact that Dr. Thomas D. Stewart (MD), a graduate of Johns Hopkins Medical School and one of physical anthropology's pioneers, had examined the very skeletons that I was reexamining. I will forever be embarrassed to admit that for a split second I was absolutely certain that my interpretation of some lesions and behavioral markers in the skeletons was correct and that Dr. Stewart's findings were wrong (I, of course, was the one who was wrong!). I am happy to say that as the years passed this feeling of confidence is something that I have occasionally seen in novice anthropologists and with which I can completely empathize. I am certainly not the first to say it, but it bears repeating that we are all students regardless of how much experience we have, how many skeletons we have examined, or how utterly confident we are that we have it right and that someone else has it wrong.

All of this brings me to Dr. Biehler-Gomez's and Dr. Cristina Cattaneo's "*Interpreting Bone Lesions and Pathology for Forensic Practice.*" This book is a culmination of many years of experience and expertise into the world of forensic anthropology and forensic medicine with a focus on bone disease and lesions. The authors, whom I worked with at the esteemed Laboratory of Forensic Anthropology and Odontology (LABANOF) in Milan, present a contemporary and multidisciplinary book highlighting the importance and role of recognizing, describing, and accurately interpreting bone disease in medicolegal cases, a topic that is often dealt with superficially, if at all. This book will no doubt help answer many medicolegal questions associated with the human skeleton and is a reference source that should be within a hands' reach in any medicolegal or human skeletal laboratory.

I applaud the authors for their vision and wish that I had a textbook such as this the day that I pondered Dr. Stewart's findings. My apologies, admiration, and a smile to Dr. Stewart, with whom I would later study under and a few years later would share a hallway in the department of anthropology at the Smithsonian Institution. Although 40 years have passed since anthropology first grabbed ahold of me, I still feel as though I am that young student captivated by seeing my first skeleton and seeking to answer its silent questions. I'm pleased to say that Dr. Biehler-Gomez's and Dr. Cattaneo's book will go a long way toward achieving that goal and that it will indeed have a special place on my desk.

Robert W. Mann, PhD, D-ABFA, F-CPP[1,2,3,4]

[1]Department of Anatomy, John A. Burns School of Medicine, University of Hawaii, Honolulu, United States, [2]Department of Pathology, John A. Burns School of Medicine, University of Hawaii, Honolulu, United States, [3]US Department of Defense Forensic Science Academy (FSA), Honolulu, United States, [4]Joint POW/MIA Accounting Command's Central Identification Laboratory (CIL), Honolulu, United States

FOREWORD

I welcome this book that discusses bone diseases from a forensic perspective, it fills an existing gap and is undoubtedly useful for forensic practitioners, in particular, forensic anthropologists. Over the 11 chapters, the authors go through a large number of diseases that can make a difference to solve forensic cases. From apparently small details which, after all, can tell a long story—the case of calcified residues of soft tissue disease—to more common and easy to diagnose pathologies (as it is the case of some diseases of the joints), this book has both a structure and organization, which makes it easy to find the help we need when doing a case. It covers a large range of diseases (e.g., infectious, degenerative, neoplastic) with the added value to approach some whose capacity to affect the skeletal system and be detected on dry bones may not be known to many readers. That is the case, for instance, of diabetes mellitus or pellagra. In this respect, this book is an important step forward showing us that the wealth of information that may be obtained from bones is considerable and that it can be revealed through the application of modern technologies and resorting to other disciplines such as imagiology and histology. In addition, this book is well-achieved since it emphasizes the truly interdisciplinary nature of reading bone lesions. The interpretation of bone lesions has to be done by interdisciplinary teams and the understanding of the effects of the pathologies in the daily lives, which could constitute key identity factors, is a complex task which also requires the inclusion of medical doctors. While medical practitioners are used to see the living and not dry bones, forensic anthropologists might be able to make a small bone fragment talk. It is that interdisciplinarity that can unlock the secrets of small bones or even soft tissue details and provide clues to solve the case.

This book is also full of good and didactic illustrations, the majority of them from the CAL Milano Cemetery Skeletal Collection, an amazing reference series which has been very well exploited in terms of lesions and pathologies, mainly by the first author who has been able to publish an impressive number of papers about different nosological entities. This book makes use of all of them, doing a state-of-the-art. In other words, the CAL (the anthropological collection of the LABANOF) is the research lab underneath this book, which provided identified cases of many of the diseases here discussed. The authors were then wise enough to detect, understand, and exploit the potential of such a true atlas of nowadays disorders. The first chapters give important clues and guidelines on how to approach a case and discuss terminology, where I would highlight the recommendation of not using the term "paleopathology" within forensic cases, which makes sense. The pragmatic and well-achieved boxes in all chapters also have to be detached since they function both as a sum up and a guideline. Two other chapters are worth mentioning: one about trauma, a central issue in forensic anthropology where key clues are provided to unravel what might have happened both in life and at the time of death; the other one is about pseudopathologies and taphonomic alterations which can truly mimic lesions and, consequently, constitutes a mandatory chapter in a book like this one. In the end, we have two major achievements: one is a chapter with practical cases where we can see the application of what was told until then and how important lesions and pathologies are to solve forensic cases. In other words, it works like a guide on how to apply all the knowledge gathered, answering the obvious question: "so what do we do with all that?" Finally, the authors go further and look to the future. They do not doubt that there is still a lot that can be done to unlock more secrets of the bones and they exemplify that with the synergies not yet fully exploited with toxicology.

This book proves how much we can learn with bones and how worthwhile it is to research to make them talk even more. The message is: don't ever give up talking with a bone.

Well done, Lucie and Cristina. Congratulations.

Eugénia Cunha, PhD
Laboratory of Forensic Anthropology, Centre for Functional Ecology – CFE,
Department of Life Sciences, University of Coimbra, Coimbra, Portugal

PREFACE

The study of bone pathology on dry bone has always been at the crossroads between anthropology and medicine. One can frequently hear osteologists sustain that medical doctors know nothing about dry bone and therefore cannot appropriately interpret bone pathology and, on the other hand, pathologists claim that anthropologists are not well acquainted enough with medicine to diagnose disease. The truth, as usual, lies in between, and both professions are needed. Furthermore, bone pathology has always been closely related and associated to paleopathology and the study of the past, which has created a bit of a bias in the evaluation of its actual potential for forensics.

This book stems largely and mainly from the PhD thesis of Dr. Lucie Biehler Gomez on the study of bone pathology in the known 20st–21st century skeletal collection Collezione Antropologica Labanof (CAL). To this we have added the contributions of anthropologists, pathologists, odontologists, and radiologists who have worked on forensic cases or research within or in collaboration with Laboratorio di Antropologia e Odontologia Forense of the University of Milan (LABANOF) in the past 25 years.

We are well aware that by no means can this text be exhaustive in educating and training in pathology on dry bone and have aimed at producing a user-friendly guide to a sound approach to the examination and interpretation of pathological lesions on bone particularly for forensic practice. We have therefore tried to steer clear of the ambiguity and tautological circularity of referring largely to ancient unknown specimens as certain examples of the osteological manifestations of disease, and have tried instead, where possible, to explain bone disease through diagnosed lesions on bone from known cases.

Along with a more classical and traditional approach to unraveling the mysteries behind signs on bones and their association to specific classes of disease (infectious, metabolic, neoplastic, and so on) mixed with a focus on pathologic manifestations from skeletons of individuals diagnosed with that specific disease and a perspective on more rarely treated topics (e.g., proliferative and osteolytic metastases), specific attention has been taken to explain how objective and very meticulous descriptions of lesions are fundamental before proceeding to what must be only a differential diagnosis—according to the strictest forensic approach. These teachings are then extrapolated to forensic scenarios, namely that of identification and of verifying maltreatment, torture, or physical abuse, with several examples of these applications on real forensic cases.

We hope that all those who approach this book will gain from the wealth of known collections and from the sharing of forensic cases and method, as well as appreciate the thrill and fascination of reconstructing life and death from bones.

Cristina Cattaneo and Lucie Biehler-Gomez

ACKNOWLEDGMENTS

We would like to acknowledge the contribution of Professor Charlotte Roberts and Professor Gérald Quatrehomme for having read and critically reviewed the PhD thesis this work stems from and for their helpful comments.

We express our deepest gratitude to Dr. Laurent Martrille and his team in Nancy (France) for their collaboration and support.

We thank and acknowledge Professor Chiarella Sforza and Professor Riccardo Zoia of the Department of Biomedical Sciences for Health of the *Università degli Studi di Milano.*

We would like to acknowledge and thank the *IRCCS Policlinico San Donato* and *Istituto Ortopedico Galeazzi* for allowing us to perform radiographic imaging of our skeletal material and for their collaboration.

We wish to acknowledge the municipality of Milano and in particular the personnel of the Morgue and Cimitero Maggiore, especially Dr. Maistri e Zuccotti, Ing. Massimo Borrelli, Mr. Mauro Marrapodi, Mr. Girolamo Facchini, Ing. Luigi Vigani, and Dr. Donatella Malloggi; of the Cimitero di Lambrate and Baggio, in particular Dr. Sandra Da Ros. We also wish to thank Dr. Luca D'auria for legal assistance.

Many thanks to the personnel of the ASL (*Azienda Sanitaria Locale*), Dr. Mariangela Autelitano, Dr. Antonio Vitello, and Dr. Gabriella Salvati.

We also acknowledge the *Soprintendenza Archeologia, Belle Arti e Paesaggio* of Milan and in particular Dr. Anna Maria Fedelli, as well as Dr. Paolo Maria Galimberti of the Foundation *IRCCS Ca' Granda, Ospedale Maggiore Policlinico.*

Finally, we want to thank all the students who contributed to cleaning and studying the osteological material and Professor Marco Grandi who started it all.

CHAPTER 1

The Study of Bone Disease: Principles and Application to Forensics

Lucie Biehler-Gomez and Cristina Cattaneo
LABANOF, Department of Biomedical Sciences for Health, University of Milan, Milan, Italy

The Potential of Bone Disease in Forensic Sciences

Terminology is fundamental in science. It allows us to communicate, understand, and discuss issues within a field, explain methodology, and divulge results. Scientific terminology is also intrinsically precise in order to provide unambiguous and detailed information. Each discipline uses standard terminology in order to permit exchanges between researchers and avoid misinterpretations. Accurate terminology is therefore necessary and of the utmost importance in scientific research and practice.

Traditionally, the study and diagnosis of bone lesions on skeletal remains is referred to as "paleopathology." However, this is a misguiding term which leads to the belief that its application is limited to archeological specimens. Paleopathology, formed of *paleo* = "ancient" and *pathology* = "the study of diseases," literally signifies "the study of ancient diseases or of diseases in the past." But what are these "ancient diseases"? Or why only in the past? Tuberculosis can be dated back thousands of years—which qualifies as "ancient"—but it is still prevalent today with an estimated 10 million new cases and 1.5 million deaths in 2018 according to the World Health Organization (WHO). Thus tuberculosis is most definitely not just ancient. Are we talking of diseases that are extinct or eradicated? Because that would represent a very small number of diseases. In its preface, one of the main manuals in paleopathology, *The Cambridge Encyclopedia of Human Paleopathology*, defines the discipline as "the study of disease in ancient populations by the examination of human remains" (Aufderheide and Rodríguez-Martín, 1998). Hence, the study of bone disease at times seems to be limited to archaeological specimens, or it seems to be conceptually separated from modern specimens. Why? Are modern remains not also affected by

Interpreting Bone Lesions and Pathology for Forensic Practice. DOI: https://doi.org/10.1016/B978-0-323-85162-6.00001-5

disease? Shouldn't pathology also apply to what is not "paleo," such as skeletons in forensic scenarios? If so, then why do we continue to refer to "paleopathology" when we are simply talking about bone disease?

In the forensic anthropology practice, just like in bioarchaeology, skeletal remains are the most valuable material at our disposal. Their examination is a long and detailed process because the smallest element can provide crucial clues to better understand the identity, life, and even death of the individual. An evident and striking sign as massive "holes" in a cranium would of course be investigated, but disease is not always this obvious on the skeleton. Pathological osseous lesions can be insidious, presenting as a reaction on the surface of the bone, a change within the bone or a concretion outside of the skeletal system; it can leave signs scattered across the skeleton or cause a unique lesion on a single bone. Bioarchaeologists are very mindful of signs of disease on skeletal remains and this should also be the case in forensic anthropology.

This leads to the heart of the question: Why study diseases on dry bone? Why should we care if the person had arthritis or suffered from malnutrition during childhood? How is that going to help in a forensic setting? We would argue that professional exactitude could be reason enough. Anthropologists are masters of osteology and superb investigators of dry bones. They are careful analysts of the smallest osseous details, even if broken, damaged, or burnt, and can reconstruct the life history of an individual or a lethal traumatic event in incredible detail where most people only see a pile of bones. If we can interpret the lesions and diagnose the disease, why not do it? But time and budget constraints are important factors limiting the analysis. As much as they would like to spend more time and money on additional analyses, forensic anthropologists work on a timeframe set by the justice system and sometimes on a limited budget. Why then should forensic scientists dedicate time to interpret bone lesions? The answer is simple: because disease is of forensic relevance.

A correct interpretation of bone disease can provide substantial information to the analysis of skeletal remains. First of all, it can provide a (tentative) diagnosis. Putting a name on the disease permits to identify it, clearly state its presence, at that time and on that person. Diseases produce symptoms and it is therefore possible that the person suffering from a specific disorder may have experienced one or more of its symptoms. Moreover, the person may have received treatment for his or her ailment. For instance, a prosthesis or a surgical intervention involving the skeletal system would be particularly useful in a forensic setting for personal identification. Second, the interpretation of the bone lesion itself can also give valuable information, including the disease process, its etiology, symptoms, pain, and/or disabilities caused by the lesion, thus providing specific details on the life and death of the individual and disease burden.

To answer the previous question, the interpretation of bone disease is of particular interest in forensic anthropology in two areas: for the construction of a generic identity and potentially even the identification of a specific identity. Indeed, one of the main objectives of the anthropological analysis of a skeletonized individual is the construction of a generic identity, commonly referred to in the discipline under the term "biological profile." The biological profile corresponds to a set of criteria determinable from skeletal remains after death but describing the individual during life. These criteria include the estimations of sex, age-at-death, anatomical variants, population affinity and stature, as well as the analysis of traumatic and/or pathological lesions. In forensic identification, the biological profile permits us to narrow the search among a missing persons list. While sex, age-at-death, and population affinity allow one to considerably reduce the list of possibilities in the identification of an unknown deceased, these criteria are generally not enough and additional descriptors are necessary to orient the search.

Imagine the mass catastrophe scenario of the crash of a large aircraft with on board 300 passengers. The victims include the passengers, the staff, and the pilot, for a total of 320 people. The plane is completely destroyed, the victims are reduced to burnt bone. In this "closed disaster"—that is, in an event resulting in the death of a more easily identifiable group of individuals—you have a list of the names of the passengers, staff, and pilot, but the individuals are no longer in their original seats on the plane, complicating their identification. For the purpose of this example, DNA analysis may not give the results one expected, perhaps because there are no close relatives or biological reference samples for some of the "missing." As a forensic anthropologist, your analysis of the skeleton currently under examination reveals a male, middle aged (30–40 years old), and European. Sex estimation may reduce the possible matches to half (so 160 possible individuals), age-at-death estimation and population affinity will also reduce the list of compatible passengers. Furthermore, dental analysis shows 32 perfect teeth and antemortem dental records have not been found, and fingerprint identification is out of the question. In such a case, you must find something to narrow down this list. What if there were lesions on the pelvic bones and lumbar vertebrae most likely caused by a metastatic solid cancer? Probably prostate. And what if the skeleton you are examining had a fracture on the proximal femur? Probably a pathologic fracture. The fracture was consolidated by a metal bar and two screws. Now, how many European men of 30–40 years are there with a prostate cancer metastasized to the bone and a pathologic fracture on the femur needing orthopedic surgical intervention on that list? Probably not many.

The bottom line of this convoluted example is that bone disease can help orient the search. Here, the diagnosis (although it is best to refer to a process of differential diagnosis) of a neoplastic disease and the surgical treatment of the fracture were given as an example of important clues for the biological profile, but bone disease can also provide information on ways of life and potential symptoms and disabilities. The purpose of the biological profile is not to reach a positive identification but to provide as much information on the individual as possible and as detailed as possible. As the estimation of population affinity and facial reconstruction are not always certain and unequivocal, the information relating to pathological conditions that the person could have suffered from must be interpreted as possible pieces of information within a larger mosaic. In fact, specifying that the person might be anemic or have a certain disease (even if it must always be clear that it is not a definitive diagnosis but a likely possibility within a larger process of differential diagnosis) is of extreme utility, so long as one tells the ultimate stakeholders how to cautiously use this information in the search for missing persons. Thus, bone disease holds an equal value to other criteria in the biological profile, such as the estimations of age-at-death, stature, and population affinity in the forensic practice.

The potential of bone disease is not limited to the biological profile in forensics. More rarely, the specific morphological features of a bone lesion can be compared to antemortem records (i.e., data concerning the missing person in life) and lead to a specific identity. Let's go back to our example of the air crash: by comparing the morphological characteristics of the osseous bone lesions interpreted as metastases on the pelvic bones and lumbar vertebrae, as well as the fracture of the femur, with antemortem imaging (such as CT or radiographs) obtained shortly before the flight, we can evidence points of correspondence in the shape, contour, and morphological details of the lesions between the images in a similar manner as dental profiles (De Angelis et al., 2007). Indeed, as skeletal features that distinguish one individual from another, pathological markers on bones can act as factors of individualization (Cunha, 2006). However, for this comparison to be valid, the time passed between antemortem and postmortem images must be relatively short as bone lesions can evolve with time and treatment (i.e., healing or worsening). Consequently, the study of bone disease has the potential to provide further postmortem data that, in combination with other personal descriptors, may be compared with antemortem information and result in a positive identification. In forensic identification, all details matter. It is important to remember that the fields of legal medicine and forensic anthropology are constituted of particular cases, and it is often the smallest details that make the difference.

Thus, terminology is fundamental, and the term "paleopathology" has prompted the idea that the study of bone disease is limited to archaeological contexts or, even worse, uses evidence from an unknown past to formulate diagnoses of bone disease. As a consequence, over the past decades in traditional anthropological literature, diseases have usually been incorporated in a non-systematic manner into the biological profile and sometimes skeptically approached as a possible contributor to personal identification, despite their large potential in the discipline. As more accurate terms, we propose to refer to the study of bone disease in skeletal remains instead of "paleopathology"; this terminology will be used throughout this book.

Principles of Bone Disease Diagnosis

A distinction between modern and ancient populations in bone disease has no sense as the same reasoning and methodology are used in both situations. Although diseases affecting humans, pathogenesis and our biological responses to disease may have changed over time, the diagnosis of bone disease will follow the same approach, whether the individual under analysis died in the 1st century BC or in the 21st century AD.

Nonetheless, several basic principles to bone disease should always be considered. First and foremost, as the material at our disposal consists of skeletal remains, we can only interpret diseases that are seen on dry bone. This implies that for many diseases, such as the flu and the common cold or even potentially lethal conditions like pneumonia and cholera, there is nothing the anthropologist can say as they do not affect bones. Only a small number of conditions have the potential to involve the skeletal system, but even those that can do not systematically affect all the individuals who have the disease. For instance, skeletal tuberculosis occurs in 1%–5% of all tuberculosis cases, so having tuberculosis does not mean that skeletal lesions will develop, restricting our possibility to read health in bones. Second, the skeleton can only react in a limited number of ways to a stimulus: with abnormal bone proliferation (osteoblastic activity) or abnormal bone loss (osteolysis)—abnormal bone shape and abnormal bone size are other skeletal markers of disease, but they are generally easily identifiable and attributable to specific conditions. This limited array of physiological response to insult leads to a considerable overlap of skeletal manifestations between bone disorders, rendering their diagnosis particularly challenging. Some patterns of lesions however are typical and even pathognomonic (in other words, specifically characteristic or distinctive of a single condition or group of conditions) of certain diseases (e.g., Pott's disease in tuberculosis) but normal variation in skeletal lesions of a given disease complicates the matter as not all disorders affect the skeleton in the same way. For instance, spinal involvement occurs in less than 1% of all patients with tuberculosis (Rezai et al., 1995). Consequently, in most cases, a certain diagnosis of disease cannot be ascertained and can only be narrowed down to a broad list of disorders that could be responsible for the lesions observed, or "differential diagnosis." The objective is therefore to construct a differential diagnosis as narrow and accurate as possible. And third, the living individual may have had more than one condition at the same time and so the bone lesions observed in a given skeleton may not be the result of a single disease. Comorbidity is an important bias that may alter the aspect and distribution of bone lesions, confusing the diagnosis.

Different frameworks may be used for the diagnosis of disease: the lesion-based approach, the direct measurement of a diagnostic parameter (e.g., bone mineral density and cortical thickness) or the direct identification of the causative microorganism (for infectious disease, e.g., DNA and biomolecular markers such as mycolic acids) (Mays, 2018). In spite of the efficiency of biomolecular methods, they are destructive and costly analyses subject to strict protocols that cannot be systematically applied to every skeleton. While they may complement macroscopic analyses, the lesion-based approach remains the foundation of the study of bone disease. This approach consists in the analysis of the morphology, position and distribution of the skeletal lesions by comparison with the clinical literature, while considering the basic biological profile of the individual (i.e., sex, age, and population affinity). Indeed, pathological conditions often favor specific subsets of the population; for example, metastatic solid cancers are more common in individuals over 40 years than in children and gout is 3 to 10 times more frequent in males than females. Hence, basic biological information on the individual may orient the diagnosis. Considering this information, the morphological aspect of bone lesions, their anatomical position on the bone and their pattern of distribution on the skeleton are interpreted by comparing them to clinical or previously published cases presenting the same evidence of disease. This intuitive approach working from the "known" to the "unknown" (Mays, 2018) assures a sound diagnosis of disease (Box 1.1).

Box 1.1 How to Approach Bone Lesions

Step 1: Make sure the bone abnormality is pathological: discard the possibility of an anatomical variation (also called non-metric or discrete traits) and of taphonomic alterations mimicking disease (see Chapter 10: The Challenge of Taphonomic Alterations).

Step 2: Describe the characteristic features of the bone abnormality (see Section "The Foundation: Describing Bone Disease") as they may give you a quantity of information useful for bone disease diagnosis.

Step 3: Draw the location of the lesions on a blank skeleton to understand the distribution of the bone abnormalities across the skeleton (see Section "The Foundation: Describing Bone Disease").

Step 4: If possible, take an X-ray of the bone and think of sampling for biomolecular and/or histological analyses.

Step 5: Consider the basic biological profile of the individual, that is, sex, age-at-death, and population affinity, as the prevalence of diseases is not even in the entire population.

Step 6: Compare this data, namely the features of the bone abnormalities (macroscopic and radiological), distribution of the lesions, and biological profile of the individual, with the clinical and dry bone literature.

Step 7: Formulate carefully your pathological interpretation (see Section "A Proposed Framework for Diagnosis in Forensic Anthropology") and always consider a differential diagnosis.

However, clinical standards and diagnostic criteria may not be adapted to the diagnosis of disease on dry bones because they were developed with a different aim: diagnosing, and treating living patients. As the main interest of medical practitioners lies within diagnosis, management, and treatment, skeletal manifestations of disease are incomplete for many disorders (Ortner, 2011; Ortner and Aufderheide, 1991, p. 6). In addition, many traits visible on radiographs cannot be appreciated on dry bone. For instance, matrix changes (with gradients of radiolucent and radiopaque areas) cannot be observed macroscopically and “moth-eaten,” “permeated,” “ill-defined,” and “sclerotic” margins are part of the standard radiological terminology and are not recognizable through visual examination of bone. Furthermore, when available, clinical data on skeletal manifestations of disease is dependent upon the sensitivity of the medical imaging technique. In fact, a change of about 40% in bone density is required to be discernible on plain radiographs (Ortner and Aufderheide, 1991, p. 8). While the morphological details of some lesions may not be completely and appropriately assessed by conventional radiography, others can virtually appear invisible. For instance, the clinical literature states that tuberculosis predilects vertebral bodies, but this may be due to the fact that the involvement of vertebral arches is rarely seen on radiographs (Ortner and Aufderheide, 1991, p. 6). New bone deposition on the medial diaphysis of tibiae is commonly observed by paleopathologists but rarely reported in clinical studies (Ortner and Aufderheide, 1991, p. 7). Another example is the periosteal reactions on the visceral surface of ribs undetected by radiography and routine autopsies (Mays, 2018) but clearly identifiable through naked eye observation and proved to be related to intrathoracic chronic infections and tuberculosis (Kelley and Micozzi, 1984; Matos and Santos, 2006; Roberts et al., 1994; Santos and Roberts, 2006). In fact, in a study of osteoarthritis on 24 knee joints, Rogers et al. (1990) report that abnormalities were detectable radiographically in only 2 specimens, whereas 16 showed evidence of macroscopic bone changes. Another study by Biehler-Gomez et al. (2019) compared the macroscopic morphology and radiographic visualization of osteolytic and proliferative bone lesions from 14 skeletons with antemortem clinical diagnoses of rheumatoid arthritis, diabetes, multiple myeloma, metastatic cancer, and osteomalacia. As a result, the study demonstrated that many lesions were not perceived on radiographs due to contrast, including periosteal reactions, osteolytic lesions, and spongiosclerosis. Additionally, medical imaging is performed in response to a patient's complaint and limited to a particular anatomical area, suggesting that "the total pattern of skeletal involvement in orthopedic diseases may not be well known" (Ortner and Aufderheide, 1991, p. 8). Sense of position and distribution are essential in the macroscopic study of bone disease as the limited array of skeletal physiological response to insult may overlap between diseases and this information may be crucial in distinguishing them.

The Foundation: Describing Bone Disease

The first stage in the study of bone disease, before even thinking of diagnosis, consists in the careful and precise recording of pathological bone abnormalities (e.g., see Fig. 1.1). This stage is the most important one. The diagnosis of the condition is secondary as it may be implemented by other techniques and performed even without the skeleton within reach. Nonetheless, one would lose tremendous precious time by not following a simple yet crucial exercise: a meticulous recording and description of pathological bone abnormalities. In fact, the description of bone disease should be clear and objective so that, just by reading it, a person can understand exactly where the bone lesion is

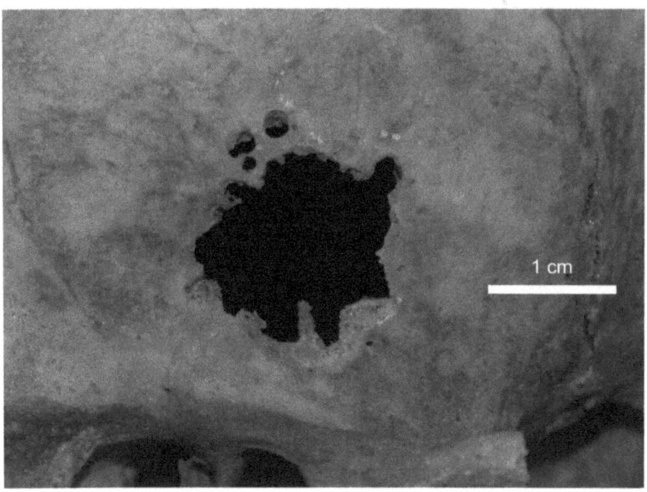

Figure 1.1 Example of a bone lesion description. Squama of the right temporal bone, circa 2 cm posterior to the coronal suture and 1 cm above the external auditory meatus, circular area of loss of bone substance of about 15 mm maximum in diameter. The lesion presents denticulated margins with absence of visible bone apposition. Skeleton #459 of the CAL Milano Cemetery Skeletal Collection with a clinical diagnosis of breast carcinoma.

and what it looks like—the main elements needed for a diagnosis. If you have a limited time to examine a skeleton (which is more than likely), you cannot afford to miss a detail on a bone lesion because when the body or skeleton is given back to the family, you will not be able to go back a second time to make sure of what you wrote in your notes. So, this stage must be both methodical and thorough.

Step 1: Location, location, location

Each bone lesion, whether it is a solitary lesion (i.e., only one lesion on the skeleton) or one of multiple bone lesions, should be first precisely anatomically located.

It is not enough to say that there is a lesion on the femur. Where on the femur? Are we talking of the diaphysis, the metaphysis, or the epiphysis? Be precise. Do you mean the left or the right femur? Use anatomical topographical terms (i.e., proximal, distal, anterior, posterior, medial, lateral, dorsal, palmar, and plantar) and planes (i.e., sagittal, transverse, and coronal) as well as anatomical landmarks (i.e., anatomical bone features). Mention the bones by name (e.g., the pelvis and cranium are not bones). Imagine that another person, without access to any photographs of the lesion, should be able to position it exactly by your description. Now that we know where the lesion is on the bone, where is it *within* the bone? On the cortical surface of the bone, the subcortical area, in the trabecular bone structure, or in the medullary cavity? Be mindful of anatomical terms. For instance, for the cranium we refer to the external and internal tables and the diploe.

This step will permit the understanding of the position of each lesion on the bone but also the visualization of the distribution of bone lesions. Remember that some diseases have specific characteristics. Is the lesion only bilateral or also symmetrical? Count the lesions. Are they all on the same side? This is particularly useful for trauma: can you understand the traumatic event that occurred?

To make sure that you do this exercise correctly, imagine that you are presented with the drawing of a blank skeleton. You do not know the skeleton or have any photographic support; you can only read the description of the location of the lesions in your notes. Are you able to draw the lesions in their exact anatomical location with their exact characteristics?

Step 2: Morphological Details Using Standard Terminology

Describe the lesions but do it methodically and using standard terminology. First, what type of abnormality are you observing? Define the character of the lesion: is it an abnormal bone resorption (i.e., an osteolytic lesion) or an abnormal bone formation (i.e., a proliferative bone lesion or osteoblastic lesion). Actually, some forensic practitioners prefer to describe the lesion as objectively as possible. If we use the term "osteolytic area" to characterize a "hole" we are already suggesting an active vital process—whereas we may be wrong and actually be looking at something taphonomic. The term "osteolytic" is for the most rigid scientists already an interpretation. Hence European academics prefer to use the terms "loss of substance," instead of "cavity" or "hole"; "discontinuation" or "break in continuity of the tissue" instead of "fracture"; and "excess" or "exuberance of bone tissue" instead of "proliferation."

Second, describe the morphological features of the lesion. If it is a bone resorption, is it bone porosity, borings, or a larger lesion? Specify even further. Is the osteolytic activity concentrated in the cortical and subcortical areas or is the resorption more important in the trabecular structure? This information allows you to understand where the lesion started, its progression and severity. Describe the margins: are they remodeled or not? If it is bone formation, is it a periosteal bone deposition, a thickening of the existing trabeculae or an endosteal bone deposition? Specify the type of bone: is it woven non-remodeled new bone or lamellar and remodeled bone? Is it a spiculated periosteal reaction? This information will provide information on the disease etiology, process, rapidity, and aggressivity. Standard terminology allows researchers to use a comparable vocabulary understood by all. A "hole" in a bone is not a scientific description and be careful of not using terms that may cause confusion: for example, a "foramen" defines an anatomical feature, not a pathological abnormality.

Finally, measure the lesions and document them photographically. If possible, implement with other imaging techniques (e.g., radiographs, CT). If this is the last time you see the skeleton, your notes and the photographs will be the only documentation you will be left with (Box 1.2).

Standard terminology for a general description of bone lesion can be found in the *Nomenclature in Paleopathology* (Manchester et al., 2016), one of the most important works in the discipline, as well as in

Box 1.2 How to Describe Bone Lesions

Step 1: Locate the bone abnormalities: name the bones and the precise anatomical locations of the lesions (use directional terms and planes as well as anatomical terms and landmarks); be as precise as possible with positionings; for example, how many millimeter anterior to the bregma and/or lateral?

Step 2: Describe the character of the lesion: discontinuity, abnormal bone resorption (loss of bone substance), abnormal bone formation/bone excess, abnormal bone shape, or abnormal bone size.

Step 3: Describe the bone abnormality: the degree of bone resorption and the margins of the lesion, the type of abnormal bone formation, and/or the abnormal shape or size.

Step 4: Describe meticulously (or draw) the distribution of bone lesions across the skeleton.

Step 5: Measure the lesions and document them with photographs. Photographs should be taken from several angles, with a metric reference and an object (e.g., a coin) which can help correct for morphological artefacts and warping.

guidelines for the recording of pathological bone abnormalities (Brickley and McKinley, 2004; Buikstra and Ubelaker, 1994; Mitchell and Brickley, 2017). In addition, excellent articles have endeavored to standardize the terminology used to describe bone lesions (Buikstra et al., 2017; Grauer, 2008; Klaus, 2017; Lovell, 2000; Mays, 2018; Miller et al., 1996; Ortner, 2012, 2003, chap. 4; Ragsdale et al., 2018; Rose et al., 1991).

A correct and precise description of bone lesions using comparable terminology will not only permit a detailed archiving of bone lesions but will also allow for an accurate diagnosis on dry bone, consistency between practitioners and the evaluation of proposed diagnoses by other researchers (Biehler-Gomez et al., 2020). Descriptors are potent tools for the understanding of the disease process. Osteoblastic activity in a bone resorptive lesion is evidence of a healing mechanism. In osteolytic lesions (once the loss of substance has been correctly interpreted in a second stage as an active reaction of bone), well-defined remodeled margins are indicative of a slow and chronic process. By opposition, poorly defined margins (in other words, without bone remodeling) suggest a rapid and aggressive process (Lovell, 2000; Ortner, 2012). Similarly, in osteoblastic lesions, woven bone (i.e., poorly organized porous fiber bone) is the result of a very rapid and recent bone formation. Indeed, woven bone remodels overtime into smooth, organized, and dense compact bone, called "lamellar bone." The presence of lamellar bone deposition designates a chronic and relatively slow process (Lovell, 2000; Ortner, 2012). Finally, projecting spicules of bone reveal a very rapid and aggressive process of bone formation (Lovell, 2000; Ragsdale et al., 2018).

Consequently, a correct and precise description of bone abnormalities can provide many details on the disease process and may considerably orient etiology and should therefore be carefully and meticulously considered.

A Proposed Framework for Diagnosis in Forensic Anthropology

Once the lesions are carefully described and considering the biological profile of the individual, a differential diagnosis can be formulated. This encompasses all the disorders and diseases that may have caused the observed lesions. Importantly, linguistic exactitude, required during the description of bones lesions, is also demanded in the differential diagnosis, and in particular, with regard to the level of confidence placed on the diagnosis.

Many fields of work have created specific classifications applicable to their practice for the standardization of diagnosis, including Adam's classification for the evaluation of suspected sexual abuse in children (Adams et al., 2018) and the standard terminology of the *Istanbul Protocol Manual on the Effective Investigation and Documentation of Torture and Other Cruel, Inhuman or Degrading Treatment or Punishment* (United Nations, 2004) to evaluate physical evidence of torture. In a similar approach, Appleby et al. (2015) proposed an adaptation of the Istanbul Protocol used in forensic sciences to indicate the degree of certainty of the diagnosis of trauma suffered during torture, for its application in the formulation of the certainty of a pathological diagnosis in anthropology.

The modified framework is as follows (Appleby et al., 2015):

- *Not consistent:* the lesion could not have been caused by the condition(s) described;

- *Consistent with:* the lesion could have been caused by the condition (s) described, but it is non-specific and there are many other possible causes;
- *Highly consistent:* the lesion could have been caused by the condition(s) described, and there are few other possible causes;
- *Typical of:* the lesion is usually found with this type of condition(s), but there are other possible causes;
- *Diagnostic of:* the lesion could not have been caused in any way other than by the condition(s) described (i.e., it is pathognomonic).

The application of this framework in the formulation of the degree of certainty of a diagnosis in forensic anthropology would increase consistency and reliability in dry bone diagnoses among practitioners, which is why we recommend it.

Known Collections: the Way Forward?

Manuals of paleopathology (Aufderheide and Rodríguez-Martín, 1998; Buikstra, 2019; Grauer, 2012; Mann and Hunt, 2005; Ortner, 2003; Pinhasi and Mays, 2008; Steinbock, 1976; Waldron, 2008; Zimmerman and Kelley, 1982) have accompanied and guided both novice and advanced researchers in the understanding and diagnosis of diseases on archaeological remains. These manuals are based to a greater (Zimmerman and Kelley, 1982) or lesser (Ortner, 2003) extent on established pathological museum collections and osteological collections around the globe (Mays, 2018), and on the long experience of the authors with bone pathology.

Unfortunately, most of the paleopathological literature is based on archaeological specimens. Thus the use of this material for the comparative diagnosis of an unknown skeleton (either archaeological or forensic) poses the question of the reliability of the initial diagnosis when it was not confirmed by direct identification of the causative microorganism or pathogenetic process, which, in other words, corresponds to the limitations and biases inherent to the lesion-based approach in the diagnosis of disease. These biases include the capacity of the disease to affect bones and its variability in pattern of affection, the potential non-linearity of the pathogenesis and pathological lesions through time (i.e., diseases may have become extinct (Meyer et al., 2002) or appeared later in time, pathogenesis may have evolved and produced different lesions in past populations (Grauer, 2012, p. 5), and our biological response to these disorders may not be the same as it was hundreds of years ago (Ortner, 2011)), the challenges of comorbidity and pitfalls of taphonomy, the limits of the clinical literature as a support for diagnosis on dry bone and the preservation of the material available for analysis (Grauer, 2012; Mays, 2018; Ortner, 2011). Consequently, the use of archaeological specimens as support for diagnosis of bone disease entails crucial limitations that may bias the diagnosis of disease in an unknown skeleton, which is tautological and sometimes typical of "paleopathology."

Consequently, much of the present knowledge on bone disease has been acquired from archaeological skeletons or medical literature, both of which present limitations for the diagnosis of bone disease on dry bone. In the former, the criteria for performing a differential diagnosis are tautological—diagnostic criteria frequently come from cases where the disease was unknown but inferred from somewhat hazy literature on the disease. Alternatively, while epidemiology, etiology, pathogenesis, and clinical manifestations will always be within the remit of clinical medicine, the distribution, and the exact morphology of lesions is inadequately answered by the latter, as many lesions go unperceived on radiographs and the presence of soft tissue may alter the characteristics of bone lesions visible on X-rays (Biehler-Gomez et al., 2019; Mays, 2018; Ortner and Aufderheide, 1991, pp. 6–8). To uphold the standards of the forensic field, the interpretation of signs and the differential diagnosis must be performed according to the clinical literature and known dry bone collections.

Known collections, or identified osteological collections, have become the backbone of the discipline of forensic anthropology. Their known data have made them ideal support for the development and testing of anthropological estimation techniques (Cappella et al., 2017; Marlow and Pastor, 2011; Martrille et al., 2007; Selliah et al., 2020), the development of population-specific methods (Garvin et al., 2014; Gocha et al., 2015), the analysis of secular change (Jantz and Jantz, 1999, 2016; Manthey et al., 2017; Spradley et al., 2016) and many methods for sex (Klales et al., 2012; Phenice, 1969), age (Brooks and Suchey, 1990; Iscan and Loth, 1986; Lovejoy et al., 1985; Meindl and Lovejoy, 1985; Rougé-Maillart et al., 2009), stature (Simmons et al., 1990; Trotter and Gleser, 1952), and ancestry (Navega et al., 2015) estimations were developed based on known collections.

The assemblage of known osteological collections started in the beginning of the 20th century with the Hamann–Todd (United States) (Rothschild and Rothschild, 1995), Terry (United States) (Hunt and Albanese, 2005), Raymond A. Dart (South Africa) (Dayal et al., 2009), and Huntington (United States) (Jantz and Jantz, 1999) collections constituted of cadaver-derived human skeletons and later developed around the globe (Ubelaker, 2014) (Fig. 1.2) with the 21st century Identified Skeletal Collection in Coimbra (Portugal) (Ferreira et al., 2014), the Luís Lopes Collection in Lisbon (Portugal) (Cardoso, 2006), the Athens Collection in Athens (Greece) (Eliopoulos et al., 2007), the Granada Osteological Collection of Identified Infants and Young Children in Granada (Spain) (Alemán et al., 2012), the UAB Identified Skeletal Collection in Barcelona (Spain) (Rissech and Steadman, 2011), the Sassari Collection in Bologna (Italy) (Hens et al., 2008), the Tedeschi Collection in Padua (Italy) (Carrara et al., 2018), the CAL Milano Cemetery Skeletal Collection in Milan (Italy) (Cattaneo et al., 2018), the Scheuer Juvenile Skeletal Collection in Dundee (Scotland) (Scheuer and Black, 2004), the Human Skeletal Identified Collection of Modern Colombian Population in Bogota (Colombia) (Sanabria-Medina et al., 2016), and the Pretoria Bone Collection in Pretoria (South Africa) (L'Abbé et al., 2005).

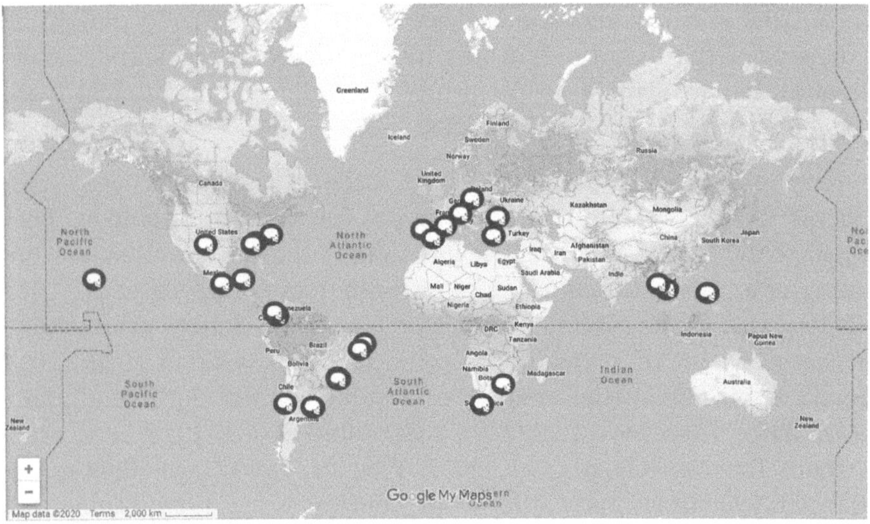

Figure 1.2 Map of modern identified osteological collections around the globe (i.e., comprised of individuals born after 1920, for whom age-at-death and sex are known). From http://forensicanthropology.eu/osteological-collections/.

Documentation in reference collections can include sex, age-at-death, population affinity, occupation, pathological conditions, and cause of death. The documentation available in each known collection will determine its potential use (e.g., an osteological collection with documented demographic information is suitable for studies on anthropological estimation techniques) and some collections have information on pathological conditions. The study of these documented skeletons with recorded diseases can provide useful information on lesion morphologies and patterns of skeletal involvement for the comparative diagnosis of further forensic anthropology cases. In addition to clinical literature, these studies illustrate and document macroscopic skeletal involvement in specific pathological conditions. The main issue with archaeological specimens is that a certain diagnosis is frequently impossible. By opposition, specimens from known collections constitute a direct model for macroscopic comparison, given that the diagnosis is ascertained and known. This concurs with Hershkovitz et al. (1998) observation: "As the life history of most archeologically derived skeletons is not usually available, information derived from clinically diagnosed cases has the potential to transform speculation into sound, data-based diagnosis."

Nonetheless, and as with any other method of research, comparative diagnoses based on known collections can also present biases and limitations that must be acknowledged (Mays, 2018). First, the presence of a pathological condition may not systematically result in bone lesions and cause of death is not necessarily cause of lesion. Therefore the associated data, while indicative and helpful, must still be considered with care and perspective in the analysis of the skeletal lesions. Second, the question of the reliability of the diagnosis remains when it was not assessed by modern medical standards and so details of diagnostic methods are of crucial importance. As our understanding of etiologies and pathogenesis considerably increased over the past century, so did our recognition, classification, and diagnosis of diseases. In fact, the 2018 WHO International Classification of Diseases (ICD-11) repertories around 55,000 injuries, diseases, and causes of death (World Health Organization, 2018). Third, while individuals often have only one condition reported in their documentation, they may have had multiple conditions during life which may bias the interpretation of lesions (Brickley and Ives, 2010). Fourth, the argument in paleopathology that the introduction of antibiotics and modern medical treatment influences the presence, frequency, and aspect of lesions in individuals who died in the postantibiotic era (as they may have received treatment), constitutes a bias for the comparison and diagnosis of conditions in archaeological specimens (preantibiotic era and so unaltered by treatment). However, the idea that preantibiotic specimens represent authentic pathological cases, unaltered by modern medicine, presupposes that individuals in the past either did not resort to medical treatments or that past medicine was perfectly ineffective on the etiology and aspect of bone lesions (in either healing or worsening the lesions). If reasoning is not enough to suggest that this postulate constitutes a profound bias in the study of bone disease, examples have also shown this to be untrue: for instance, we know of mercury used as a treatment of syphilis in the past; while the efficiency of this treatment in the survival of the individual remains unclear (Zuckerman, 2016), we do know it to be responsible for abnormalities in the development of permanent teeth in infants (Hutchinson, 1887), as well as dental defects referred to as "mercurial teeth" (Ioannou et al., 2016), and Ortner (2003, p. 279) reported that the treatment with mercury exacerbated the extent and severity of bone lesions, exceeding classic manifestations of the disease. Thus just as we cannot ascertain that individuals did not resort to some treatment in the preantibiotic era, we cannot assume that preantibiotic specimens exhibit authentic signs of disease untouched by treatment. As Ortner concludes "At the very least, the implication is that we need to be very careful before assuming that a preantibiotic anatomical case of any skeletal disease is typical of the natural, untreated expression of the disease. Throughout human history medical practitioners used various substances to treat their patients and some of these treatments could easily have had adverse effects on the patients that could affect the skeletal manifestations." In addition, this reasoning is not applicable to forensic cases (generally postantibiotic era) and modern examples might prove insightful as the manifestations of disease evolve with treatment. Fifth, the state of preservation and completeness of the skeletons in osteological collections (especially if not cadaver-derived) may constitute an important factor affecting the reliability of comparative diagnoses as it may impact the recovery and recognition of pathological lesions as well as the understanding of skeletal involvement. This state of preservation of the skeletal remains results from the conditions of conservation of the skeletal assemblages in museums, laboratories, or universities, the method of recovery of the skeletons and the potential effect of taphonomic alterations. Finally, pathological museums present a particular situation as their sample selection strategies consisted in collecting the most unusual pathological cases. As a result, their specimens tend to present more severe and extreme expressions of disease, often unrepresentative of archaeological or forensic anthropology cases (Mays, 2018).

Despite their limitations, known collections can provide direct comparison of lesion morphologies and distributions in skeletons with known age and sex. Thus the diagnosis remains built working from the "known" (here, a skeleton in which the disease is reported and ascertained) to the "unknown" (a skeleton under study), warranting scientific reliability for forensic scenarios. For this reason, we decided in this book that most of the skeletal material presented should be based on skeletons from a known collection with documented diagnoses of disease, and in our case specifically, the CAL Milano Cemetery Skeletal Collection (Cattaneo et al., 2018) which we have at hand (Figs. 1.3 and 1.4) and which this work stems from.

Figure 1.3 Skeletal remains laid out before cleaning and analysis, note the presence of clothing (e.g., tights), a pacemaker and personal belongings (e.g., cross necklace). Photograph taken in the Laboratory of Forensic Anthropology and Odontology (LABANOF), University of Milan, Italy. Skeleton #371 of the CAL Milano Cemetery Skeletal Collection.

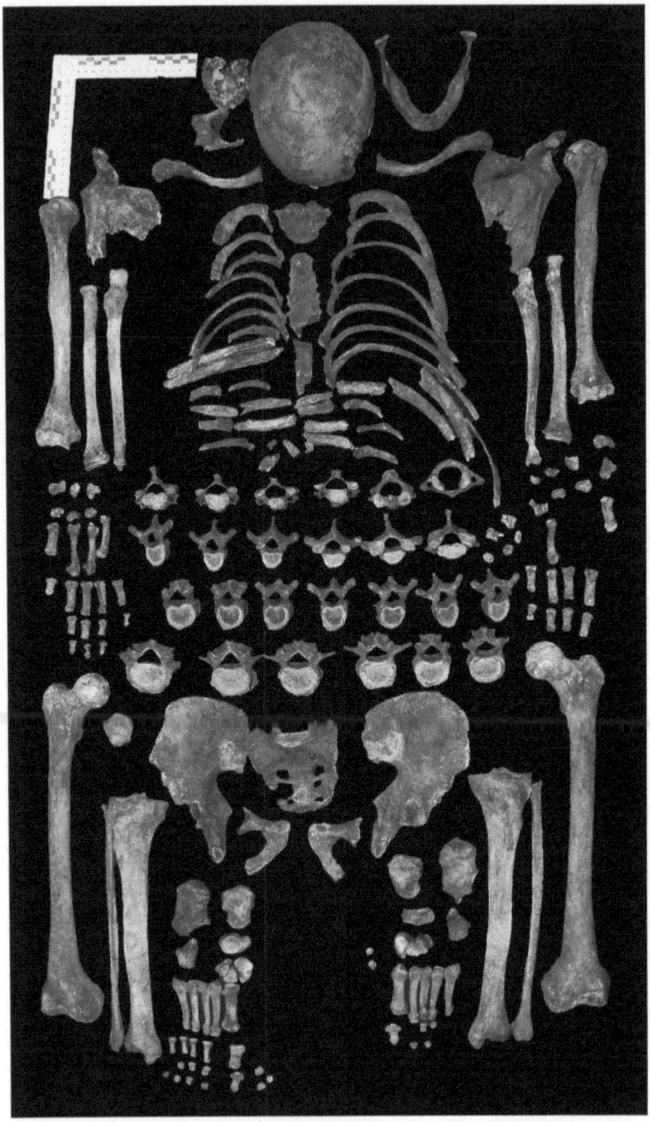

Figure 1.4 Skeleton laid out in anatomical position for analysis at the Laboratory of Forensic Anthropology and Odontology, University of Milan, Italy. Skeleton #1010 of the CAL Milano Cemetery Skeletal Collection.

References

Adams, J.A., Farst, K.J., Kellogg, N.D., 2018. Interpretation of medical findings in suspected child sexual abuse: an update for 2018. J. Pediatr. Adolesc. Gynecol. 31 (3), 225–231.

Alemán, I., Irurita, J., Valencia, A.R., Martínez, A., López-Lázaro, S., Viciano, J., et al., 2012. Brief communication: the Granada osteological collection of identified infants and young children. Am. J. Phys. Anthr. 149, 606–610. Available from: https://doi.org/10.1002/ajpa.22165.

Appleby, J., Thomas, R., Buikstra, J., 2015. Increasing confidence in paleopathological diagnosis – application of the Istanbul terminological framework. Int. J. Paleopathol. 8, 19–21. Available from: https://doi.org/10.1016/j.ijpp.2014.07.003.

Aufderheide, A.C., Rodríguez-Martín, C., 1998. The Cambridge Encyclopedia of Human Paleopathology. Cambridge University Press, Cambridge, UK.

Biehler-Gomez, L., Indra, L., Martino, F., Campobasso, C.P., Cattaneo, C., 2020. Observer error in bone disease description: a cautionary note. Int. J. Osteoarchaeol. Available from: https://doi.org/10.1002/oa.2885.

Biehler-Gomez, L., Tritella, S., Martino, F., Campobasso, C.P., Franchi, A., et al., 2019. The synergy between radiographic and macroscopic observation of skeletal lesions on dry bone. Int. J. Leg. Med. Available from: https://doi.org/10.1007/s00414-019-02122-0.

Brickley, M., Ives, R., 2010. The Bioarchaeology of Metabolic Bone Disease. Elsevier Academic Press, London.

Brickley, M., McKinley, J.I., 2004. Guidelines to the Standards for Recording Human Remains. British Association for Biological Anthropology and Osteoarchaeology and Institute of Field Archaeologists, Southampton.

Brooks, S., Suchey, J.M., 1990. Skeletal age determination based on the os pubis: A comparison of the Acsádi-Nemeskéri and Suchey-Brooks methods. Hum. Evol. 5, 227–238. Available from: https://doi.org/10.1007/BF02437238.

Buikstra, J.E., 2019. Ortner's Identification of Pathological Conditions in Human Skeletal Remains. Academic Press.

Buikstra, J.E., Cook, D.C., Bolhofner, K.L., 2017. Introduction: scientific rigor in paleopathology. Int. J. Paleopathol. 19, 80–87. Available from: https://doi.org/10.1016/j.ijpp.2017.08.005.

Buikstra, J.E., Ubelaker, D.H., 1994. Standards for Data Collection from Human Skeletal Remains. Arkansas Archaeological Survey Report Number 44, Fayetteville, Arkansas.

Cappella, A., Cummaudo, M., Arrigoni, E., Collini, F., Cattaneo, C., 2017. The issue of age estimation in a modern skeletal population: are even the more modern current aging methods satisfactory for the elderly? J. Forensic Sci. 62, 12–17. Available from: https://doi.org/10.1111/1556-4029.13220.

Cardoso, H.F.V., 2006. Brief communication: The collection of identified human skeletons housed at the Bocage Museum (National Museum of Natural History), Lisbon, Portugal. Am. J. Phys. Anthr. 129, 173–176. Available from: https://doi.org/10.1002/ajpa.20228.

Carrara, N., Scaggion, C., Holland, E., 2018. The Tedeschi collection: a collection of documented and undocumented human skeletal remains at the Museum of Anthropology, Padua University (Italy). Am. J. Phys. Anthropol. 166, 930–933. Available from: https://doi.org/10.1002/ajpa.23471.

Cattaneo, C., Mazzarelli, D., Cappella, A., Castoldi, E., Mattia, M., Poppa, P., et al., 2018. A modern documented Italian identified skeletal collection of 2127 skeletons: the CAL Milano Cemetery Skeletal Collection. Forensic Sci. Int. 287, 219.e1–219.e5. Available from: https://doi.org/10.1016/j.forsciint.2018.03.041.

Cunha, E., 2006. Pathology as a factor of personal identity in forensic anthropology. In: Schmitt, A., Cunha, E., Pinheiro, J. (Eds.), Forensic Anthropology and Medicine. Springer, pp. 333–358.

Dayal, M.R., Kegley, A.D.T., Strkalj, G., Bidmos, M.A., Kuykendall, K.L., 2009. The history and composition of the Raymond A. Dart Collection of Human Skeletons at the University of the Witwatersrand, Johannesburg, South Africa. Am. J. Phys. Anthropol. 140, 324–335. Available from: https://doi.org/10.1002/ajpa.21072.

De Angelis, D., Cattaneo, C., Grandi, M., 2007. Dental superimposition: a pilot study for standardising the method. Int. J. Leg. Med. 121, 501–506. Available from: https://doi.org/10.1007/s00414-007-0198-y.

Eliopoulos, C., Lagia, A., Manolis, S., 2007. A modern, documented human skeletal collection from Greece. HOMO 58, 221–228. Available from: https://doi.org/10.1016/j.jchb.2006.10.003.

Ferreira, M.T., Vicente, R., Navega, D., Gonçalves, D., Curate, F., Cunha, E., 2014. A new forensic collection housed at the University of Coimbra, Portugal: the 21st century identified skeletal collection. Forensic Sci. Int. 245, 202.e1–202.e5. Available from: https://doi.org/10.1016/j.forsciint.2014.09.021.

Garvin, H.M., Sholts, S.B., Mosca, L.A., 2014. Sexual dimorphism in human cranial trait scores: effects of population, age, and body size. Am. J. Phys. Anthropol 154, 259–269. Available from: https://doi.org/10.1002/ajpa.22502.

Gocha, T.P., Ingvoldstad, M.E., Kolatorowicz, A., Cosgriff-Hernandez, M.-T.J., Sciulli, P.W., 2015. Testing the applicability of six macroscopic skeletal aging techniques on a modern Southeast Asian sample. Forensic Sci. Int. 249, 318.e1–7. Available from: https://doi.org/10.1016/j.forsciint.2014.12.015.

Grauer, A.L., 2008. Macroscopic analysis and data collection in palaeopathology. In: Pinhasi, R., Mays, S. (Eds.), Advances in Human Palaeopathology. Wiley Online Library, Chichester, England, pp. 57–76.

Grauer, A.L., 2012. A Companion to Paleopathology. John Wiley & Sons.

Hens, S.M., Rastelli, E., Belcastro, M.G., 2008. Age estimation from the human Os Coxa: a test on a Documented Italian Collection. J. Forensic Sci. 53, 1040–1043. Available from: https://doi.org/10.1111/j.1556-4029.2008.00818.x.

Hershkovitz, I., Rothschild, B.M., Dutour, O., Greenwald, C.M., 1998. Clues to recognition of fungal origin of lytic skeletal lesions. Am. J. Phys. Anthropol. 106, 47–60. https://doi.org/10.1002/(SICI)1096-8644(199805)106:1 < 47::AID-AJPA4 > 3.0.CO;2-A.

Hunt, D.R., Albanese, J., 2005. History and demographic composition of the Robert J. Terry anatomical collection. Am. J. Phys. Anthropol. 127, 406–417. Available from: https://doi.org/10.1002/ajpa.20135.

Hutchinson, J., 1887. Syphilis. Cassell & Company Limited, London, UK.

Ioannou, S., Sassani, S., Henneberg, M., Henneberg, R.J., 2016. Diagnosing congenital syphilis using Hutchinson's method: differentiating between syphilitic, mercurial, and syphilitic-mercurial dental defects. Am. J. Phys. Anthropol. 159, 617–629. Available from: https://doi.org/10.1002/ajpa.22924.

Iscan, M.Y., Loth, S.R., 1986. Estimation of age and determination of sex from the sternal rib. Forensic Osteol. 68–89.

Jantz, L.M., Jantz, R.L., 1999. Secular change in long bone length and proportion in the United States, 1800–1970. Am. J. Phys. Anthropol. 110, 57–67. https://doi.org/10.1002/(SICI)1096-8644(199909)110:1 < 57::AID-AJPA5 > 3.0.CO;2-1.

Jantz, R.L., Jantz, L.M., 2016. The remarkable change in Euro-American cranial shape and size. Hum. Biol. 88, 56–64. Available from: https://doi.org/10.13110/humanbiology.88.1.0056.

Kelley, M.A., Micozzi, M.S., 1984. Rib lesions in chronic pulmonary tuberculosis. Am. J. Phys. Anthropol. 65, 381–386. Available from: https://doi.org/10.1002/ajpa.1330650407.

Klales, A.R., Ousley, S.D., Vollner, J.M., 2012. A revised method of sexing the human innominate using Phenice's nonmetric traits and statistical methods. Am. J. Phys. Anthropol. 149, 104–114. Available from: https://doi.org/10.1002/ajpa.22102.

Klaus, H.D., 2017. Paleopathological rigor and differential diagnosis: case studies involving terminology, description, and diagnostic frameworks for scurvy in skeletal remains. Int. J. Paleopathol. 19, 96–110. Available from: https://doi.org/10.1016/j.ijpp.2015.10.002.

L'Abbé, E.N., Loots, M., Meiring, J.H., 2005. The Pretoria Bone Collection: a modern South African skeletal sample. HOMO 56, 197–205. Available from: https://doi.org/10.1016/j.jchb.2004.10.004.

Lovejoy, C.O., Meindl, R.S., Pryzbeck, T.R., Mensforth, R.P., 1985. Chronological metamorphosis of the auricular surface of the ilium: a new method for the determination of adult skeletal age at death. Am. J. Phys. Anthr. 68, 15–28. Available from: https://doi.org/10.1002/ajpa.1330680103.

Lovell, N.C., 2000. Paleopathological description and diagnosis. In: Saunders, S.R., Katzenberg, A.M. (Eds.), Biological Anthropology of the Human Skeleton. Wiley-Liss, New York, pp. 217–248.

Manchester, M., Ogden, A., Storm, R., 2016. Nomenclature in Paleopathology, Paleopathology Association Newsletter.

Mann, R.W., Hunt, D.R., 2005. Photographic regional atlas of bone disease, 3rd ed. Charles Thomas Publisher, Springfield, IL.

Manthey, L., Jantz, R.L., Bohnert, M., Jellinghaus, K., 2017. Secular change of sexually dimorphic cranial variables in Euro-Americans and Germans. Int. J. Leg. Med. 131, 1113–1118. Available from: https://doi.org/10.1007/s00414-016-1469-2.

Marlow, E.J., Pastor, R.F., 2011. Sex determination using the second cervical vertebra--a test of the method. J. Forensic Sci. 56, 165–169. Available from: https://doi.org/10.1111/j.1556-4029.2010.01543.x.

Martrille, L., Ubelaker, D.H., Cattaneo, C., Seguret, F., Tremblay, M., Baccino, E., 2007. Comparison of four skeletal methods for the estimation of age at death on White and Black Adults. J. Forensic Sci. 52, 302–307. Available from: https://doi.org/10.1111/j.1556-4029.2006.00367.x.

Matos, V., Santos, A.L., 2006. On the trail of pulmonary tuberculosis based on rib lesions: results from the human identified skeletal collection from the Museu Bocage (Lisbon, Portugal). Am. J. Phys. Anthropol. 130, 190–200. Available from: https://doi.org/10.1002/ajpa.20309.

Mays, S., 2018. How should we diagnose disease in palaeopathology? Some epistemological considerations. Int. J. Paleopathol. 20, 12–19. Available from: https://doi.org/10.1016/j.ijpp.2017.10.006.

Meindl, R.S., Lovejoy, C.O., 1985. Ectocranial suture closure: a revised method for the determination of skeletal age at death based on the lateral-anterior sutures. Am. J. Phys. Anthr. 68, 57–66. Available from: https://doi.org/10.1002/ajpa.1330680106.

Meyer, C., Jung, C., Kohl, T., Poenicke, A., Poppe, A., Alt, K., 2002. Syphilis 2001 a palaeopathological reappraisal. HOMO-Journal of Comparative Human Biology. Urban & Fischer 53 (1), 39–58.

Miller, E., Ragsdale, B.D., Ortner, D.J., 1996. Accuracy in dry bone diagnosis: a comment on palaeopathological methods. Int. J. Osteoarchaeol. 6, 221–229. https://doi.org/10.1002/(SICI)1099-1212(199606)6:3<221::AID-OA267>3.0.CO;2-2.

Mitchell, P.D., Brickley, M., 2017. Updated guidelines to the standards for recording human remains. Chartered Institute for Archaeologists.

Navega, D., Coelho, C., Vicente, R., Ferreira, M.T., Wasterlain, S.N., Cunha, E., 2015. AncesTrees: ancestry estimation with randomized decision trees. Int. J. Leg. Med. 129, 1145–1153. Available from: https://doi.org/10.1007/s00414-014-1050-9.

Ortner, D.J., 2003. Identification of Pathological Conditions in Human Skeletal Remains, 3rd ed. Smithsonian Institution Press, New York.

Ortner, D.J., 2011. Human skeletal paleopathology. Int. J. Paleopathol. 1, 4–11. Available from: https://doi.org/10.1016/j.ijpp.2011.01.002.

Ortner, D.J., 2012. Differential diagnosis and issues in disease classification. In: Grauer, A.L. (Ed.), A Companion to Paleopathology. Wiley Online Library, Chichester, England, pp. 250–267.

Ortner, D.J., Aufderheide, A.C., 1991. Human Paleopathology: Current Syntheses and Future Options. Smithsonian Institution Press, Washington, DC.

Phenice, T.W., 1969. A newly developed visual method of sexing the os pubis. Am. J. Phys. Anthr. 30, 297–301. Available from: https://doi.org/10.1002/ajpa.1330300214.

Pinhasi, R., Mays, S., 2008. Advances in human palaeopathology. John Wiley & Sons, Chichester, England.

Ragsdale, B.D., Campbell, R.A., Kirkpatrick, C.L., 2018. Neoplasm or not? General principles of morphologic analysis of dry bone specimens. Int. J. Paleopathol. 21, 27–40. Available from: https://doi.org/10.1016/j.ijpp.2017.02.002.

Rezai, A.R., Lee, M., Cooper, P.R., Errico, T.J., Koslow, M., 1995. Modern management of spinal tuberculosis. Neurosurgery 36, 87–88.

Rissech, C., Steadman, D.W., 2011. The demographic, socio-economic and temporal contextualisation of the Universitat Autònoma de Barcelona collection of identified human skeletons (UAB collection). Int. J. Osteoarchaeol. 21, 313–322. Available from: https://doi.org/10.1002/oa.1145.

Roberts, C.A., Lucy, D., Manchester, K., 1994. Inflammatory lesions of ribs: an analysis of the Terry Collection. Am. J. Phys. Anthropol. 95, 169–182. Available from: https://doi.org/10.1002/ajpa.1330950205.

Rogers, J., Watt, I., Dieppe, P., 1990. Comparison of visual and radiographic detection of bony changes at the knee joint. BMJ 300, 367–368.

Rose, J.C., Anton, S., Aufderheide, A.C., Eisenberg, L., Gregg, J.B., Neiburger, E.J., et al., 1991. Skeletal database committee recommendations.

Rothschild, B.M., Rothschild, C., 1995. Comparison of radiologic and gross examination for detection of cancer in defleshed skeletons. Am. J. Phys. Anthr. 96, 357–363. Available from: https://doi.org/10.1002/ajpa.1330960404.

Rougé-Maillart, C., Vielle, B., Jousset, N., Chappard, D., Telmon, N., Cunha, E., 2009. Development of a method to estimate skeletal age at death in adults using the acetabulum and the auricular surface on a Portuguese population. Forensic Sci. Int. 188, 91–95. Available from: http://doi.org/10.1016/j.forsciint.2009.03.019.

Sanabria-Medina, C., González-Colmenares, G., Restrepo, H.O., Rodríguez, J.M.G., 2016. A contemporary Colombian skeletal reference collection: A resource for the development of population specific standards. Forensic Sci. Int. 266, 577.e1–577.e4. Available from: https://doi.org/10.1016/j.forsciint.2016.06.020.

Santos, A.L., Roberts, C.A., 2006. Anatomy of a serial killer: differential diagnosis of tuberculosis based on rib lesions of adult individuals from the Coimbra identified skeletal collection, Portugal. Am. J. Phys. Anthropol. 130, 38–49. Available from: https://doi.org/10.1002/ajpa.20160.

Scheuer, L., Black, S., 2004. The Juvenile Skeleton. Elsevier.

Selliah, P., Martino, F., Cummaudo, M., Indra, L., Biehler-Gomez, L., Campobasso, C., et al., 2020. Sex estimation of skeletons in middle and late adulthood: reliability of pelvic morphological traits and long bone metrics on an Italian skeletal collection. Int. J. Leg. Med. Available from: https://doi.org/10.1007/s00414-020-02292-2.

Simmons, T., Jantz, R.L., Bass, W., 1990. Stature estimation from fragmentary femora: a revision of the Steele Method BT. J. Forensic Sci. 35, 628–636.

Spradley, K., Stull, K.E., Hefner, J.T., 2016. Craniofacial secular change in recent Mexican migrants. Hum. Biol. 88, 15–29.

Steinbock, R.T., 1976. Paleopathological diagnosis and interpretation: bone diseases in ancient human populations. Charles Thomas Publisher, Springfield, IL.

Trotter, M., Gleser, G.C., 1952. Estimation of stature from long bones of American Whites and Negroes. Am. J. Phys. Anthropol. 10, 463–514.

Ubelaker, D.H., 2014. Osteology reference collections. In: Smith, C. (Ed.), Encyclopedia of Global Archaeology. Springer, New York, pp. 5632–5641.

United Nations, 2004. Istanbul Protocol Manual on the Effective Investigation and Documentation of Torture and Other Cruel, Inhuman or Degrading Treatment or Punishment. Office of the United Nations High Commissioner for Human Rights, New York/Geneva.

Waldron, T., 2008. Palaeopathology. Cambridge University Press, Cambridge, UK.

World Health Organization, 2018. WHO releases new International Classification of Diseases (ICD 11) [WWW Document]. <https://www.who.int/news-room/detail/18-06-2018-who-releases-new-international-classification-of-diseases-(icd-11)> (accessed 3.8.19).

Zimmerman, M.R., Kelley, M.A., 1982. Atlas of human paleopathology. Praeger Publishers, New York.

Zuckerman, M.K., 2016. More harm than healing? Investigating the iatrogenic effects of mercury treatment on acquired syphilis in post-medieval London. Open. Archaeol. 2, 42–55. Available from: https://doi.org/10.1515/opar-2016-0003.

CHAPTER 2

Bone Homeostasis and Mechanisms

Lucie Biehler-Gomez and Cristina Cattaneo
LABANOF, Department of Biomedical Sciences for Health, University of Milan, Milan, Italy

What is Bone?

Let's face it: next to the beautiful rhythm of the incredible beating muscle that is the heart and the mysterious and astounding complexity of the human brain, bones make for a pale comparison in the wonders of the human body. Since antiquity, the interest in bones focused on their hardness and solidity and was seen as only necessary for the structural integrity of the human body. As famous roman physician Galen explained: "Nature consequently did not merely entrust its [the brain] defense to the skin, as she did for the parts in the abdomen, but first, before the skin was put on, she invested it with bone like a helmet." Initial studies resulted in rather unflattering descriptions: Galen claimed that bones were made of sperm because of their pale color and Persian physician Avicenna, considered the father of early modern medicine, argued that as bones are cold and dry, they were primarily made of earth. Today, bones generally represent death or the end of life in the collective mind and are only "celebrated" during Halloween festivities. Let's restore their image and explain why anthropologists, anatomists, and other bone specialists such as orthopedic surgeons marvel at bones.

Bone is a living tissue. Bones grow with us, they endure trauma and repair themselves, adapt to our activities and ways of life, and suffer from our diseases. They are highly vascularized and in constant remodeling and so they are sponges full of information absorbed during the life of the individual. Skeletons are not, in fact, bland articulated structures devoid of identity. Quite the opposite, much of the history and identity of a person may be read on bare bones.

The bone matrix is constituted of multistrand collagen fibers and hydroxyapatite, an inorganic mineral in the form of small crystals,

Interpreting Bone Lesions and Pathology for Forensic Practice. DOI: https://doi.org/10.1016/B978-0-323-85162-6.00002-7

organized in a woven design. This unique composition and structure confers bones their solidity, strength, and flexibility as highly resistant to compression forces, while remaining lightweight. The bone tissue assumes several functions in the human body: (1) the skeleton acts as a framework for attachment of the muscles and ligaments and thus provide structural support for the body; (2) it protects vital organs by shielding the brain in the cranium, the spinal cord within the vertebrae, and the heart, lungs, and major blood vessels with the sternum, rib cage, and spine; (3) it allows movement of the body by providing articulations; (4) it is the center for hematopoiesis, that is, blood cell production in the bone marrow; and (5) it functions as a storage area for calcium and iron in the body.

The bone structure can be divided into two morphological types: cortical and spongy bone. Cortical or compact bone forms the hard exterior of the bone or cortex. It shields the bone marrow and is constituted of structural units called osteons or Haversian systems. Osteons are formed of concentric layers of compact matrix, called lamellae, with embedded osteocytes, enclosing a Haversian canal, which allows for the passage of blood vessels and nerve fibers. The cortical bone is enveloped by two membranes: the periosteum, which covers the outer surface of the bones, with the exception of the areas of articulation; and the endosteum, separating the cortical bone from the medullary cavity. The spongy bone, also named cancellous or trabecular bone, can be found at the ends of long bones (i.e., metaphysis and epiphysis), near articular areas and in the body of the vertebrae. Spongy bone is highly vascularized and has a non-compact structure similar to a sponge (hence its name), making it less resistant to fracture than cortical bone.

Bone Modeling and Remodeling

Before we can understand the bone modeling and remodeling processes, we need to spend a little bit of time on the different types of bone cells, as these will be fundamental to understand bone lesions. We will focus here in particular on three types of cells: osteoblasts, osteocytes, and osteoclasts.

- *Osteoblasts* (meaning "bone germinator") derive from mesenchymal stem cells from the bone marrow. They are mononucleate cells located close to the external surface of bones. They are responsible for the formation of osteoid, the unmineralized bone matrix, primarily composed of type I collagen. The osteoblasts also produce hydroxyapatite which is deposited in a regular fashion in the matrix. The osteoid then becomes mineralized, forming bone. Osteoblasts operate by creating new bone around themselves, comfortably wrapping themselves in cocoons of bone before maturing into osteocytes.

- *Osteocytes* (meaning "mature bone cells") are star-shaped cells located in lacunae between the lamellae in Haversian systems and remain connected through canaliculi. These mature cells derived from osteoblasts are not completely retired: they are responsible for the maintenance of the bone structure, in particular, they regulate the flow of oxygen and minerals (i.e., calcium and phosphorus) in and out of the bone matrix.
- *Osteoclasts* (meaning "cells that break down bone") are large multinucleated cells derived from monocyte–macrophage lineage cells. They are responsible for bone resorption in a mechanism akin to phagocytosis in circulating macrophages.

Bone modeling refers to the process of bone formation and resorption until complete skeletal maturation, in other words, during bone growth. The activity of both osteoblasts and osteoclasts permits the gain of bone mass (through bone formation) and the shaping of skeletal form (through bone resorption). Nonetheless, the activity of osteoblasts and osteoclasts remains constant throughout life, although it slows with increasing age. In this process, called bone remodeling, old bone is replaced by new bone tissue to maintain bone mass and respond to functional stress demands (i.e., in areas of mechanical loading as a result of piezoelectric signals) (Fig. 2.1). Rapid osteoid

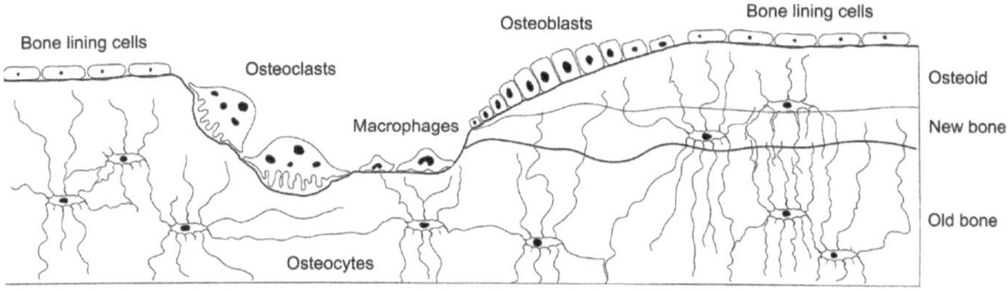

Figure 2.1 Bone remodeling process. From left to right: bone covered with lining cells; the osteoclasts remove bone (i.e., bone resorption); osteoblasts form the osteoid and mineralize it; new bone is formed, covered with lining cells. Drawing by Davide Porta.

production by osteoblasts leads to woven bone deposition, an immature bone tissue with a disorganized collagen fiber structure. This mechanically weak tissue is found in fetal bones and in sites of fractures as an initial bone repairing structure (i.e., callus formation). Woven bone gradually remodels into lamellar bone, a mature bone organized in lamellae of parallel collagen fibers, conferring mechanical bone strength. Bone turnover is also essential to maintain calcium levels in the body: as bone acts as a storage area of calcium, bone resorption releases calcium contained in the bone tissue into the system enabling physiological functions of the blood and heart. Bone metabolism is a highly regulated chemical process, coordinated through hormones—parathyroid, thyroid, and growth hormones—as well as cytokines (i.e., signaling proteins) and enforced through the differentiation of bone remodeling cells (i.e., osteoblasts and osteoclasts) as well as the stimulation and inhibition of their activity to control the rate of bone formation and resorption.

Loss of Equilibrium

The constant process of bone remodeling, operated by osteoblasts and osteoclasts conjointly, assures a biological balance referred to as bone homeostasis. This homeostasis maintains the body environment in equilibrium to continue the healthy functions of the organism. By opposition, the disturbance of homeostasis, that is, when the balance is no longer equilibrated, results in bone disease.

For instance, osteoporosis occurs when poor osteoblasts can't keep up with hyperefficient osteoclasts, offsetting the delicate balance of bone homeostasis. In this condition, osteoclasts degrade the bone matrix at a faster rate than osteoblasts are at rebuilding it; this causes excessive bone resorption and leads to lower bone mass density. In addition, the new bone tissue produced by osteoblasts is mechanically weak, rendering it prone to fracture. Osteoporosis and its precursor, osteopenia, are accurately diagnosed by measuring bone mineral density. Contrary to other conditions, this is not a disorder that can be diagnosed just by macroscopic examination on dry bone. We have often seen students "weighing" the bones in their hands and firmly saying that the individual had osteoporosis (i.e., a lower weight than normal could indicate a depletion of the internal bone structure, in other words, a low bone mass density, characteristic of osteopenia, and osteoporosis); since weight loss may depend enormously on taphonomic degradation, making assumptions without scientific evidence leads to misdiagnoses. Although it will not endanger the health of your patient as in clinical cases, it can have dramatic consequences in forensic settings. You can absolutely *suspect* osteoporosis based on light bones, but you will need further radiological and structural analyses to confirm it, when possible.

Another example is bone metastases. Metastatic cancer cells can manipulate the activity of osteoblasts and osteoclasts through the release of stimulators to incite the chemoattraction of cancer cells as well as support their survival. Indeed, the bone microenvironment is also the site of storage of considerable growth factors. By activating bone turnover, cancer cells feed on growth factors and proliferate. In multiple myeloma, a cancer of plasma cells, osteoblastic activity and differentiation is inhibited while malignant cells promote osteoclastic differentiation and activity (in other words, bone formation is chemically stopped, and bone resorption is put on steroids), resulting in a dramatic loop of bone destruction. Consequently, bone lesions in multiple myeloma are exclusively osteolytic with no chance of bone healing.

Metabolically, this excessive bone resorption leads to high levels of calcium released in the blood or hypercalcemia, which is an important factor of morbidity and mortality, especially in cancer patients.

Bone Response to Insult

Considering that the bone remodeling team is constituted of two types of cells (i.e., osteoblasts and osteoclasts), bone response to insult (that is to say, any type of injury) is limited and consists in either bone formation or bone resorption.

Typically, when not due to a metabolic, neoplastic, or autoimmune dysfunction, bone resorptive lesions are the result of an external agent causing the insult (e.g., mechanical or infectious) and can appear as an erosion of the bone surface with bone porosity, borings, larger osteolytic lesions, or even bone atrophy (i.e., the complete resorption of part of a bone) (Figs. 2.2 and 2.3). Then, sometimes, bone formation ensues as an attempt at bone repair. The margins of osteolytic bone lesions can inform on the rapidity and aggressiveness of the disease process: round

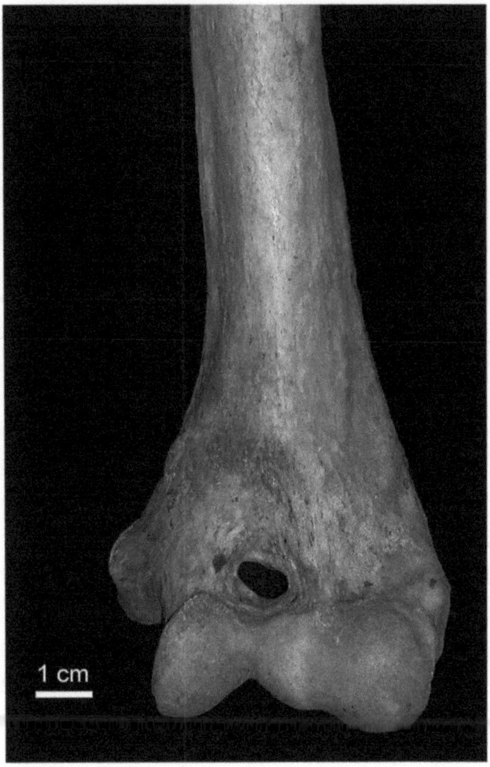

Figure 2.2 Septal aperture (anterior view of a distal left humerus). You can see here a large boring in the coronoid fossa, be careful that this is in fact not pathological but a normal anatomical variation (also called nonmetric or discrete trait) referred to as "septal aperture." Skeleton #27 of the CAL Milano Cemetery Skeletal Collection with a clinical diagnosis of rheumatoid arthritis.

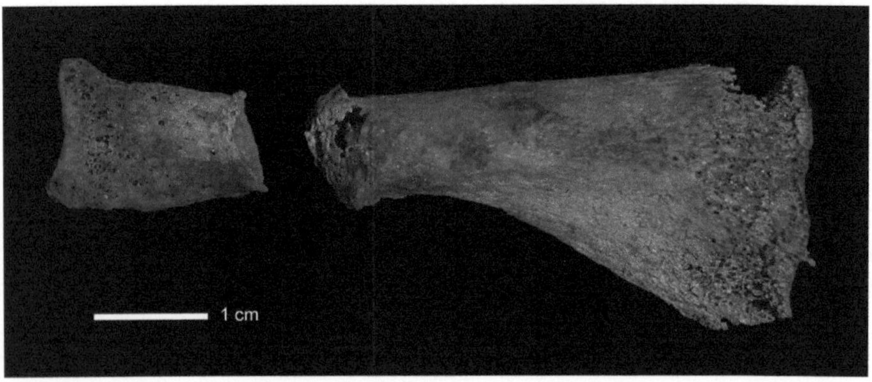

Figure 2.3 Atrophy of the base of the phalanx and head of the first metatarsal deforming the metatarsophalangeal articulation (medial view of first right metatarsal and dorsal view of first right proximal phalanx). Skeleton #277 of the CAL Milano Cemetery Skeletal Collection with a clinical diagnosis of rheumatoid arthritis.

and/or remodeled margins (the latter signaling the activity of osteoblasts consolidating the outer rim of the bone) and seen as well-defined geographic lesions with or without a sclerotic rim on radiographs, reveal a slow-growing process (Fig. 2.4); by opposition, non-remodeled margins, appearing denticulated or scalloped ("moth-eaten" on X-rays) suggest a rapid and aggressive process, leaving no time for osteoblasts to lay down new bone (Fig. 2.5).

The periosteum, the membrane covering the outer surface of all bones with the exception of their articular surfaces, is a very sensitive connective tissue: almost anything that breaks, tears, stretches, or even touches the periosteum can result in periosteal new bone (Richardson, 2001). Periosteal new bone is often referred to as "periostitis" which, according to some authors, is misguiding: the prefix "-itis" connotes a cellular inflammation that may not always be present, which is why the terms "periosteal new bone" should be preferred for linguistic exactitude. Just like with resorptive lesions, the pattern of osteoblastic bone lesions can be informative on the speed and temporality of the disease process. Woven bone (immature and disorganized new bone) suggests

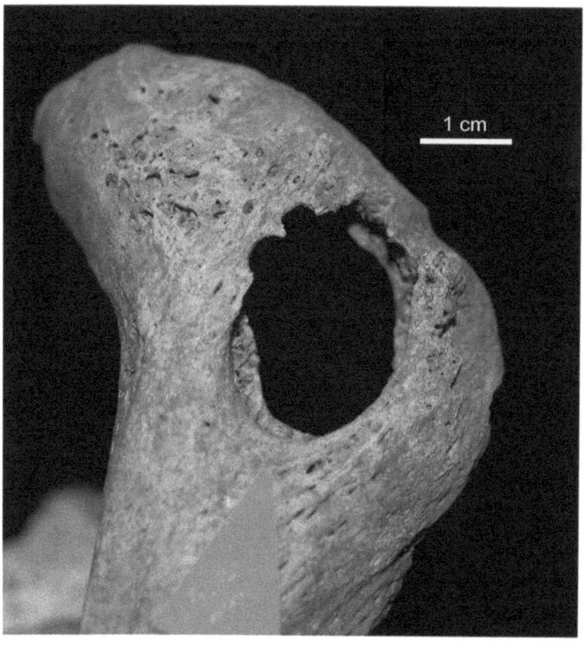

Figure 2.4 Round osteolytic lesion with remodeled margins (superior view of the acromion of the right scapula). Archaeological specimen #1300 of the CAL with probable tuberculosis dated c. CE 9th century.

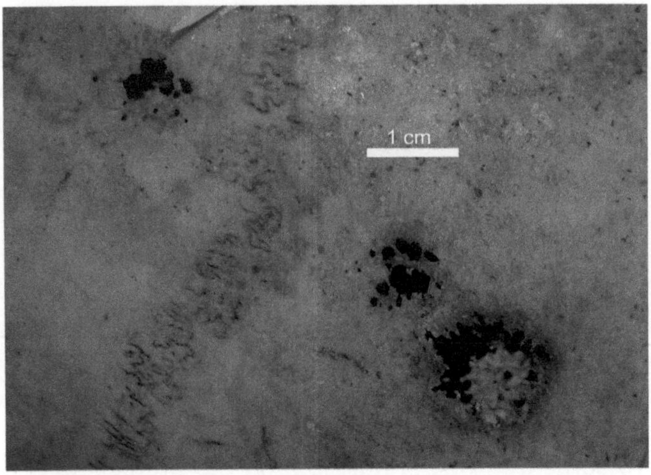

Figure 2.5 Small osteolytic lesions with scalloped margins (lateral view of the frontal and left parietal bones with the coronal suture in the middle). Skeleton #10 of the CAL Milano Cemetery Skeletal Collection with a clinical diagnosis of liver carcinoma.

a process still active at the time of death. On dry bone, woven bone appears as a porous bone layer deposited on the cortical surface (Fig. 2.6). As woven bone remodels into lamellar bone over time, lamellar or remodeled periosteal new bone suggests a healed process (Fig. 2.7). Spiculated periosteal reactions, appearing as parallel or divergent projecting spicules of fiber bone indicate a rapid and aggressive process, as osteoblasts do not have the time to lay down new bone in a regular and organized fashion (Fig. 2.8). Another osteoproliferative lesion also occurring as a form of bone repair consists in trabecular thickening, a subcortical osteoblastic activity within the trabeculae of the spongy bone structure, making it appear visually thickened, which Ortner (2003, p. 52) referred to as "spongiosclerosis" (Fig. 2.9). These lesions are visible on radiographs as radiopaque or sclerotic areas.

The extent of the lesion can be indicative of the duration and repetition of the insult and/or the aggressiveness of the causative agent/mechanism. Consequently, given the informative capacity of bone lesions on the process responsible for their formation, bone response to insult should be careful recorded.

Throughout the rest of this book, we will discuss the various categories of pathology, including infectious, metabolic, endocrine, and

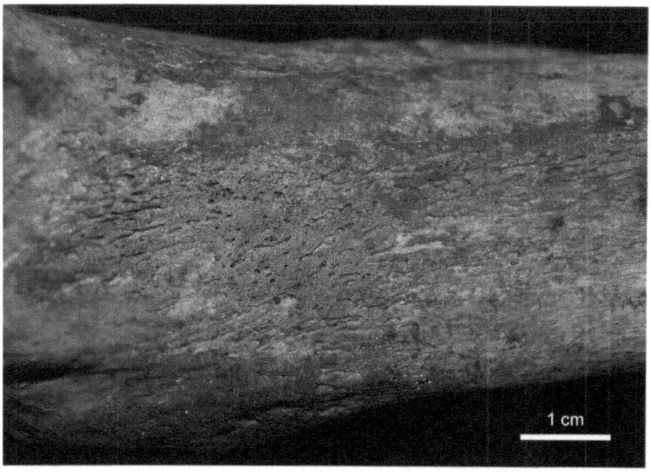

Figure 2.6 Woven periosteal new bone on a proximal tibia. Skeleton #854 of the CAL Milano Cemetery Skeletal Collection. Reproduced with permission from Biehler-Gomez, L., Cabrini, A., De Angelis, D., Cattaneo, C., 2018. How do skeletons with HIV present? A study on the identified CAL Milano Cemetery Skeletal Collection. Leg. Med. 33, 11–16. https://doi.org/10.1016/j.legalmed.2018.04.007.

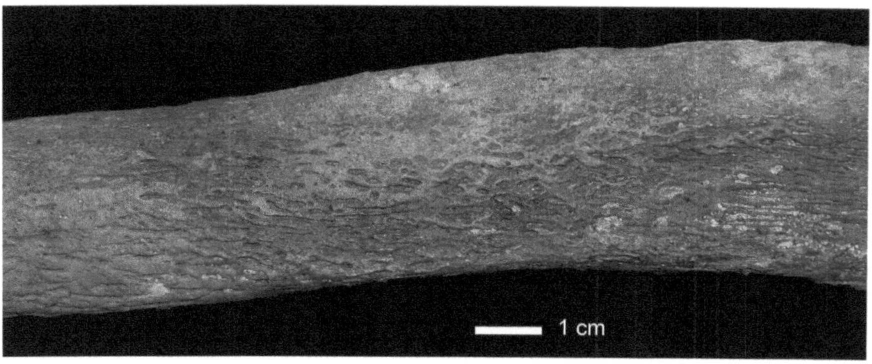

Figure 2.7 Remodeled or lamellar periosteal new bone on a proximal tibia. Skeleton #25 of the CAL Milano Cemetery Skeletal Collection.

neoplastic diseases, stress markers, calcified residues of soft tissue disease and trauma, before finishing with the challenge of taphonomy and the potential of toxicology. We chose to primarily follow the classification of diseases of Roberts and Manchester (2007), as it is simple, clear and widely used in the discipline. Skeletal dysplasias were not included because of their rare incidence in the population; moreover, their severe skeletal abnormalities render them more easily recognizable (Beighton et al., 1993; Oostra et al., 1998; Rimoin et al., 2007).

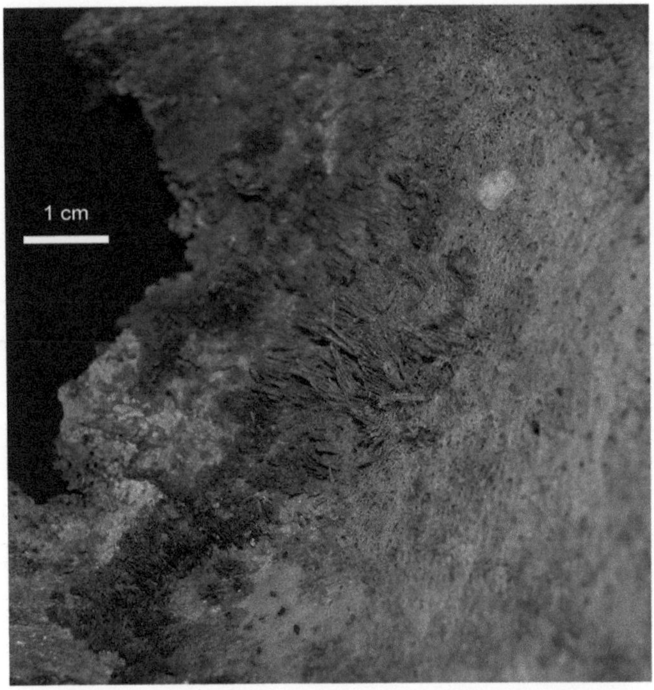

Figure 2.8 Spiculated periosteal reaction on the right iliac fossa (anterior view) of skeleton #366 of the CAL Milano Cemetery Skeletal Collection with a clinical diagnosis of prostate carcinoma.

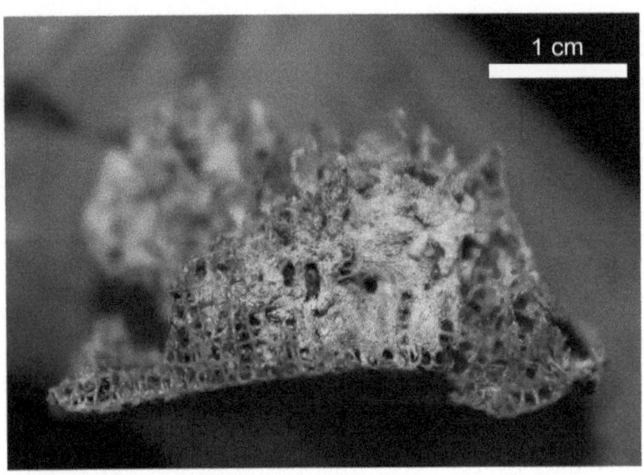

Figure 2.9 Spongiosclerosis or thickening of the trabecular bone in a fragmented vertebral body from skeleton #425 of the CAL Milano Cemetery Skeletal Collection with a clinical diagnosis of breast carcinoma. Reproduced with permission from Biehler-Gomez, L., Giordano, G., Cattaneo, C., 2019. The appearance of breast cancer metastases on dry bone: implications for forensic anthropology. J. Forensic Leg. Med. 61, 5–12. https://doi.org/10.1016/j.jflm.2018.10.007.

Dental diseases result from a combination of genetic and environmental factors and can thus provide substantial information on diet, oral hygiene, and stress. They will not be addressed in a single chapter but included when relevant in the specific sections.

References

Beighton, P., Sujansky, E., Patzak, B., Portele, K.A., 1993. Genetic skeletal dysplasias in the Museum of Pathological Anatomy, Vienna. Am. J. Med. Genet. 47, 843–847. Available from: https://doi.org/10.1002/ajmg.1320470609.

Oostra, R., Baljet, B., Dijkstra, P.F., Hennekam, R.C.M., 1998. Congenital anomalies in the teratological collection of Museum Vrolik in Amsterdam, The Netherlands. II: Skeletal dysplasias. Am. J. Med. Genet. 77, 116–134. Available from: https://doi.org/10.1002/(SICI)1096-8628(19980501)77:2 < 116::AID-AJMG4 > 3.0.CO;2-Q.

Ortner, D.J., 2003. Identification of Pathological Conditions in Human Skeletal Remains, 3rd ed. Smithsonian Institution Press, New York.

Richardson, M., 2001. Periosteal reaction. Approaches to Differential Diagnosis in Musculoskeletal Imaging. University of Washington, Department of Radiology.

Rimoin, D.L., Cohn, D., Krakow, D., Wilcox, W., Lachman, R.S., Alanay, Y., 2007. The skeletal dysplasias. Ann. N. Y. Acad. Sci. 1117, 302–309. Available from: https://doi.org/10.1196/annals.1402.072.

Roberts, C.A., Manchester, K., 2007. The Archaeology of Disease, 3rd ed. Cornell University Press, Ithaca, NY.

CHAPTER 3

Infectious Diseases: Non-Specific and Specific Infections

Lucie Biehler-Gomez and Cristina Cattaneo
LABANOF, Department of Biomedical Sciences for Health, University of Milan, Milan, Italy

Inflammation Versus Infection

One thing that must be clear before entering in the details of infectious diseases and their recognition on dry bone is that inflammation and infection are two very distinct entities and are sometimes initially confused by anthropology or non-medical students in general. Inflammation corresponds to a set of vascular, cellular, and molecular mechanisms from the immune system and operates as a physiological response to any harmful external (e.g., infection, trauma) or internal (e.g., autoimmune, cancer) insult. In vivo, the four cardinal signs of inflammation or "Celsus tetrad" (Celsus AC, *De Medicina*, CE 25), are *calor* (warmth), *dolor* (pain), *rubor* (redness), and *tumor* (swelling).

By opposition, an infection consists in the "invasion" of a host organism by a foreign living agent (i.e., microorganisms such as viruses, bacteria, parasites, or fungi), where they multiply causing disease. The disease progress and outcome from infection depend on the entry route of the pathogen, its quantity and virulence, and the immune status of the host body. Inflammatory response to infection initiates with vascular changes, including vasodilatation (i.e., enlargement of blood vessels), increased permeability (allowing for the passage of plasma, proteins, and cells), and increased blood flow. White blood cells can then migrate through the capillaries to the site of infection (by chemotaxis, i.e., chemical attraction) and will degrade the pathogenic cells, eliminate them through phagocytosis and maintain the inflammation until complete victory of the immune system. Most acute infections do not have the time to involve the skeletal system before resolving or causing death and so bone changes in infectious conditions tend to be the result of subacute or chronic diseases. Thus

Interpreting Bone Lesions and Pathology for Forensic Practice. DOI: https://doi.org/10.1016/B978-0-323-85162-6.00003-9

and paradoxically, infectious and inflammatory bone changes are manifestations of long-standing conditions with a relatively healthy and strong immune system (Roberts and Manchester, 2007).

Inflammation is part of the innate immune response of the organism to a pathogen, and infection is one of the causes of inflammation. The two terms are semantically different and should not be used synonymously.

Non-Specific Infections

On dry bone, bacterial infections are generally divided into specific and non-specific. Bone lesions that may be ascribed to a particular infection based on their distinctive pattern of bone involvement are referred to as "specific infections," the most commonly described being tuberculosis (TB), syphilis, and leprosy. On the opposite side, "non-specific infections" comprise pathological bone changes that cannot be attributed to a particular infectious agent. In these cases, skeletal manifestations are indistinguishable between bacteria impeding the identification of the bacterial cause responsible for the observed osseous lesions through macroscopic examination (Roberts and Manchester, 2007).

Bone infection may affect each of its layers: endosteal, cortical, and periosteal. The endosteal layer of bone (i.e., the inner or medullary surface) is primarily involved in osteomyelitis (i.e., inflammation and infection of bone "osteitis" and bone marrow "myelitis"), starting from the marrow spaces and spreading to the bone. The microorganisms may infect the bone through various possible routes: (1) contiguous spread from an adjacent infected tissue (e.g., direct extension from pressure ulcers in diabetic feet); (2) direct infection from a penetrating injury (i.e., open wound) or bone surgery; (3) bloodstream dissemination to the bone from a distant site of infection (hematogenous osteomyelitis). *Staphylococcus aureus* is the microorganism responsible for osteomyelitis in about 90% of cases (although infectious causes other than the pyogenic bacteria including fungi, viruses, and parasites may also lead to bone marrow infection). Vertebral osteomyelitis, spread hematogenously from the lungs and due to TB, is known as Pott's disease. The radiological and dry bone markers of osteomyelitis include three characteristic features: (1) the sequestrum, which corresponds to devitalized fragments of avascular bone (in other words, a bone necrosis); (2) the involucrum, an envelope of new bone surrounding the necrotic sequestrum; and (3) the cloaca, which is an opening in the involucrum allowing for drainage of pus (Aufderheide and Rodríguez-Martín, 1998, pp. 178–181; Gold et al., 1991; Lew and Waldvogel, 2004, 1997; Ortner, 2003, pp. 181–186). Thus, although we cannot ascertain the bacterial agent responsible for the infectious lesion, we can implement the biological profile with symptoms the individual probably suffered from and even disabilities: for instance, fever, local pain, swelling and limp, or reduced mobility caused by osteomyelitis on a lower limb.

Inflammation of the compact bone is referred to as "osteitis" (an ambiguous term preferable not to use) and appears radiographically as a cortical thickening with increased density (Chhem and Brothwell, 2008, pp. 93–99). On dry bone, this abnormal thickening of the cortical bone can only be seen in transverse sections.

Finally, periostitis is frequently derived from an inflammation of the periosteum resulting in the deposition of new bone on the cortex (i.e., the outer surface of bone). Radiographically, periosteal reactions are separated in benign and aggressive types and can morphologically appear single-layered or multilayered, continuous, interrupted, or complex (Ragsdale et al., 2018; Rana et al., 2009).

Periosteal reactions are not bone changes specific to bacterial infections and may be found in other conditions (Aufderheide and Rodríguez-Martín, 1998; Ortner, 2003). However, the problem of their non-specificity prevents a certain diagnosis for this bone abnormality. For instance, periosteal reactions appearing as plaque-like new bone formation with fine pitting and longitudinal striation (in other words, woven periosteal new bone) were frequently observed on the cortical surface of the medial diaphysis of tibiae in archaeological skeletons but not noted in clinical contexts (Ortner and Aufderheide, 1991, p. 7). Several hypotheses were proposed to account for this bone change including physiological stress indicators, recurrent minor trauma on this bone area close to the skin and ulceration induced from venous stasis in varicose veins (Roberts and Manchester, 2007, pp. 129–130), but the exact etiology of the lesion remains unknown.

Dental caries, attrition, and fractures can expose the pulp, allowing microorganisms to enter and cause inflammation, especially in the

Figure 3.1 Large osteolytic lesion with remodeled margins caused by a periapical abscess at the level of the second left premolar of the mandible (tooth 35).

surrounding bone. In periapical lesions, this may lead to abscesses, resulting in bone loss and periosteal new bone deposition (Hillson, 2019, 2005) (Fig. 3.1).

These characteristics of infection can also be appreciated on histological thin sections of dry bone lesions and through microtomography (micro-CT), through bone resorption and bone formation features (De Boer et al., 2013; Kuhn et al., 2007; Rühli et al., 2007; Schultz, 2001).

The Big Three: Tuberculosis, Syphilis, and Leprosy

Tuberculosis

TB remains one of the top 10 causes of death worldwide responsible for about 1.5 million deaths yearly (World Health Organization, 2019a). Due to the AIDS epidemic which predisposes to TB, extrapulmonary TB occurs in 20%–40% of TB cases (Hopewell, 1994; Pigrau-Serrallach and Rodríguez-Pardo, 2013). Therefore, given the prevalence of TB in the population, even in western countries, knowing how to recognize TB on dry bones may be of forensic relevance and the condition should not be disregarded.

TB is a chronic and progressive infectious condition caused by the bacillus *Mycobacterium tuberculosis.* After the asymptomatic primary contact with the infectious agent, the infection may become either latent or active. The immune system contains the bacilli preventing their replication in caseous and necrotic centers of granulomas in the lungs, but the bacteria can survive in this material for years. The host's resistance against the microbial virulence will determine if the infection becomes latent (and asymptomatic), also called persistent TB, or if it reactivates (with symptoms). Only 5%–10% of healthy people infected develop an active disease. Factors weakening the immune system such as HIV infection, immunosuppressive drugs, malnutrition, aging, and diabetes, may precipitate reactivation. At this point, the bacilli are revived and able to replicate in an uncontrolled manner, escape the granuloma, spread within the lungs, and to other tissues (including bones and joints) via lymphatic route or the bloodstream (Smith, 2003; Tierney and Nardell, 2018).

Clinical features of pulmonary TB include cough, chest pain, hemoptysis (i.e., coughing up blood), and respiratory failure. After physical examination, chest X-rays are usually performed and allow the observation of lung infiltrates with adenopathy and cavitation (Hopewell, 1994). Extrapulmonary TB, resulting from a failure to contain the bacilli, presents non-specific symptoms depending on the severity of the condition such as fever, weight loss, and weakness, and may be concomitant with pulmonary TB, in particular in patients with HIV infection (Hopewell, 1994; Pigrau-Serrallach and Rodríguez-Pardo, 2013).

Skeletal TB is slowly progressive; it causes pain, soft tissue swelling, and limitation of joint movement. TB is described as rarely affecting the skeleton (Ortner, 2011), but when it does, the spine and metaphyses of long bones (and by extension the joints) are most commonly involved due to the rich vascular supply of these areas. Spinal TB favors the thoracic and lumbar spine, causing paravertebral and epidural abscesses in about 50%–80% of cases and lesions with virtually no new bone reaction ranging from contiguous focal erosions on the anterior corners of the vertebral bodies to fragmentation of the vertebral bodies, disc space narrowing to intervertebral disc destruction, and a progressive vertebral body collapse creating the characteristic gibbus deformation called "Pott's disease" (Figs. 3.2–3.4) (Golden and Vikram, 2005; Hopewell,

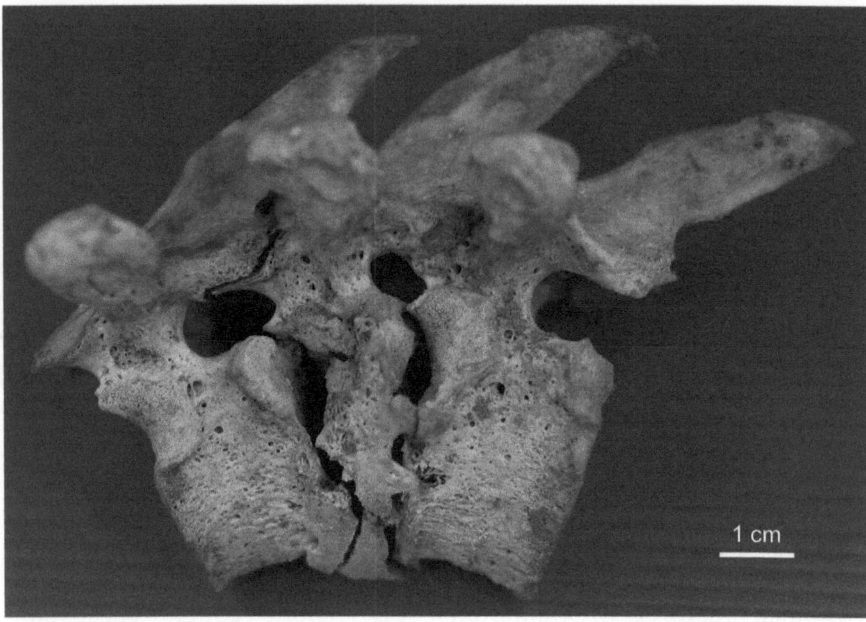

Figure 3.2 Pott's disease, lateral view (thoracic vertebrae 5, 6, and 7). Osteolytic destruction of the body of T6 and preservation of its neural arch leading to the structural collapse of the body and a kyphosis at the level of T5–T7 in a deformation known as "Pott's disease" (Martrille et al., 2020). Courtesy of Dr. Laurent Martrille, University of Nancy.

1994; Jain et al., 1993; Shanley, 1995). Neurological complications of spinal TB include spinal cord compression and in extreme cases, paraplegia or tetraplegia. Articular TB, much less common than spinal TB, typically consists in a slowly progressive monoarticular arthritis of the hip or knee (Golden and Vikram, 2005; Pigrau-Serrallach and Rodríguez-Pardo, 2013). Lesions may heal without treatment and may terminate in the ankylosis of the articulation affected (Aufderheide and Rodríguez-Martín, 1998; Golden and Vikram, 2005; Hopewell, 1994; Jain et al., 1993; Ortner, 2011, 2003; Pigrau-Serrallach and Rodríguez-Pardo, 2013; Roberts and Buikstra, 2003; Roberts and Manchester, 2007; Shanley, 1995; Waldron, 2008).

Although Pott's disease is a known sign of the infectious condition, Kelley and El-Najjar (1980) showed, based on skeletons with recorded TB from the Hamann–Todd collection, the importance of knowing the range of variation of the lesions in TB bone disease which may be circumferential (on the anterior and lateral sides of the bodies of the vertebrae), central (within the bodies), or paradiscal (on either side of

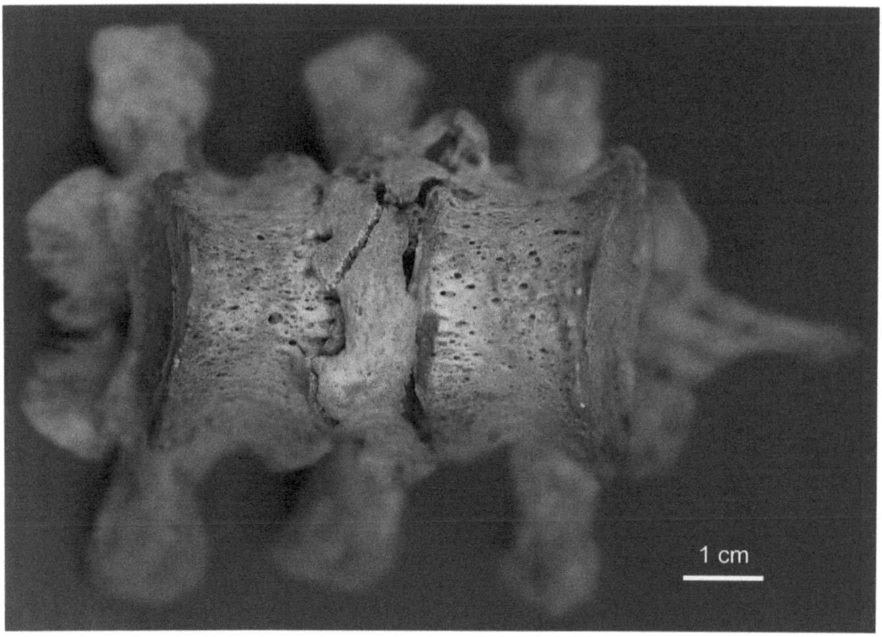

Figure 3.3 Pott's disease, anterior view. Note the compression fractures on the body of T6 due to its central pathological destruction and the normal pressure applied by the superior vertebra (T5) (Martrille et al., 2020). Courtesy of Dr. Laurent Martrille, University of Nancy.

intervertebral disc). In addition, while the neural arches have been described in the clinical literature as spared from the infection, Kelley and El-Najjar (1980) report three cases of neural arch involvement evidencing the issues of clinical diagnostic criteria (Ortner and Aufderheide, 1991, pp. 6–7). Mariotti et al. (2015) furthered the research on TB bone lesions through the examination of erosions, cavities, enlarged vascular foramina, and periosteal new bone on the ribs of 244 skeletons (including 61 with known TB) from the Certosa cemetery in Bologna (Italy). Indeed, from the 1980s, studies suggested a positive (but not exclusive) correlation between TB and periosteal new bone on the visceral surfaces of ribs based on the Hamann–Todd (Kelley and Micozzi, 1984), Terry (Roberts et al., 1994), Coimbra (Santos and Roberts, 2006, 2001), and Lisbon (Matos and Santos, 2006) collections. Hershkovitz et al. (2002) investigated the relationship between the occurrence of *serpens endocrania symmetrica* lesions which are endocranial labyrinth-like impressions and intrathoracic diseases, in particular TB, based on material from the Hamann–Todd collection, providing yet another skeletal marker suggestive of the condition.

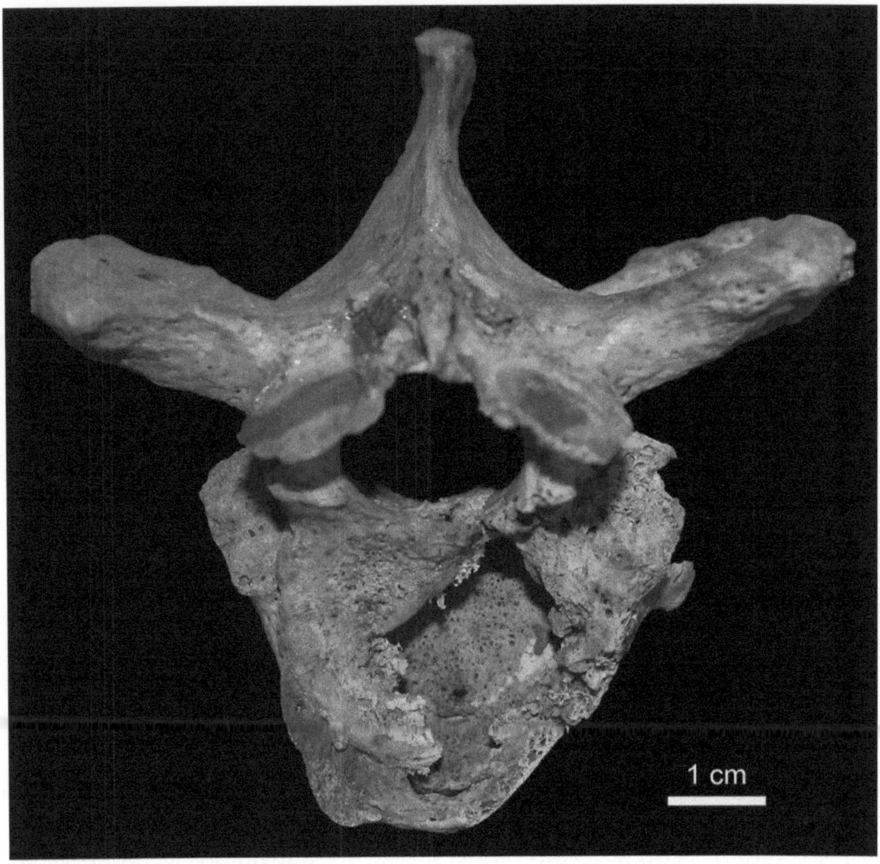

Figure 3.4 Central osteolytic destruction of the body of T6 (Martrille et al., 2020). Courtesy of Dr. Laurent Martrille, University of Nancy.

Ten years later, Pálfi et al. (2012) provided valuable illustration and details of the extreme osseous involvement in three juvenile skeletons from the Terry collection who died of TB and Holloway et al. (2013) examined 69 cases of skeletal TB from the Galler collection, before and after the introduction of pharmaceutical treatments to assess the impact of healing and treatment on the skeletal diagnosis of TB. Recent research (Steyn et al., 2013; Steyn and Buskes, 2016) studied the evolution of TB bone changes in 205 skeletons who died of TB from South Africa known collections (including the Pretoria bone collection (L'Abbé et al., 2005) and the Raymond A. Dart Collection (Dayal et al., 2009)), before, during, and after the emergence of antibiotics and evidenced interesting changes. Not only did the number of lesions increase despite the introduction of antibiotics but the distribution of lesions also varied: while costal and intracranial lesions increased, spinal manifestations, the most characteristic lesions of TB, decreased. These studies (Holloway et al., 2013; Steyn et al., 2013; Steyn and Buskes, 2016) illustrating the changes in TB lesions in post-antibiotic era may prove crucial in the pathological diagnosis of disease in forensic skeletonized cases.

A certain diagnosis is often difficult to assess on dry bones as many lesions due to TB are not specific to the infection (periosteal new bone on ribs, *serpens endocrania symmetrica*, erosions of the vertebral bodies, enlarged vertebral vascular foramina, osteolytic lesions, etc.). In these cases, biomolecular studies of ancient pathogens, such as mycobacterial DNA or mycolic acids, can allow the diagnosis of the disease in skeletal remains (Donoghue et al., 2004; Mays et al., 2001; Nerlich et al., 1997; Redman et al., 2009; Salo et al., 1994) (Box 3.1).

Treponematoses

To this date, the treponematoses remain endemic in many parts of the world. Treponematosis infection is divided into four types: yaws, bejel (endemic syphilis or Treponarid), venereal syphilis, and pinta, but only the first three can affect the skeleton (Farnsworth and Rosen, 2006; Marks et al., 2014; Mitjà et al., 2013).

Venereal syphilis is caused by the spirochete *Treponema pallidum* subspecies *pallidum*. While this treponeme lacks metabolic activity as well as oxygen and temperature adaptability, it possesses high invasive and attachment capabilities as well as a high motility allowing it to invade and survive in a wide variety of tissues for years. Even more challenging, *T. pallidum* cannot be cultured or genetically manipulated, hindering our

Box 3.1 Bone Features of Tuberculosis

Features	Diagnostic strength
Pott's disease	Diagnostic
Osteolytic lesions in the vertebrae	Typical
Periosteal new bone on the visceral surface of ribs	Consistent
Serpens endocrania symmetrica	Consistent
Enlarged vascular foramina	Consistent
Articular erosions and ankylosis	Consistent

understanding of its pathogenesis (Ho and Lukehart, 2011; LaFond and Lukehart, 2006; Peeling and Hook, 2006; Singh and Romanowski, 1999).

Syphilis develops in a multistage process and is responsible for protean clinical manifestations confusing the diagnosis, earning the alias of "great mimicker." Infection occurs by direct contact with active primary or secondary lesions. The replication of *T. pallidum* at the site of the inoculation induces a local inflammation classically resulting in a painless chancre 3–6 weeks after infection and a moderate lymphadenopathy. This primary chancre spontaneously heals within 3–8 weeks, signaling the local clearance of the spirochete. However, at this point, *T. pallidum* has already spread systematically to deep and distant tissues and organs. About 3 months after the onset of the infection, secondary symptoms develop. The most common is a disseminated rash which may appear inconspicuous and can go undetected. Other, although less common, clinical signs include malaise, sore throat, muscle aches, weight loss, general lymphadenopathy, meningitis, ocular inflammation, inflammation of mucosal tissues, and hepatitis (Ho and Lukehart, 2011; LaFond and Lukehart, 2006; Peeling and Hook, 2006; Singh and Romanowski, 1999). Symptoms of secondary syphilis usually resolve spontaneously within 3 months, when the host enters an asymptomatic latent stage leading, if kept untreated, to tertiary syphilis: *T. pallidum* evades immune detection and reactivates to cause symptoms in multiple invaded organs (Ho and Lukehart, 2011; LaFond and Lukehart, 2006). The Oslo Study (Gjestland, 1955) reported that about a third of patients with latent syphilis developed clinical signs of tertiary syphilis, often 20–40 years after primary contact. Gummatous lesions are localized tissue (usually skin) and bone destruction appearing as nodular ulcerative or necrotic lesions (15% of untreated syphilis); they rarely heal spontaneously but can resolve with appropriate antibiotic treatment. They are considered signs of "late benign syphilis" as they do not cause life-threatening complications unless they affect critical organs. Cardiovascular syphilis, another complication of tertiary syphilis, can manifest as aortic insufficiency, aortic aneurysms, or coronary stenosis (10% of untreated syphilis). The primary invasion of the spirochetes may reach the central nervous system and left untreated or inadequately treated, the early neurosyphilis (6.5% of untreated syphilis) may spontaneously resolve or evolve either in asymptomatic meningitis or in acute syphilitic meningitis. In tertiary syphilis, the infection progresses to late neurosyphilis with general paresis and *tabes dorsalis* (Ho and Lukehart, 2011; LaFond and Lukehart, 2006; Peeling and Hook, 2006; Singh and Romanowski, 1999).

Primary yaws and bejel do not affect the skeletal system and lesions in both primary and secondary syphilis generally resolve spontaneously; however, if left untreated, the treponematoses can affect bones and thus may be recognized on skeletons. Nonetheless, the medical literature shows a considerable overlap in bone involvement of most cases of the three syndromes. Secondary yaws can cause bone changes including periostitis and osteitis, in particular in hands and feet (dactylitis) and in long bones, creating an onion-layering aspect on X-rays. Tertiary yaws is rare but can cause gummatous lesions and bone deformities including the saddle-nose deformity, bowing of long bones or saber shin, destruction of the palate and maxilla (rhinopharyngitis obliterans or gangosa), and exostosis of the paranasal maxilla (goundou) (Farnsworth and Rosen, 2006; Marks et al., 2014; Mitjà et al., 2013). Secondary bejel can be accompanied by osteitis and periostitis, and in its late form may evidence bowing of bones, bony gummata, and osteolytic changes (Farnsworth and Rosen, 2006; Marks et al., 2014; Mitjà et al., 2013). Periostitis and osteitis are also observed in secondary syphilis, but are transient and resolve spontaneously (Ortner, 2003, pp. 278–279). In the clinical literature, changes in tertiary syphilis include periostitis and gummatous lesions, particularly involving the cranial bones, tibia, and clavicle, and *tabes dorsalis* resulting in Charcot's joints (Singh and Romanowski, 1999).

Therefore the argument in the discipline is that a differential diagnosis between the three syndromes is likely to be difficult if not impossible on the basis of dry bone lesions. After the analysis of 424 crania and calvariae and 250 long bones in 22 medical museums in Europe and based on his first-hand medical experience with yaws in Uganda, Hackett (1976, 1975) concluded that caries sicca (gummatous lesions on the cranium) (Fig. 3.5) and "nodes/expansions with superficial cavitation in long bones" (gummatous lesions on long bones) are pathognomonic traits of syphilis and of yaws and treponarid in relevant geographical areas (subtropical humid regions for yaws and subtropical non-humid areas for bejel (Aufderheide and Rodríguez-Martín, 1998, p. 154)). Other lesions suggestive of syphilis but not diagnostic, which Hackett (1975) referred to as "on trial," include cortical thickening of long bones or periosteal new bone on the cortical surface creating the appearance of enlarged bones with "larger than usual striae and pits." In addition, given the cardiovascular and neurological complications of syphilis, Hackett (1975) legitimately evokes sternal or vertebral erosions from aortic aneurysms and Charcot's joints from *tabes*

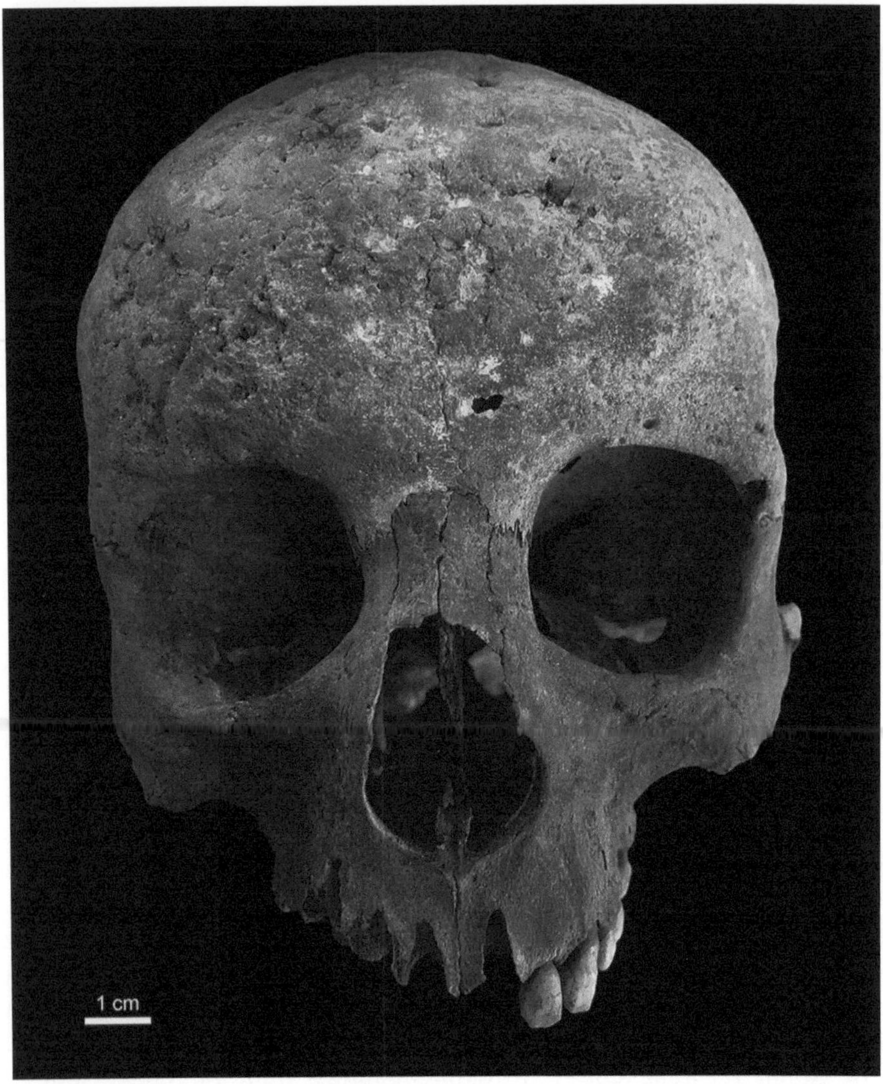

Figure 3.5 Gummatous lesions (frontal bone) or caries sicca due to tertiary syphilis. Source: Archaeological specimen #CG19O-706 from the 17th century Ca' Granda crypt.

dorsalis as potential lesions due to syphilis. Nonetheless, only about 8% of crania/calvariae and one long bone in Hackett's study had documentation supporting the diagnosis of syphilis beyond the morphological appearance of the bone. In spite of this, his work on treponematoses remains a reference for paleopathological analyses (Harper et al., 2013; Mays and Vincent, 2013). Other lesions of tertiary venereal syphilis include saddle-nose deformity, destruction and perforation of the palate, nasal septum and maxillary sinuses, and pathologic fractures due to gummatous osteoperiostitis (Aufderheide and Rodríguez-Martín, 1998; Ortner, 2003). Rothschild and Rothschild (1995) later performed a more "quantitative" analysis on Bedouin and Guam archaeological remains (with bejel and yaws, respectively) and 135 skeletons with diagnosed syphilis from the Hamann–Todd collection, determining the different skeletal distribution of the infectious conditions: syphilis and bejel appear to usually spare hands and feet, while yaws tends to affect more bones than the other treponemal conditions; but all involve principally the tibiae (most commonly bilaterally), femora, fibulae, and cranium. However, this research was met with criticism, particularly given the fact that the authors base their conclusions on a differentiation of the syndromes from undocumented cases (the Guam and Bedouin archaeological specimens) and refute the accepted consensus on the etiology of the disease (Harper et al., 2011; Heathcote et al., 1998).

Congenital syphilis consists in the transmission of the infection from the mother to the fetus through the placenta. Untreated cases are associated with a high risk of stillbirths and neonatal deaths. Manifestations of congenital syphilis are classified into two forms: early congenital syphilis (from birth to about 2 years) and late congenital syphilis (after the age of 2 years). Bone changes in early congenital syphilis include subperiosteal bone deposition, symmetric syphilitic osteochondritis of long bones (areas of increased radiodensities at the epiphyseal–metaphyseal junction) and Wimberger's sign (i.e., bilateral metaphyseal radiolucency of the medial proximal tibia). Manifestations of the late form are similar to those of acquired syphilis (with saber-shin tibiae, gummatous and non-gummatous lesions) and can also include dactylitis and dental stigmata, in particular Hutchinson's incisors (i.e., notched upper permanent central incisors), Moon's molars (i.e., small dome-shaped permanent first molars) and mulberry molars (i.e., permanent first molars with large nodules and tubercles on the occlusal surface) (Aufderheide and Rodríguez-Martín, 1998, pp. 164–166; Hillson et al., 1998; Ioannou et al., 2016; Tesini, 2018).

Contrary to TB, ancient DNA does not seem to be adequate for the study of the condition in dry bones as treponemal DNA is not preserved in human bone (Barnes and Thomas, 2006; Bouwman and Brown, 2005; von Hunnius et al., 2007). Histomorphological features have also been examined as a potential tool for dry bone diagnosis.

Box 3.2 Bone Features of Acquired Syphilis

Features	Diagnostic strength
Gummatous lesions on cranium and long bones	Diagnostic
Saber tibia	Typical
Periosteal new bone	Consistent
Erosions due to aneurysms	Consistent
Charcot's joints	Consistent
Rhinomaxillary changes	Consistent
Histomorphometric features: pollsters and grenzstreifen	Consistent

Unfortunately, "polsters" and "grenzstreifen," suggested to be hallmarks of syphilis (Schultz, 2001), are in fact not pathognomonic for the disease and cannot be used as diagnostic characteristics; interestingly, however, they are indicators of a slow and long-standing infection (De Boer et al., 2013) (Box 3.2).

Leprosy

About 200,000 new cases of leprosy are reported every year making its consideration on dry bone still relevant today (World Health Organization, 2019b). Leprosy is a chronic granulomatous infection caused by the obligate intracellular organism *Mycobacterium leprae*. The transmission of the disease is very low and poorly understood, although we know that risk factors include overcrowding and prolonged contacts. The bacillus enters the body via the nose and spreads through the circulation to the peripheral nerves and skin (Abulafia and Vignale, 1999; Eichelmann et al., 2013; Walker, 1983). The clinical setting of the condition depends on the immune status of the host at and during the infection and is expressed in a spectrum with two opposite poles. At one pole, tuberculoid leprosy is stable, rarely contagious and characterized by high cell–mediated immunity, a limited number of bacilli and a few limited lesions. These lesions are well-defined hypopigmented anesthetic macules or plaques with elevated borders, called "epithelioid granulomas," that may resolve spontaneously; however, the granulomatous inflammation of peripheral nerves will enlarge, causing an impairment of the peripheral nerves with sensory and motor loss and potential necrosis. At the opposite pole of the spectrum, lepromatous leprosy is defined as progressive and systemic with low cell–mediated immunity, high mycobacterial loads in skin and nerves, symmetrical and bilateral wide lesions as confluent papules and nodules named "lepromatous granulomas," greater nerve involvement and more severe disability. Nonetheless, most patients exhibit manifestations intermediate to both polar forms, called borderline leprosy, where both granulomas may appear (Abulafia and Vignale, 1999; Eichelmann et al., 2013; Gulia et al., 2010; Sehgal, 1987; Walker and Lockwood, 2006). Nerve involvement in leprosy leads to thickening of the peripheral nerves, pain, sensory, and motor impairment causing disability and deformity. This impaired sense of touch can result in undetected trauma causing secondary infections and tissue damage, such as ulcers, osteomyelitis, and neuropathic arthropathy. Other complications include osteoporosis, testicular damage, and eye involvement with blindness occurring in 3.2% of patients (Eichelmann et al., 2013; Walker and Lockwood, 2006).

Nonetheless, this clinical classification of leprosy cannot be achieved on dry bones as in living patients, although Andersen et al. (1994) suggest that symmetrical lesions in the extremities may be attributed to lepromatous leprosy or borderline lepromatous leprosy. The small bones of the hands and feet are the preferred locations for bone lesions in leprosy, but the tibiae and fibulae may also be affected (Andersen et al., 1994; Ortner, 2003, pp. 278–289). These lesions are the result of ulcerations and infections secondary to long-standing nerve involvement and unperceived microtrauma; they include periosteal new bone, osteomyelitis, destruction of the joints, and ankylosis (Andersen et al., 1994; Faget and Mayoral, 1944). Two lesions in particular are characteristic of the infectious condition: severe erosion of the tubular bones of the hands and feet, particularly in the phalanges, and rhinomaxillary changes. The former is a late manifestation of leprosy, classically described as "concentric bone atrophy" of the phalanges (Faget and Mayoral, 1944; Møller-Christensen et al., 1952; Talhari et al., 2015). The latter corresponds to the clinical "Bergen syndrome," a facial disfigurement associated with a rhinomaxillary syndrome occurring in severe, advanced and long-standing lepromatous or near-lepromatous leprosy patients (Andersen and Manchester, 1992). Møller-Christensen (1961, 1953, 1952) described these rhinomaxillary changes osteologically based on his study of skeletal material from medieval Danish leper cemeteries and referred to them as "facies leprosa." In living patients, progressive changes may be observed: first, the infiltration of the mycobacteria in the nasal septum will induce a mucosal swelling; if the olfactory nerves are involved, anosmia may occur; later, the perforation of the nasal septum with sparing of the nasal bones will lead to "saddle-nose" deformity and the swollen mucosa may ulcerate resulting in its atrophy; finally, late manifestations include perforation of the palate and loss of the central and lateral maxillary incisors (Andersen and Manchester, 1992). In skeletonized material, rhinomaxillary changes include resorption of the anterior nasal spine (present in about 80% of leprosy skeletons), bilateral symmetrical resorption of the alveolar process of the maxilla (first extending anteroposteriorly and then progressing superiorly) leading to the loss of the central and lateral maxillary incisors, bilateral symmetrical resorption of the margins of the nasal aperture, erosive changes on the nasal and oral surfaces of the palatine process of the maxilla leading to perforation of the hard palate, pitting on the nasal septum, and resorption on the inferior nasal conchae (Andersen and Manchester, 1992; Møller-Christensen et al., 1952).

However, all rhinomaxillary changes—except for the resorption of the anterior nasal spine caused directly by the bacilli—are signs of inflammatory reactions that may not be necessarily attributed to leprosy. For instance, a resorption of the alveolar process of the maxilla is not significant in the absence of upper incisors. Similarly, leprosy bone lesions in the post-cranial skeleton may be identical to lesions in osteomyelitis (from other causes), diabetic gangrene, gout, psoriatic arthritis, TB, dactylitis, sarcoidosis, and *tabes dorsalis* in tertiary syphilis. Although just like venereal syphilis, histomorphological features of leprosy are not specific to the disease (De Boer et al., 2013; Schultz, 2001), aDNA amplification and lipid biomarkers can be used for its identification in ancient remains (Inskip et al., 2017, 2015; Michael Taylor et al., 2018; Rafi et al., 1994; Taylor et al., 2009) (Box 3.3).

Box 3.3 Bone Features of Leprosy

Features	Diagnostic strength
Rhinomaxillary changes	Typical
Concentric atrophy of the phalanges	Typical
Histomorphological features	Consistent

Fungal Diseases

Today, nearly a billion people are estimated to have a fungal infection (Bongomin et al., 2017). Bone changes in fungal disease can occur via systemic hematological dissemination to the skeleton or via direct extension from soft tissue lesions (Hay, 2006; Lupi et al., 2005; Ortner, 2003). The disease is rarely reported in the paleopathological record; in fact, only five cases were reported in the archaeological literature (Micarelli et al., 2019; Ortner, 2003) in which a diagnosis of mycosis was plausible. Mycoses (in particular, blastomycosis, paracoccidioidomycosis, coccidioidomycosis, histoplasmosis, criptococcosis, candidiasis, aspergillosis, mucormycosis, sporotrichosis, maduromycosis) tend to present similar lesions, that is, osteolytic lesions with well-defined margins and punched-out appearance, and possible periosteal new bone of variable extension, and a random distribution (Aufderheide and Rodríguez-Martín, 1998; Bradsher, 1992; Gehweiler et al., 1970; Hay, 2006; Lupi et al., 2005; Moore and Green, 1982; Ortner, 2003). This random distribution of bone changes may allow their distinction from other infectious diseases, whereas it renders the differential diagnosis among mycoses impossible (Aufderheide and Rodríguez-Martín, 1998; Ortner, 2003). Bone lesions in blastomycosis, coccidioidomycosis, paracoccidioidomycosis, and aspergillosis may simulate TB as well as primary and metastatic neoplasia, often causing misdiagnoses (Aufderheide and Rodríguez-Martín, 1998; Bradsher, 1992; Gehweiler et al., 1970; Moore and Green, 1982; Ortner, 2003). Similarly, nasomaxillary bone changes in mucormycosis may be confused with treponematosis and leprosy (Ortner, 2003). Hershkovitz et al. (1998) worked to answer this question by comparing a skeleton diagnosed in life with blastomycosis from the Terry collection with skeletons diagnosed with metastatic cancer and TB from the Hamann–Todd collection. They demonstrated that both the distribution and the aspect of lesions of the skeleton with the fungal disease are distinguishable from TB and metastatic cancer. For instance, both the cortical and trabecular bone are equally affected in blastomycosis, while this is not true in metastatic cancer and TB. However, this research was performed on only one skeleton with blastomycosis; it would therefore be interesting to see if the same analysis and distinguishing features are shared by other skeletons with the diagnosed fungal disease.

Parasitic Infections

Parasitic infection in humans may be caused by endoparasites (including protozoa and helminth) or ectoparasites (flea, ticks, head, and body lice). The first parasite in archaeological material was found by Sir Armand Ruffer (1910) in his recovery of well-preserved calcified eggs in the kidney tissue of Egyptian mummies dated c.1200 BCE. Parasitic infection can thus be identified in skeletal remains through the recovery of hydatid cysts (in particular for echinococcosis), ova, and worms in (rehydrated) coprolites (Araújo et al., 2015; Aufderheide and Rodríguez-Martín, 1998; Ortner, 2003; Reinhard et al., 2013; Roberts and Manchester, 2007) but also on dry bones such as in malaria.

Malaria is an infection affecting about 220 million people caused by the parasites *Plasmodium falciparum* and to a lesser extent *Plasmodium vivax* in endemic regions of the world. After a mosquito bite injects the parasites in the subcutaneous tissue, they migrate via the bloodstream and invade the liver where they bind to red blood cells. These merozoites destroy both parasitized and non-parasitized red blood cells, cause microvascular obstruction and induce systemic inflammation. Clinical presentation may be acute, with metabolic acidosis, severe anemia, cerebral malaria, and respiratory distress or chronic, with a severe anemia in spite of a low parasitemia (Miller et al., 2002; Wickramasinghe and Abdalla, 2000). Anemia is a common complication of both acute and chronic malaria (Ghosh and Ghosh, 2007). It may vary on a spectrum from mild, and thus benign, to severe and life-threatening. Hemolysis and impaired erythropoiesis, both direct and indirect consequences of the parasitic infection, are major factors in the etiology of anemia in malaria (Wickramasinghe and Abdalla, 2000). Nonetheless, comorbidities including iron, folate, and vitamin B12 deficiencies, other nutritional deficiencies may cause anemia in malaria infection and antimalarial therapy may aggravate it by hemolysis and bone marrow suppression (Ghosh and Ghosh, 2007).

Anemia is of special interest as it is a common complication of malaria found to cause bone lesions (Ghosh and Ghosh, 2007; Nagel, 2002). Indeed, while past studies have demonstrated the potential of biomolecular analyses to directly identify *Plasmodium falciparum* in ancient human remains (Nerlich et al., 2008), Rabino Massa et al. (2000) performed immunological tests on Egyptian mummies dated 3200 BCE and report porotic hyperostosis and *cribra orbitalia* (bone lesions commonly associated with anemia) in 92% of mummies tested positive for malaria. More recently, Smith-Guzmán (2015) furthered

Box 3.4 Bone Features of Malaria

Features	Diagnostic strength
Cribra orbitalia	Consistent
Porotic hyperostosis	Consistent
Humeral cribra	Consistent
Femoral cribra	Consistent

this question by performing a study on 98 individuals, including 27 with a reported cause-of-death of either malaria or anemia from the Galloway Osteological Collection, a documented collection of 592 unclaimed donated individuals from the Mulago hospital in Uganda (a region known to be holoendemic for malaria), and concludes that *cribra orbitalia*, spinal porosity, humeral cribra, and femoral cribra are lesions indicative of malarial disease (Box 3.4).

Viral Infections

While measles and influenza do not affect the skeleton, other viral infections such as smallpox, rubella, poliomyelitis, and the Human Immunodeficiency Virus (HIV) may lead to bone changes.

Smallpox is caused by the variola virus, specific to humans (Henderson, 1999; Moore et al., 2006). The virus must pass from one individual to the next in a continuing chain of transmission to sustain itself (Henderson, 1999; Moore et al., 2006). Thanks to a coordinated international effort initiated in 1966, the World Health Organization announced the worldwide eradication of smallpox in 1980 (Breman and Arita, 1980). The virus spreads by inhalation and infects the respiratory tract mucosa where it replicates, resulting in a primary viremia. During the immune response, the macrophages take on the virus which enters the reticuloendothelial system where it replicates, causing a second viremia and the onset of symptoms. Two variants of smallpox are described: variola major (with a fatality rate of about 30%) and variola minor (less virulent, extremely contagious and a fatality rate of less than 1%). In the former, the disease may be expressed according to several types, among which ordinary smallpox, by far the most common (about 90% of cases), is characterized by raised pustular lesions (Moore et al., 2006). During the clinical evolution of the infection, pain increases, febrility is maintained and a papular rash appears on the face and spreads to the extremities; the rash becomes pustular and further heals in scabs (Henderson, 1999; Moore et al., 2006). Skeletal complications may occur in up to 20% of young children (Davidson and Palmer, 1963) 1–6 weeks after the onset of smallpox (Cockshott and MacGregor, 1958) and manifest as "osteomyelitis variolosa." Initially, the lesions start as an arthritis with diffuse periarticular swelling, in particular in the elbows (about 80% of patients). The separation of the epiphysis at the epiphyseal junction is characteristic of osteomyelitis variolosa; severe lesions may provoke the detachment and destruction of the epiphysis causing disorganization of the joint. Marked periosteal new bone ensues and bone destruction may be observed in the small tubular bones of the hands and feet, also resulting in deformation of the joints. Lesions develop symmetrically, bilaterally and multifocally, primarily in the elbows but also in the wrist, knees, and ankles, resulting in severe disability. Sequellae include ankylosis of the joints, reduction of the longitudinal growth with deformation, and secondary osteoarthritis (Cockshott and MacGregor, 1958; Davidson and Palmer, 1963; Eeckels et al., 1964; Jackes, 1983). Transverse bands of juxtametaphyseal osteoporosis can be seen on roentgenographic images (Eeckels et al., 1964). Nonetheless, these lesions may appear similar to TB, syphilis, leprosy, and sarcoidosis on dry bones (Lefort and Bennike, 2007) and a certain diagnosis based on the morphological appearance of the lesions may be impossible.

Rubella, also known as German measles, is an acute airborne infection preventable by vaccination. While it is harmless in children and adults, it may have serious consequences on fetuses. In adults, arthritis of the small joints of the hands and feet may be seen; in infants, rubella can provoke skeletal changes in the metaphysis of the long bones, manifesting as radiolucent bands due to poor mineralization, coarsening of the trabeculae, and retardation of growth. In particular, "beaklike projections" may be observed in metaphyses during healing. If the infant survives the viral infection, bone changes may spontaneously resolve in a few months. However, these changes may appear similar to early rickets and congenital syphilis and may be due to nutritional deficiencies (Aufderheide and Rodríguez-Martín, 1998, pp. 209–210; Lewis, 2017, pp. 152–153; Ortner, 2003, pp. 336–337; Reed, 1969).

Like smallpox, poliovirus only affects humans and spreads through person-to-person contact. *Poliomyelitis* is still not eradicated; it is highly infectious and mainly affects children under 5 years of age. It may lead to osteoporosis, pathologic fractures as well as underdevelopment and deformities in children including scoliosis, limb shortening (due to post-polio paralysis), talipes cavus and talipes equinovarus (i.e., high arched foot deformities) and coxa valga (i.e., increased femoral head to neck angle) (Aufderheide and Rodríguez-Martín, 1998, p. 212; Faraj, 2006; Lewis, 2017, pp. 153–155; Sharma et al., 1991). A possible case of poliomyelitis from the 15th century Portugal was reported by Umbelino et al. (1996) based on an asymmetry of the lower limbs with a shortening of the right leg and differential muscular activity, coxa valga, a scoliosis, a fracture on the right tibia, and stress markers (specifically, Harris lines, *cribra orbitalia*, and enamel hypoplasia).

HIV is a virus that attacks and damages the immune system ultimately leading to Acquired Immunodeficiency Syndrome (AIDS), leaving the immune system vulnerable to opportunistic infections. Although HIV does not directly affect bones, HIV/AIDS-induced infections and inflammations and HIV-related risk factors may produce skeletal changes. Long-standing HIV and antiretroviral therapy are associated with low bone mineral density, osteopenia, osteoporosis, osteonecrosis, osteomalacia, and a higher rate of fractures (Ahmad et al., 2017; Cotter and Powderly, 2011). Other

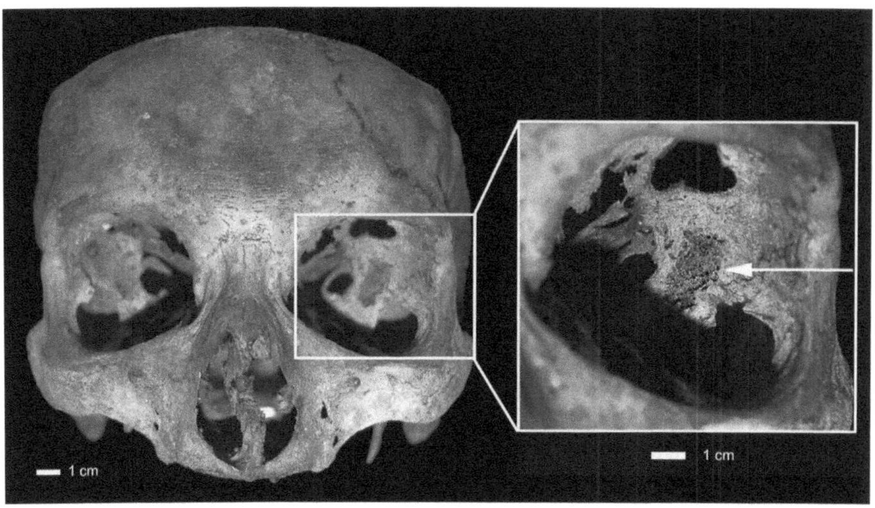

Figure 3.6 Porotic lesion (white arrow) on the orbital plate of the greater wing of the sphenoid bone (left orbit) consistent with an eye infection, common in immunodepressed individuals such as HIV infected patients. Skeleton #289 of the CAL Milano Cemetery Skeletal Collection with a clinical diagnosis of HIV. Reproduced with permission from Biehler-Gomez, L., Cabrini, A., De Angelis, D., Cattaneo, C., 2018. How do skeletons with HIV present? A study on the identified CAL Milano Cemetery Skeletal Collection. Leg. Med. 33, 11–16. doi:10.1016/j.legalmed.2018.04.007.

complications of HIV infection include septic arthritis, reactive arthritis, TB, and osteomyelitis (Greenberg and Lahart, 2000; Vigorita et al., 2016). In addition, neuropathy has been mentioned as a possible complication of antiretroviral therapy (Greenberg and Lahart, 2000) potentially leading to Charcot's joints (i.e., neuropathic arthropathy). Finally, a recent study (Biehler-Gomez et al., 2018) examined nine skeletons with an antemortem record of HIV (including four with AIDS) from the CAL Milano Cemetery Skeletal Collection (Fig. 3.6). While the authors explain that HIV infection cannot be diagnosed on dry bones, they also evidenced lesions consistent with HIV/AIDS-induced infections noted in the antemortem data. However, the identification of HIV biomolecular markers in decomposed bloodstains (Cattaneo et al., 1996) and in dry bone (Pérez-Martínez et al., 2016) constitute a reliable technique to identify the disease in decomposed or skeletonized remains.

References

Abulafia, J., Vignale, R.A., 1999. Leprosy: pathogenesis updated. Int. J. Dermatol. 38, 321–334. Available from: https://doi.org/10.1046/j.1365-4362.1999.00650.x.

Ahmad, A.N., Ahmad, S.N., Ahmad, N., 2017. HIV Infection and bone abnormalities. Open. Orthop. J. 11, 777–784. Available from: https://doi.org/10.2174/1874325001711010777.

Andersen, J.G., Manchester, K., 1992. The rhinomaxillary syndrome in leprosy: a clinical, radiological and palaeopathological study. Int. J. Osteoarchaeol. 2, 121–129. Available from: https://doi.org/10.1002/oa.1390020204.

Andersen, J.G., Manchester, K., Roberts, C.A., 1994. Septic bone changes in leprosy: a clinical, radiological and palaeopathological review. Int. J. Osteoarchaeol. 4, 21–30. Available from: https://doi.org/10.1002/oa.1390040105.

Araújo, A., Reinhard, K.J., Ferreira, L.F., 2015. Chapter nine - palaeoparasitology — human parasites in ancient material. In: De Baets, K., Littlewood, D.T. (Eds.), Fossil Parasites. Academic Press, pp. 349–387. Available from: https://doi.org/10.1016/bs.apar.2015.03.003.

Aufderheide, A.C., Rodríguez-Martín, C., 1998. The Cambridge Encyclopedia of Human Paleopathology. Cambridge University Press, Cambridge, United Kingdom.

Barnes, I., Thomas, M.G., 2006. Evaluating bacterial pathogen DNA preservation in museum osteological collections. Proc. R. Soc. B Biol. Sci. 273, 645–653. Available from: https://doi.org/10.1098/rspb.2005.3339.

Biehler-Gomez, L., Cabrini, A., De Angelis, D., Cattaneo, C., 2018. How do skeletons with HIV present? A study on the identified CAL Milano Cemetery Skeletal Collection. Leg. Med. 33, 11–16. Available from: https://doi.org/10.1016/j.legalmed.2018.04.007.

Bongomin, F., Gago, S., Oladele, R.O., Denning, D.W., 2017. Global and multi-national prevalence of fungal diseases-estimate precision. J. Fungi 3, 57. Available from: https://doi.org/10.3390/jof3040057.

Bouwman, A.S., Brown, T.A., 2005. The limits of biomolecular palaeopathology: ancient DNA cannot be used to study venereal syphilis. J. Archaeol. Sci. 32, 703–713. Available from: https://doi.org/10.1016/j.jas.2004.11.014.

Bradsher, R.W., 1992. Blastomycosis. Clin. Infect. Dis. 14, S82–S90.

Breman, J.G., Arita, I., 1980. The confirmation and maintenance of smallpox eradication.

Cattaneo, C., Nuttall, P.A., Sokol, R.J., 1996. Detection of HIV, hepatitis B and hepatitis C markers in discarded syringes and bloodstains. Sci. Justice 36, 271–274. Available from: https://doi.org/10.1016/S1355-0306(96)72613-8.

Chhem, R.K., Brothwell, D., 2008. Paleoradiology: Imaging Mummies and Fossils. Springer, Berlin (Germany).

Cockshott, P., MacGregor, M., 1958. Osteomyelitis Variolosa. Q. J. Med. 27, 369–387.

Cotter, A.G., Powderly, W.G., 2011. Endocrine complications of human immunodeficiency virus infection: hypogonadism, bone disease and tenofovir-related toxicity. Best. Pract. Res. Clin. Endocrinol. Metab. 25, 501–515. Available from: https://doi.org/10.1016/j.beem.2010.11.003.

Davidson, J.C., Palmer, P.E.S., 1963. Osteomyelitis variolosa. J. Bone Joint Surg. Br. 45-B, 687–693. Available from: https://doi.org/10.1302/0301-620X.45B4.687.

Dayal, M.R., Kegley, A.D.T., Strkalj, G., Bidmos, M.A., Kuykendall, K.L., 2009. The history and composition of the Raymond A. Dart Collection of Human Skeletons at the University of the Witwatersrand, Johannesburg, South Africa. Am. J. Phys. Anthropol. 140, 324–335. Available from: https://doi.org/10.1002/ajpa.21072.

De Boer, H.H., Van der Merwe, A.E., Maat, G.J.R., 2013. The diagnostic value of microscopy in dry bone palaeopathology: a review. Int. J. Paleopathol. 3, 113–121. Available from: https://doi.org/10.1016/j.ijpp.2013.03.004.

Donoghue, H.D., Spigelman, M., Greenblatt, C.L., Lev-Maor, G., Bar-Gal, G.K., Matheson, C., et al., 2004. Tuberculosis: from prehistory to Robert Koch, as revealed by ancient DNA. Lancet Infect. Dis. 4, 584–592.

Eeckels, R., Vincent, J., Seynhaeve, V., 1964. Bone lesions due to smallpox. Arch. Dis. Child. 39, 591–597.

Eichelmann, K., González González, S.E., Salas-Alanis, J.C., Ocampo-Candiani, J., 2013. Leprosy. An update: definition, pathogenesis, classification, diagnosis, and treatment. Actas Dermosifiliogr. 104, 554–563 (English Ed.). Available from: https://doi.org/10.1016/j.adengl.2012.03.028.

Faget, G.H., Mayoral, A., 1944. Bone changes in leprosy: a clinical and roentgenologic study of 505 cases. Radiology 42, 1–13. Available from: https://doi.org/10.1148/42.1.1.

Faraj, A.A., 2006. Poliomyelitis: orthopaedic management. Curr. Orthop. 20, 41–46. Available from: https://doi.org/10.1016/j.cuor.2005.10.005.

Farnsworth, N., Rosen, T., 2006. Endemic treponematosis: review and update. Clin. Dermatol. 24, 181–190. Available from: https://doi.org/10.1016/j.clindermatol.2005.11.004.

Gehweiler, J.A., Capp, M.P., Chick, E.W., 1970. Observations on the roentgen patterns in blastomycosis of bone: a review of cases from the blastomycosis cooperative study of the Veterans Administration and Duke University Medical Center. Am. J. Roentgenol. 108, 497–510.

Ghosh, K., Ghosh, K., 2007. Pathogenesis of anemia in malaria: a concise review. Parasitol. Res. 101, 1463–1469. Available from: https://doi.org/10.1007/s00436-007-0742-1.

Gjestland, T., 1955. The Oslo study of untreated syphilis; an epidemiologic investigation of the natural course of the syphilitic infection based upon a re-study of the Boeck-Bruusgaard material. Acta Derm. Venereol. Suppl. (Stockh) 35, 3.

Gold, R.H., Hawkins, R.A., Katz, R.D., 1991. Bacterial osteomyelitis: findings on plain radiography, CT, MR, and scintigraphy. Am. J. Roentgenol. 157, 365–370. Available from: https://doi.org/10.2214/ajr.157.2.1853823.

Golden, M.P., Vikram, H.R., 2005. Extrapulmonary tuberculosis: an overview. Am. Fam. Physician 72, 1761–1768.

Greenberg, S.B., Lahart, C.J., 2000. HIV/AIDS: clinical considerations. In: Humes, H.D., DuPont, H.L., Gardner, L.B., Griffin, J.W., Harris, E.D., Hazzard, W.R., King, T.E., Loriaux, D.L., Nabel, E.G., Todd, R.F., Traber, P.G. (Eds.), Kelley's Textbook of Internal Medicine. Lippincott Williams & Wilkins, Philadelphia, PA, pp. 2320–2328.

Gulia, A., Fried, I., Massone, C., 2010. New insights in the pathogenesis and genetics of leprosy. F1000 Med. Rep. 2, 30. Available from: https://doi.org/10.3410/M2-30.

Hackett, C.J., 1975. An introduction to diagnostic criteria of syphilis, treponarid and yaws (treponematoses) in dry bones, and some implications. Virchows Arch. A 368, 229–241. Available from: https://doi.org/10.1007/BF00432525.

Hackett, C.J., 1976. Diagnostic Criteria of Syphilis, Yaws and Treponarid (Treponematoses) and Some Other Diseases in Dry Bones. Springer-Verlag, Berlin (Germany).

Harper, K.N., Zuckerman, M.K., Armelagos, G.J., 2013. Correspondence: a possible (but not probable?) case of treponemal disease. Int. J. Osteoarchaeol. 23, 626–627. Available from: https://doi.org/10.1002/oa.1283.

Harper, K.N., Zuckerman, M.K., Harper, M.L., Kingston, J.D., Armelagos, G.J., 2011. The origin and antiquity of syphilis revisited: an appraisal of old world pre-Columbian evidence for treponemal infection. Am. J. Phys. Anthropol. 146, 99–133. Available from: https://doi.org/10.1002/ajpa.21613.

Hay, R.J., 2006. Fungal infections. Clin. Dermatol. 24, 201–212. Available from: https://doi.org/10.1016/j.clindermatol.2005.11.011.

Heathcote, G.M., Stodder, A.L.W., Buckley, H.R., Hanson, D.B., Douglas, M.T., Underwood, J.H., et al., 1998. On treponemal disease in the Western Pacific: corrections and critique. Curr. Anthropol. 39, 359–368. Available from: https://doi.org/10.1086/204745.

Henderson, D.A., 1999. Smallpox: clinical and epidemiologic features. Emerg. Infect. Dis. 5, 537–539. Available from: https://doi.org/10.3201/eid0504.990415.

Hershkovitz, I., Greenwald, C.M., Latimer, B.M., Jellema, L.M., Wish-Baratz, S., Eshed, V., et al., 2002. Serpens endocrania symmetrica (SES): a new term and a possible clue for identifying intrathoracic disease in skeletal populations. Am. J. Phys. Anthropol. 118, 201–216. Available from: https://doi.org/10.1002/ajpa.10077.

Hershkovitz, I., Rothschild, B.M., Dutour, O., Greenwald, C.M., 1998. Clues to recognition of fungal origin of lytic skeletal lesions. Am. J. Phys. Anthropol. 106, 47–60. Available from: https://doi.org/10.1002/(SICI)1096-8644(199805)106:1<47::AID-AJPA4>3.0.CO;2-A.

Hillson, S., 2005. Teeth, 2nd ed. Cambridge University Press.

Hillson, S., 2019. Dental pathology. In: Katzenberg, M.A., Grauer, A.L. (Eds.), Biological Anthropology of the Human Skeleton. John Wiley & Sons, New York, pp. 295–334.

Hillson, S., Grigson, C., Bond, S., 1998. Dental defects of congenital syphilis. Am. J. Phys. Anthropol. 107, 25–40. Available from: https://doi.org/10.1002/(SICI)1096-8644(199809)107:1<25::AID-AJPA3>3.0.CO;2-C.

Ho, E.L., Lukehart, S.A., 2011. Syphilis: using modern approaches to understand an old disease. J. Clin. Invest. 121, 4584–4592. Available from: https://doi.org/10.1172/JCI57173.

Holloway, K.L., Link, K., Rühli, F.J., Henneberg, M., 2013. Skeletal lesions in human tuberculosis may sometimes heal: an aid to palaeopathological diagnoses. PLoS One 8, e62798.

Hopewell, P.C., 1994. Overview of clinical tuberculosis. In: Bloom, B.R. (Ed.), Tuberculosis: Pathogenesis, Protection, and Control. American Society for Microbiology, Washington, DC, pp. 25–46. Available from: https://doi.org/10.1128/9781555818357.ch3.

Inskip, S.A., Taylor, G.M., Anderson, S., Stewart, G., 2017. Leprosy in pre-Norman Suffolk, UK: biomolecular and geochemical analysis of the woman from Hoxne. J. Med. Microbiol. 66, 1640–1649.

Inskip, S.A., Taylor, G.M., Zakrzewski, S.R., Mays, S.A., Pike, A.W.G., Llewellyn, G., et al., 2015. Osteological, biomolecular and geochemical examination of an early anglo-saxon case of lepromatous leprosy. PLoS One 10, e0124282–e0124282. Available from: https://doi.org/10.1371/journal.pone.0124282.

Ioannou, S., Sassani, S., Henneberg, M., Henneberg, R.J., 2016. Diagnosing congenital syphilis using Hutchinson's method: differentiating between syphilitic, mercurial, and syphilitic-mercurial dental defects. Am. J. Phys. Anthropol. 159, 617–629. Available from: https://doi.org/10.1002/ajpa.22924.

Jackes, M.K., 1983. Osteological evidence for smallpox: a possible case from seventeenth century Ontario. Am. J. Phys. Anthropol. 60, 75–81. Available from: https://doi.org/10.1002/ajpa.1330600112.

Jain, R., Sawhney, S., Berry, M., 1993. Computed tomography of vertebral tuberculosis: patterns of bone destruction. Clin. Radiol. 47, 196–199.

Kelley, M.A., El-Najjar, M.Y., 1980. Natural variation and differential diagnosis of skeletal changes in tuberculosis. Am. J. Phys. Anthropol. 52, 153–167. Available from: https://doi.org/10.1002/ajpa.1330520202.

Kelley, M.A., Micozzi, M.S., 1984. Rib lesions in chronic pulmonary tuberculosis. Am. J. Phys. Anthropol. 65, 381–386. Available from: https://doi.org/10.1002/ajpa.1330650407.

Kuhn, G., Schultz, M., Müller, R., Rühli, F.J., 2007. Diagnostic value of micro-CT in comparison with histology in the qualitative assessment of historical human postcranial bone pathologies. HOMO 58, 97–115. Available from: https://doi.org/10.1016/j.jchb.2006.11.002.

L'Abbé, E.N., Loots, M., Meiring, J.H., 2005. The Pretoria Bone Collection: a modern South African skeletal sample. HOMO 56, 197–205. Available from: https://doi.org/10.1016/j.jchb.2004.10.004.

LaFond, R.E., Lukehart, S.A., 2006. Biological basis for syphilis. Clin. Microbiol. Rev. 19, 29–49. LP.

Lefort, M., Bennike, P., 2007. A case study of possible differential diagnoses of a medieval skeleton from Denmark: leprosy, ergotism, treponematosis, sarcoidosis or smallpox? Int. J. Osteoarchaeol. 17, 337–349. Available from: https://doi.org/10.1002/oa.905.

Lew, D.P., Waldvogel, F.A., 1997. Osteomyelitis. N. Engl. J. Med. 336, 999–1007. Available from: https://doi.org/10.1056/NEJM199704033361406.

Lew, D.P., Waldvogel, F.A., 2004. Osteomyelitis. Lancet 364, 369–379.

Lewis, M., 2017. Paleopathology of Children: Identification of Pathological Conditions in the Human Skeletal Remains of Non-adults. Academic Press.

Lupi, O., Tyring, S.K., McGinnis, M.R., 2005. Tropical dermatology: fungal tropical diseases. J. Am. Acad. Dermatol. 53, 931–951. Available from: https://doi.org/10.1016/j.jaad.2004.10.883.

Mariotti, V., Zuppello, M., Pedrosi, M.E., Bettuzzi, M., Brancaccio, R., Peccenini, E., et al., 2015. Skeletal evidence of tuberculosis in a modern identified human skeletal collection (Certosa cemetery, Bologna, Italy). Am. J. Phys. Anthropol. 157, 389–401. Available from: https://doi.org/10.1002/ajpa.22727.

Marks, M., Solomon, A.W., Mabey, D.C., 2014. Endemic treponemal diseases. Trans. R. Soc. Trop. Med. Hyg. 108, 601–607. Available from: https://doi.org/10.1093/trstmh/tru128.

Martrille, L., De Angelis, D., Blum, A., Gauchotte, G., Cattaneo, C., Biehler-Gomez, L., 2020. The potential of bone disease for personal identification: a case of tuberculosis. Int. J. Leg. Med. 1–6. Available from: https://doi.org/10.1007/s00414-020-02348-3.

Matos, V., Santos, A.L., 2006. On the trail of pulmonary tuberculosis based on rib lesions: results from the human identified skeletal collection from the Museu Bocage (Lisbon, Portugal). Am. J. Phys. Anthropol. 130, 190–200. Available from: https://doi.org/10.1002/ajpa.20309.

Mays, S., Taylor, G.M., Legge, A.J., Young, D.B., Turner-Walker, G., 2001. Paleopathological and biomolecular study of tuberculosis in a medieval skeletal collection from England. Am. J. Phys. Anthropol. 114, 298–311. Available from: https://doi.org/10.1002/ajpa.1042.

Mays, S., Vincent, S., 2013. Correspondence: probable and possible cases of treponematosis: a response to the comment 'A Possible (But not Probable) Case of Treponemal Disease' by Harper, Zuckerman and Armelagos. Int. J. Osteoarchaeol. 23, 628–629. Available from: https://doi.org/10.1002/oa.1282.

Micarelli, I., Paine, R.R., Tafuri, M.A., Manzi, G., 2019. A possible case of mycosis in a post-classical burial from La Selvicciola (Italy). Int. J. Paleopathol. 24, 25–33. Available from: https://doi.org/10.1016/j.ijpp.2018.09.001.

Michael Taylor, G., Murphy, E.M., Mendum, T.A., Pike, A.W.G., Linscott, B., Wu, H., et al., 2018. Leprosy at the edge of Europe—Biomolecular, isotopic and osteoarchaeological findings from medieval Ireland. PLoS One 13, 1–27. Available from: https://doi.org/10.1371/journal.pone.0209495.

Miller, L.H., Baruch, D.I., Marsh, K., Doumbo, O.K., 2002. The pathogenic basis of malaria. Nature 415, 673.

Mitjà, O., Asiedu, K., Mabey, D., 2013. Yaws. Lancet 381, 763–773. Available from: https://doi.org/10.1016/S0140-6736(12)62130-8.

Møller-Christensen, V., 1953. Ten Lepers From Næstved in Denmark: A Study of Skeletons From a Medieval Danish Leper Hospital. Danish Science Press.

Møller-Christensen, V., 1961. Bone Changes in Leprosy. Munksgaard, Denmark, Copenhagen.

Møller-Christensen, V., Bakke, S.N., Melsom, R.S., Waaler, E., 1952. Changes in the anterior nasal spine and the alveolar process of the maxillary bone in leprosy. Internat. J. Lepr. 20, 335–340.

Moore, R.M., Green, N.E., 1982. Blastomycosis of bone. A report of six cases. JBJS 64.

Moore, Z.S., Seward, J.F., Lane, J.M., 2006. Smallpox. Lancet 367, 425–435. Available from: https://doi.org/10.1016/S0140-6736(06)68143-9.

Nagel, R.L., 2002. Malarial anemia. Hemoglobin 26, 329–343. Available from: https://doi.org/10.1081/HEM-120016370.

Nerlich, A.G., Haas, C.J., Zink, A., Szeimies, U., Hagedorn, H.G., 1997. Molecular evidence for tuberculosis in an ancient Egyptian mummy. Lancet 350, 1404.

Nerlich, A.G., Schraut, B., Dittrich, S., Jelinek, T., Zink, A., 2008. Plasmodium falciparum in ancient Egypt. Emerg. Infect. Dis. 14, 1317–1319. Available from: https://doi.org/10.3201/eid1408.080235.

Ortner, D.J., 2003. Identification of Pathological Conditions in Human Skeletal Remains, 3rd ed. Smithsonian Institution Press, New York.

Ortner, D.J., 2011. What skeletons tell us. The story of human paleopathology. Virchows Arch. 459, 247–254. Available from: https://doi.org/10.1007/s00428-011-1122-x.

Ortner, D.J., Aufderheide, A.C., 1991. Human Paleopathology: Current Syntheses and Future Options. Smithsonian Institution Press, Washington, DC.

Pálfi, G., Bereczki, Z., Ortner, D.J., Dutour, O., 2012. Juvenile cases of skeletal tuberculosis from the Terry Anatomical collection (Smithsonian Institution, Washington, DC, USA). Acta Biol. Szeged. 56, 1–12.

Peeling, R.W., Hook, E.W., 2006. The pathogenesis of syphilis: the Great Mimicker, revisited. J. Pathol. 208, 224–232. Available from: https://doi.org/10.1002/path.1903.

Pérez-Martínez, C., Prieto-Bonete, G., Pérez-Cárceles, M.D., Luna, A., 2016. Usefulness of protein analysis for detecting pathologies in bone remains. Forensic Sci. Int. 258, 68–73. Available from: https://doi.org/10.1016/j.forsciint.2015.11.009.

Pigrau-Serrallach, C., Rodríguez-Pardo, D., 2013. Bone and joint tuberculosis. Eur. Spine J. 22, 556–566. Available from: https://doi.org/10.1007/s00586-012-2331-y.

Rabino Massa, E., Cerutti, N., Marin, D., Savoia, A., 2000. Malaria in Ancient Egypt: paleoimmunological investigation on predynastic mummified remains. Chungará (Arica) 32 (1).

Rafi, A., Spigelman, M., Stanford, J., Lemma, E., Donoghue, H., Zias, J., 1994. DNA of Mycobacterium leprae detected by PCR in ancient bone. Int. J. Osteoarchaeol. 4, 287–290. Available from: https://doi.org/10.1002/oa.1390040403.

Ragsdale, B.D., Campbell, R.A., Kirkpatrick, C.L., 2018. Neoplasm or not? General principles of morphologic analysis of dry bone specimens. Int. J. Paleopathol. 21, 27–40. Available from: https://doi.org/10.1016/j.ijpp.2017.02.002.

Rana, R.S., Wu, J.S., Eisenberg, R.L., 2009. Periosteal reaction. Am. J. Roentgenol. 193, W259–W272. Available from: https://doi.org/10.2214/AJR.09.3300.

Redman, J.E., Shaw, M.J., Mallet, A.I., Santos, A.L., Roberts, C.A., Gernaey, A.M., et al., 2009. Mycocerosic acid biomarkers for the diagnosis of tuberculosis in the Coimbra Skeletal Collection. Tuberculosis 89, 267–277. Available from: https://doi.org/10.1016/j.tube.2009.04.001.

Reed, G.B., 1969. Rubella bone lesions. J. Pediatr. 74, 208–213.

Reinhard, K.J., Ferreira, L.F., Bouchet, F., Sianto, L., Dutra, J.M.F., Iniguez, A., et al., 2013. Food, parasites, and epidemiological transitions: a broad perspective. Int. J. Paleopathol. 3, 150–157. Available from: https://doi.org/10.1016/j.ijpp.2013.05.003.

Roberts, C.A., Buikstra, J.E., 2003. The Bioarchaeology of Tuberculosis: A Global View on a Reemerging Disease. University Press of Florida.

Roberts, C.A., Lucy, D., Manchester, K., 1994. Inflammatory lesions of ribs: an analysis of the Terry Collection. Am. J. Phys. Anthropol. 95, 169–182. Available from: https://doi.org/10.1002/ajpa.1330950205.

Roberts, C.A., Manchester, K., 2007. The Archaeology of Disease, 3rd ed. Cornell University Press, Ithaca, NY.

Rothschild, B.M., Rothschild, C., 1995. Treponemal disease revisited: skeletal discriminators for Yaws, Bejel, and Venereal Syphilis. Clin. Infect. Dis. 20, 1402–1408.

Ruffer, M.A., 1910. Note on the presence of "Bilharzia Haematobia" in Egyptian mummies of the twentieth dynasty [1250-1000 BC]. Br. Med. J. 1, 16.

Rühli, F.J., Kuhn, G., Evison, R., Müller, R., Schultz, M., 2007. Diagnostic value of micro-CT in comparison with histology in the qualitative assessment of historical human skull bone pathologies. Am. J. Phys. Anthropol. 133, 1099–1111. Available from: https://doi.org/10.1002/ajpa.20611.

Salo, W.L., Aufderheide, A.C., Buikstra, J.E., Holcomb, T.A., 1994. Identification of mycobacterium tuberculosis DNA in a pre-Columbian Peruvian mummy. Proc. Natl. Acad. Sci. 91, 2091–2094.

Santos, A.L., Roberts, C.A., 2001. A picture of tuberculosis in young Portuguese people in the early 20th century: a multidisciplinary study of the skeletal and historical evidence. Am. J. Phys. Anthropol. 115, 38–49. Available from: https://doi.org/10.1002/ajpa.1054.

Santos, A.L., Roberts, C.A., 2006. Anatomy of a serial killer: differential diagnosis of tuberculosis based on rib lesions of adult individuals from the Coimbra identified skeletal collection, Portugal. Am. J. Phys. Anthropol. 130, 38–49. Available from: https://doi.org/10.1002/ajpa.20160.

Schultz, M., 2001. Paleohistopathology of bone: a new approach to the study of ancient diseases. Am. J. Phys. Anthropol. 116, 106–147. Available from: https://doi.org/10.1002/ajpa.10024.

Sehgal, V., 1987. Reactions in leprosy clinical aspects. Int. J. Dermatol. 26, 278–285. Available from: https://doi.org/10.1111/j.1365-4362.1987.tb00188.x.

Shanley, D.J., 1995. Tuberculosis of the spine: imaging features. Am. J. Roentgenol. 164, 659–664. Available from: https://doi.org/10.2214/ajr.164.3.7863889.

Sharma, J.C., Gupta, S.P., Sankhala, S.S., Mehta, N., 1991. Residual poliomyelitis of lower limb-pattern and deformities. Indian. J. Pediatr. 58, 233–238. Available from: https://doi.org/10.1007/BF02751127.

Singh, A.E., Romanowski, B., 1999. Syphilis: review with emphasis on clinical, epidemiologic, and some biologic features. Clin. Microbiol. Rev. 12, 187–209. LP.

Smith, I., 2003. Mycobacterium tuberculosis pathogenesis and molecular determinants of virulence. Clin. Microbiol. Rev. 16, 463–496. LP.

Smith-Guzmán, N.E., 2015. The skeletal manifestation of malaria: an epidemiological approach using documented skeletal collections. Am. J. Phys. Anthropol. 158, 624–635. Available from: https://doi.org/10.1002/ajpa.22819.

Steyn, M., Buskes, J., 2016. Skeletal manifestations of tuberculosis in modern human remains. Clin. Anat. 29, 854–861. Available from: https://doi.org/10.1002/ca.22688.

Steyn, M., Scholtz, Y., Botha, D., Pretorius, S., 2013. The changing face of tuberculosis: trends in tuberculosis-associated skeletal changes. Tuberculosis 93, 467–474. Available from: https://doi.org/10.1016/j.tube.2013.04.003.

Talhari, C., Talhari, S., Penna, G.O., 2015. Clinical aspects of leprosy. Clin. Dermatol. 33, 26–37. Available from: https://doi.org/10.1016/j.clindermatol.2014.07.002.

Taylor, G.M., Blau, S., Mays, S., Monot, M., Lee, O.Y.-C., Minnikin, D.E., et al., 2009. Mycobacterium leprae genotype amplified from an archaeological case of lepromatous leprosy in Central Asia. J. Archaeol. Sci. 36, 2408–2414. Available from: https://doi.org/10.1016/j.jas.2009.06.026.

Tesini, B.L., 2018. Congenital Syphilis - Merck Manual for Health Professionals [WWW Document]. <https://www.msdmanuals.com/professional/pediatrics/infections-in-neonates/congenital-syphilis>.

Tierney, D., Nardell, E.A., 2018. Tuberculosis (TB) - Merck Manual For Health Professionals [WWW Document]. <https://www.merckmanuals.com/professional/infectious-diseases/mycobacteria/tuberculosis-tb> (accessed 9.6.19.).

Umbelino, C., Cunha, E., Silva, A.M., 1996. A possible case of poliomyelitis in a Portuguese skeleton dated from the 15th century. In: Salud, Enfermedad Y Muserte en el Pasado Consucuencìas biológicas del esters y lapatología. Fund. Uriach 1838, pp. 229–235.

Vigorita, V.J., Ghelman, B., Mintz, D., 2016. Osteomyelitis and septic arthritis. In: Vigorita, V. J., Ghelman, B., Mintz, D. (Eds.), Orthopaedic Pathology. Lippincott Williams & Wilkins, Philadelphia.

von Hunnius, T.E., Yang, D., Eng, B., Waye, J.S., Saunders, S.R., 2007. Digging deeper into the limits of ancient DNA research on syphilis. J. Archaeol. Sci. 34, 2091–2100. Available from: https://doi.org/10.1016/j.jas.2007.02.007.

Waldron, T., 2008. Palaeopathology. Cambridge University Press, Cambridge, UK.

Walker, E.G., 1983. Evidence for prehistoric cardiovascular disease of syphilitic origin on the Northern Plains. Am. J. Phys. Anthr. 60, 499–503. Available from: https://doi.org/10.1002/ajpa.1330600412.

Walker, S.L., Lockwood, D.N.J., 2006. The clinical and immunological features of leprosy. Br. Med. Bull. 77–78, 103–121.

Wickramasinghe, S.N., Abdalla, S.H., 2000. Blood and bone marrow changes in malaria. Best. Pract. Res. Clin. Haematol. 13, 277–299. Available from: https://doi.org/10.1053/beha.1999.0072.

World Health Organization, 2019a. Tuberculosis Fact Sheet [WWW Document]. <https://www.who.int/en/news-room/fact-sheets/detail/tuberculosis> (accessed 11.4.19.).

World Health Organization, 2019b. Leprosy Fact Sheet [WWW Document].

CHAPTER 4

Indicators of Stress: Metabolic and Endocrine Disorders

Lucie Biehler-Gomez and Cristina Cattaneo
LABANOF, Department of Biomedical Sciences for Health, University of Milan, Milan, Italy

Metabolic diseases refer to disorders that disrupt the normal metabolism of the organism. They generally revolve around a nutritional or hormonal imbalance, such as deficiency or excess. Metabolic disorders constitute indicators of stress as skeletal and dental changes correspond to an adaptative response to stressors during growth and through life in general. Skeletal manifestations as a response to stressors are influenced by multiple factors, including the individuals' immune status and age, genetic predisposition, environmental constraints as well as cultural systems. Nonetheless, stressors do not affect individuals proportionately and a skeleton exhibiting no indicators of metabolic stress may have been healthy or did not survive from the insults to the body (Roberts and Manchester, 2007). In this chapter, we will discuss the metabolic and endocrine conditions affecting bone and present skeletal markers of physiological metabolic stress.

Anemia

It is important to remember that anemia does not refer to a specific disease but to a sign of an underlying condition. Anemia consists in a decline in the number of red blood cells, hematocrit, or hemoglobin as a result of one of three basic mechanisms: significant blood loss, a deficient erythropoiesis (in other words, a decreased production of red blood cells), or an excessive hemolysis (i.e., an increased destruction of red blood cells) (Braunstein, 2017). Causes of anemia are numerous and may be classified in nutritional anemias (i.e., iron-deficiency anemia and megaloblastic anemia—due to vitamin B_{12}/folate deficiency), anemia of chronic disease (subsequent to rheumatoid arthritis, kidney disease, cancer, HIV/AIDS, Crohn's disease as well as other chronic

Interpreting Bone Lesions and Pathology for Forensic Practice. DOI: https://doi.org/10.1016/B978-0-323-85162-6.00004-0

inflammatory conditions), aplastic anemia (consequent to infections, medical drugs, autoimmune diseases, or exposure to toxic chemicals), hemolytic anemias (acquired or inherited, including the hemoglobinopathies with thalassemia and sickle cell anemia), malarial anemia, and anemias due to other causes (Tefferi, 2003). Symptoms of anemia are consequent to hypoxia (i.e., low blood oxygen, thus tissues are not oxygenated adequately), as red blood cells function as oxygen carriers, and most commonly include general fatigue, weakness, pale skin, coldness of hands and feet, and dyspnea (i.e., shortness of breath) (Braunstein, 2017).

Bone lesions in anemia result from marrow hyperplasia: in a hypoxic state, the kidneys release erythropoietin hormone to increase red blood cells production by the bone marrow in a powerful stimulus. The idea is that, regardless of the cause, in anemia, red blood cells are not carrying enough oxygen to the body tissues; so, the body tries to compensate by increasing the number of red blood cells in circulation, thus augmenting the overall supply of oxygen to the tissues. This powerful stimulus leads to bone marrow hyperplasia (i.e., increased number of hematopoietic cells in the bone marrow). Marrow hyperplasia will then induce bone resorption (Fig. 4.1), in particular of the external table or cortex (depending on its location) leading to skeletal lesions including thickening of the cranial vault, "hair-on-end" appearance in the skull, metaphyseal widening, cortical thinning, trabecular coarsening, and osteopenia (Aufderheide and Rodríguez-Martín, 1998, pp. 345–351; Ortner, 2003, pp. 363–376; Vilter et al., 1960). Bone lesions of anemia occur in severe, chronic, and long-standing cases and mild manifestations are not specific of the condition. Indeed, *cribra orbitalia* is a potential lesion of anemia but other causes include local inflammation, scurvy, trauma, osteoporosis, and pseudopathology (Klaus, 2017; Wapler et al., 2004). While porotic hyperostosis (Fig. 4.2) is a possible manifestation of anemia, debate in the scientific community has questioned the validity of the iron-deficiency anemia hypothesis as its cause (McIlvaine, 2015; Oxenham and Cavill, 2010; Rothschild, 2012; Rothschild et al., 2002; Walker et al., 2009).

Hershkovitz et al. (1997) and Lagia et al. (2007) examined single cases of sickle cell anemia and thalassemia respectively from the Hamann–Todd collection and the Athens collection—constituted of

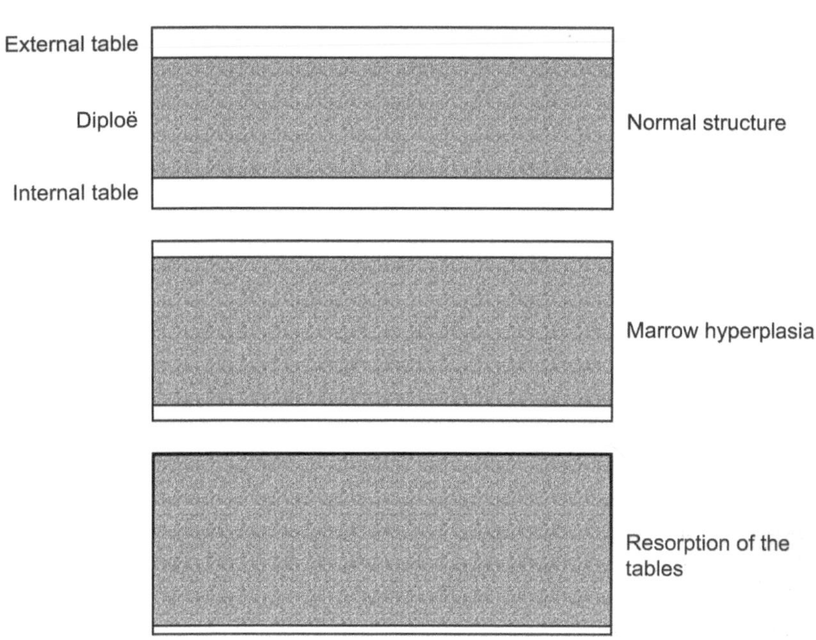

Figure 4.1 Mechanisms of bone changes due to marrow hyperplasia. Increase of red blood cells production as a response to the hypoxic state leading to marrow hyperplasia and bone resorption of the internal and external tables. Source: Drawing by Davide Porta.

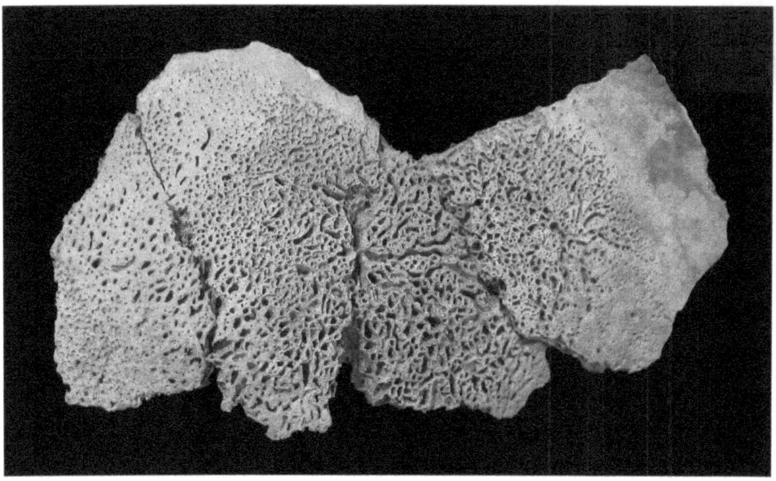

Figure 4.2 Porotic hyperostosis on a fragmented occipital bone (ectocranial view). Archaeological specimen of the CAL dated CE 17th century.

Box 4.1 Bone Features of Anemia

Features	Diagnostic strength
Cribra orbitalia	Consistent
Porotic hyperostosis	Consistent
"Hair-on-end" cranial lesions	Consistent
Osteopenia	Consistent

individuals exhumed from cemeteries with known demographic data and causes of death (Eliopoulos et al., 2007). In the second study, however, the associated record only mentioned "anemia—heart failure" but a diagnosis of thalassemia was assessed by the authors from the analysis of bone lesions. After literature review and examination of their own cases, the authors suggest criteria allowing the distinction between the three main types of anemia: while all types of anemia may affect the cranium, facial involvement and severe lesions are characteristic of thalassemia, long bone and spinal involvement (with H-shaped vertebrae on X-rays and enlarged basivertebral foramina) are typical of sickle cell anemia, and iron-deficiency anemia tends to cause generalized osteopenia (Hershkovitz et al., 1997; Lagia et al., 2007). Additional case studies of skeletons with clinical diagnoses of anemia would strengthen the diagnosis of the different types of anemia on dry bone (Box 4.1).

Vitamin D Deficiency

Vitamin D holds a key role in the metabolic regulation of calcium and phosphorus and subsequently, in the mineralization of the osteoid. The most common causes of vitamin D deficiency include a lack of sunlight exposure associated with dietary insufficiencies, intestinal malabsorption as well as renal disease, and result in an insufficient mineralization of the newly formed bone (Berry et al., 2002; Brickley and Ives, 2010, Chapter 5). In the pathological analysis of dry bones, the pathological condition resulting from vitamin D deficiency is called "rickets" in infants, children, and adolescents and "osteomalacia" in the grown skeleton (Mays and Brickley, 2018). The most severe manifestations of rickets occur in period of rapid growth, when poor mineralization of bones causes bending to weight-bearing bones and skeletal deformities: in crawling children the deformities affect the upper limbs while the

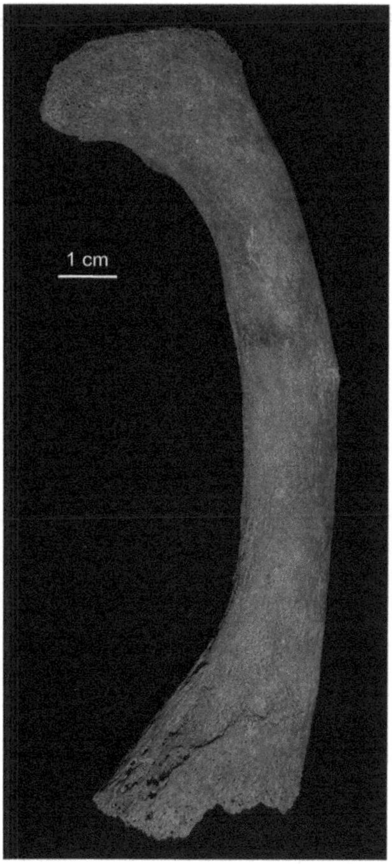

Figure 4.3 Left femur of 3-year-old child (± 12 months) showing lateral bending, porosity, woven periosteal new bone, and distal metaphyseal fraying probably due to rickets. Source: Archaeological specimen #2321 of the CAL dated CE 3rd–5th century.

lower limbs will be more commonly involved in walking children. In addition, rickets is associated with retarded growth, joint swelling, muscle weakness, and delay in tooth eruption. In adolescents, both tetany and hypercalcemia may be observed. Moreover, delayed skeletal maturity may occur if the vitamin D deficiency is due to renal disease or intestinal malabsorption (Berry et al., 2002). The classical sign of osteomalacia is the pseudofracture or "Looser's zone," a small area of increased radiolucency on radiograph and corresponding to an accumulation of osteoid.

Considerable research has been devoted to the study of the skeletal complications of vitamin D deficiency over the past decades

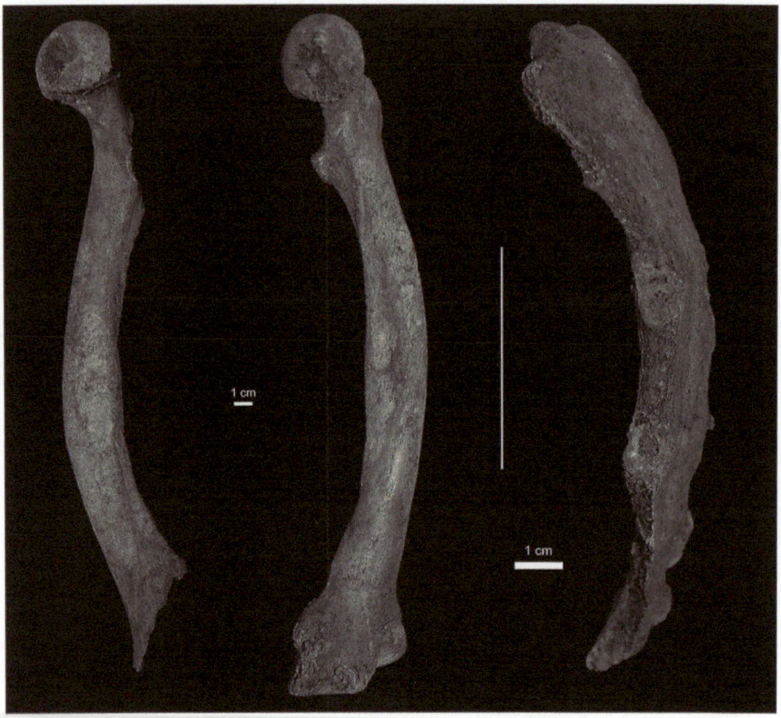

Figure 4.4 Medial views of the right (left image) and left femora (middle image) and right lateral view of the sternum (right image) showing anterior bending deformities due to osteomalacia. Source: Skeleton #7 of the CAL Milano Cemetery Skeletal Collection.

(Mankin, 1974; Mays and Brickley, 2018) based on pathology museum collections (Brickley et al., 2005; Schamall et al., 2003) and refined with the study of archaeological specimens (Brickley et al., 2010, 2007; Ives and Brickley, 2014; Mays et al., 2006; Ortner and Mays, 1998) allowing a confident diagnosis of the disease in skeletonized remains. Rickets is thus recognizable by the presence of cortical porosity in particular on the cranium but also on growth plates, flaring and thickening of rib ends and long bone metaphyses, medial bending of the tibia as well as distortion of the bones due to mechanical loading (Fig. 4.3). Osteomalacia is characterized by pseudofractures and bending deformities (Figs. 4.4 and 4.5). Pseudofractures appear macroscopically as small, usually bilateral, linear fractures with almost systematically evidence of repair forming an irregular callus. Their most frequent locations are on the ribs, spinous process and lateral border of the scapula, ilium,

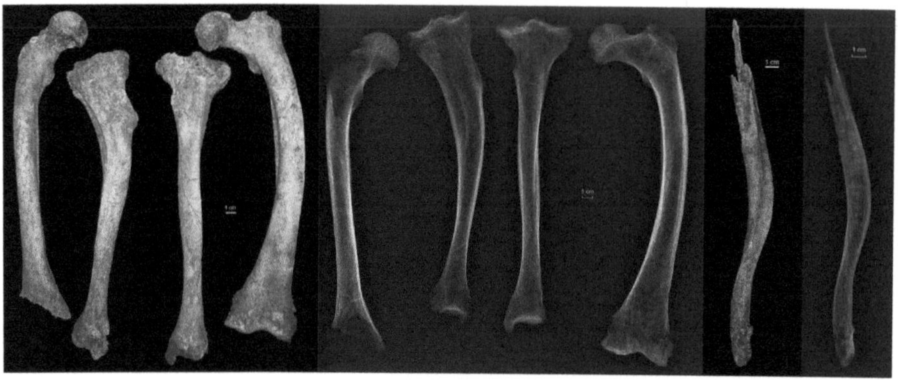

Figure 4.5 Radiological and macroscopic anterior views of the femora and tibiae showing bending deformities, and lateral view of the left fibula showing torsion and bending due to osteomalacia. Skeleton #7 of the CAL Milano Cemetery Skeletal Collection. Reproduced with permission from Biehler-Gomez, L., Tritella, S., Martino, F., Campobasso, C.P., Franchi, A., Spairani, R., et al., 2019. The synergy between radiographic and macroscopic observation of skeletal lesions on dry bone. Int. J. Leg. Med. doi:10.1007/s00414-019-02122-0.

Box 4.2 Bone Features of Rickets

Features	Diagnostic strength
Bending deformities	Typical
Metaphyseal flaring	Typical
Growth plate porosity	Typical
Defects adjacent to cement lines (histomorphometric feature)	Typical
Retarded growth	Consistent

clavicle, distal ulna, pubic rami, and femoral neck and shaft, respectively. Bending deformities occur as a distortion of the bone under normal weight-bearing, due to the weakening and softening of the insufficiently mineralized bone and may affect the long bones, pelvis, sternum, and cause kyphosis as well as scoliosis. Nonetheless, Ives and Brickley (2014) concluded in their large-scale study of 1181 skeletons that the manifestations of vitamin D deficiency observed in pathology museums (Brickley et al., 2005) were much more severe than what they found in archaeological excavations. At the microscopic level, Brickley's et al. (2007) "defective cement lines" may constitute a pathognomonic histomorphological feature of osteomalacia (De Boer et al., 2013) (Boxes 4.2 and 4.3).

Box 4.3 Bone Features of Osteomalacia.

Features	Diagnostic strength
Bending deformities	Typical
Pseudofractures	Typical
Incomplete and poor bone mineralization (histomorphometric feature)	Typical
Defectively mineralized bone adjacent to cement lines (histomorphometric feature)	Typical

Vitamin C Deficiency

Vitamin C (ascorbic acid) is essential for collagen synthesis and thus significantly contributes to bone and blood vessel health as well as wound healing. The human body is only able to store a limited amount of vitamin C and its reservoir can depleted in as little as 30 days (Venes, 2017, p. 2116). Therefore continuous vitamin C intake is needed to maintain physiological functions. Deficient vitamin C or scurvy was known to be a disease of sailors and soldiers over the 17th and 18th centuries. As global wars and trading sent ships on increasingly long voyages and land soldiers in long active duties, scurvy became a prominent condition (Harrison, 2013). In fact, and according to historian Stephen Bown (2005), scurvy was responsible for more mariners deaths than storms, shipwrecks, war, and all other diseases combined. Citrus fruits were a known cure for scurvy, giving rise to the saying "a lime a day keeps scurvy away." Today, studies have shown that smoking lowers serum vitamin C levels (Schectman et al., 1989), making smokers with a poor diet more at risk for scurvy in addition to individuals with a deficient vitamin C diet.

Deficient vitamin C intake causes severe impairment of collagen synthesis, especially in the vascular structure, leading to the main feature of scurvy: subperiosteal hemorrhages. These result primarily from a fragility of blood vessels susceptible to rupture and microfractures and may occur throughout the skeleton. Histomorphological features of ossified hematomas on dry bone have been described in the paleohistopathological literature (Maat, 2004; Schultz, 2001; Van der Merwe et al., 2010); however, as ossified hematomas are not exclusive to scurvy, histomorphology cannot constitute a method of diagnosis in itself and requires macroscopic gross examination for the diagnosis of scurvy on dry bone (De Boer et al., 2013). Vitamin C depletion also causes a depressed osteoblastic activity with a continuing or increased osteoclastic activity, resulting in a defective osteoid matrix formation. Radiographic changes thus include osteopenia, osteonecrosis, cortical thinning with periosteal new bone formation and demineralization with metaphyseal fractures in juveniles. Nonetheless, reintroduction of vitamin C in the diet will completely resolve lesions after a few months (Brickley and Ives, 2010, pp. 41–74, 2006; Fain, 2005).

As a consequence of the inflammatory response to scorbutic chronic bleeding, diffuse abnormal bone porosity may be observed on the skull, and in particular the greater wings of the sphenoid, the roof and lateral margins of the orbit, the posterior maxilla, the interior surface of the zygomatic bone, the infraorbital foramen, the palate, the alveolar process of the maxilla and the coronoid process of the mandible as well as on the scapula, and the metaphyseal ends of subadult bones (Fig. 4.6). Other scorbutic bone lesions include new bone formation in the orbits and on the vault (due to the stripping of the periosteum from the underlying bone) and enlargement of the costochondral junction of the ribs ("scorbutic rosary"). In adults, affection of the gums may result in antemortem tooth loss (Aufderheide and Rodríguez-Martín, 1998, pp. 310–316; Brickley and Ives, 2010, pp. 41–74, 2006; Ortner, 2003, pp. 383–392; Ortner et al., 2001). Documentations of dry bone lesions of scurvy were

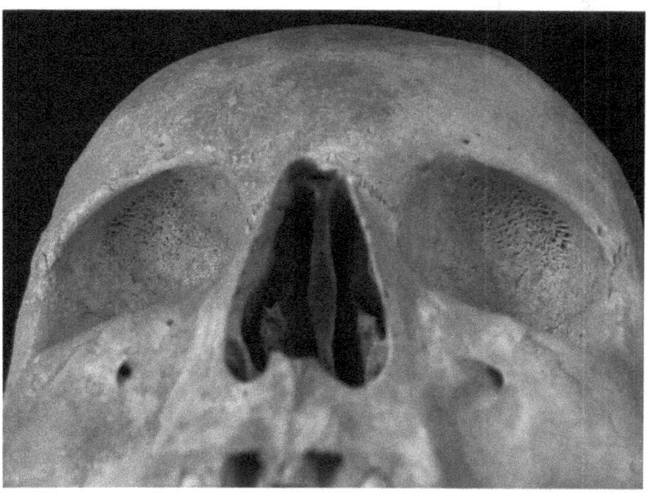

Figure 4.6 Cribra orbitalia *in the orbital roof.* Source: Roman archaeological specimen from the CAL.

Box 4.4 Bone Features of Scurvy

Features	Diagnostic strength
Porosity of bone cortex	Typical
New bone formation in orbits	Typical
Scorbutic rosary	Typical
Antemortem tooth loss	Consistent
Ossified hematoma (histomorphometric feature)	Consistent

obtained from archaeological cases with probable diagnoses. As Ortner et al. (2001) points out, "confirmation of these findings with medically documented cases of scurvy would be very helpful" for future diagnoses (Box 4.4).

Pellagra

Pellagra, from the Italian *pelle agra* or "rough skin," is a systemic and potentially lethal disease characterized by a niacin (vitamin B_3) and/or tryptophan deficiency. Described since the 18th century, it was endemic among Italian and Spanish peasants because of their high-maize and low-protein diets. Mild niacin deficiency is asymptomatic, but in its chronic state, clinical manifestations are known as the four D's: Dermatitis, Diarrhea, and Dementia, eventually leading to Death. However, symptoms of the condition would resolve with niacin intake. Pellagra remained widespread until the 20th century, when food such as breads and cereals were fortified with niacin (Paine and Brenton, 2006; Savvidou, 2014).

Knowledge on bone lesions due to pellagra is very limited and its diagnosis on dry bone is not standardized (Klaus, 2017; Paine and Brenton, 2006). Possible skeletal manifestations (notable through gross examination and light microscopy) include osteoporosis, rickets, delayed healing of fractures, cortical bone loss of the rib, periostitic lesions, *cribra orbitalia*, cranial pitting, alveolar bone loss, and dental caries (Paine and Brenton, 2006). None of these lesions is pathognomonic of the condition as these are non-specific signs of disease. Further studies based on individuals with known pellagra are required to reliably diagnose the condition on dry bone.

Diabetes Mellitus

Diabetes is a metabolic disorder characterized by chronic hyperglycemia and classified in to two main categories: type 1, which may be idiopathic or autoimmune and type 2, representing about 90% of diabetic cases (Alberti and Zimmet, 1998; Arkkila and Gautier, 2003; Brutsaert, 2017a). The pathogenesis of both etiologies remains incompletely understood but includes a combination of genetic and environmental factors. In type 1, the autoimmune destruction of pancreatic β-cells debilitates insulin secretion and results in insulin deficiency, while type 2 ranges from a predominant insulin resistance to a predominant insulin deficiency (Alberti and Zimmet, 1998; Arkkila and Gautier, 2003; Brutsaert, 2017a). Complications of diabetes are generally separated into microvascular (also known as "small blood vessel disease") and macrovascular (or "large blood vessel disease"). Microvascular complications include retinopathy (i.e., eye impairment through retina damage), nephropathy (also known as diabetic kidney disease, i.e., kidney impairment) and neuropathy (i.e., damage to peripheral nerves) resulting from blood vessel damage. Neuropathy in diabetes can cause a peripheral loss of the sense of touch, proprioception, temperature, and vibration. This loss of feeling leaves the feet vulnerable to undetected microtrauma which can later lead to foot ulcerations and infections, fractures, dislocations, destructions, and deformities of feet bones (such as Charcot's joints) (Brutsaert, 2017b; Crispin and Alcocer-Varela, 2003; Fowler, 2008). Macrovascular complications include myocardial infarction, stroke, and peripheral artery disease (i.e., atherosclerosis) and constitute a major cause of morbidity and mortality in diabetes (Beckman et al., 2002; Brutsaert, 2017b; Fowler, 2008).

Musculoskeletal complications of diabetic neuropathy should therefore be observable on skeletal remains and include markers of infections, osteomyelitis, Charcot's joints, "claw foot" deformity, and diabetic osteolysis (Belcastro et al., 2005; Giurato and Uccioli, 2006; Hartemann-Heurtier and Senneville, 2008; Husni et al., 2005). Nonetheless, the condition was only diagnosed in Egyptian mummies based on CT observation of lower extremity arterial calcifications (Marx and D'Auria, 1986). Biehler-Gomez et al. (2019) examined 38 skeletons from the CAL Milano Cemetery Skeletal Collection with an antemortem diagnosis of diabetes as well as 11 "control" skeletons and

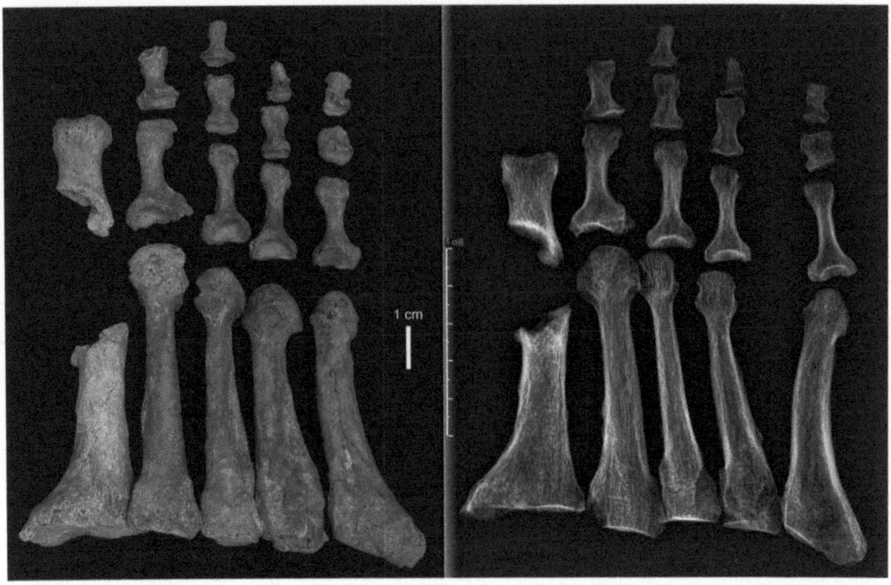

Figure 4.7 Radiographic and macroscopic images of the bones of the right foot (metatarsals and phalanges) showing an osteolytic deformation of the first metatarsophalangeal articulation with the resorption of the head of the metatarsal and the base of the phalanx. Skeleton #20 of the CAL Milano Cemetery Skeletal Collection with a clinical diagnosis of diabetes mellitus. Reproduced with permission from Biehler-Gomez, L., Tritella, S., Martino, F., Campobasso, C.P., Franchi, A., Spairani, R., et al., 2019. The synergy between radiographic and macroscopic observation of skeletal lesions on dry bone. Int. J. Leg. Med. doi:10.1007/s00414-019-02122-0.

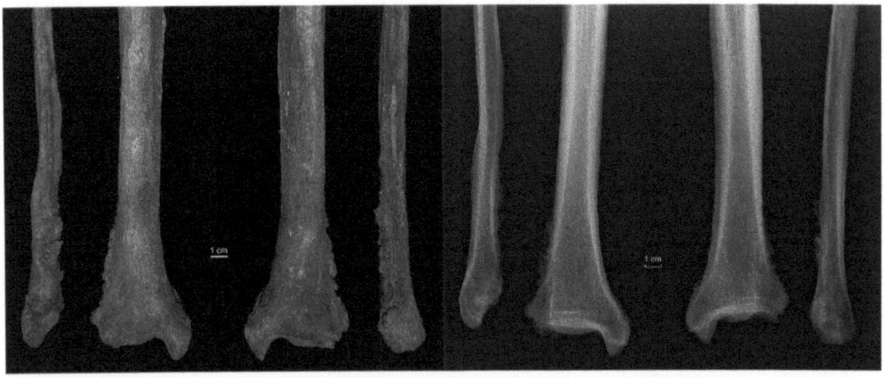

Figure 4.8 Radiographic and macroscopic images of the distal half of the fibulae and tibiae showing extensive lamellar periosteal bone deposition. Skeleton #25 of the CAL Milano Cemetery Skeletal Collection with a clinical diagnosis of diabetes mellitus. Reproduced with permission from Biehler-Gomez, L., Tritella, S., Martino, F., Campobasso, C.P., Franchi, A., Spairani, R., et al., 2019. The synergy between radiographic and macroscopic observation of skeletal lesions on dry bone. Int. J. Leg. Med. doi:10.1007/s00414-019-02122-0.

Box 4.5 Bone Features of Diabetes Mellitus

Features	Diagnostic strength
Periosteal new bone	Consistent
Osteolytic lesions	Consistent
Osteolysis of digital tufts	Consistent
Osteomyelitis	Consistent
Traumatic lesions	Consistent
Vascular calcifications	Consistent
Osteochondritis dissecans	Consistent

found several types of lesions consistent with the disease process including periosteal new bone formation, lysis of tuft, osteolytic lesions, evidence of trauma, osteomyelitis, osteochondritis dissecans, and vascular calcifications which may, in a multifactorial approach, suggest the disorder in the differential diagnosis but are not specific enough for a definitive diagnosis (Figs. 4.7 and 4.8). Indeed, as Dupras et al. (2010) remark in their study of bilateral amputations in ancient Egypt: "diagnosing diabetes from skeletal material alone is very difficult as no skeletal changes are specific to diabetes" (Box 4.5).

Paget's Disease

Paget's disease of bone, previously known as "osteitis deformans" was named after the English surgeon James Paget who first described it in 1877. It is a non-inflammatory chronic condition of unknown etiology altering metabolic bone homeostasis through an increased bone turnover (i.e., bone resorption and formation). It affects about 1.5% of the population with a male predominance (3:2 male-to-female ratio) and is more frequent in individuals with a family history. The disease occurs after 40 years with a prevalence increasing with age and is more common in Europeans and individuals of British descent, in particular in Australia, New Zealand, and North America (Nebot Valenzuela and Pietschmann, 2017).

Paget's disease affects the skeletal system in three progressive stages. It may involve one bone (monostotic) or a few (polyostotic) generally affecting the axial skeleton and the end of the long bones, specifically the pelvic bones (70 %), femur (55 %), lumbar spine (53 %), skull (42 %), and tibia (32 %), although virtually any bone may be affected.

Initially, an osteolytic phase results in localized regions of sharply demarcated radiolucency known as "osteoporosis circumscripta." Lesions on the calvarium show marked reduction of the trabeculae in the diploe accompanied by thinning of the internal and external tables and may slowly coalesce. However, this type of lesion is not specific to the condition and may mimic cancer metastases. Subsequently, a compensatory increased osteoblastic activity occurs in a mixed osteolytic-osteoblastic phase and leads to and excessive production of poorly organized fibroblastic new bone in areas of the skeleton previously exhibiting a purely osteolytic character, terminating in a predominant sclerotic phase. On dry bones, this osteoblastic overstimulation is observable through enlargement of bones by periosteal new bone formation causing an increased circumference of the osseous element and thickening of the cranial vault by endocranial and ectocranial bone formation. Nonetheless, pagetic lesions never affect the entire skeleton, they are circumscribed to the affected bones and do not spread to adjacent skeletal elements. Skeletal deformity and pathologic fractures are common features due to the biomechanical weakness and unstability of the excessive abnormal bone apposition; they may occur in the skull, weight-bearing bones with bowing and vertebrae with vertebral compression and kyphosis. Additional complications of the condition include osteoarthritis and more rarely, osteosarcoma (in up to 1% of patients) (Aufderheide and Rodríguez-Martín, 1998, pp. 413–417; Nebot Valenzuela and Pietschmann, 2017; Ortner, 2003, pp. 435–442; Singer, 2016; Whyte, 2006).

Histology (specifically, light microscopy) is a particularly helpful method to confirm Paget's disease in dry bone material because of its characteristic "mosaic" pattern of woven and lamellar tissue, and pathognomonic "patchwork" architecture (De Boer et al., 2013); allowing for its diagnosis in archaeological material (Aaron et al., 1992; Roches et al., 2002) (Box 4.6).

Box 4.6 Bone Features of Paget's Disease

Features	Diagnostic strength
Histomorphological "patchwork"	Diagnostic
Enlargement of bones	Typical
Fractures and deformities	Consistent
Osteolytic lesions	Consistent

Endocrine Diseases

The endocrine system consists in a series of glands that produce and secrete hormones in the circulatory system in order to regulate metabolic processes in the body, including growth, development, and maintenance of skeletal tissue. In particular, disorders of the pituitary, parathyroid, and thyroid glands may affect the skeletal system.

Hyperpituitarism is a rare disease defined by an excessive production of growth hormone by the pituitary gland most often due to a secretory non-cancerous tumor (i.e., adenoma) resulting in excessive skeletal proportions; for instance, gigantism and acromegaly. In addition, the association of increased size and weight with muscle weakness may cause degenerative changes and skeletal distortions such as kyphosis and scoliosis (Aufderheide and Rodríguez-Martín, 1998, pp. 326–330; Ortner, 2003, pp. 422–425; Roberts and Manchester, 2007).

Just like hyperpituitarism is characterized by a hypersecretion of pituitary hormones, *hypopituitarism* refers to a hyposecretion of pituitary hormones or pituitary deficiency. Thus, in this rare condition, the destruction of pituitary function leads to a form of dwarfism characterized by normally proportioned bones but reduced in size as well as retarded skeletal maturation and dental eruption due to the loss of growth hormone effect (Aufderheide and Rodríguez-Martín, 1998, pp. 326–330; Ortner, 2003, pp. 422–425; Roberts and Manchester, 2007).

Hyperparathyroidism is characterized by an overstimulation of the parathyroid glands resulting in a hypersecretion of parathyroid hormone. As parathyroid hormone acts as a messenger regulating serum calcium concentration, hyperparathyroidism results in an increased level of calcium in the blood plasma or hypercalcemia, a potentially life-threatening complication. Primary hyperparathyroidism is most commonly caused by a benign tumor (i.e., adenoma) in the parathyroid glands and is a frequent complication of kidney disease. The most common symptoms are chronic fatigue, depression, difficulty sleeping, body aches, bone and joint pain, muscle spasms, loss of concentration, nausea, and may cause kidney stones. Hyperparathyroidism may affect the skeleton with diffuse osteopenia, subperiosteal porosity, and in more advanced cases, osteitis fibrosa cystica (i.e. focal and well-defined osteolytic lesions such as brown tumors) (Aufderheide and Rodríguez-

Martín, 1998, pp. 330–334; Marx, 2000; Ortner, 2003, pp. 429–430). In addition, histomorphological resorptive features on dry bone, and in particular "tunneling resorption," are pathognomonic for hyperparathyroidism in well-preserved specimens (De Boer et al., 2013).

Hypoparathyroidism corresponds to an underproduction of parathyroid hormone. This leads to decreased blood levels of calcium (i.e. hypocalcemia) and increased serum levels phosphorus (i.e. hyperphosphatemia). This rare condition may be acquired, autoimmune, congenital, or idiopathic. Symptoms are due to hypocalcemia and include muscle cramps and spasms, pain, paresthesia and twitching. Hypoparathyroidism can lead to osteopenia and unspecific skeletal lesions (Aufderheide and Rodríguez-Martín, 1998, pp. 330–334; Marx, 2000; Ortner, 2003, pp. 429–430).

Hyperthyroidism, regardless of its cause (e.g. Graves' disease, thyroiditis, adenoma of the thyroid gland, excessive iodine intake) results from an overactive thyroid gland producing too much thyroid hormones and leads to thyrotoxicosis, that is, high serum thyroid hormone concentration. Hyperthyroidism may cause various clinical manifestations including nervousness, irritability, increased sweating, heart racing, hand tremors, anxiety, trouble sleeping, and mood swings, among others. Bone changes in hyperthyroidism are generally mild, asymptomatic and unspecific, they include increased bone resorption leading to osteopenia, mildly increased stature and/or accelerated skeletal maturation (Aufderheide and Rodríguez-Martín, 1998, pp. 334–339; Ortner, 2003, pp. 426–428).

Hypothyroidism is a clinical state resulting from an insufficient production of thyroid hormones. The most common cause today of hypothyroidism is iodine deficiency; in iodine-replete areas, the causes are congenital, due to chronic autoimmune disease (such as atrophic autoimmune thyroiditis or goitrous autoimmune thyroiditis), or iatrogenic, caused by destructive treatment for hyperthyroidism or thyroid cancer (Garber et al., 2012; Hall and Scanlon, 1979; Vanderpump and Tunbridge, 2002). Any tissue may be affected in hypothyroidism. Clinical manifestations include fatigue, dry skin and hair, cold sensitivity, hoarseness of voice, constipation, muscle cramps, mental retardation, and hearing loss (Gruber, 2012; Hall and Scanlon, 1979). Donald J. Ortner examined 12 skeletons with hypothyroidism from the Galler

Collection and observed marked dwarfism in all 12 cases (with statures ranging from 105 to 145 cm), disproportionate bone development, delayed epiphyseal and apophyseal union as well as severe osteoarthrosis in particular in the hip and shoulder (Ortner and Hotz, 2005). It is however important to remember, as already mentioned, that specimens in pathology museums tend to present severe pathological manifestations (motivating their selection for entry in the museum) unrepresentative of archaeological cases (Mays, 2018; Mays and Brickley, 2018); therefore it would be interesting to compare Ortner's descriptions with additional material from other sources to improve diagnostic methods for the condition.

Markers of Non-Mechanical Stress

The living individual may be submitted to considerable stress from external factors during his lifetime (e.g., famine, malnutrition, heavy workload, repetitive movements, disease, etc.). These may affect the skeleton and are referred to in anthropology as "stress markers." Their interpretation can provide substantial information about the life history, activity, and even occupation of the individual and therefore should not be disregarded in the forensic practice. Here, we will explore in particular the markers of physiological stress.

Growth is not perfectly linear relative to age; it follows a predictable pattern allowing us to estimate age from bones (i.e., bone length and epiphyseal fusion) and teeth (i.e., dental eruption) and is increased during infancy and adolescence. Growth can be affected by genetic influences, growth hormone deficiencies, diseases, and nutrition. Thus by disturbing normal growth, physiological stress can lead to *skeletal growth retardation* (i.e., late epiphyseal closure) as well as a *shortened adult stature* relative to that of the population (Larsen, 2015). Growth disruption caused by pathologic or nutritional stress may also be perceptible through growth arrest lines or *Harris lines* (Harris, 1931), which appear as radiopaque (i.e., due to increased bone density) transverse lines in the metaphyses of long bones on radiographs (Fig. 4.9). Specifically, Harris lines result from alternating cycles of osseous growth arrest and growth resumption, which is why it has been suggested that the term "recovery lines" may be more accurate, given that they result from periods of bone formation following a period of inhibited bone growth (Ameen et al., 2005; Park and Riohter, 1953). Harris lines can

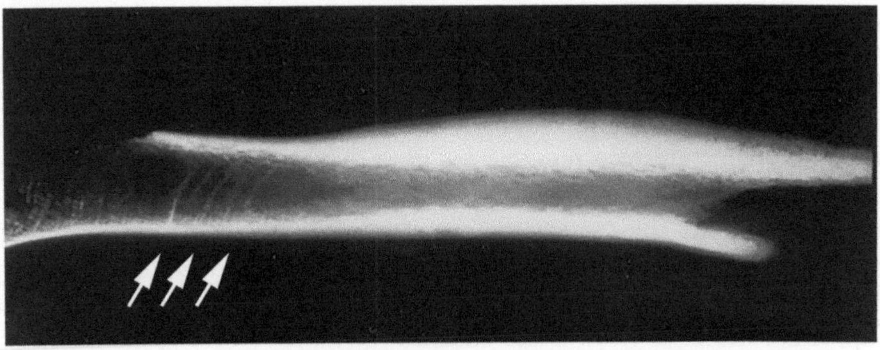

Figure 4.9 Harris lines (arrows) in a long bone of a child with possible congenital syphilis (thickening of the cortex and narrowing of the medullary cavity). Archaeological specimen of the CAL dated CE 3rd–4th century.

vary in thickness from less than 1 mm to more than 1 cm, they are thickest and more numerous in areas of rapid growth, such as the distal tibia and femur and may resolve through bone remodeling with age (Larsen, 2015). Therefore the lack of transverse radiopaque lines on a radiograph may either be the result of an absence of physiological stress during growth or the resorption of the stress marker. Moreover, the occurrence of Harris lines is highly variable from one individual to the next, regardless of the stress endured, complicating their interpretation. Indeed, individuals with known health histories of stress may not manifest Harris lines, whereas others, with no evident stress in their health history, may show some on X-rays (Larsen, 2015). Harris lines should therefore be interpreted with care to assess stress in past populations.

On dental tissue, growth disruption from physiological stress manifest may manifest as *enamel hypoplasia*, which corresponds to developmental defects of the thickness of the enamel, resulting from disturbances to ameloblasts (i.e., enamel-producing cells) during enamel formation. Enamel hypoplasia may appear morphologically as small pits (also known as "pitted enamel hypoplasia"), horizontal lines, furrows or grooves (also called "linear enamel hypoplasia") and even areas of missing enamel (Fig. 4.10). This quantitative enamel defect may affect all forming teeth during the period of stress (in other words, both deciduous and permanent teeth). Unlike Harris lines, defects of enamel hypoplasia remain permanent (as enamel does not remodel), although they can be damaged by abrasion and attrition. Interestingly, and in a similar manner as dendrochronology using tree rings, the period of stress leading to growth disturbance can be precisely

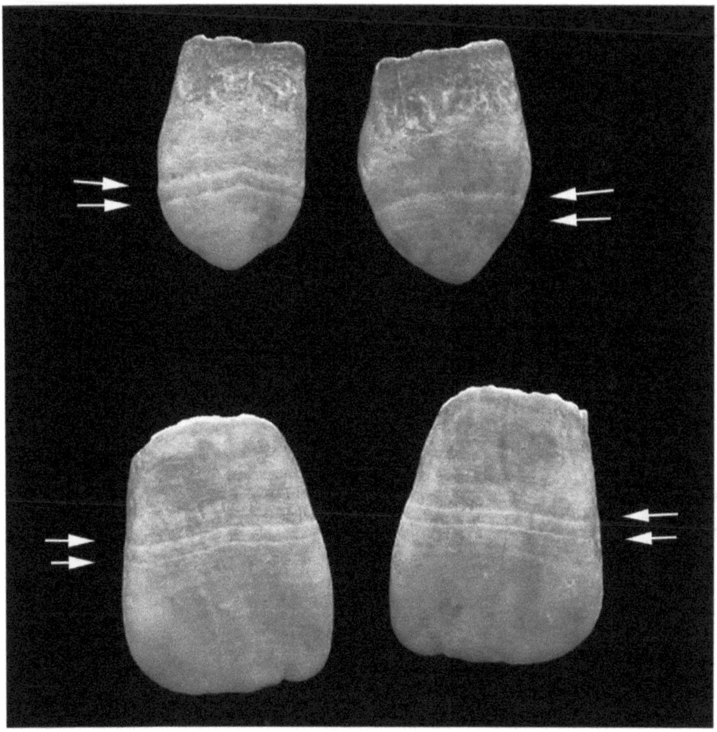

Figure 4.10 Enamel hypoplasia (arrows) in the maxillary permanent premolars (top) and incisors (bottom). Archaeological specimen of the CAL.

determined by counting dental growth increments (Hillson, 2019, 1996). Physiological stress may also be observable through microdefects in the enamel such as Wilson bands (FitzGerald and Saunders, 2005), in the same manner as the neonatal line, a histological defect caused by the metabolic stress of birth in deciduous teeth.

References

Aaron, J.E., Rogers, J., Kanis, J.A., 1992. Paleohistology of Paget's disease in two medieval skeletons. Am. J. Phys. Anthropol. 89, 325–331. Available from: https://doi.org/10.1002/ajpa.1330890306.

Alberti, K.G.M.M., Zimmet, P., 1998. Definition, diagnosis and classification of diabetes mellitus and its complications. Part 1: diagnosis and classification of diabetes mellitus. Provisional report of a WHO Consultation. Diabet. Med. 15, 539–553. Available from: https://doi.org/10.1002/(SICI)1096-9136(199807)15:7 < 539::AID-DIA668 > 3.0.CO;2-S.

Ameen, S., Staub, L., Ulrich, S., Vock, P., Ballmer, F., Anderson, S.E., 2005. Harris lines of the tibia across centuries: a comparison of two populations, medieval and contemporary in Central Europe. Skelet. Radiol. 34, 279–284. Available from: https://doi.org/10.1007/s00256-004-0841-3.

Arkkila, P.E.T., Gautier, J.-F., 2003. Musculoskeletal disorders in diabetes mellitus: an update. Best. Pract. Res. Clin. Rheumatol. 17, 945–970. Available from: http://doi.org/10.1016/j.berh.2003.11.001.

Aufderheide, A.C., Rodríguez-Martín, C., 1998. The Cambridge Encyclopedia of Human Paleopathology. Cambridge University Press, Cambridge, UK.

Beckman, J.A., Creager, M.A., Libby, P., 2002. Diabetes and atherosclerosis: epidemiology, pathophysiology, and management. JAMA 287, 2570–2581. Available from: https://doi.org/10.1001/jama.287.19.2570.

Belcastro, M.G., Mariotti, V., Facchini, F., Dutour, O., 2005. Leprosy in a skeleton from the 7th century necropolis of Vicenne-Campochiaro (Molise, Italy). Int. J. Osteoarchaeol. 15, 431–448. Available from: https://doi.org/10.1002/oa.799.

Berry, J.L., Davies, M., Mee, A.P., 2002. Vitamin D metabolism, rickets, and osteomalacia. Seminars in Musculoskeletal Radiology. Thieme Medical Publishers, pp. 173–182.

Biehler-Gomez, L., Castoldi, E., Baldini, E., Cappella, A., Cattaneo, C., 2019. Diabetic bone lesions: a study on 38 known modern skeletons and the implications for forensic scenarios. Int. J. Leg. Med. 133, 1225–1239. Available from: https://doi.org/10.1007/s00414-018-1870-0.

Bown, S.R., 2005. Scurvy: How a Aurgeon, a Mariner, and a Gentlemen Solved the Greatest Medical Mystery of the Age of Sail. Macmillan.

Braunstein, E.M., 2017. Evaluation of Anemia - Merck Manual For Health Professionals [WWW Document]. <https://www.msdmanuals.com/professional/hematology-and-oncology/approach-to-the-patient-with-anemia/evaluation-of-anemia>.

Brickley, M., Ives, R., 2006. Skeletal manifestations of infantile scurvy. Am. J. Phys. Anthropol. 129, 163–172. Available from: https://doi.org/10.1002/ajpa.20265.

Brickley, M., Ives, R., 2010. The Bioarchaeology of Metabolic Bone Disease. Elsevier Academic Press, London.

Brickley, M., Mays, S., Ives, R., 2005. Skeletal manifestations of vitamin D deficiency osteomalacia in documented historical collections. Int. J. Osteoarchaeol. 15, 389–403. Available from: https://doi.org/10.1002/oa.794.

Brickley, M., Mays, S., Ives, R., 2007. An investigation of skeletal indicators of vitamin D deficiency in adults: Effective markers for interpreting past living conditions and pollution levels in 18th and 19th century Birmingham, England. Am. J. Phys. Anthropol. 132, 67–79. Available from: https://doi.org/10.1002/ajpa.20491.

Brickley, M., Mays, S., Ives, R., 2010. Evaluation and interpretation of residual rickets deformities in adults. Int. J. Osteoarchaeol. 20, 54–66. Available from: https://doi.org/10.1002/oa.1007.

Brutsaert, E., 2017a. Diabetes Mellitus (DM) - Merck Manual for Health Professionals [WWW Document]. <https://www.msdmanuals.com/professional/endocrine-and-metabolic-disorders/diabetes-mellitus-and-disorders-of-carbohydrate-metabolism/diabetes-mellitus-dm>.

Brutsaert, E., 2017b. Complications of Diabetes Mellitus - Merck Manual for Health Professionals [WWW Document]. <https://www.merckmanuals.com/professional/endocrine-and-metabolic-disorders/diabetes-mellitus-and-disorders-of-carbohydrate-metabolism/complications-of-diabetes-mellitus>.

Crispin, J.C., Alcocer-Varela, J., 2003. Rheumatologic manifestations of diabetes mellitus. Am. J. Med. 114, 753–757. Available from: http://doi.org/10.1016/S0002-9343(03)00140-2.

De Boer, H.H., Van der Merwe, A.E., Maat, G.J.R., 2013. The diagnostic value of microscopy in dry bone paleopathology: a review. Int. J. Paleopathol. 3, 113–121. Available from: https://doi.org/10.1016/j.ijpp.2013.03.004.

Dupras, T.L., Williams, L.J., De Meyer, M., Peeters, C., Depraetere, D., Vanthuyne, B., et al., 2010. Evidence of amputation as medical treatment in ancient Egypt. Int. J. Osteoarchaeol 20, 405–423. Available from: https://doi.org/10.1002/oa.1061.

Eliopoulos, C., Lagia, A., Manolis, S., 2007. A modern, documented human skeletal collection from Greece. HOMO 58, 221–228. Available from: https://doi.org/10.1016/j.jchb.2006.10.003.

Fain, O., 2005. Musculoskeletal manifestations of scurvy. Joint Bone Spine 72, 124–128. Available from: https://doi.org/10.1016/j.jbspin.2004.01.007.

FitzGerald, C.M., Saunders, S.R., 2005. Test of histological methods of determining chronology of accentuated striae in deciduous teeth. Am. J. Phys. Anthropol. 127, 277–290. Available from: https://doi.org/10.1002/ajpa.10442.

Fowler, M.J., 2008. Microvascular and macrovascular complications of diabetes. Clin. Diabetes 26, 77.

Garber, J.R., Cobin, R.H., Gharib, H., Hennessey, J.V., Klein, I., Mechanick, J.I., et al., 2012. Clinical practice guidelines for hypothyroidism in adults: cosponsored by the American Association of Clinical Endocrinologists and the American Thyroid AssociationWoeber for the American Association of Clinical Endocrinologists and American Thyroid Association Taskforce on Hypothyroidism in AdultsThyroid 22, 1200–1235. Available from: https://doi.org/10.1089/thy.2012.0205.

Giurato, L., Uccioli, L., 2006. The diabetic foot: charcot joint and osteomyelitis. Nucl. Med. Commun. 27, 745–749. Available from: https://doi.org/10.1097/01.mnm.0000230066.23823.cc.

Gruber, R., 2012. Reader's digest of the pathophysiology of bone metastases. Wien. Med. Wochenschr. 162, 370–373. Available from: https://doi.org/10.1007/s10354-012-0110-3.

Hall, R., Scanlon, M.F., 1979. Hypothyroidism: clinical features and complications. Clin. Endocrinol. Metab. 8, 29–38. Available from: https://doi.org/10.1016/S0300-595X(79)80007-9.

Harris, H.A., 1931. Lines of arrested growth in the long bones in childhood: the correlation of histological and radiographic appearances in clinical and experimental conditions. Br. J. Radiol. 4, 561–588.

Harrison, M., 2013. Scurvy on sea and land: political economy and natural history, c. 1780-c. 1850. J. Marit. Res. 15, 7–25. Available from: https://doi.org/10.1080/21533369.2013.783167.

Hartemann-Heurtier, A., Senneville, E., 2008. Diabetic foot osteomyelitis. Diabetes Metab. 34, 87–95.

Hershkovitz, I., Rothschild, B.M., Latimer, B.M., Dutour, O., Léonetti, G., Greenwald, C.M., et al., 1997. Recognition of sickle cell anemia in skeletal remains of children. Am. J. Phys. Anthropol. 104, 213–226. Available from: https://doi.org/10.1002/(SICI)1096-8644(199710)104:2 < 213::AID-AJPA8 > 3.0.CO;2-Z.

Hillson, S., 1996. Dental anthropology. Cambridge University Press.

Hillson, S., 2019. Dental pathology. In: Katzenberg, M.A., Grauer, A.L. (Eds.), Biological Anthropology of the Human Skeleton. John Wiley & Sons, New York, pp. 295–334.

Husni, M.E., Kroop, S.F., Simon, L.S., 2005. Joint and bone manifestations of diabetes mellitus. In: Kahn, C.R., King, G.L., Moses, A.C., Weir, G.C., Jacobson, A.M., Smith, R.J. (Eds.), Joslin's Diabetes Mellitus, 14th Edition Lippincott Williams & Wilkins, Boston, MA.

Ives, R., Brickley, M., 2014. New findings in the identification of adult vitamin D deficiency osteomalacia: results from a large-scale study. Int. J. Paleopathol. 7, 45–56. Available from: https://doi.org/10.1016/j.ijpp.2014.06.004.

Klaus, H.D., 2017. Paleopathological rigor and differential diagnosis: case studies involving terminology, description, and diagnostic frameworks for scurvy in skeletal remains. Int. J. Paleopathol. 19, 96–110. Available from: https://doi.org/10.1016/j.ijpp.2015.10.002.

Lagia, A., Eliopoulos, C., Manolis, S., 2007. Thalassemia: macroscopic and radiological study of a case. Int. J. Osteoarchaeol. 17, 269–285. Available from: https://doi.org/10.1002/oa.881.

Larsen, C.S., 2015. Bioarchaeology: Interpreting Behavior from the Human Skeleton, 2nd ed. Cambridge University Press.

Maat, G.J.R., 2004. Scurvy in adults and youngsters: the Dutch experience. A review of the history and pathology of a disregarded disease. Int. J. Osteoarchaeol. 14, 77–81.

Mankin, H.J., 1974. Review article, rickets, osteomalacia, and renal osteodystrophy. J. Bone Joint Surg. 56, 101–128.

Marx, M., D'Auria, S.H., 1986. CT examination of eleven Egyptian mummies. RadioGraphics 6, 321–330. Available from: https://doi.org/10.1148/radiographics.6.2.3317542.

Marx, S.J., 2000. Hyperparathyroid and hypoparathyroid disorders. N. Engl. J. Med. 343, 1863–1875. Available from: https://doi.org/10.1056/NEJM200012213432508.

Mays, S., 2018. How should we diagnose disease in palaeopathology? Some epistemological considerations. Int. J. Paleopathol. 20, 12–19. Available from: https://doi.org/10.1016/j.ijpp.2017.10.006.

Mays, S., Brickley, M., 2018. Vitamin D deficiency in bioarchaeology and beyond: the study of rickets and osteomalacia in the past. Int. J. Paleopathol. 23, 1–5. Available from: https://doi.org/10.1016/j.ijpp.2018.05.004.

Mays, S., Brickley, M., Ives, R., 2006. Skeletal manifestations of rickets in infants and young children in a historic population from England. Am. J. Phys. Anthropol. 129, 362–374. Available from: https://doi.org/10.1002/ajpa.20292.

McIlvaine, B.K., 2015. Implications of reappraising the iron-deficiency anemia hypothesis. Int. J. Osteoarchaeol. 25, 997–1000. Available from: https://doi.org/10.1002/oa.2383.

Nebot Valenzuela, E., Pietschmann, P., 2017. Epidemiologie und Pathologie des Morbus Paget – ein Überblick. Wien. Med. Wochenschr. 167, 2–8. Available from: https://doi.org/10.1007/s10354-016-0496-4.

Ortner, D.J., 2003. Identification of Pathological Conditions in Human Skeletal Remains, third ed. Smithsonian Institution Press, New York.

Ortner, D.J., Butler, W., Cafarella, J., Milligan, L., 2001. Evidence of probable scurvy in subadults from archeological sites in North America. Am. J. Phys. Anthropol. 114, 343–351. Available from: https://doi.org/10.1002/ajpa.1046.

Ortner, D.J., Hotz, G., 2005. Skeletal manifestations of hypothyroidism from Switzerland. Am. J. Phys. Anthropol. 127, 1–6. Available from: https://doi.org/10.1002/ajpa.20033.

Ortner, D.J., Mays, S., 1998. Dry-bone manifestations of rickets in infancy and early childhood. Int. J. Osteoarchaeol. 8, 45–55. Available from: https://doi.org/10.1002/(SICI)1099-1212(199801/02)8:1 < 45::AID-OA405 > 3.0.CO;2-D.

Oxenham, M.F., Cavill, I., 2010. Porotic hyperostosis and cribra orbitalia: the erythropoietic response to iron-deficiency anaemia. Anthropol. Sci. 118, 199–200. Available from: https://doi.org/10.1537/ase.100302.

Paine, R.R., Brenton, B.P., 2006. The paleopathology of pellagra: investigating the impact of prehistoric and historical dietary transitions to maize. J. Anthropol. Sci. 84, 125–135.

Park, E.A., Riohter, C.P., 1953. Transverse lines in bone: the mechanism of their development. Bull. Johns Hopkins Hosp. 93, 234–248.

Roberts, C.A., Manchester, K., 2007. The Archaeology of Disease, third ed. Cornell University Press, Ithaca, New York.

Roches, E., Blondiaux, J., Cotten, A., Chastanet, P., Flipo, R.-M., 2002. Microscopic evidence for Paget's disease in two osteoarchaeological samples from early northern France. Int. J. Osteoarchaeol. 12, 229–234. Available from: https://doi.org/10.1002/oa.617.

Rothschild, B.M., 2012. Extirpolation of the mythology that porotic hyperostosis is caused by iron deficiency secondary to dietary shift to maize. Adv. Anthropol. 2, 157.

Rothschild, B.M., Manzi, G., Ricci, F., Salvadei, L., 2002. Letter to the editor, Am. J. Hum. Biol., 14. pp. 417–420. Available from: https://doi.org/10.1002/ajhb.10078.

Savvidou, S., 2014. Pellagra : a non-eradicated old disease. Clin. Pract. 4, 637.

Schamall, D., Teschler-Nicola, M., Kainberger, F., Tangl, S., Brandstätter, F., Patzak, B., et al., 2003. Changes in trabecular bone structure in rickets and osteomalacia: the potential of a medico-historical collection. Int. J. Osteoarchaeol. 13, 283–288. Available from: https://doi.org/10.1002/oa.688.

Schectman, G., Byrd, J.C., Gruchow, H.W., 1989. The influence of smoking on vitamin C status in adults. Am. J. Public Health 79, 158–162. Available from: https://doi.org/10.2105/ajph.79.2.158.

Schultz, M., 2001. Paleohistopathology of bone: a new approach to the study of ancient diseases. Am. J. Phys. Anthropol. 116, 106–147. Available from: https://doi.org/10.1002/ajpa.10024.

Singer, F., 2016. Paget's disease of bone. In: Endotext [Internet]. MDText.com, Inc.

Tefferi, A., 2003. Anemia in adults: a contemporary approach to diagnosis. Mayo Clin. Proc. 78, 1274–1280. Available from: https://doi.org/10.4065/78.10.1274.

Van der Merwe, A.E., Maat, G.J.R., Steyn, M., 2010. Ossified haematomas and infectious bone changes on the anterior tibia: histomorphological features as an aid for accurate diagnosis. Int. J. Osteoarchaeol. 20, 227–239.

Vanderpump, M.P.J., Tunbridge, W.M.G., 2002. Epidemiology and prevention of clinical and subclinical hypothyroidism. Thyroid 12, 839–847. Available from: https://doi.org/10.1089/105072502761016458.

Venes, D., 2017. Taber's Cyclopedic Medical Dictionary, twenty third ed. FA Davis Company.

Vilter, R.W., Jarrold, T., Will, J.J., Mueller, J.F., Friedman, B., Hawkins, V.R., 1960. Refractory anemia with hyperplastic bone marrow. Blood 15, 1–29. Available from: https://doi.org/10.1182/blood.V15.1.1.1.

Walker, P.L., Bathurst, R.R., Richman, R., Gjerdrum, T., Andrushko, V.A., 2009. The causes of porotic hyperostosis and cribra orbitalia: a reappraisal of the iron-deficiency-anemia hypothesis. Am. J. Phys. Anthropol. 139, 109–125. Available from: https://doi.org/10.1002/ajpa.21031.

Wapler, U., Crubézy, É., Schultz, M., 2004. Is cribra orbitalia synonymous with anemia? Analysis and interpretation of cranial pathology in Sudan. Am. J. Phys. Anthropol. 123, 333–339. Available from: https://doi.org/10.1002/ajpa.10321.

Whyte, M.P., 2006. Paget's disease of bone. N. Engl. J. Med. 355, 593–600. Available from: https://doi.org/10.1056/NEJMcp060278.

CHAPTER 5

Diseases of Joints

Lucie Biehler-Gomez and Cristina Cattaneo
LABANOF, Department of Biomedical Sciences for Health, University of Milan, Milan, Italy

Arthropathies are diseases affecting the joints and associated bones. Despite the ample clinical and dry bone literature on bone manifestations of the arthropathies, their diagnosis on dry bones remains particularly challenging. This is mainly due to their variability in skeletal manifestations, the impossibility to apply clinical tests and the frequent absence of parts of the skeleton necessary for a diagnosis. In this chapter we will explore the most commonly addressed joint diseases and discuss their diagnosis.

Osteoarthrosis or Degenerative Joint Disease

Osteoarthritis is a misnomer as it implies with the suffix *-itis* an inflammatory process which is not systematic. Thus the terms "osteoarthrosis" or "degenerative joint disease" are a more accurate representation of the condition on dry bone and should be preferred for linguistic exactitude.

Osteoarthrosis is one of the major causes of skeletal pathology and the most common joint disease. Whether the cause is pathomechanical or due to another etiology, the pathogenesis of the condition is characterized by an enzymatic breakdown of the cartilage matrix. This leads to subchondral bone exposition, bone growth with sclerosis, bony cysts due to microfractures, and osteophytes. The clinical diagnosis of the arthropathy relies on joint pain, swelling, and stiffness. About 15% of the population and more than 58% of the individuals over 65 years are affected by the condition with a higher rate for American Indians, Caucasian, and African Americans compared to Hispanics, and Asian and Pacific Islanders. There is a slight female predominance in the epidemiology of the disease and risk factors include advanced age (especially after 50 years), excessive joint loading (high body mass index), repetitive physical activity, previous trauma, and anatomic variants such as muscle strength and alignment (Dominick and Baker, 2004; Johnson and Hunter, 2014). Osteoarthrosis

Interpreting Bone Lesions and Pathology for Forensic Practice. DOI: https://doi.org/10.1016/B978-0-323-85162-6.00005-2

can virtually affect any joint but the most typical locations are the hips, knees, spine, the acromioclavicular joint, hands, and feet (in particular, the first carpometacarpal and tarsometatarsal joints) (Banks, 2010; Chew, 2012; Fitzgerald et al., 2002; Johnson and Hunter, 2014; Roberts and Manchester, 2007; Rogers, 2000; Rogers et al., 1987). The asymmetric loss of cartilage in the joint (due to differences in weight-bearing areas and/or mechanical impairment) induces a bone-to-bone contact of the exposed bone surfaces resulting in focal abrasion with pitting, subchondral cysts due to microfractures with surrounding and underlying reactive new bone formation (seen as sclerosis on X-rays), highly polished areas from prolonged bone-to-bone friction known as eburnation, marginal bone remodeling related to joint repair (i.e., marginal osteophytes) and widening and flattening of the joint contour with the passage of time (Figs. 5.1–5.3) (Aufderheide and Rodríguez-Martín, 1998;

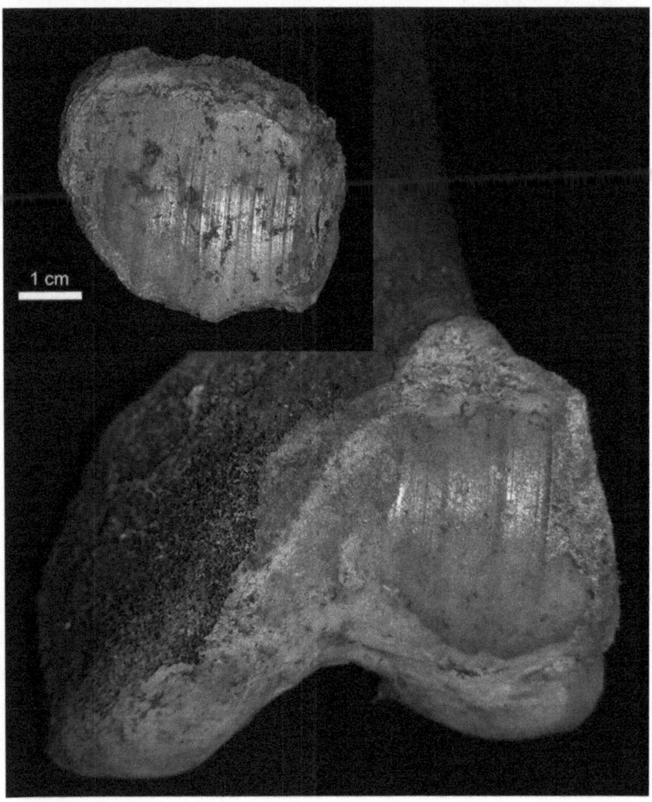

Figure 5.1 Articulation of the femur and patella showing eburnation (i.e., polished area caused by bone-to-bone friction) and striation due to osteoarthrosis of the patellofemoral articulation. Source: Skeleton #1022 of the CAL Milano Cemetery Skeletal Collection.

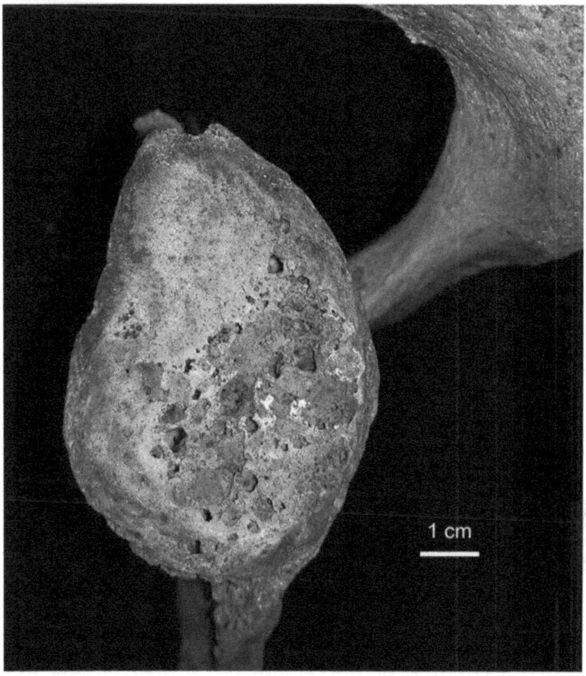

Figure 5.2 Glenoid fossa of the left scapula showing bone porosity, marginal osteophytes, flattening of the articular surface, and eburnation due to osteoarthrosis of the glenohumeral articulation. Source: Skeleton #32 of the CAL Milano Cemetery Skeletal Collection.

Braun and Gold, 2012; Fitzgerald et al., 2002; Hochberg, 2000; Ortner, 2003; Roberts and Manchester, 2007; Rogers, 2000; Rogers et al., 1987, 1981; Vigorita and Ghelman, 2016; Waldron, 2008). In addition to these, in the spine, intervertebral disc herniations or Schmorl's nodes may be seen. First described in 1927 by pathologist Christian Georg Schmorl, Schmorl's nodes are herniation of nucleus pulposus, protruding through the cartilaginous and bony end plate into the body of an adjacent vertebra, causing pressure and erosion of one or more foci (Fig. 5.4). This herniated defect may appear in a variety of shapes, typically in the center of the surface of the vertebral body and are particularly common in the thoracic and lumbar spine (although they may be seen on any spinal vertebra). Both etiology and pathogenesis of Schmorl's nodes remain unclear, but degenerative disk disease and thoracolumbar stress are predisposing factors (Aufderheide and Rodríguez-Martín, 1998, p. 97; Dar et al., 2010; Kyere et al., 2012; Ortner, 2003, p. 558; Waldron, 2008, p. 45). While eburnation is considered a pathognomonic sign of osteoarthrosis (Roberts and

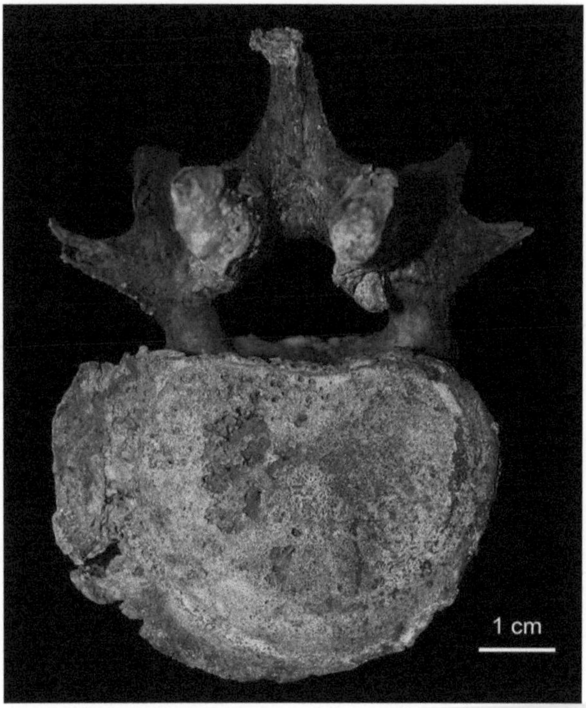

Figure 5.3 Inferior view of a lumbar vertebra showing extensive marginal osteophytes, new bone formation and porosity on the vertebral body and inferior articular facets due to spondylarthrosis. Source: Skeleton #917 of the CAL Milano Cemetery Skeletal Collection.

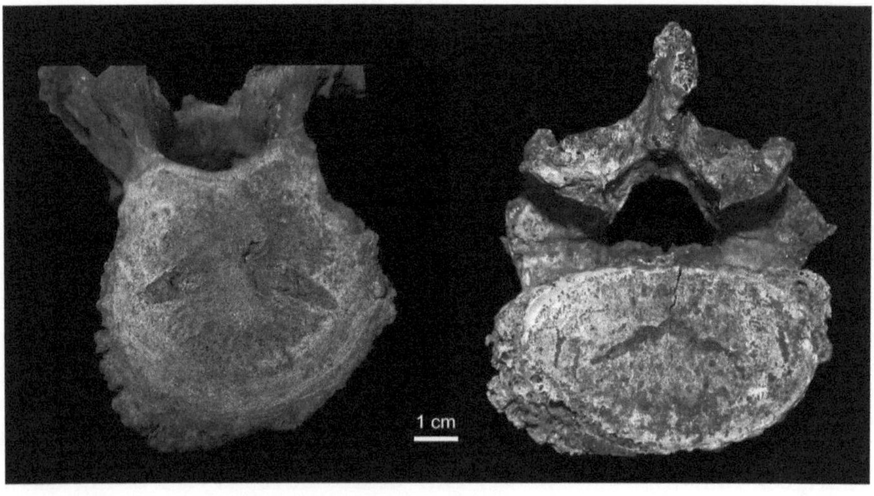

Figure 5.4 Schmorl's nodes on thoracic (left) and lumbar (right) vertebral bodies. Source: Skeletons #1160 (left) and #623 (right) of the CAL Milano Cemetery Skeletal Collection.

Box 5.1 Bone Features of Osteoarthrosis

Features	Diagnostic strength
Eburnation	Diagnostic
Marginal osteophytes	Typical
Pitting on the articular surface	Consistent
New bone on the articular surface	Consistent
Alteration of the articular contour	Consistent

Manchester, 2007; Rogers, 2000), marginal osteophytes alone are not a sufficient indicator as their formation can be related to the ageing process (Roberts and Manchester, 2007; Waldron, 2008).

A study by Zampetti et al. (2016) was performed on 332 individuals of the Frasseti collection, a modern skeletal collection, to investigate the link between bone changes associated with the degenerative condition and factors such as sex, age, and occupation and evidenced no differences among different occupations, indicating that advanced age was a stronger factor on the development of degenerative bone changes.

Bone changes is osteoarthrosis are well-known, but diagnosis based solely on the presence of marginal osteophytes should be avoided (Roberts and Manchester, 2007; Waldron, 2008) (Box 5.1).

Markers of Mechanical Stress

As the bone adapts to repetitive mechanical stresses, bone changes may be seen throughout the skeleton. The interpretation of skeletal markers of mechanical stress, also called "occupational markers" can suggest additional information on the life of the individual regarding activity, occupation, repeated movements, workload, disuse of specific muscles, and even socioeconomic status.

Indeed, as they result from mechanical loading and repetitive motions, the location and pattern of distribution of osteoarthrosis or degenerative bone changes in the skeleton can be indicative of activity, workload, occupation, and even socioeconomic status.

Other markers of mechanical stress are enthesophytes. Muscles are connected to the skeletal system through tendons and ligaments in areas of articulations. The tendons and ligaments are joined to the bone in a site of insertion known as "enthesis," which facilitates joint motion through biomechanical properties. Entheses can be divided into two types: fibrous and fibrocartilaginous entheses. In fibrous entheses, the tendon or ligament is directly attached to the bone or periosteum through fibrous tissue. This type of entheses is most commonly found in the diaphysis and metaphysis of long bones. By opposition, fibrocartilaginous entheses are joined to bone via a layer of fibrocartilage. They represent the majority of entheses and are typical of epiphyses and apophyses (Apostolakos et al., 2014). *Entheseal changes*, also referred to as musculoskeletal stress markers or enthesopathies, manifest through bone changes at the site of enthesis including porosity and new bone formation (called enthesophytes) and typically occur under heavy muscular activity (Figs. 5.5 and 5.6). As a result, the pattern of entheseal changes may be used to reconstruct activity and occupation: as each enthesis corresponds to a muscle insertion, the mechanical activity of specific muscles can be identified. Similarly, asymmetry may be indicative of handedness or a dominant limb (Christensen et al., 2014). However, some pathological conditions may also induce entheseal changes, in particular, diffuse idiopathic skeletal hyperostosis (DISH) and the seronegative spondyloarthropathies, and advanced age, male sex and high body mass index are contributing factors in healthy individuals, and so entheseal changes should be interpreted with care, especially in forensic practice.

Erosive Osteoarthritis

Erosive osteoarthritis is considered to be an aggressive subtype of osteoarthritis typically affecting the hands of middle-aged women

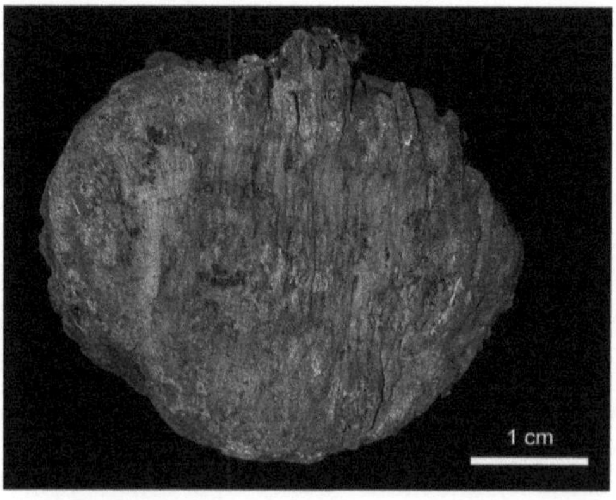

Figure 5.5 Entheseal changes (enthesophytes) at the insertion of the quadriceps tendon (for attachment of the quadriceps muscle). Skeleton #32 of the CAL Milano Cemetery Skeletal Collection.

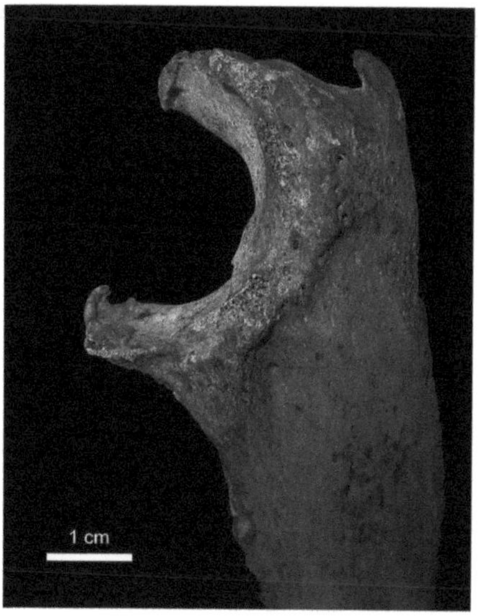

Figure 5.6 Entheseal changes (enthesophytes) at the insertion of the triceps tendon (for attachment of the triceps muscle). Source: Skeleton #389 of the CAL Milano Cemetery Skeletal Collection.

(Marshall et al., 2013; Mas and Rotés-Querol, 2007; Punzi et al., 2004). Its etiology is unclear and tends to be more common among Caucasians. In fact, it is present in about 2.8% of the general population and in 4%–15% of patients with osteoarthritis of the hands (Banks, 2010; Ehrlich, 2001; Marshall et al., 2013; Punzi et al., 2004).

Erosive osteoarthritis produces both erosions and bone proliferation. The most characteristic lesion is the central erosion of the interphalangeal joints that differentiates it from the other arthropathies affecting the hands (Fig. 5.7) (Aufderheide and Rodríguez-Martín, 1998; Punzi et al., 2004; Rogers, 2000). This central erosion generates a collapse of the subchondral bone resulting in two typical erosive osteoarthritic deformities of interphalangeal joints: "gull-wing" and "saw-tooth" (Fig. 5.8) (Banks, 2010; Jacobson et al., 2008; Marshall et al., 2013; Punzi et al., 2004; Rogers, 2000; Waldron, 2008). Osteophytes and eburnation are a common feature of the condition and ankyloses of interphalangeal joints are described as being more common in erosive osteoarthritis than in any other arthropathy (Aufderheide and Rodríguez-Martín, 1998; Banks, 2010; Punzi et al., 2004; Waldron, 2008). The radiographic lesions reflect the aforementioned macroscopic lesions and also include subchondral cysts and

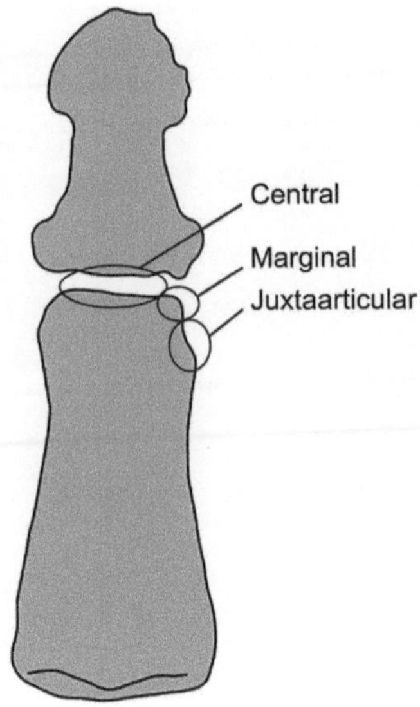

Figure 5.7 Differential location of articular erosions. Central erosions are typical of erosive osteoarthritis, whereas marginal or para-articular erosions are seen in rheumatoid arthritis and juxtaarticular erosions are characteristic of gout. Drawing by Davide Porta.

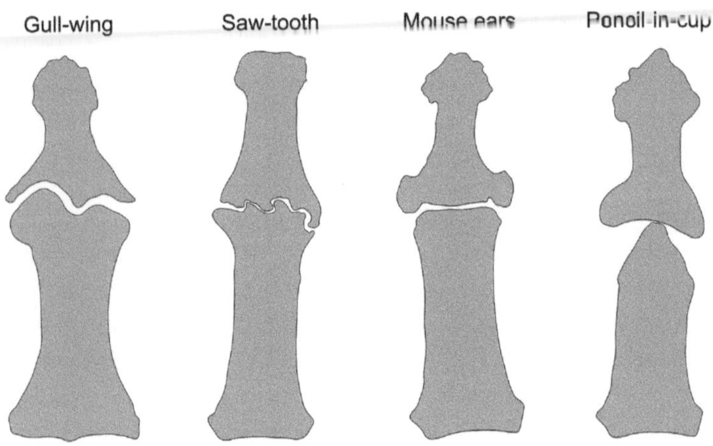

Figure 5.8 Drawing showing different articular deformations. Drawing by Davide Porta.

surrounding sclerosis (Banks, 2010; Jacobson et al., 2008; Waldron, 2008). The lesions are found most commonly in the distal interphalangeal and the proximal interphalangeal joints, more often symmetrical than asymmetrical. In decreasing frequency, erosive osteoarthritis also affects respectively the first carpometacarpal joint, the metacarpophalangeal

Box 5.2 Bone Features of Erosive Osteoarthritis

Features	Diagnostic strength
"Gull-wing" and "sawtooth" interphalangeal deformities	Diagnostic
Interphalangeal joint ankylosis	Typical
Marginal osteophytes	Consistent
Eburnation	Consistent
Subchondral cysts	Consistent

joints and, lastly, the feet (Aufderheide and Rodríguez-Martín, 1998; Banks, 2010; Punzi et al., 2004).

The most reliable features of the condition are the central erosions and deformities of the interphalangeal joints. As a subset of osteoarthritis, erosive osteoarthritic lesions can appear very similar (Vigorita and Ghelman, 2016). In addition, about 15% of all patients with erosive osteoarthritis will develop rheumatoid arthritis in their lifetimes, and since both diseases affect primarily the hands, a correct diagnosis may be challenging (Marshall et al., 2013). Rogers and Waldron (1995) mention that only one case of erosive osteoarthritis has been reported in the paleopathological literature (Rogers et al., 1991); thus documentation from clinically diagnosed dry bone cases could help the recognition of the condition in the future (Box 5.2).

Septic Arthritis

Septic arthritis may be caused by spreading of the infectious agent (most commonly, bacteria and in particular *Staphylococcus aureus*) to the joint cavity via hematogenous dissemination from a distant source, by direct inoculation (i.e., skin wound) or through contiguous infected bone. The infectious arthritis may involve one joint (classically, the hip or knee) or more. No changes can be noted on dry bones in acute septic arthritis. As the infection progresses, joint space narrowing, subchondral bone changes, and complications such as subluxations or dislocations may manifest. Untreated septic arthritis is a potentially fatal condition which often terminates in bony ankylosis.

The main differential diagnosis of the condition is tuberculous arthritis: the latter tends to be more destructive and affects primarily children, whereas septic arthritis may affect all ages (Aufderheide and Rodríguez-Martín, 1998,

Box 5.3 Bone Features of Septic Arthritis

Features	Diagnostic strength
Joint ankylosis	Typical
Erosions	Consistent

pp. 106–107; García-Arias et al., 2011; Ortner, 2003, pp. 222–226; Roberts and Manchester, 2007). Nonetheless, both conditions may be undistinguishable on dry bones. In addition, as Roberts and Manchester (2007) explain: "septic arthritis may also be complicated by non-septic osteoarthritis or other joint diseases, so that, in any one individual, a number of joint diseases may present themselves but are impossible to differentiate from one another" (Box 5.3).

Rheumatoid Arthritis

Rheumatoid arthritis is a chronic, systemic, progressive, and proinflammatory multifactorial disease. The disorder manifests through a pathological autoimmune response and affects primarily women (female-to-male ratio of 3:1) around 30–50 years (Choy, 2012; Firestein, 2000; Henrique da Mota et al., 2013). With a prevalence between 0.8% and 2% in the general population, rheumatoid arthritis presents its highest rates of incidence among Native Americans (5%–7%) and its lowest in Africa and South-East Asia, which suggests the presence of a genetic role in disease risk, mainly accounted for by genetic variation of the HLA DRB1 alleles (Alamanos and Drosos, 2005; Lee and Weinblatt, 2001; Rindfleisch and Muller, 2005; Silman and Pearson, 2002; Smolen et al., 2016; Watts et al., 2013). There is also evidence that occurrence and severity of rheumatoid arthritis are related to genetic factors (Alamanos and Drosos, 2005). Environmental risk factors include increasing age, obesity, family history, and cigarette smoking. In fact, smoking and infections might trigger the development of rheumatoid arthritis on genetically predisposed individuals and may influence the rate of development and severity of the pathology (Choy, 2012; Entezami et al., 2011; Majithia and Geraci, 2007; Rindfleisch and Muller, 2005).

The initiation of the lesion is characterized by an infiltration of leukocytes in the synovium leading to its inflammation due to a combination of genetic, environmental, and immunological factors. This synovitis generates a massive and uncontrolled immune response resulting in the formation of an aggressive front of tissue or "pannus." Three types of white blood cells will interplay at this point: T-cells, B-cells, and macrophages. T-cells, also known as T-lymphocytes, are basically the Navy Seals of the body, they are specialized units and can be divided in two main teams: Killer T-cells (i.e., cytotoxic $CD8^+$ cells) eliminate the target, that is, the infected host cells and Helper T-cells (i.e., $CD4^+$ cells) coordinate the attack (they suppress or regulate the immune response through cytokines that stimulate B-cells to make antibodies and induce the development of other killer T-cells). B-cells, also known as B-lymphocytes, are major players in the adaptive humoral immunity through the secretion of specific antibodies; basically, they are the intelligence analysts of the body, they monitor and gather information on threats at first contact and should they come back, they know exactly how to neutralize them (they produce antibodies that attach to the surface of the foreign agent) and call for backup (i.e., other immune cells) for their elimination. Macrophages (from the Greek "large eaters") are police first responders: they patrol for pathogens throughout the body migrating using blood vessels, mediate inflammation through cytokines, eliminate threats directly through phagocytosis, recruit specific immune cells (e.g., lymphocytes), and participate in tissue repair. However, in autoimmune conditions, the immune system attacks its own organism by mistake, thinking there is a foreign invader and tragically sends its armed forces against its own tissues.

Thus interactions between these cells (i.e., T-cells, B-cells, and macrophages) in the pannus induce the overproduction of proinflammatory cytokines and chemokines (including interleukin 1, 6 and tumor necrosis factor-α) and the activation of osteoclasts rendering the pannus persistently inflammatory. This leads to the destruction of local articular structures and the demineralization of subchondral bone as the pannus spreads and invades cartilage and bone (Firestein, 2003, 2000; Fitzgerald et al., 2002; Lee and Weinblatt, 2001; McInnes and Schett, 2011; Smolen et al., 2016). Rheumatoid arthritis also causes extra-articular manifestations in about 40% of patients due to a progressive and systemic inflammation with skin (rheumatoid nodules), ocular (keratoconjunctivitis sicca, iritis), oral, gastrointestinal, respiratory (pulmonary fibrosis, pleural effusion), cardiac (atherosclerosis, myocarditis, endocarditis, pericardial inflammation), neurological (neuropathy, myelopathy), hepatic, hematological (anemia, thrombocytopenia, neutropenia), and vascular (vasculitis) involvement causing major morbidity and mortality, as well as a generally heightened mortality rate (Cojocaru et al., 2010; Henrique da Mota et al., 2013; Lee and Weinblatt, 2001; Smolen et al., 2016).

On dry bone, rheumatoid arthritis is described as mostly erosive with minimal new bone formation to no bony proliferation (Aufderheide and Rodríguez-Martín, 1998, pp. 99–101; Ortner, 2003, pp. 561–570; Rogers et al., 1987; Waldron, 2008, pp. 46–49). The rheumatologic definition of rheumatoid arthritis postulates that the condition affects at least three joints, mainly interphalangeal, metacarpophalangeal or wrist joints, in a symmetrical pattern with radiological erosions and/or periarticular osteopenia in hand and/or wrist joints (Arnett et al., 1988). Thus rheumatoid arthritis lesions are polyarticular (i.e., affecting more than four joints), symmetrical, articular, or para-articular affecting the small bones of the wrist and hands (carpal, carpometacarpal, metacarpophalangeal, and interphalangeal joints) (Figs. 5.7 and 5.9), as well as the feet (metatarsophalangeal and interphalangeal joints) (Fig. 5.10), and may spread to more distant weight-bearing joints (elbows, shoulders, ankles, knees, temporomandibular, and atlantoaxial joints) (Fig. 5.11) (Brahee et al., 2003; Firestein, 2000;

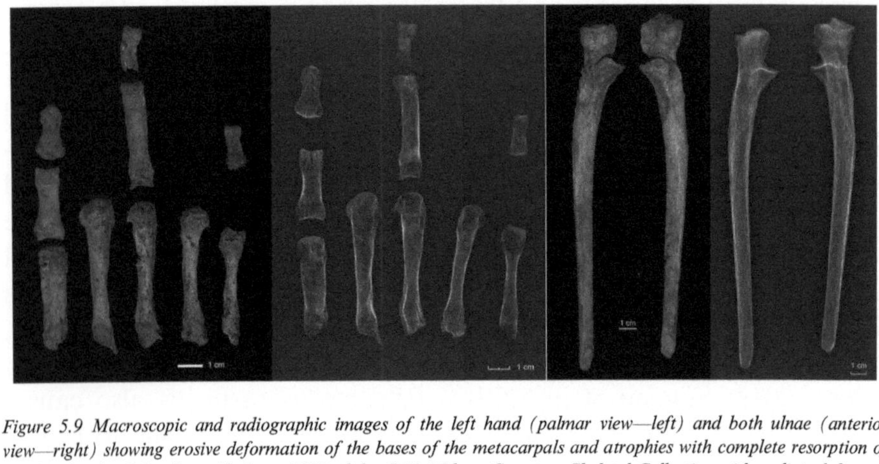

Figure 5.9 Macroscopic and radiographic images of the left hand (palmar view—left) and both ulnae (anterior view—right) showing erosive deformation of the bases of the metacarpals and atrophies with complete resorption of the distal ends of the ulnae. Skeleton #277 of the CAL Milano Cemetery Skeletal Collection with a clinical diagnosis of rheumatoid arthritis. Reproduced with permission from Biehler-Gomez, L., Tritella, S., Martino, F., Campobasso, C., Pietro, Franchi, A., et al., 2019. The synergy between radiographic and macroscopic observation of skeletal lesions on dry bone. Int. J. Leg. Med. https://doi.org/10.1007/s00414-019-02122-0.

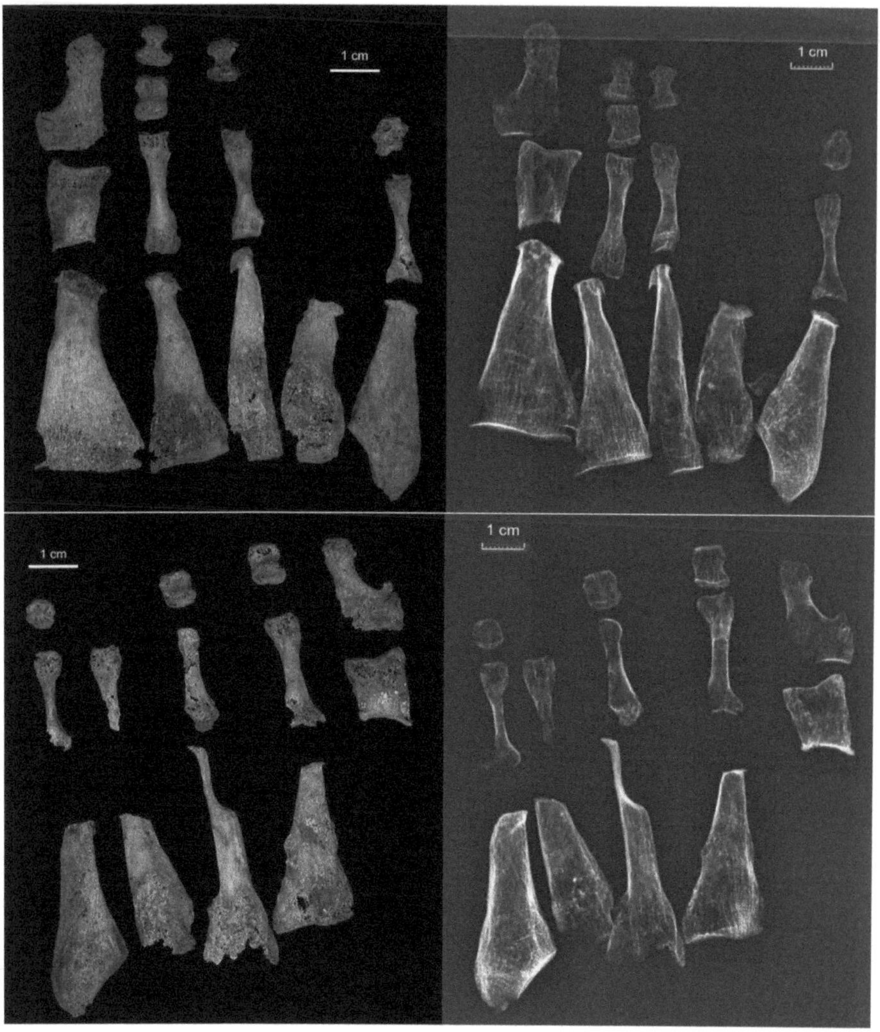

Figure 5.10 Macroscopic and radiographic images of both feet (dorsal views—right foot on the top) showing atrophies of the heads of the metatarsals and base of the first proximal phalanges as well as erosive deformation (i.e., widening) of the bases of the proximal phalanges. Skeleton #277 of the CAL Milano Cemetery Skeletal Collection with a clinical diagnosis of rheumatoid arthritis. Reproduced with permission from Biehler-Gomez, L., Tritella, S., Martino, F., Campobasso, C., Pietro, Franchi, A., et al., 2019. The synergy between radiographic and macroscopic observation of skeletal lesions on dry bone. Int. J. Leg. Med. https://doi.org/10.1007/s00414-019-02122-0.

Fitzgerald et al., 2002; Rogers et al., 1987; Sommer et al., 2005; Vigorita and Ghelman, 2016). The involvement of the thoracic and lumbar spine is infrequent. The prevalence of involvement of the cervical spine (typically, the atlantoaxial joint) ranges between 17% and

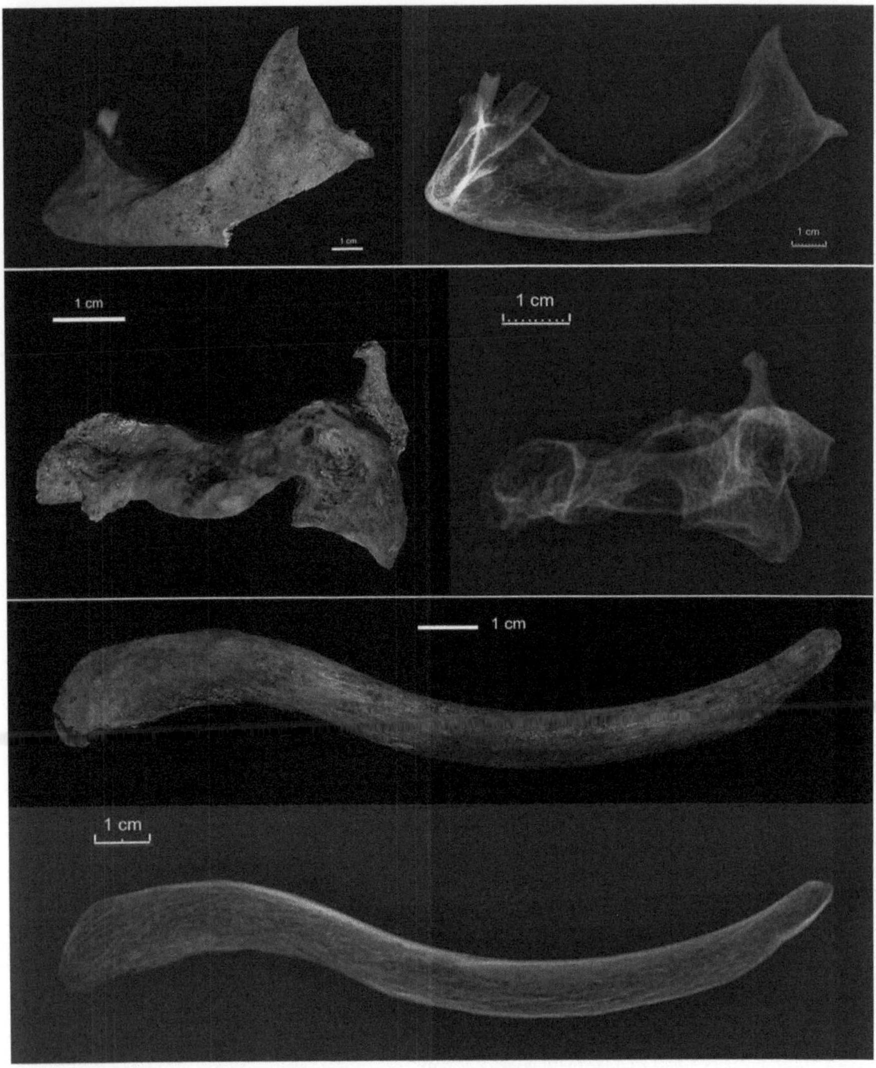

Figure 5.11 Macroscopic and radiographic images of the mandible (left lateral side—top), axis (right lateral view—middle), and right clavicle (superior view—bottom) showing atrophies of the mandibular condyle, odontoid process (causing subluxation of the atlantoaxial joint), and sternal end of the clavicle. Skeleton #277 of the CAL Milano Cemetery Skeletal Collection with a clinical diagnosis of rheumatoid arthritis. Reproduced with permission from Biehler-Gomez, L., Tritella, S., Martino, F., Campobasso, C., Pietro, Franchi, A., et al., 2019. The synergy between radiographic and macroscopic observation of skeletal lesions on dry bone. Int. J. Leg. Med. https://doi.org/10.1007/s00414-019-02122-0.

88% (Kim et al., 2015). It is a late manifestation of long-standing rheumatoid arthritis associated with subluxation and reduced life expectancy (Jurik, 2011). Contrary to the spondyloarthropathies, rheumatoid arthritis is characterized by a relative sparing of distal interphalangeal joints as well as sacroiliac and/or spinal fusion (Erickson et al., 2017; Henrique da Mota et al., 2013; Ortner, 2003, pp. 561–580; Rothschild and Woods, 1991; Veale and Fearon, 2015). Complications of bone erosions in rheumatoid arthritis include subluxation and dislocation of the atlantoaxial joint, ulnar deviation of the hand, and carpal and/or tarsal ankyloses (the latter is considered a sign of extreme severity of the disease). On radiographs, subchondral cysts, osteopenia, and more generally osteoporosis can also be observed (Brahee et al., 2003; Kim et al., 2015; Leden et al., 2012). More recently, a study of two skeletons from the CAL Milano Cemetery Skeletal Collection with recorded rheumatoid arthritis in their antemortem medical data showed bone lesions consistent with the rheumatological and paleopathological literature, specifically, symmetric para-articular or articular erosions of multiple bones of the hands and wrists as well as of more distant joints, sparing the distal interphalangeal joints and sacroiliac and spinal fusion, thus strengthening the criteria for the diagnosis of rheumatoid arthritis on dry bones (Biehler-Gomez and Cattaneo, 2018).

Despite the fact that pathological bone markers for rheumatoid arthritis are well-known in both clinical and dry bone literature, a certain diagnosis may not always be possible as the presence of the bones of the hands and/or feet is capital to achieve a diagnosis (Rogers et al., 1987) (Box 5.4).

Spondyloarthropathies

The spondyloarthropathies commonly refer to the seronegative spondyloarthritides, which include ankylosing spondylitis, inflammatory bowel disease-related arthritis or enteropathic arthritis, psoriatic arthritis, Reiter's disease or reactive arthritis, and undifferentiated

Box 5.4 Bone Features of Rheumatoid Arthritis

Features	Diagnostic strength
Symmetric (para)articular erosions of small joints of hands and/or feet	Diagnostic
Sparing of distal interphalangeal joints	Typical
Absence of sacroiliac or spinal fusion	Typical
Symmetric (para)articular erosions of weight-bearing joints	Consistent
Carpal and/or tarsal ankylosis	Consistent
Minimal new bone formation	Consistent

spondyloarthropathy (Dougados et al., 1991). The spondyloarthropathies are inflammatory arthritides with poorly understood etiologies; they are also clinically negative to rheumatoid factors, associated with the major histocompatibility complex class 1 antigen HLA-B27 and share characteristic clinical features (Arnett, 2000; Olivieri et al., 2002; Zochling and Smith, 2010), including spinal inflammation and/or synovitis, sacroiliitis, asymmetrical peripheral oligoarthritis (mainly in the lower limbs), peripheral and central enthesitis, dactylitis, eye inflammation, and skin lesions (Akgul and Ozgocmen, 2011; Wendling et al., 2010). Consequently, dry bone diagnoses of the spondyloarthropathies may be particularly challenging.

Rothschild and Woods (1991) and Martin-Dupont et al. (2006) examined respectively 2906 skeletons from the Hamann–Todd collection and 505 human remains from the Coimbra identified skeletal collection for evidence of spondyloarthropathies and enhanced the criteria for diagnosis; however, while these studies were performed on identified collections, no diagnosis of spondyloarthropathies was recorded in the associated documentation. In addition, the considerable overlap still existing within the spondyloarthropathies and with other inflammatory arthritides renders a certain diagnosis on dry bones difficult.

Ankylosing Spondylitis

Ankylosing spondylitis is by far the most common of the spondyloarthropathies (between 0.2% and 1% in the general population), it predominates in males (male-to-female ratio of 2–9:1) and begins in the third decade of life. The pathogenesis of ankylosing spondylitis remains obscure; at present, it is known that it is an autoimmune and inflammatory arthritis and enthesitis with a clear genetic predisposition (Arnett, 2000; Olivieri et al., 2002; Watts et al., 2013; Zochling and Smith, 2010).

The pathognomonic bone signs for ankylosing spondylitis are bilateral symmetrical sacroiliitis and spondylitis (Braun and Sieper, 2007). Spine involvement in ankylosing spondylitis consists of syndesmophytes (vertically oriented osteophytes) and the consequent ascending ankylosis of the vertebrae creating a “bamboo spine” appearance, as well as osteopenia of the vertebral bodies resulting in the “squaring effect” of the vertebrae on X-rays (Aufderheide and Rodríguez-Martín, 1998; Buikstra, 2019; Ortner, 2003; Raychaudhuri

Box 5.5 Bone Features of Ankylosing Spondylitis

Features	Diagnostic strength
Symmetric fusion of the sacroiliac joints	Diagnostic
Spinal fusion through syndesmophytes	Diagnostic
Bamboo spine	Diagnostic
Entheseal changes	Typical
Erosions in peripheral joints	Consistent

and Deodhar, 2014; Rogers et al., 1987; Sieper et al., 2002). Entheseal and ligamentous (including apophyseal joints) ossification are particularly marked in ankylosing spondylitis and sacroiliitis is typically bilateral and symmetric (Arnett, 2000; Aufderheide and Rodríguez-Martín, 1998; Chew, 2012; Ortner, 2003; Raychaudhuri and Deodhar, 2014; Rogers et al., 1987; Waldron, 2008; Zochling and Smith, 2010). Peripheral joint involvement in ankylosing spondylitis is variable. It may be absent, or present as either a non-destructive mono/oligoarthritis of the large joints leading with time to their ankylosis or an asymmetric polyarthritis affecting mostly the hips, shoulders, and knees (Aufderheide and Rodríguez-Martín, 1998; Braun and Sieper, 2007; Fitzgerald et al., 2002; Ortner, 2003; Rogers et al., 1987; Šlaus et al., 2012; Watts et al., 2013) (Box 5.5)

Enteropathic Arthritis

Enteropathic arthritis is an inflammatory arthropathy present in 2%–22% of inflammatory bowel disease patients that includes Crohn's disease and ulcerative colitis, both idiopathic pathological conditions. Enteropathic arthritis affects both sexes, with perhaps a slight female predominance, and shows geographical differences in disease risk due to immunological and genetic factors (Arnett, 2000; Holden et al., 2003; Olivieri et al., 2002; Resende et al., 2013; Voulgari, 2011; Waldron, 2008).

The exact mechanism responsible for the development of this arthritis is uncertain and consists of a reaction to an extra-articular infection, probably linked to abnormal bowel permeability combined with genetic and immunological influences (Holden et al., 2003; Voulgari, 2011). Axial involvement consists of bilateral symmetric or asymmetric (Ortner, 2003; Vigorita and Ghelman, 2016; Voulgari, 2011; Waldron, 2008) sacroiliitis with spinal fusion. The symmetric sacroiliitis pattern with spinal involvement may be similar to ankylosing spondylitis (Bruintjes and Panhuysen, 1992; Jadon and McHugh, 2014; Jurik, 2011; Ortner, 2003; Rogers et al., 1987; Voulgari, 2011; Waldron, 2008). Entheseal changes are marked in enteropathic arthritis, mostly in the heels and knees (Rogers, 2000; Voulgari, 2011). Peripheral joint involvement can follow two different types: Type 1 is a non-erosive asymmetrical arthritis of the large joints of the lower limbs affecting at most four articulations; whereas Type 2 displays symmetrical involvement of at least five small joints consisting of erosive lesions (Holden et al., 2003; Jadon and McHugh, 2014; Ortner, 2003; Rogers, 2000; Vigorita and Ghelman, 2016; Voulgari, 2011; Waldron, 2008; Zochling and Smith, 2010)

Enteropathic arthritis is quite challenging to diagnose on skeletonized individuals without a medical history. The non-specificity of the lesions and their similarities with other arthropathies raises the problem of the identification of enteropathic arthritis in skeletal remains. As Waldron (2008, pp. 65–66) explains: "Although it is probable that both ulcerative colitis and Crohn's disease occurred in the past, it is not very likely that those who contracted either would have survived very long," thus precluding the possibility to affect bones. Waldron concludes that in any case, enteropathic arthritis could not be differentiated from classical ankylosing spondylitis or undifferentiated forms of spondyloarthropathies.

Psoriatic Arthritis

Psoriatic arthritis is an inflammatory arthritis affecting 6%–42% of patients with psoriasis. In over half of the cases, psoriatic arthritis is the result of long-standing psoriasis of about 7–12 years' duration (Dhir and Aggarwal, 2013). It affects both sexes with a slight female predominance in individuals around 40–50 years of age (Arnett, 2000; Fitzgerald et al., 2002; Myers et al., 2006; Olivieri et al., 2002; Zochling and Smith, 2010). The etiology responsible for the arthritis remains unclear: it consists of a combination of genetic predisposition (antigen HLA-B27) and environmental factors (e.g., an infection) triggering an abnormal immune response.

Like in rheumatoid arthritis, T-cells, B-cells, macrophages, and fibroblasts infiltrate the synovial tissue resulting in its hypertrophy.

Cytokines, including tumor necrosis factor-α, stimulate both osteoclastic activity and the proliferation of inflammatory cells within the synovium, leading to its inflammation as well as to bone erosion and new bone formation (Jadon and McHugh, 2014; Myers et al., 2006). Moll and Wright (1973) initially described four types of articular involvement that may accompany spondylitis and sacroiliitis: one consists of the extensive erosion of the distal interphalangeal joints and represents less than 5% of cases; another, as uncommon as the first, is called *arthritis mutilans* and presents sacroiliitis and severe osteolysis in the interphalangeal, metacarpophalangeal, and metatarsophalangeal joints; the third type and most common (about 70% of cases), is an asymmetrical oligoarthritis of the distal interphalangeal, interphalangeal, metacarpophalangeal, and metatarsophalangeal joints; and the last type, occurring in about 15% of cases, is a symmetrical polyarthritis indistinguishable from rheumatoid arthritis. Recent research suggests that the asymmetrical oligoarthritic type gradually evolves into the symmetric polyarthritic type over time (Dhir and Aggarwal, 2013; Myers et al., 2006).

More than the pattern of involvement, what differentiates psoriatic arthritis from the other arthropathies is its characteristic lesions. Acroosteolysis or the resorptions of the apical tufts in the hands and the "mouse ear" lesions of the interphalangeal joints are pathognomonic of the disease (Waldron, 2008). Whittling of the metacarpals and metatarsals or "pencil-in-cup" deformities of the metacarpophalangeal and metatarsophalangeal joints is also more typical of psoriatic arthritis (Fig. 5.12)

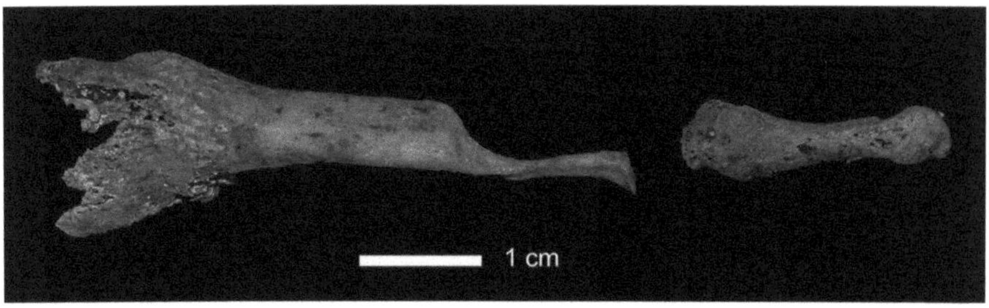

Figure 5.12 Medial view of the fourth metatarsal and proximal phalanx with "pencil-in-cup" deformity of the metatarsophalangeal joint: note the tapered deformation of the distal end of the metatarsal with atrophy of the head (assuming a pencil shape) and widening of the base of the phalanx (cup-shaped). "Pencil-in-cup" deformities are more typical of psoriatic arthritis but may also be found in other conditions including rheumatoid arthritis. Source: Skeleton #277 of the CAL Milano Cemetery Skeletal Collection with a clinical diagnosis of rheumatoid arthritis.

(Aufderheide and Rodríguez-Martín, 1998; Dhir and Aggarwal, 2013; Ortner, 2003; Roberts and Manchester, 2007; Rogers, 2000; Vigorita and Ghelman, 2016; Waldron, 2008). Similarly to rheumatoid arthritis, psoriatic arthritis affects mostly the hands with marginal erosions as well as subchondral cysts and can present ankyloses of the interphalangeal, carpal, and tarsal joints. Unlike rheumatoid arthritis, the lesions are Ω-shaped (by opposition to U-shaped in rheumatoid arthritis), both erosive and proliferative and can affect entire rays of the hands and feet, marginal erosions are poorly demarcated on X-rays, distal interphalangeal joints are more affected than the proximal interphalangeal and metacarpophalangeal joints and the involvement of the temporomandibular joint is uncommon (Aufderheide and Rodríguez-Martín, 1998; Chew, 2012; Finzel et al., 2011; Helliwell and Taylor, 2005; Henrique da Mota et al., 2013; Ortner, 2003; Rogers, 2000; Veale and Fearon, 2015; Vigorita and Ghelman, 2016; Waldron, 2008).

Entheseal changes are common occurrences in psoriatic arthritis. Peripheral psoriatic arthritis can also be accompanied by sacroiliitis and spine involvement. Sacroiliitis can be similar to reactive arthritis (bilaterally asymmetric) (Aufderheide and Rodríguez-Martín, 1998; Helliwell and Taylor, 2005; Rogers, 2000; Waldron, 2008), or ankylosing spondylitis (bilateral symmetric) (Vigorita and Ghelman, 2016). Spine involvement in psoriatic arthritis may simulate that of reactive arthritis with asymmetrical large paravertebral bridging and skip lesions (Aufderheide and Rodríguez-Martín, 1998; Baraliakos et al., 2015; Waldron, 2008), or be indistinguishable from ankylosing spondylitis (Helliwell and Taylor, 2005; Ortner, 2003; Vigorita and Ghelman, 2016). Cervical spine involvement, in particular the atlantoaxial joint, is possible and may be similar to that of rheumatoid arthritis (Helliwell and Taylor, 2005; Laiho and Kauppi, 2002; Ortner, 2003; Rogers, 2000).

Reactive Arthritis

Reactive arthritis is part of the "Reiter's syndrome" and develops in 2%–4% of patients in response to an infection in the gastrointestinal or urogenital tract, affecting mainly young adults, from 20 to 40 years of age (Kim et al., 2009). This inflammatory arthritis and spondyloarthropathy has a genetic predisposition and an onset as an overstimulated autoimmune response to a triggering infection caused by a specific microorganism, including *Salmonella, Shigella, Yersinia, Campylobacter, Clostridium, Eschridia, Chlamydia, Ureaplasma*, or *Mycoplasma* species of bacteria (Hannu, 2011; Lahu et al., 2015; Selmi and Gershwin, 2014). However, it is "not clear how and in what form the bacterial components reach the joint and whether there are viable bacteria in the joint" (Kim et al., 2009).

Reactive arthritis presents marked entheseal changes, typically in the heel as well as in the axial joints. Sacroiliitis is asymmetrical and spinal fusion generally occurs with skip lesions and paravertebral bridging. Peripheral joints are involved in an asymmetrical mono- or oligoarthritis. The pathology involves the lower limbs most commonly, including the joints of the feet, knees, ankles, and tarsals, but the hands can also be affected, although less often and only very mildly. The lesions are erosive with reactive new bone and possible ankylosis of the tarsals (Aufderheide and Rodríguez-Martín, 1998; Cawley and Paine, 2015; Hannu, 2011; Kim et al., 2009; Lahu et al., 2015; Mays et al., 2016; Ortner, 2003; Rogers, 2000; Selmi and Gershwin, 2014; Vigorita and Ghelman, 2016; Waldron, 2008). Reactive arthritis, although very different from ankylosing spondylitis in its axial joint involvement, can also coexist with the latter (Olivieri et al., 2002), making its diagnosis in these cases dependent solely on the peripheral bone lesions.

Diffuse Idiopathic Skeletal Hyperostosis

DISH is a skeletal disease of unknown etiology, more common in men over 40 years, inducing entheseal calcification and ossification. Specifically, it is characterized by the ossification of the anterior longitudinal ligament of the spine, and in particular of the thoracic segment, with the production of flowing ossifications with a "dripping candle wax" appearance, leading to the fusion of at least four contiguous vertebrae (Figs. 5.13 and 5.14). This spinal ligamentous ossification is limited to the right side of the vertebral bodies while preserving the intervertebral disc space. Another typical feature of the condition consists in the absence of changes associated with a degenerative disc disease or apophyseal joint ankylosis. DISH may also involve the heterotopic ossification of other entheses (e.g., peripheral joints), and is frequently associated with the ossification of the posterior longitudinal ligament and

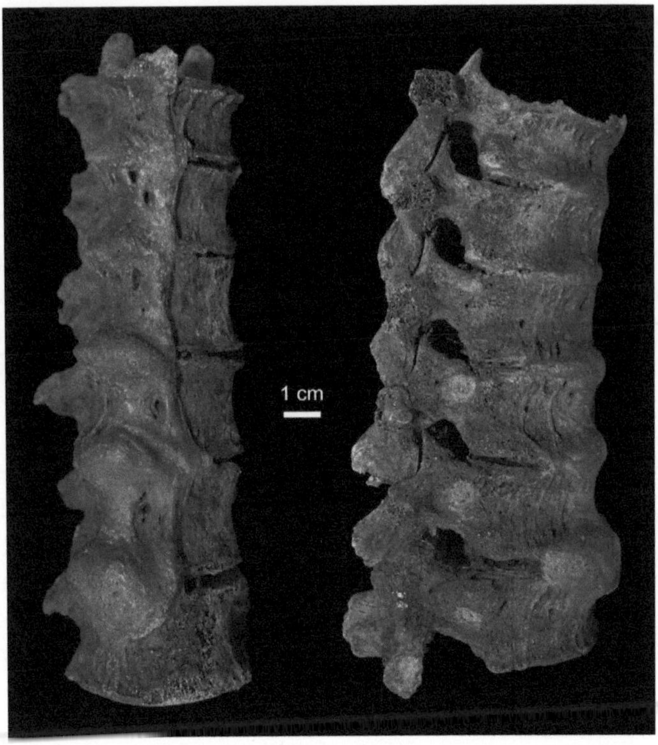

Figure 5.13 Anterior and right lateral views of the 7th–12th thoracic vertebrae fused through DISH, note the "dripping candle wax" appearance on the right side of the vertebral bodies. Source: Skeleton #21 of the CAL Milano Cemetery Skeletal Collection.

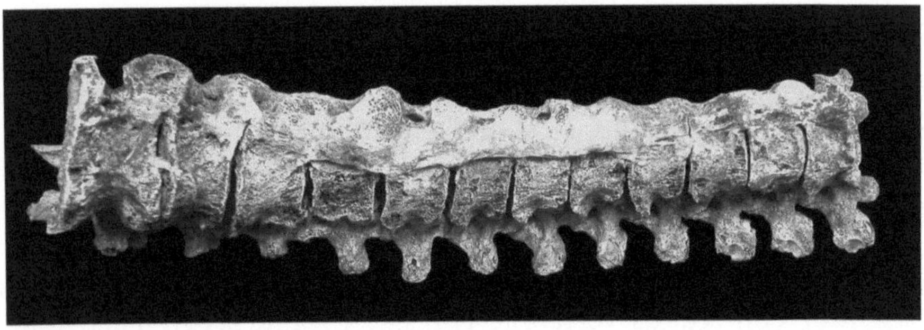

Figure 5.14 Anterior view of the 1st–12th thoracic vertebrae fused through DISH. Archaeological specimen of the CAL.

that of the ligamentum flavum in the spine (Aufderheide and Rodríguez-Martín, 1998, pp. 97–99; Holgate and Steyn, 2016; Ortner, 2003, pp. 558–560; Resnick and Niwayama, 1976; Rogers and Waldron, 2001; Sarzi-Puttini and Atzeni, 2004).

Box 5.6 Bone Features of DISH

Features	Diagnostic strength
Flowing ossification and fusion of the right side of at least four contiguous vertebrae	Diagnostic
Peripheral and spinal entheseal changes	Consistent

On dry bones, the earliest evidence of DISH dates back over 40,000 BP in the Shanidar 1 skeleton and is supported by flowing ossifications on L3 and L5, as well as diffuse ossifications of entheses (Crubézy and Trinkaus, 1992). The standardization of the diagnostic criteria of the condition by Resnick and Niwayama (1976) allowed the diagnosis of numerous cases (Aufderheide and Rodríguez-Martín, 1998, pp. 97–99; Ortner, 2003, pp. 558–560; Weisz et al., 2011) and the reevaluation of previous diagnoses of ankylosing spondylitis. For instance, the radiographic reexamination of 13 royal Ancient Egyptian mummies (CE 1492–1153) permitted the exclusion of the diagnosis of ankylosing spondylitis based on the absence of sacroiliac joint erosions or fusion of the facet joints, including in two pharaohs initially diagnosed with the condition: Ramesses II, and his son Merneptah; and instead, allowed the diagnosis of DISH based on the ossification of the anterior longitudinal ligament along at least four contiguous vertebrae for four pharaohs: Amenhotep III, Ramesses II, his son Merneptah, and Ramesses III (Saleem and Hawass, 2014) (Box 5.6).

Gouty Arthritis

Gout, already recorded in the Hippocratic corpus and named "the disease of kings" because of its association with rich diets, is a form of arthritis caused by a disorder of urate metabolism affecting predominantly males (male-to-female ratio of 3–10:1) over 40–50 years of age. Risk factors for the condition include hypertension, hyperlipidemia, obesity, insulin resistance, renal disease, low-level lead poisoning, uric acid calculi, and endocrine disorders, although about 80% of patients also had a family history of gout (Falasca, 2006; Kim et al., 2003; Monu and Pope, 2004; Nuki and Simkin, 2006). Gout is characterized by hyperuricemia (i.e., an excess of uric acid in blood), which occurs as a result of either an overproduction or an under-excretion of uric acids by the kidneys. Hyperuricemia elicits the deposition of monosodium urate crystals in and around the joints. The presence of these foreign bodies at the articulation induces an immune response, which occurs as a synovitis (i.e., inflammation of the synovial membrane). The synovitis promotes the phagocytosis of the crystals that causes the release of proinflammatory mediators. The interaction between the urate crystals and the inflammatory response ultimately results in nodules, called "tophi," containing the uric crystals. The tophi deposited in sites of articulation finally lead to joint destruction through pressure and erosion (Aufderheide and Rodríguez-Martín, 1998; Fitzgerald et al., 2002; Monu and Pope, 2004; Ortner, 2003; Richette and Bardin, 2010; Waldron, 2008).

The arthropathy is generally monoarticular and asymmetrical and involves the first metatarsophalangeal joint in 85%–90% of cases, referred to as "podagra." Other commonly affected joints include the feet, ankles, knees, shoulders, elbows, wrists, and hands. Lesions in chronic tophaceous gout typically appear as singular juxta-articular osteolytic erosions with a "punched-out" appearance surrounded by a sclerotic rim and manifest the pathognomonic "overhanging edge" or Martel's hook, identifiable on X-rays (Figs. 5.7 and 5.15) (Aufderheide and Rodríguez-Martín, 1998; Monu and Pope, 2004; Richette and Bardin, 2010; Rogers, 2000; Waldron, 2008). However, articular gouty lesions (by opposition to para-articular lesions in tophaceous gout previously described) including joint erosion, subchondral cystic changes, deformities, subluxations, and ankyloses, may appear indistinguishable from those of osteoarthritis (Aufderheide and Rodríguez-Martín, 1998).

The paleopathological examination of the skeletal remains of several members of the Medici demonstrated that the historically documented "gout" they suffered from referred in fact to three separate conditions: rheumatoid arthritis, DISH, and true uric acid gout. The latter was found in one Medici, Ferdinand I (1549–1609) based on suggestive lesions on his left foot (Fornaciari and Giuffra, 2013). While the clinical diagnosis of gout relies on the finding of monosodium urate crystals in the joints of patients, histopathology, polarizing light microscopy, and scanning electron microscopy allowed the detection of urate crystals and the identification of gouty tophi in the

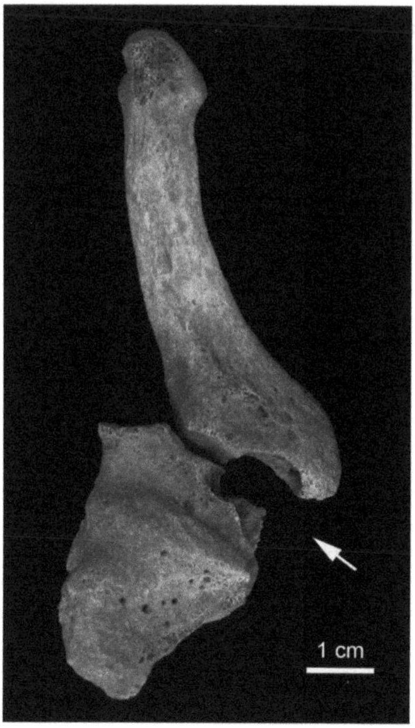

Figure 5.15 Right fifth metatarsal and cuboid exhibiting a loss of substance potentially attributable to an osteolytic lesion due to tophaceous gout (the diagnosis cannot be ascertained but it corresponds to what gouty lesions should look like). Archaeological specimen of the CAL dated CE 8th century.

Box 5.7 Bone Features of Gouty Arthritis

Features	Diagnostic strength
Asymmetric juxtaarticular erosion with Martel's hook	Diagnostic
Joint erosion and subchondral cysts	Consistent
Joint deformities	Consistent

rehydrated mummified remains of the emperor Charles V (Ordi et al., 2006). Limbrey et al. (2011) identified monosodium urate crystals using polarizing light microscopy in the white powder associated to the gouty erosion of two archaeological skeletons from Britain and in the bone particles from an erosion suggestive of gout in a skeleton from the Bocage museum collection in Lisbon (Portugal) (Cardoso, 2006) (Box 5.7).

Neuropathic Arthropathy

Neuropathic arthropathy, also referred to as Charcot's joint, is the arthropathic result of continued weight-bearing and undetected microfractures due to primary disturbances in the sensory and neurovascular innervation, produced in the absence of sensitivity to pain and altered proprioception. The primary causes of neuropathic arthropathy include syringomyelia, *tabes dorsalis*, diabetic neuropathy, neural leprosy, traumatic nerve damage, pernicious anemia, and poliomyelitis. In syringomyelia, a rare pathology that produces a central lesion in the spinal cord, about 25% of patients develop neuropathic arthropathy, mostly in the large upper limb joints and unilaterally. Five to ten percent of patients suffering from *tabes dorsalis*, a manifestation of tertiary neurosyphilis, present Charcot's joints, usually unilaterally in the large lower limb joints (often the knees). Neuropathic arthropathy tends to affect feet more commonly the ankles in both neural leprosy and diabetes mellitus (Canoso, 2000; Gupta, 1993; Levy and Valabhji, 2008; Stanley and Collier, 2008; Vigorita and Ghelman, 2016; Wukich and Sung, 2009).

The neurotraumatic hypothesis, first developed by Virchow in 1886, postulates a mechanical cause to neuropathic arthropathy: peripheral neuropathy permits continued and unnoticed microtrauma because of the loss of proprioception associated with regular load-bearing, making the ligaments excessively relaxed and the unstable joint structures susceptible to microfractures, bone, and cartilage fragmentation with debris formation, demineralization of the affected bones, subluxations, and deformities. The neurovascular hypothesis, introduced under the influence of Charcot's neurotrophic hypothesis, advances that the autonomic neuropathy causes vascular sympathetic dysfunction with a loss of thermoregulation. Reflex vasodilatation then leads to higher blood flow, which activates osteoclastic activity and resorption of the mineral matrix. This osteolysis and demineralization weakens the bone and predisposes it to minor trauma and, as a consequence, to neuropathic arthropathy (Chantelau and Onvlee, 2006; Fitzgerald et al., 2002; Giurato and Uccioli, 2006; Ortner, 2003; Stanley and Collier, 2008; Trepman et al., 2005; Wukich and Sung, 2009). However, these two hypotheses do not explain why lesions in neuropathic arthropathy are unilateral when neuropathy is most

Box 5.8 Bone Features of Neuropathic Arthropathy

Features	Diagnostic strength
Joint destruction and bone fragmentation	Typical
Osteophytes	Consistent
Osteopenia	Consistent

commonly bilateral, or why neuropathic arthropathy is so uncommonly observed today compared to the high frequency of diabetic neuropathy. As a result, an inflammatory hypothesis arose and is now recognized. It presupposes a local inflammatory response and the release of proinflammatory cytokines in the joint as responsible for bone resorption (Molines et al., 2010).

Therefore neuropathic arthropathy typically causes severe joint destruction and bone fragmentation with pathognomonic bone debris around the affected joint. Osteoporosis and/or sclerosis can be observed on X-rays, ankyloses are common, and osteophytes can be present (Aufderheide and Rodríguez-Martín, 1998; Fitzgerald et al., 2002; Ortner, 2003; Stanley and Collier, 2008; Trepman et al., 2005; Vigorita and Ghelman, 2016; Wukich and Sung, 2009).

The dry bone diagnosis of neuropathic arthropathy is relatively straightforward if the lesion is unilateral, monoarticular, and surrounded by bone debris. However, it is important to note that lesions in neuropathic arthropathy may also appear similar to those of osteoarthrosis, post-traumatic osteoarthrosis, bone complications due to an infection, osteonecrosis, gout, or even rheumatoid arthritis (Stanley and Collier, 2008; Trepman et al., 2005); however, the condition is uncommon (Box 5.8).

The collective data regarding the morphology, location, and pattern of involvement of each of the arthropathies is compiled and summarized in Table 5.1. Table 5.2 presents the characteristics that permit the discrimination and differentiation of the arthropathies.

Table 5.1 Macroscopic Bone Lesions for Each Arthropathy.

	Macroscopic Lesions			Location	Pattern
	On joint surface	*On joint contour*			
Osteoarthrosis	• Eburnation • New bone formation • Abrasion • Pitting	• Marginal osteophytes • Widening and flattening		Hips, knees, spine, hands, feet	Rarely monoarticular
	Erosions	*Proliferations*	*Deformities*		
Erosive osteoarthritis	• Central erosions of IP joints	• Osteophytes • Eburnation	• IP ankylosis • "Gull-wing" • "Saw-tooth"	DIP of hands > PIP of hands > CMC1 > MCP > feet	• Pauciarticular or polyarticular • Asymmetrical or symmetrical
Septic arthritis	• Subchondral bone changes	• New bone formation	• Subluxations/dislocation • Joint ankylosis	Typically, hip or knee	One joint or more
Rheumatoid arthritis	• Articular/para-articular erosions	Minimal new bone formation	• Carpal and tarsal ankylosis possible • Ulnar deviation	MCP, PIP, wrists > elbows, hips, knees, shoulders, ankles, atlantoaxial, feet, radiocarpal, radioulnar, and TMJ	• Polyarticular • Symmetrical
	Axial Joints	**Peripheral Joints**		**Other**	
Ankylosing spondylitis	• Symmetrical bilateral sacroiliitis • Syndesmophytes	Either sparing or mono-/oligoarticular in large joints without destruction		• Entheseal changes • Ossifications of connective tissue	
Enteropathic arthritis	• Bilateral asymmetrical/symmetrical sacroiliitis • Spinal fusion	*Type 1* • Asymmetrical • Oligoarticular • Large joints of lower limbs • Non-erosive	*Type 2* • Symmetrical • Polyarticular • Small joints • Erosive	• Entheseal changes	

Psoriatic arthritis	• Symmetrical/asymmetrical sacroiliitis • Paravertebral bridging with skip lesions or ankylosing spondylitis	• Mostly hands, DIP > PIP and MCP joints • Acroosteolysis • "Pencil-in-cup" of MC and MT • "Mouse ear" of IP joints • Ankylosis and bone proliferation • Marginal erosions		• Entheseal changes
Reactive arthritis	• asymmetric sacroiliitis • spine fusion with paravertebral bridging and skip lesions	• Asymmetric • Mono-/oligoarticular • Lower limbs • Erosive and proliferative		• Entheseal changes
	Macroscopic Lesions		**Location**	**Pattern**
	Erosions	***Proliferations***		
Gout	• Juxtaarticular • "Punched-out"	• "Overhanging edges"	Typically MTP1	• Usually monoarticular and asymmetrical • Chronic: may be polyarticular
Neuropathic arthropathy	• Severe joint destruction • Bone debris	• Ankylosis • Osteophytes	Depends on primary disease	Typically monoarticular unilateral

CMC, *Carpometacarpal joint;* DIP, *distal interphalangeal joint;* IP, *interphalangeal joint;* MC, *metacarpal;* MT, *metatarsal;* MTP, *metatarsophalangeal joint;* PIP, *proximal interphalangeal joint;* TMJ, *temporomandibular joint.*

Table 5.2 Discriminating Characteristics of the Arthropathies.

	Osteoarthrosis	Erosive Osteoarthritis	Septic Arthritis	Rheumatoid Arthritis	Ankylosing Spondylitis	Enteropathic Arthritis	Psoriatic Arthritis	Reactive Arthritis	Gout	Neuropathic Arthropathy
Osteoarthrosis	–	Large joints usually affected	Eburnation	Proliferation and eburnation	Bone abrasion and eburnation	Bone abrasion and eburnation	Bone abrasion and eburnation	Upper and lower limbs affected	Proliferation and eburnation	Usually more than one joint
Erosive osteoarthritis	Central erosion, "sawtooth," and "gull-wing" deformities, only in hands	–	"Saw-tooth" and "gull-wing" deformities	DIP affected, central erosion	Only hands	Only hands	Central erosion, "saw-tooth," and "gull-wing" deformities	Only hands	Central erosion, "saw-tooth," and "gull-wing" in hands	Central erosion, "saw-tooth," and "gull-wing" in hands
Septic arthritis	Joint ankylosis	Typically, hip or knee affected	–	Typically, hip or knee affected	Spine and sacroiliac joints are not affected, absence of entheseal changes	Spine and sacroiliac joints are not affected, absence of entheseal changes	Spine and sacroiliac joints are not affected, absence of entheseal changes	Spine and sacroiliac joints are not affected, absence of entheseal changes	Typically, hip or knee affected and terminates in ankylosis	Typically, hip or knee affected and terminates in ankylosis
Rheumatoid arthritis	DIP not affected, only osteolytic	DIP not affected, marginal erosion	Symmetrical polyarticular erosions of hands and wrists	–	Only osteolytic and mostly hands and wrists	DIP not affected	DIP not affected	Symmetrical polyarticular erosions of hands and wrists	Symmetrical polyarticular of hands and wrists	Symmetrical polyarticular of hands and wrists
Ankylosing spondylitis	Entheseal changes, spinal fusion, and sacroiliitis	Entheseal changes, spinal fusion, and sacroiliitis	Entheseal changes, spinal fusion, and sacroiliitis	Entheseal changes, spinal fusion, and sacroiliitis	–	"Bamboo spine"	Symmetrical sacroiliitis	Symmetrical sacroiliitis	Entheseal changes, spinal fusion, and sacroiliitis	Entheseal changes, spinal fusion, and sacroiliitis
Enteropathic arthritis	Entheseal changes, spinal fusion, and sacroiliitis	Entheseal changes, spinal fusion, and sacroiliitis	Entheseal changes, spinal fusion, and sacroiliitis	Entheseal changes, spinal fusion, and sacroiliitis	Can coexist, can be Type 2, can have asymmetric sacroiliitis	–	Can be Type 1	Can have symmetrical sacroiliitis and be Type 2	Entheseal changes, spinal fusion, and sacroiliitis	Entheseal changes, spinal fusion, and sacroiliitis
Psoriatic arthritis	Acroosteolysis, "mouse ears" and "pencil-in-cup", spinal fusion, and sacroiliitis	Bone proliferation, entheseal changes, spinal fusion, and sacroiliitis	Entheseal changes, spinal fusion, and sacroiliitis	Bone proliferation and DIP affected, spinal fusion and sacroiliitis, entheseal changes	Mostly osteolytic	Acroosteolysis, "mouse ear" and "pencil-in-cup" lesions	–	Mostly hands, acroosteolysis, "mouse ear," and "pencil-in-cup" lesions	Mostly hands, entheseal changes, spinal fusion, and sacroiliitis	Mostly hands, entheseal changes, spinal fusion, and sacroiliitis
Reactive arthritis	Entheseal changes, spinal fusion, and sacroiliitis	Entheseal changes, spinal fusion, and sacroiliitis	Entheseal changes, spinal fusion, and sacroiliitis	Entheseal changes, spinal fusion, and sacroiliitis	Asymmetrical sacroiliitis	Paravertebral bridging and can be erosive	Mostly lower limbs	–	Entheseal changes, spinal fusion, and sacroiliitis	Entheseal changes, spinal fusion, and sacroiliitis
Gout	"Punched-out" lesion with "overhanging edge," mostly monoarticular	"Punched-out" lesion with "overhanging edge," mostly monoarticular	"Punched-out" lesion with "overhanging edge"	"Punched-out" lesion with "overhanging edge," mostly monoarticular	Osteolytic lesion	"Punched-out" lesion with "overhanging edge"	"Punched-out" lesion with "overhanging edge," mostly monoarticular	"Punched-out" lesion with "overhanging edge"	–	"Punched-out" lesion with "overhanging edge"
Neuropathic arthropathy	Bone debris	Osteophytes and sclerosis, bone debris	Bone debris	Osteophytes and sclerosis, bone debris	Bone debris	Bone debris	Bone debris	Bone debris	Bone debris	–

The table presents characteristic lesions of the arthropathies listed in the rows allowing their distinction with the arthropathies listed in the columns, for example, in osteoarthrosis, large joints are usually affected, which differentiates it from erosive osteoarthritis. DIP, *distal interphalangeal joint.*

References

Akgul, O., Ozgocmen, S., 2011. Classification criteria for spondyloarthropathies. World J. Orthop. 2, 107–115. Available from: https://doi.org/10.5312/wjo.v2.i12.07.

Alamanos, Y., Drosos, A.A., 2005. Epidemiology of adult rheumatoid arthritis. Autoimmun. Rev. 4, 130–136. Available from: http://doi.org/10.1016/j.autrev.2004.09.002.

Apostolakos, J., Durant, T.J., Dwyer, C.R., Russell, R.P., Weinreb, J.H., Alaee, F., et al., 2014. The enthesis: a review of the tendon-to-bone insertion. Muscles Ligaments Tendons J. 4, 333–342.

Arnett, F.C., 2000. Spondyloarthropathies. In: Humes, H.D., DuPont, H.L., Gardner, L.B., Griffin, J.W., Harris, E.D., Hazzard, W.R., et al.,Kelley's Textbook of Internal Medicine. Lippincott Williams & Wilkins, Philadelphia, PA, pp. 1364–1370.

Arnett, F.C., Edworthy, S.M., Bloch, D.A., McShane, D.J., Fries, J.F., Cooper, N.S., et al., 1988. The American Rheumatism Association 1987 revised criteria for the classification of rheumatoid arthritis. Arthritis Rheum. 31, 315–324. Available from: https://doi.org/10.1002/art.1780310302.

Aufderheide, A.C., Rodríguez-Martín, C., 1998. The Cambridge Encyclopedia of Human Paleopathology. Cambridge University Press, Cambridge, UK.

Banks, S.E., 2010. Erosive osteoarthritis: a current review of a clinical challenge. Clin. Rheumatol. 29, 697–706. Available from: https://doi.org/10.1007/s10067-009-1369-7.

Baraliakos, X., Coates, L.C., Braun, J., 2015. The involvement of the spine in psoriatic arthritis. Clin. Exp. Rheumatol. 33, S31–S35.

Biehler-Gomez, L., Cattaneo, C., 2018. The diagnostic implications of two cases of known rheumatoid arthritis from the CAL Milano Cemetery Skeletal Collection. J. Forensic Sci. 63, 1880–1887. Available from: https://doi.org/10.1111/1556-4029.13799.

Brahee, D.D., Pierre-Jerome, C., Kettner, N.W., 2003. Clinical and radiological manifestations of the rheumatoid wrist. A comprehensive review. J. Manipulative Physiol. Ther. 26, 323–329. Available from: http://doi.org/10.1016/S0161-4754(03)00046-0.

Braun, H.J., Gold, G.E., 2012. Diagnosis of osteoarthritis: imaging. Bone 51, 278–288. Available from: http://doi.org/10.1016/j.bone.2011.11.019.

Braun, J., Sieper, J., 2007. Ankylosing spondylitis. Lancet 369, 1379–1390. Available from: http://doi.org/10.1016/S0140-6736(07)60635-7.

Bruintjes, T., Panhuysen, R., 1992. The paleopathological diagnosis of seronegative spondylarthropathies. In: 9th European Meeting of the Paleopathology Association. Barcelona, Spain, pp. 73–77.

Buikstra, J.E., 2019. Ortner's Identification of Pathological Conditions in Human Skeletal Remains. Academic Press.

Canoso, J.J., 2000. Infiltrative, neoplastic, and endocrinologic causes of musculoskeletal complaints. In: Humes, H.D., DuPont, H.L., Gardner, L.B., Griffin, J.W., Harris, E.D., Hazzard, W. R., et al.,Kelley's Textbook of Internal Medicine. Lippincott Williams & Wilkins, Philadelphia, PA, pp. 1431–1436.

Cardoso, H.F.V., 2006. Brief communication: the collection of identified human skeletons housed at the Bocage Museum (National Museum of Natural History), Lisbon, Portugal. Am. J. Phys. Anthr. 129, 173–176. Available from: https://doi.org/10.1002/ajpa.20228.

Cawley, W.D., Paine, R.R., 2015. Skeletal indicators of reactive arthritis: a case study comparison to other skeletal conditions, such as rheumatoid arthritis, ankylosing spondylitis, ankylosing sero-negative SpA, and DISH. Int. J. Paleopathol. 11, 70–74. Available from: http://doi.org/10.1016/j.ijpp.2015.10.001.

Chantelau, E., Onvlee, G.J., 2006. Charcot foot in diabetes: farewell to the neurotrophic theory. Horm. Metab. Res. 38, 361–367. Available from: https://doi.org/10.1055/s-2006-944525.

Chew, F.S., 2012. Skeletal Radiology: The Bare Bones, third ed. Lippincott Williams & Wilkins, Philadelphia, PA.

Choy, E., 2012. Understanding the dynamics: pathways involved in the pathogenesis of rheumatoid arthritis. Rheumatology 51, v3–v11. Available from: https://doi.org/10.1093/rheumatology/kes113.

Christensen, A.M., Passalacqua, N.V., Bartelink, E.J., 2014. Forensic Anthropology: Current Methods and Practice. Elsevier.

Cojocaru, M., Cojocaru, I.M., Silosi, I., Vrabie, C.D., Tanasescu, R., 2010. Extra-articular manifestations in rheumatoid arthritis. Mædica 5, 286–291.

Crubézy, É., Trinkaus, E., 1992. Shanidar 1: a case of hyperostotic disease (DISH) in the middle paleolithic. Am. J. Phys. Anthropol. 89, 411–420. Available from: https://doi.org/10.1002/ajpa.1330890402.

Dar, G., Masharawi, Y., Peleg, S., Steinberg, N., May, H., Medlej, B., et al., 2010. Schmorl's nodes distribution in the human spine and its possible etiology. Eur. Spine J. 19, 670–675. Available from: https://doi.org/10.1007/s00586-009-1238-8.

Dhir, V., Aggarwal, A., 2013. Psoriatic arthritis: a critical review. Clin. Rev. Allergy Immunol. 44, 141–148. Available from: https://doi.org/10.1007/s12016-012-8302-6.

Dominick, K.L., Baker, T.A., 2004. Racial and ethnic differences in osteoarthritis: prevalence, outcomes, and medical care. Ethn. Dis. 14, 558–566.

Dougados, M., Van Der Linden, S., Juhlin, R., Huitfeldt, B., Amor, B., et al., 1991. The European Spondylarthropathy Study Group Preliminary Criteria for the Classification of Spondylarthropathy. Arthritis Rheum. 34, 1218–1227. Available from: https://doi.org/10.1002/art.1780341003.

Ehrlich, G.E., 2001. Erosive osteoarthritis: presentation, clinical pearls, and therapy. Curr. Rheumatol. Rep. 3, 484–488. Available from: https://doi.org/10.1007/s11926-001-0062-x.

Entezami, P., Fox, D.A., Clapham, P.J., Chung, K.C., 2011. Historical perspective on the etiology of rheumatoid arthritis. Hand Clin. 27, 1–10. Available from: https://doi.org/10.1016/j.hcl.2010.09.006.

Erickson, A.R., Cannella, A.C., Mikuls, T.R., 2017. Clinical features of rheumatoid arthritis. In: Firestein, G.S., Budd, R., Gabriel, S.E., McInnes, I.B., O'Dell, J.R. (Eds.), Kelley and Firestein's Textbook of Rheumatology. Elsevier Health Sciences, Philadelphia, PA, pp. 1167–1186.

Falasca, G.F., 2006. Metabolic diseases: gout. Clin. Dermatol. 24, 498–508. Available from: http://doi.org/10.1016/j.clindermatol.2006.07.015.

Finzel, S., Englbrecht, M., Engelke, K., Stach, C., Schett, G., 2011. A comparative study of periarticular bone lesions in rheumatoid arthritis and psoriatic arthritis. Ann. Rheum. Dis. 70, 122–127. Available from: https://doi.org/10.1136/ard.2010.132423.

Firestein, G.S., 2000. Rheumatoid arthritis. In: Humes, H.D., DuPont, H.L., Gardner, L.B., Griffin, J.W., Harris, E.D., Hazzard, W.R., et al.,Kelley's Textbook of Internal Medicine. Lippincott Williams & Wilkins, Philadelphia, PA, pp. 1347–1359.

Firestein, G.S., 2003. Evolving concepts of rheumatoid arthritis. Nature 423, 356–361.

Fitzgerald, R.H., Kaufer, H., Malkani, A.L., 2002. Orthopaedics. Mosby, St Louis.

Fornaciari, G., Giuffra, V., 2013. The "Gout of the Medici": making the modern diagnosis using paleopathology. Gene 528, 46–50. Available from: https://doi.org/10.1016/j.gene.2013.04.056.

García-Arias, M., Balsa, A., Mola, E.M., 2011. Septic arthritis. Best. Pract. Res. Clin. Rheumatol. 25, 407–421. Available from: https://doi.org/10.1016/j.berh.2011.02.001.

Giurato, L., Uccioli, L., 2006. The diabetic foot: Charcot joint and osteomyelitis. Nucl. Med. Commun. 27, 745–749. Available from: https://doi.org/10.1097/01.mnm.0000230066.23823.cc.

Gupta, R., 1993. A short history of neuropathic arthropathy. Clin. Orthop. Relat. Res. 43–49.

Hannu, T., 2011. Reactive arthritis. Best. Pract. Res. Clin. Rheumatol. 25, 347–357. Available from: http://doi.org/10.1016/j.berh.2011.01.018.

Helliwell, P., Taylor, W., 2005. Classification and diagnostic criteria for psoriatic arthritis. Ann. Rheum. Dis. 64, ii3–ii8. Available from: https://doi.org/10.1136/ard.2004.032318.

Henrique da Mota, L.M., Afonso Cruz, B., Viegas Brenol, C., Alves Pereira, I., Rezende-Fronza, L.S., Barros Bertolo, M., et al., 2013. Guidelines for the diagnosis of rheumatoid arthritis. Rev. Bras. Reumatol. 53, 141–157. Available from: http://doi.org/10.1016/S2255-5021(13)70019-1.

Hochberg, M.C., 2000. Osteoarthritis and polychondritis. In: Humes, H.D., DuPont, H.L., Gardner, L.B., Griffin, J.W., Harris, E.D., Hazzard, W.R., et al.,Kelley's Textbook of Internal Medicine. Lippincott Williams & Wilkins, Philadelphia, PA, pp. 1359–1364.

Holden, W., Orchard, T., Wordsworth, P., 2003. Enteropathic arthritis. Rheum. Dis. Clin. North. Am. 29, 513–530. Available from: http://doi.org/10.1016/S0889-857X(03)00043-7.

Holgate, R.L.V., Steyn, M., 2016. Diffuse idiopathic skeletal hyperostosis: diagnostic, clinical, and paleopathological considerations. Clin. Anat. 29, 870–877. Available from: https://doi.org/10.1002/ca.22716.

Jacobson, J.A., Girish, G., Jiang, Y., Sabb, B.J., 2008. Radiographic evaluation of arthritis: degenerative joint disease and variations. Radiology 248, 737–747. Available from: https://doi.org/10.1148/radiol.2483062112.

Jadon, D.R., McHugh, N.J., 2014. Other seronegative spondyloarthropathies. Med. (Baltim.) 42, 257–261. Available from: http://doi.org/10.1016/j.mpmed.2014.02.008.

Johnson, V.L., Hunter, D.J., 2014. The epidemiology of osteoarthritis. Best. Pract. Res. Clin. Rheumatol. 28, 5–15. Available from: http://doi.org/10.1016/j.berh.2014.01.004.

Jurik, A.G., 2011. Imaging the spine in arthritis—a pictorial review. Insights Imaging 2, 177–191. Available from: https://doi.org/10.1007/s13244-010-0061-4.

Kim, P.S., Klausmeier, T.L., Orr, D.P., 2009. Reactive arthritis: a review. J. Adolesc. Heal. 44, 309–315. Available from: http://doi.org/10.1016/j.jadohealth.2008.12.007.

Kim, H.J., Nemani, V.M., Riew, K.D., Brasington, R., 2015. Cervical spine disease in rheumatoid arthritis: incidence, manifestations, and therapy. Curr. Rheumatol. Rep. 17, 9. Available from: https://doi.org/10.1007/s11926-014-0486-8.

Kim, K.Y., Ralph Schumacher, H., Hunsche, E., Wertheimer, A.I., Kong, S.X., 2003. A literature review of the epidemiology and treatment of acute gout. Clin. Ther. 25, 1593–1617. Available from: http://doi.org/10.1016/S0149-2918(03)80158-3.

Kyere, K.A., Than, K.D., Wang, A.C., Rahman, S.U., Valdivia-Valdivia, J.M., Marca, F., et al., 2012. Schmorl's nodes. Eur. Spine J. 21, 2115–2121. Available from: https://doi.org/10.1007/s00586-012-2325-9.

Lahu, A., Backa, T., Ismaili, J., Lahu, V., Saiti, V., 2015. Modes of presentation of reactive arthritis based on the affected joints. Med. Arch. 69, 42–45. Available from: https://doi.org/10.5455/medarh.2015.69.42-45.

Laiho, K., Kauppi, M., 2002. The cervical spine in patients with psoriatic arthritis. Ann. Rheum. Dis. 61, 650–652.

Leden, I., Forslind, K., Svensson, B., 2012. Ankylosis of wrist and small joints of the hand occurs in rheumatoid arthritis: diagnostic implication in paleopathology. Int. J. Paleopathol. 2, 249–251. Available from: https://doi.org/10.1016/j.ijpp.2012.09.001.

Lee, D.M., Weinblatt, M.E., 2001. Rheumatoid arthritis. Lancet 358, 903–911. Available from: https://doi.org/10.1016/s0140-6736(01)06075-5.

Levy, M.J., Valabhji, J., 2008. The diabetic foot. Surg 26, 25–28. Available from: http://doi.org/10.1016/j.mpsur.2007.10.013.

Limbrey, S., Brickley, M., Marques, C., Swinson, D., 2011. Identification of urate crystals in gouty individuals. J. Archaeol. Sci. 38, 2497–2501. Available from: https://doi.org/10.1016/j.jas.2010.06.015.

Majithia, V., Geraci, S.A., 2007. Rheumatoid arthritis: diagnosis and management. Am. J. Med. 120, 936–939. Available from: http://doi.org/10.1016/j.amjmed.2007.04.005.

Marshall, M., Nicholls, E., Kwok, W.-Y., Peat, G., Kloppenburg, M., van der Windt, D., et al., 2013. Erosive osteoarthritis: a more severe form of radiographic hand osteoarthritis rather than a distinct entity? Ann. Rheum. Dis. 74, 136–141.

Martin-Dupont, S., Cunha, E., Rougé, D., Crubézy, É., 2006. Spondylarthropathy striking prevalence in a 19th–20th century Portuguese collection. Joint Bone Spine 73, 303–310. Available from: https://doi.org/10.1016/j.jbspin.2005.05.005.

Mas, A.J., Rotés-Querol, J., 2007. Erosive osteoarthritis of the feet: description of two patients. Joint Bone Spine 74, 296–298. Available from: http://doi.org/10.1016/j.jbspin.2006.08.006.

Mays, S., Watt, I., Loe, L., 2016. An unusual erosive arthropathy from medieval England. Int. J. Osteoarchaeol. 27, 693–699. Available from: https://doi.org/10.1002/oa.2574.

McInnes, I.B., Schett, G., 2011. The pathogenesis of rheumatoid arthritis. N. Engl. J. Med. 365, 2205–2219. Available from: https://doi.org/10.1056/NEJMra1004965.

Molines, L., Darmon, P., Raccah, D., 2010. Charcot's foot: newest findings on its pathophysiology, diagnosis and treatment. Diabetes Metab. 36, 251–255. Available from: http://doi.org/10.1016/j.diabet.2010.04.002.

Moll, J.M.H., Wright, V., 1973. Psoriatic arthritis. Semin. Arthritis Rheum. 3, 55–78. Available from: http://doi.org/10.1016/0049-0172(73)90035-8.

Monu, J.U.V., Pope Jr, T.L., 2004. Gout: a clinical and radiologic review. Radiol. Clin. North. Am. 42, 169–184. Available from: http://doi.org/10.1016/S0033-8389(03)00158-1.

Myers, W.A., Gottlieb, A.B., Mease, P., 2006. Psoriasis and psoriatic arthritis: clinical features and disease mechanisms. Clin. Dermatol. 24, 438–447. Available from: http://doi.org/10.1016/j.clindermatol.2006.07.006.

Nuki, G., Simkin, P.A., 2006. A concise history of gout and hyperuricemia and their treatment. Arthritis Res. Ther. 8 (Suppl 1), S1. Available from: https://doi.org/10.1186/ar1906.

Olivieri, I., van Tubergen, A., Salvarani, C., van der Linden, S., 2002. Seronegative spondyloarthritides. Best. Pract. Res. Clin. Rheumatol. 16, 723–739. Available from: http://doi.org/10.1053/berh.2002.0263.

Ordi, J., Alonso, P.L., de Zulueta, J., Esteban, J., Velasco, M., Mas, E., et al., 2006. The Severe Gout of Holy Roman Emperor Charles V. N. Engl. J. Med. 355, 516–520. Available from: https://doi.org/10.1056/NEJMon060780.

Ortner, D.J., 2003. Identification of Pathological Conditions in Human Skeletal Remains, third ed. Smithsonian Institution Press, New York.

Punzi, L., Ramonda, R., Sfriso, P., 2004. Erosive osteoarthritis. Best. Pract. Res. Clin. Rheumatol. 18, 739–758. Available from: http://doi.org/10.1016/j.berh.2004.05.010.

Raychaudhuri, S.P., Deodhar, A., 2014. The classification and diagnostic criteria of ankylosing spondylitis. J. Autoimmun. 48–49, 128–133. Available from: http://doi.org/10.1016/j.jaut.2014.01.015.

Resende, G.G., Lanna, C.C.D., Bortoluzzo, A.B., Gonçalves, C.R., Sampaio-Barros, P.D., Silva, J.A.B., et al., 2013. Enteropathic arthritis in Brazil: data from the Brazilian registry of spondyloarthritis. Rev. Bras. Reumatol. 53, 452–459. Available from: http://doi.org/10.1016/j.rbre.2013.04.001.

Resnick, D., Niwayama, G., 1976. Radiographic and pathologic features of spinal involvement in diffuse idiopathic skeletal hyperostosis (DISH). Radiology 119, 559–568. Available from: https://doi.org/10.1148/119.3.559.

Richette, P., Bardin, T., 2010. Gout. Lancet 375, 318–328. Available from: http://doi.org/10.1016/S0140-6736(09)60883-7.

Rindfleisch, J.A., Muller, D., 2005. Diagnosis and management of rheumatoid arthritis. Am. Fam. Physician 72, 1037–1047.

Roberts, C.A., Manchester, K., 2007. The Archaeology of Disease, third ed Cornell University Press, Ithaca, NY.

Rogers, J., 2000. The palaeopathology of joint disease. In: Cox, M., Mays, S. (Eds.), Human Osteology in Archaeology and Forensic Science. Cambridge University Press, pp. 163–182.

Rogers, J., Waldron, T., 1995. A field guide to joint disease in archaeology. Wiley, Chichester.

Rogers, J., Waldron, T., 2001. DISH and the monastic way of life. Int. J. Osteoarchaeol. 11, 357–365. Available from: https://doi.org/10.1002/oa.574.

Rogers, J., Waldron, T., Dieppe, P., Watt, I., 1987. Arthropathies in palaeopathology: the basis of classification according to most probable cause. J. Archaeol. Sci. 14, 179–193. Available from: https://doi.org/10.1016/0305-4403(87)90005-7.

Rogers, J., Waldron, T., Watt, I., 1991. Erosive osteoarthritis in a medieval skeleton. Int. J. Osteoarchaeol. 1, 151–153. Available from: https://doi.org/10.1002/oa.1390010212.

Rogers, J., Watt, I., Dieppe, P., 1981. Medical history: arthritis in saxon and mediaeval skeletons. Br. Med. J. 283, 1668–1670 (Clin. Res. Ed.). Available from: https://doi.org/10.1136/bmj.283.6307.1668.

Rothschild, B.M., Woods, R.J., 1991. Spondyloarthropathy: erosive arthritis in representative defleshed bones. Am. J. Phys. Anthropol. 85, 125–134. Available from: https://doi.org/10.1002/ajpa.1330850202.

Saleem, S.N., Hawass, Z., 2014. Brief report: ankylosing spondylitis or diffuse idiopathic skeletal hyperostosis in Royal Egyptian Mummies of the 18th–20th Dynasties? Computed tomography and archaeology studies. Arthritis Rheumatol. 66, 3311–3316. Available from: https://doi.org/10.1002/art.38864.

Sarzi-Puttini, P., Atzeni, F., 2004. New developments in our understanding of DISH (diffuse idiopathic skeletal hyperostosis). Curr. Opin. Rheumatol. 16 (3), 287–292.

Selmi, C., Gershwin, M.E., 2014. Diagnosis and classification of reactive arthritis. Autoimmun. Rev. 13, 546–549. Available from: http://doi.org/10.1016/j.autrev.2014.01.005.

Sieper, J., Braun, J., Rudwaleit, M., Boonen, A., Zink, A., 2002. Ankylosing spondylitis: an overview. Ann. Rheum. Dis. 61, iii8.

Silman, A.J., Pearson, J.E., 2002. Epidemiology and genetics of rheumatoid arthritis. Arthritis Res. Ther. 4, S265. Available from: https://doi.org/10.1186/ar578.

Šlaus, M., Novak, M., Čavka, M., 2012. Four cases of ankylosing spondylitis in medieval skeletal series from Croatia. Rheumatol. Int. 32, 3985–3992. Available from: https://doi.org/10.1007/s00296-011-2343-7.

Smolen, J.S., Aletaha, D., McInnes, I.B., 2016. Rheumatoid arthritis. Lancet 388, 2023–2038. Available from: http://doi.org/10.1016/S0140-6736(16)30173-8.

Sommer, O.J., Kladosek, A., Weiler, V., Czembirek, H., Boeck, M., Stiskal, M., 2005. Rheumatoid arthritis: a practical guide to state-of-the-art imaging, image interpretation, and clinical implications. RadioGraphics 25, 381–398. Available from: https://doi.org/10.1148/rg.252045111.

Stanley, J.C., Collier, A.M., 2008. Charcot osteo-arthropathy. Curr. Orthop. 22, 428–433. Available from: http://doi.org/10.1016/j.cuor.2008.08.004.

Trepman, E., Nihal, A., Pinzur, M.S., 2005. Current topics review: Charcot neuroarthropathy of the foot and ankle. Foot Ankle Int. 26, 46–63.

Veale, D.J., Fearon, U., 2015. What makes psoriatic and rheumatoid arthritis so different? RMD Open 1, e000025. Available from: https://doi.org/10.1136/rmdopen-2014-000025.

Vigorita, V.J., Ghelman, B., 2016. Arthritis. In: Vigorita, V.J., Ghelman, B. (Eds.), Orthopaedic Pathology. Lippincott Williams & Wilkins, Philadelphia, pp. 710–768.

Voulgari, P.V., 2011. Rheumatological manifestations in inflammatory bowel disease. Ann. Gastroenterol. 24, 173–180.

Waldron, T., 2008. Palaeopathology. Cambridge University Press, Cambridge, UK.

Watts, R.A., Conaghan, P.G., Denton, C., Foster, H., Isaacs, J., Muller-Ladner, U., 2013. Oxford Textbook of Rheumatology, fourth ed Oxford University Press, New York.

Weisz, G.M., Matucci-Cerinic, M., Lippi, D., Albury, W.R., 2011. The ossification diathesis in the Medici family: DISH and other features. Rheumatol. Int. 31, 1649–1652. Available from: https://doi.org/10.1007/s00296-010-1563-6.

Wendling, D., Prati, C., Toussirot, É., Ornetti, P., 2010. Spondylarthrite, spondylarthropathies: critères de diagnostic et de classification. Rev. du. Rhum. Monogr. 77, 43–47. Available from: https://doi.org/10.1016/j.monrhu.2009.12.002.

Wukich, D.K., Sung, W., 2009. Charcot arthropathy of the foot and ankle: modern concepts and management review. J. Diabetes Complications 23, 409–426. Available from: http://doi.org/10.1016/j.jdiacomp.2008.09.004.

Zampetti, S., Mariotti, V., Radi, N., Belcastro, M.G., 2016. Variation of skeletal degenerative joint disease features in an identified Italian modern skeletal collection. Am. J. Phys. Anthropol. 160, 683–693. Available from: https://doi.org/10.1002/ajpa.22998.

Zochling, J., Smith, E.U.R., 2010. Seronegative spondyloarthritis. Best. Pract. Res. Clin. Rheumatol. 24, 747–756. Available from: http://doi.org/10.1016/j.berh.2011.02.002.

CHAPTER 6

Neoplastic Diseases

Lucie Biehler-Gomez[1], Francesco Sardanelli[2,3] and Cristina Cattaneo[1]
[1]LABANOF, Department of Biomedical Sciences for Health, University of Milan, Milan, Italy,
[2]Department of Biomedical Sciences for Health, University of Milan, Milan, Italy,
[3]Unit of Radiology, IRCCS Policlinico San Donato, Milan, Italy

Today, cancer is the second leading cause of death worldwide, with an expected rise of new cases of about 70% over the next twenty years (World Health Organization, 2017). It has been estimated that approximately 40% of men and women in the United States will be diagnosed with cancer at some point during their lifetime (National Cancer Institute, 2017). The high incidence and mortality of the disease has made it a subject of paramount interest for research over the past century, from early diagnosis to the search of effective treatments and cure (DeVita and Chu, 2008).

The pathology is so prevalent that its interest is not limited to the living but extends to the dead. Diagnoses of the disease have been performed in archaeological contexts (Roberts and Manchester, 2007; Strouhal and Němečková, 2009) and contributed to the understanding of the history and antiquity of the disease. In a similar way, a diagnosis of metastatic cancer in a forensic skeletonized case can provide valuable information on the individual, including in the construction of a biological profile or for comparison with antemortem data, especially if the individual is unidentified.

Tumors, Neoplasms, and Cancers

Although the terms "tumor," "neoplasm," and "cancer" are often used interchangeably in common parlance, they are not, in fact, synonymous. So, let us break it down.

A tumor is defined as a swelling (from the latin *tumor*—one of the four cardinal signs of inflammation) and thus refers to a mass of undefined etiology. Neoplasm, formed of "*neo*" meaning "new" and

Interpreting Bone Lesions and Pathology for Forensic Practice. DOI: https://doi.org/10.1016/B978-0-323-85162-6.00006-4

"*plasm*" which means "cell" or "tissue substance", is defined as an abnormal new growth of cells. Hence, tumor is a non-specific term for neoplasm. Neoplasms may be of two types: they can be benign or malignant (even though intermediate cases do exist). Benign neoplasms are non-cancerous, they tend to be localized and do not invade surrounding tissues or spread to distant parts of the body. However, they may grow too large and become harmful, for instance by compressing and obstructing organs and tissues and thus need to be removed. By opposition, malignant neoplasms are cancerous growths, they tend to spread throughout the body in a process called "metastasis," they are often resistant to treatment and can recur after their removal.

So, to sum it up, "benign cancers" do not exist, because a tumor and more specifically a neoplasm cannot be at the same time benign and malignant, in other words, non-cancerous and cancerous. However, "tumor" is still more largely used than "neoplasm" in clinical medicine, in spite of purists' protests, which is why we will use it as well.

Benign Tumors

Benign tumors tend to be more often solitary, slow growing, and of limited size. These characteristics allow their histomorphological distinction from malignant tumors (De Boer et al., 2013; Strouhal et al., 1996). However, demographic details (such as the sex and age of the individual), size and distribution of the lesions as well as their radiological aspect (including shape, density at X-ray-based imaging, contour, functional parameters at contrast-enhanced imaging, etc.) are necessary for a specific diagnosis of the type of tumor.

The osteoma, and in particular, the "button osteoma," is the most common tumor found in skeletons. It consists of a smooth rounded mass of compact bone sharply demarcated, typically on the outer surface of the cranium, and no larger than 20 mm in diameter (Fig. 6.1). Conversely, the "osteoid" osteoma occurs most often on a long bone of the legs in older children and young adults. The osteoblastoma is a rare tumor showing a slight radiolucency affecting the spine in adolescents and young adults. Chondromas are tumors of hyaline cartilage generally appearing in the bone (i.e., endochondroma); they predilect hands and feet and are found in all ages after 10 years. The osteochondroma is an osteocartilaginous exostosis appearing as a spongy mass

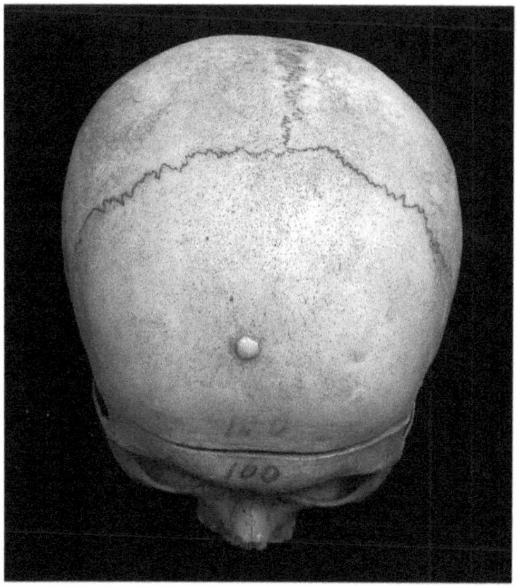

Figure 6.1 Button osteoma on the frontal bone. Specimen of the CAL from the craniological collection of Mombello di Limbiate dated end of CE 19th century.

near the growth plate on the metaphyseal surface of long bones; they tend to be solitary and to affect people younger than 21 years. Chondroblastomas are rare tumors with rounded, radiolucent, and well-defined lesions occurring in the epiphyseal area of the long bones of immature individuals. Non-ossifying fibromas exhibit expanding lesions with a lobulated "soap bubble" appearance in the metaphyses of long bones (particularly the lower leg) of subadults. Giant cell tumors are locally destructive tumors favoring the knees of young adults. Osteolytic lesions in the epiphysis may extend to involve the metaphysis and the subchondral bone; however, giant cell tumors also retain some benign characteristics including a reluctance to perforate the bone cortex. Hemangiomas are solitary and small tumors of proliferating blood vessels. They may affect the vertebrae, reducing the trabeculae, and increasing their diameter without altering the contour of the vertebral body, giving the aspect of a depleted trabecular structure with vertical striation on radiographs; or the cranium, where a "sunburst" appearance similar to osteosarcoma but with circular margins may be observed (Aufderheide and Rodríguez-Martín, 1998, pp. 371–392; Brothwell, 2012, 2008; Campanacci, 1999; Chhem and Brothwell, 2008; Greenspan, 1993; Ortner, 2003, pp. 504–523).

Antiquity of Cancer

Cancer seems to be limited to vertebrates, as no clear evidence has demonstrated its presence in invertebrates. The oldest indication of metastatic cancer potentially dates back to the Upper Devonian (about 350 million years BP) and was suggested from a dip pit on the internal surface of the lower jawbone of a *Dinichthys*, an armored fish (Capasso, 2005). The earliest evidence of the disease in humans comes from osteolytic lesions on an Egyptian skull of 3000 BCE that was diagnosed with nasopharyngeal carcinoma (Wells, 1963) but this diagnosis, being based on the sole evidence of a cranium, is disputed (Binder et al., 2014). Considering a full skeleton, the earliest diagnosis of cancer was assessed in a male of 25 – 35 years from ancient Nubia, c.1200 BCE (Binder et al., 2014). Paleopathological evidence indicates a low frequency of the condition in antiquity, even among the thousands of mummies analyzed to date (Capasso, 2005; David and Zimmerman, 2010); however, a comparative study between 905 skeletal remains from ancient Egypt (3200 – 3500 BCE) and 2457 skeletons from south Germany (CE 1400–1800) concludes that malignant tumors were not significantly fewer than expected given the changes in life expectancy (Nerlich et al., 2006). Moreover, the Papyrus of Ebers (c.1538 BCE) and the Papyrus of Kahun (c.1825 BCE) include possible descriptions of uterus and breast carcinomas (David and Zimmerman, 2010). In ancient Greece, Hippocrates (5th century BCE) used the word "carcinoma" as his diagnosis of a chest wall tumor and bleeding nipple of a woman from Abdera (Retief and Cilliers, 2011). He also described hard tumors in breast (Retief and Cilliers, 2011) and theorized that the cause of cancer was due to an excess of black bile; a theory that lasted until the Renaissance when Andrea Vesalius could not attest of the existence of black bile during anatomic dissections (Weinstein and Case, 2008).

So why is the evidence of metastatic cancer so scarce in skeletal remains of antiquity? Several factors may explain this observation. First, the shorter life span of ancient populations (about 40–50 years for the wealthy and 25–30 years for the non-elite population (David and Zimmerman, 2010; Preston, 1995)) would reduce the risks of cell mutation, carcinogen exposure, and development of bone metastases known to be associated with increasing age. However, there is growing evidence that age in ancient skeletal remains may be underestimated, in particular for older individuals (Binder et al., 2014). Second, the predominance of infectious conditions in antiquity (Marques et al., 2013) limited the increase of the life span and the potential development of cancer. Third, the decreased quality of modern lifestyle compared to ancient populations may play a role in the higher cancer incidence observed today. Indeed, modern lifestyle is associated with smoking, lack of physical activity, unhealthy dietary habits, artificial environment as well as occupational and environmental carcinogens. Nonetheless, smoke exposure from open wood fires, actively used in the past, have carcinogenic properties similar to tobacco, especially when used indoors (Binder et al., 2014; Delgado et al., 2005). Fourth, the preservation of the integrity of the bone affected by metastases is essential for the diagnosis of the disease and highly dependent upon taphonomic conditions, which after centuries in the ground may have altered and destroyed the precious evidence of the condition. Nevertheless, the mummification process allows the preservation of tumorous lesions but the search of metastatic lesions in these collections has been largely unrewarded (David and Zimmerman, 2010). Finally, as metastatic lesions develop in vascularized areas, it is the trabecular bone that is first and most commonly involved. Consequently, a macroscopic observation of the bone may not be enough for the identification of potential metastatic lesions and X-ray-based imaging proved to be an essential tool for the detection of cancer, even if not systematically used in the anthropological analysis (Binder et al., 2014; Rothschild and Rothschild, 1995).

Leukemia

Leukemia is a malignant condition of hematopoietic stem cells characterized by an excess of immature or abnormal leukocytes in the bone marrow, preventing the production of normal blood cells and leading to cytopenia. The type of leukemia may be classified as "myeloid" or "lymphoid" according to the lineage of precursor stem cell affected, as well as "acute" or "chronic" depending on the percentage of leukemia cells in the bone marrow or blood, resulting in four major categories of leukemia: acute myeloid leukemia, acute lymphoblastic leukemia, chronic myeloid leukemia, and chronic lymphocytic leukemia (Emadi and Law, 2018). Infiltration of the malignant cells in the bone marrow leads to a reduction of red blood cells (leading to anemia), platelets (thrombocytopenia), and white blood cells (granulocytopenia). Clinical symptoms result from this impaired hematopoiesis: anemia induces fatigue, weakness, pallor, malaise, dyspnea, anorexia, and tachycardia;

thrombocytopenia causes mucosal bleeding, easy bruising, petechiae and hemorrhages; and granulocytopenia leads to a severe vulnerability to bacterial, fungal or viral infection and fever. In addition, other organ infiltration can result in enlargement of the spleen (splenomegaly) or liver (hepatomegaly), skin lesions (leukemia cutis), lymphadenopathy, bone and joint pain, as well as headache, stroke, visual and auditory involvement in meningeal infiltration (Emadi and Law, 2018; Lowenberg et al., 1999; Sawyers, 1999).

Although acute and chronic forms of leukemia may involve the skeletal system, Ortner (2003, p. 376) warns that the changes are non-specific, that is, loss of bone mass (from osteopenia to osteoporosis) as well as scattered, focal and small osteolytic lesions (Aufderheide and Rodríguez-Martín, 1998, p. 355; Ortner, 2003, p. 376). Indeed, the most common osseous involvement (in up to 70% of cases) consists in radiolucent metaphyseal bands or "leukemic lines" ranging from 2 to 15 mm in length, found in particular in the distal femur and proximal tibia (Chell et al., 2001; Mostoufi-Moab and Halton, 2014; Riccio et al., 2013). Other skeletal lesions reported in the clinical literature include osteopenia and osteoporosis (13%–40% of cases), osteolytic lesions (19%–38% of cases), pathologic fractures (2%–10% of cases), periosteal reactions (2%–19% of cases) as well as osteosclerosis and osteonecrosis. Therapeutic treatments, in particular corticosteroids, are responsible for the development or worsening of osteopenia/osteoporosis, pathologic fractures and osteonecrosis, which are debilitating complications (Chell et al., 2001; Mostoufi-Moab and Halton, 2014; Riccio et al., 2013). Roberts and Manchester (2007, p. 320) mention that no individuals from antiquity have yet been diagnosed with this condition. Recently, two potential cases of leukemia from Ancient Egypt (c.2160–2000 BCE) (Isidro et al., 2019) and Peru (CE c.1533–1620) (Klaus, 2016) were published in the literature. The large spectrum of differential diagnosis in both cases demonstrates the difficulty of the diagnosis of this condition in skeletal remains.

Rothschild et al. (1997) examined in particular two skeletons from the Hamann-Todd collection who died of leukemia: a 3-year-old skeleton with acute lymphoblastic leukemia and a 60-year-old skeleton with acute myeloid leukemia. They describe superficial solitary and coalescing pits with smooth, minimally remodeled edges, minimal periosteal reaction, and sparing the joints. This study helped some of the authors to differentiate between leukemia and other conditions creating lytic lesions on the skeleton (Rothschild et al., 2002, 1998). Nonetheless, this research was focused on only two skeletons; thus, additional cases of diagnosed leukemia would strengthen the criteria for leukemia diagnosis on dry bones. In a recent study, Pérez-Martínez et al. (2016) detected proteomic markers of leukemia in one of two cemeterial skeletons with medical records of the malignancy, demonstrating the potential of lipidic biomarkers for the diagnosis of disease on dry bone.

Multiple Myeloma

Multiple myeloma is a plasma cell malignancy characterized by monoclonal protein secretion, excessive osteoclastic activity and inhibition of osteoblastic bone formation. This set of characteristics leads to progressive and destructive osteolytic bone disease manifesting as osteolytic lesions and severe osteopenia/osteoporosis (Edwards et al., 2008; Kumar et al., 2017; Vincent Rajkumar, 2009). Clinical manifestations and complications include severe bone pain, pathologic fractures, osteoporosis, hypercalcemia, renal insufficiency (the so-called "myeloma kidney"), anemia and, more infrequently, spinal cord compression, and peripheral neuropathy (Bladé and Rosiñol, 2007; Edwards et al., 2008). In addition, multiple myeloma can induce general immunodeficiency making infections a major cause of morbidity and mortality in the affected individuals (Bladé and Rosiñol, 2007).

Bone lesions in multiple myeloma are purely osteolytic. They appear as small and relatively uniform in size, with a spheroid or "bubble-like" shape, sharp and well-circumscribed margins (or "punched-out"), and the absence of new bone reaction (Figs. 6.2 and 6.3) (Aufderheide and Rodríguez-Martín, 1998, pp. 351–354; Brothwell, 2012; Ortner, 2003, pp. 376–382; Riccomi et al., 2019; Rothschild et al., 1998; Strouhal, 1991).

Rothschild et al. (1998) examined a skeleton from the Hamann-Todd collection and the pelvis, ribs, and vertebrae of a second individual from the Mutter Museum in Philadelphia, both with an antemortem diagnosis of multiple myeloma, and evidenced the different aspect of multiple myeloma lesions by opposition to those of metastatic carcinoma and leukemia. Similarly, Biehler-Gomez et al., (2019a) reported the morphological aspect and pattern of distribution of multiple myeloma lesions in two clinically diagnosed cases from the CAL Milano Cemetery Skeletal Collection, showing that multiple myeloma lesions are numerous, scattered, sometimes coalescing and located primarily in highly vascularized areas of the axial and appendicular skeleton not distal to the knees and elbows (Figs. 6.4 and 6.5). However, multiple myeloma remains the main

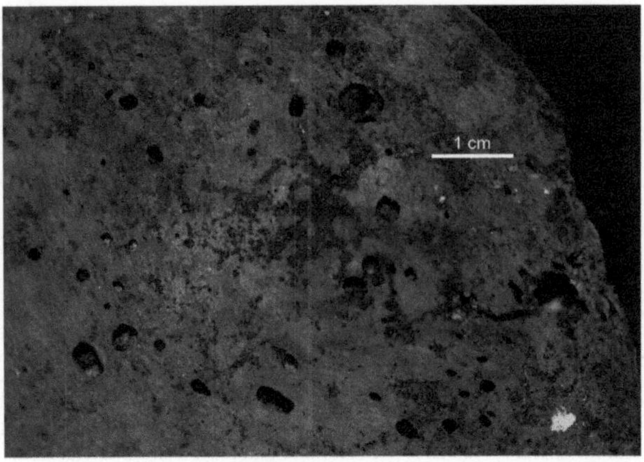

Figure 6.2 Anterior view of the iliac fossa showing the characteristic features of bone lesions in multiple myeloma: small, uniform lesions with a spheroid shape, well-circumscribed margins and the absence of new bone formation. Skeleton #156 of the CAL Milano Cemetery Skeletal Collection with a clinical diagnosis of multiple myeloma.

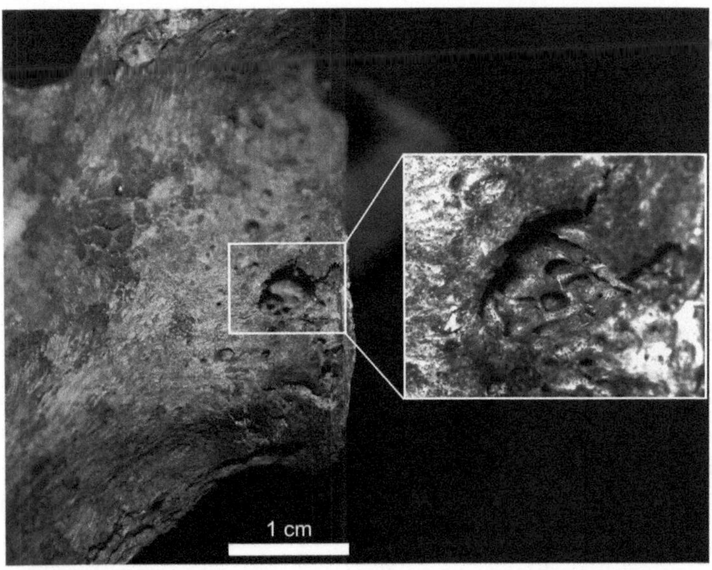

Figure 6.3 Close-up of a bone lesion in multiple myeloma showing a small osteolytic lesion on the area adjacent to the glenoid fossa (left scapula), note the spheroid lesion with well-defined margins and absence of new bone production (zoomed area) visible through the circular opening of the bone cortex. Skeleton #156 of the CAL Milano Cemetery Skeletal Collection with a clinical diagnosis of multiple myeloma. Reproduced with permission from Biehler-Gomez, L., Giordano, G., Cattaneo, C., 2019. Multiple myeloma bone lesions in skeletal remains: Report of two known cases from the 20th century CAL Milano Cemetery Skeletal Collection. Int. J. Osteoarchaeol. 101–107. https://doi.org/10.1002/oa.2721.

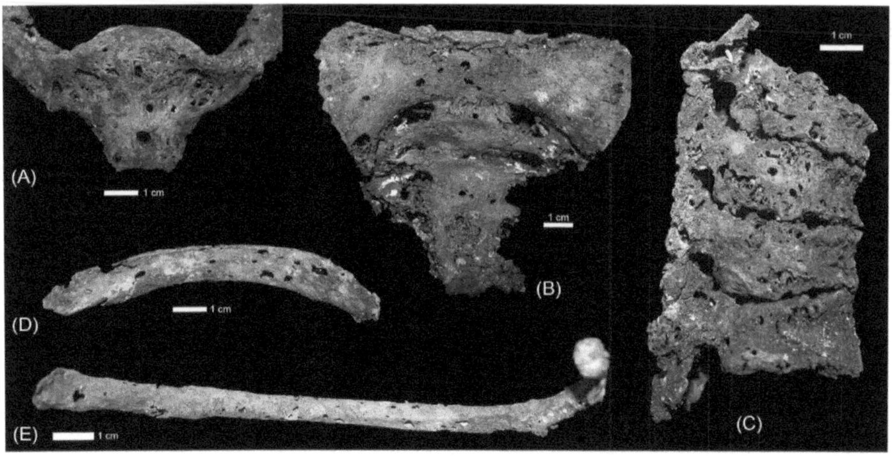

Figure 6.4 Distribution and morphology of bone lesions in multiple myeloma. (A) Anterior view of the manubrium, the cartilage of both first ribs is ossified; (B) anterior view of the sacrum; (C) right lateral view of four fused thoracic vertebrae; (D) internal view of a rib fragment; (E) internal view of a complete rib. Skeleton #156 of the CAL Milano Cemetery Skeletal Collection with a clinical diagnosis of multiple myeloma. Reproduced with permission from Biehler-Gomez, L., Giordano, G., Cattaneo, C., 2019. Multiple myeloma bone lesions in skeletal remains: Report of two known cases from the 20th century CAL Milano Cemetery Skeletal Collection. Int. J. Osteoarchaeol. 101–107. https://doi.org/10.1002/oa.2721.

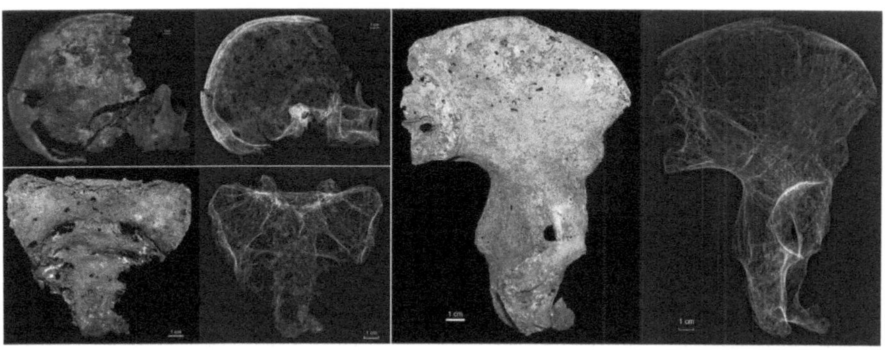

*Figure 6.5 Macroscopic and radiographic images of the cranium (*norma lateralis, *top left), sacrum (anterior view, bottom left), and right innominate bone (anterior view, right) showing scattered multiple myeloma bone lesions and diffuse osteopenia. Skeleton #156 of the CAL Milano Cemetery Skeletal Collection with a clinical diagnosis of multiple myeloma.* Reproduced with permission from Biehler-Gomez, L., Tritella, S., Martino, F., Campobasso, C.P., Franchi, A., Spairani, R., et al., 2019. The synergy between radiographic and macroscopic observation of skeletal lesions on dry bone. Int. J. Leg. Med. https://doi.org/10.1007/s00414-019-02122-0.

differential diagnosis of metastatic bone disease and both conditions may be indistinguishable on dry bones (Ortner, 2003, p. 535).

Riccomi et al. (2019) provided a thorough literature review concerning paleopathological evidence of multiple myeloma and reported a total of 72 cases, but only 25 ascertained cases after screening. In their review, they rejected the individual from the Mutter Museum (Rothschild et al., 1998) due to the lack of images documenting the case and both individuals of the CAL Milano Cemetery Skeletal Collection (Biehler-Gomez et al., 2019a) because they died after 1950 (a common practice in paleopathology, due to the possibility of having received treatment, as discussed in Chapter 1). Consequently, only four cases with antemortem diagnoses of multiple myeloma have been published in the literature, including one undocumented case (Rothschild et al., 1998). Additional reports of documented cases of multiple myeloma would help diagnose the disease on dry bones and differentiate it from metastatic bone disease. In addition to macroscopic examination, immunological analyses of bones can permit the diagnosis of multiple myeloma in dry bone, as demonstrated by Cattaneo et al. (1994).

Metastatic Bone Disease

Carcinomas are solid tumors. They result from unregulated proliferation of cells and their malignant transformation into cancerous cells in epithelial tissues. After the malignant cells invade the adjoining local tissue, they can spread to distant sites or "metastasize" (Kirkpatrick et al., 2018; Vassiliou et al., 2013). Symptoms vary depending on the primary organ of origin, but general clinical manifestations of cancer may include pain, fatigue, weight loss, bleeding, swollen lymph nodes, headaches, dizziness, nausea, and dyspnea. Metastatic cancers are far more prevalent than primary bone malignancies. Any cancer has the potential to metastasize to bone. Indeed, although sarcomas may metastasize, it is a rare occurrence in bone. Typically, bone metastasis happens late in the tumor progression. Metastatic bone disease is associated with skeletal-related events, a higher morbidity and mortality (Bussard et al., 2008; Joyce, 2012; Lipton and Vigorita, 2016; O'Sullivan et al., 2015; Roodman, 2004; Talmadge and Fidler, 2010; Vassiliou et al., 2013).

For breast and prostate cancers, bone is the third most common metastatic site in the body, after the lungs and liver (Coleman, 2001; Lipton and Vigorita, 2016; Mundy, 1997; Vassiliou et al., 2013). Multiple myeloma (75–95%), prostate and breast cancers (65%–80%) have the highest frequency of bone lesions, followed by thyroid (60%), lung (30%–40%), and kidney (20%–25%) cancers. Malignant neoplasms of the bladder, rectum, pancreas, uterus, ovary, and colon can also involve bones with a frequency varying from 9% to 30%, while other gastrointestinal cancers seldom affect the skeleton (Coleman, 2001, 1997; Lipton and Vigorita, 2016; Roodman, 2004).

Tumor metastasis to the skeleton is the result of a complex cascade of event, demonstrating the resilience of these dreadful malignant cells. The first step in this multistage process is the invasion by the primary tumor of the surrounding basement membrane. The neoplastic cells dissolve the extracellular matrix containing growth factors, stimulating their motility and develop neoangiogenesis (i.e., a process consisting in the formation of new blood vessels). This new vasculature will promote their growth and supply a route for migration through lymph or blood vessels. Hematogenous spread to the skeleton is far more frequent than direct invasion and lymphatic spread to bone is rare (Rosenthal, 1997; Rybak and Rosenthal, 2001). Individual tumor cells detach from the primary tumor and enter the layered endothelial vascular wall, a process called "intravasation." They must then survive the velocity-induced shear forces of the blood flow, evade the "anoikis" (i.e., the programmed cell death after detachment from the extracellular matrix) and shield themselves from the patrolling cells of the immune system. The surviving tumor cells arrest in the circulation by adhering to the vessel endothelium of the target organ and exit the blood vessel by a mechanism similar to intravasation, called "extravasation." The final step is the adaptation of the neoplastic cells in the new, potentially hostile, territory. In the bone, the tumor cell must survive the immune response trying to eliminate it, colonize, and adapt to the new metastatic site and develop a vascular network to sustain itself. Indeed, neoangiogenesis will provide growth factors, oxygen, nutrients, and metabolites to the metastatic lesion, allowing it to grow and proliferate. Finally, the neoplastic cells produce secondary metastases or "metastasis of metastases" that will repeat the same process and metastasize and colonize further distant sites (Bussard et al., 2008; Faraji and Eissenberg, 2013; Fidler, 1989; Gupta and Massagué, 2006; Harvey and von Reyn Cream, 2007; Lipton and Vigorita, 2016; Randall, 2015; Steeg, 2006; Talmadge and Fidler, 2010).

Why is bone such a preferential organ for metastasis? In 1889, Stephen Paget addressed the question of favored metastatic sites and posed the principles of his "seed and soil" framework: "when a plant goes to seed, its seeds are carried in all directions, but they can only live and grow if they fall on congenial soil" (Paget, 1889). Consequently, the development of the metastasis (here, the seed) is dependent upon the conditions of the metastatic site (which is the soil in Paget's metaphor) (Mundy, 2002). The target site may either support the survival of the cancer cells, if the microenvironment possesses the necessary properties, or limit it (Talmadge and Fidler, 2010). Bone is a preferred site for metastasis because the bone microenvironment is highly favorable to the survival and proliferation of tumor cells. Indeed, bones present highly vascularized and metabolically active areas with a unique vascular structure, namely large diameter vascular sinusoids, inducing a slow blood flow and facilitating the intravasation and extravasation of the neoplastic cells (Bussard et al., 2008; Lipton and Vigorita, 2016; Mastro et al., 2003; Roodman, 2004; Vassiliou et al., 2013).

Moreover, the bone microenvironment is a reservoir of immobilized growth factors released during bone remodeling that can both attract tumor cells and support them during the "vicious cycle" when in place. This "vicious cycle" is the result of the cross-talk between the migrated neoplastic cells and the bone microenvironment that feeds a disastrous loop of tumor growth and bone resorption (Bussard et al., 2008; Gruber, 2012; Guise, 2002; Guise et al., 1996; Lipton and Vigorita, 2016; Roodman, 2004; Steeg, 2006; Vassiliou et al., 2013). The mechanisms responsible for bone formation orchestrated by the cancer cells are still unclear, but they attest to a selective interaction of the tumor cells with the bone microenvironment (Guise, 2002; Guise et al., 2003; Roodman, 2004; Theriault and Theriault, 2012). Metastatic cancer cells can manipulate the activity of osteoblasts (i.e., bone forming cells) and osteoclasts (i.e., bone resorptive cells) through the release of stimulators to incite the chemoattraction of cancer cells as well as support their survival (Bussard et al., 2008; Guise, 2002; Guise et al., 2006). Finally, the bone microenvironment presents some intrinsic properties favorable to the development and thriving of neoplastic cells, including low oxygen, low pH, and high calcium and phosphate concentrations. While hypoxia (i.e., low blood oxygen) promotes the proliferation and motility of cancer cells, acidosis, high calcium and phosphate concentrations increase osteoclastic resorption contributing to the vicious cycle of tumor metastases (Vassiliou et al., 2013).

Bone Metastases

The propensity of primary tumor cells to metastasize to bone demonstrates that bone metastases are a common clinical feature (Gruber, 2012). Bone metastases are located predominantly in hematopoietic areas of the skeleton, namely the vertebrae, pelvis, ribs, skull, and ends of the long bones. Metastases distal to the knees and elbows are unusual (Aufderheide and Rodríguez-Martín, 1998; Chew, 2012; Lipton and Vigorita, 2016; Mundy, 1997; O'Sullivan et al., 2015; Ortner, 2003; Randall, 2015). Typically, bone metastases are classified into three types: osteolytic, osteoblastic, and mixed. However, they generally express both osteolytic and osteoblastic components and range from mostly blastic to mostly lytic (Brothwell, 2008; Coleman, 2001, 1997; Miler et al., 2017; Mundy, 2002, 1997; Randall, 2015).

Osteolytic metastases extend from osteoclastic resorption of cortical bone to complete focal bone destruction of the cortex. They can present as coalescing porosity, osteolytic foci or destruction of bone parts. Osteolytic foci are discrete, multiple, irregularly round osteolytic lesions of variable size with a denticulated or scalloped perimeter. On radiographs, the lesions manifest as geographic lucent areas (either well-defined or ill-defined, with or without sclerosis) or "moth-eaten" (i.e., multiple sites of osteoclasia) (Figs. 6.6–6.9) (Aufderheide and Rodríguez-Martín,

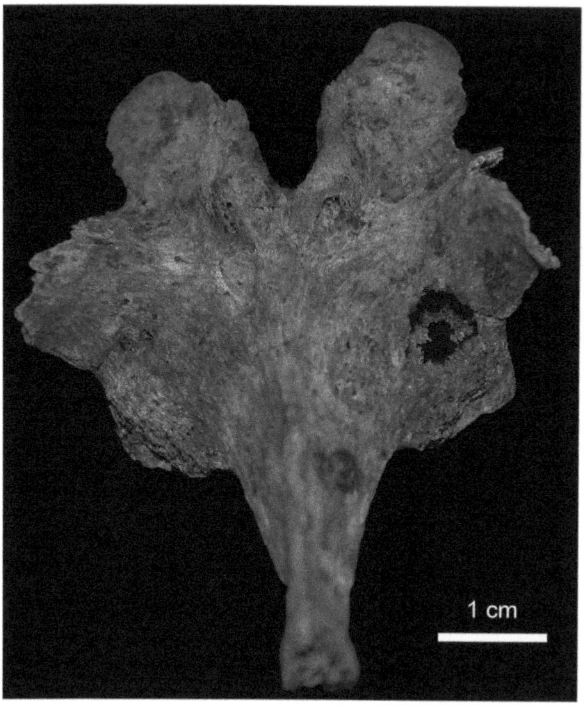

Figure 6.6 Posterior view of the ninth thoracic vertebra showing an osteolytic metastasis on the right side of neural arch with denticulated margins and a more extensive resorption of the trabecular bone. Skeleton #37 of the CAL Milano Cemetery Skeletal Collection with a clinical diagnosis of breast carcinoma.

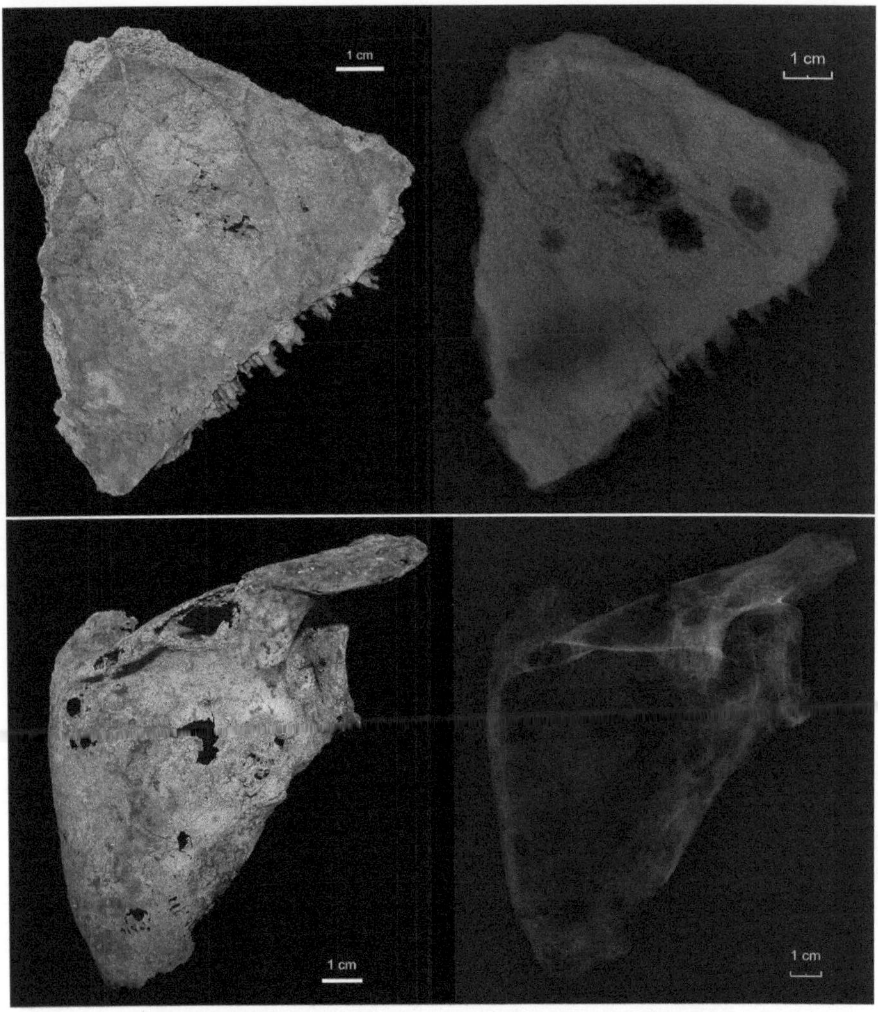

Figure 6.7 Macroscopic and radiographic images of a fragmented parietal bone (endocranial view, top) and right scapula (posterior view, bottom) showing osteolytic metastases with ill-defined or "moth-eaten" margins on X-rays. Skeletons #422 (top) and #37 of the CAL Milano Cemetery Skeletal Collection with clinical diagnoses of bladder and breast carcinomas respectively. Reproduced with permission from Biehler-Gomez, L., Tritella, S., Martino, F., Campobasso, C.P., Franchi, A., Spairani, R., et al., 2019. The synergy between radiographic and macroscopic observation of skeletal lesions on dry bone. Int. J. Leg. Med. https://doi.org/10.1007/s00414-019-02122-0.

1998; Coleman, 2001; Ortner, 2003; Ragsdale et al., 2018; Strouhal, 1991; Theriault and Theriault, 2012; Waldron, 2008).

Osteoblastic metastases can appear as new bone deposits coating the existing trabecula called "spongiosclerosis" (Ortner, 2003, p. 52),

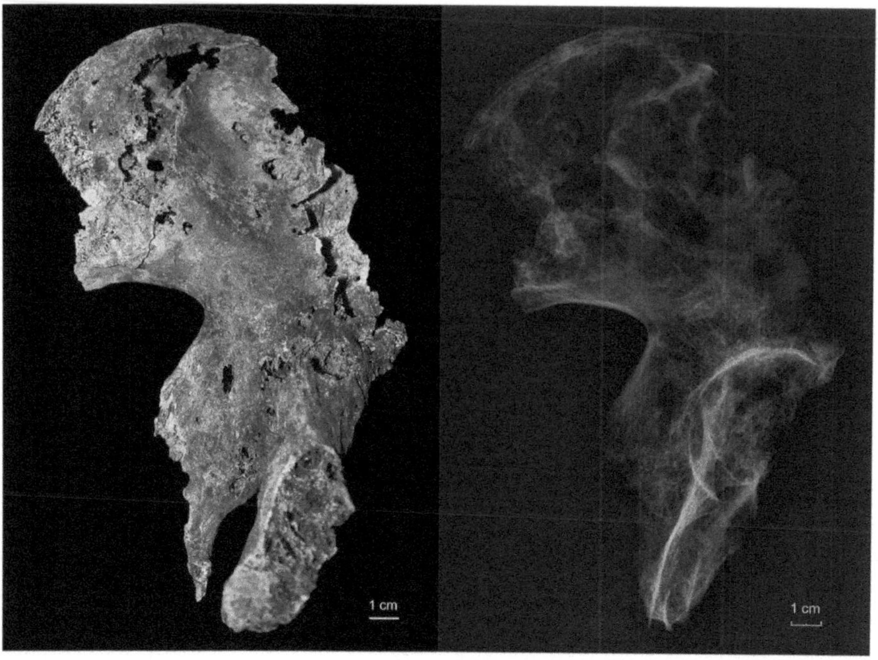

Figure 6.8 Macroscopic and radiographic images of the left innominate bone showing extensive osteolytic metastases and bone destruction. Skeleton #37 of the CAL Milano Cemetery Skeletal Collection with a clinical diagnosis of breast carcinoma. Reproduced with permission from Biehler-Gomez, L., Tritella, S., Martino, F., Campobasso, C.P., Franchi, A., Spairani, R., et al., 2019. The synergy between radiographic and macroscopic observation of skeletal lesions on dry bone. Int. J. Leg. Med. https://doi.org/10.1007/s00414-019-02122-0.

or as periosteal reactions, including woven bone, lamellar bone (i.e., remodeled woven bone), or even spiculated periosteal bone (Figs. 6.10–6.15). The excess deposition of new bone is seen radiographically as an area of increased density and opacity, defined as "osteosclerotic" (Aufderheide and Rodríguez-Martín, 1998; Ortner, 2003; Smith, 2002; Theriault and Theriault, 2012; Vilar et al., 1979; Waldron, 2008, 1997). Spiculated periosteal reactions may be "perpendicular to the cortex or slightly angulated, short or long, fine or coarse, few in numbers or forming a well-developed palisade" (Bloom et al., 1987). "Hair-on-end" periosteal reactions are defined as parallel spiculated, whereas "sunburst" are divergent spiculated periosteal reactions (Ragsdale et al., 2018). While osteolytic metastases tend to be rapidly growing and aggressive, sclerotic metastases indicate a slower progression (Galasko, 1986; O'Sullivan et al., 2015; Rybak and Rosenthal, 2001). Nonetheless, both lamellated periosteal reactions (observable on radiographs but not macroscopically recognizable) and spiculated

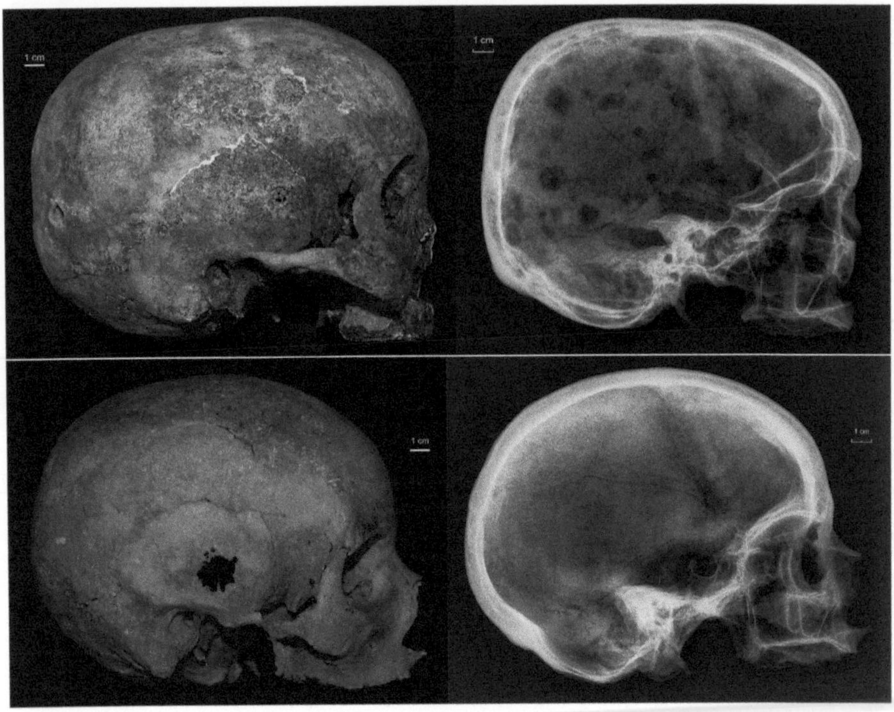

Figure 6.9 Macroscopic and radiographic images in norma lateralis *of the crania of the skeletons #37 (top) and #459 (bottom) of the CAL Milano Cemetery Skeletal Collection with clinical diagnoses of breast carcinoma. This panel shows both the strengths and limitations of radiographic imaging for the study of bone disease: on the top images, the lesions were macroscopically uncertain and may be confused with taphonomic alterations but the X-ray image clearly indicates a case of cancer, demonstrating the importance of X-ray-based imaging to support pathological diagnoses on dry bone; on the bottom images, the osteolytic bone metastasis is striking and unmistakable, yet, it is unrecognizable on the radiograph, threatening the diagnosis of the disease if the analysis was limited to radiography.* Reproduced with permission from Biehler-Gomez, L., Tritella, S., Martino, F., Campobasso, C.P., Franchi, A., Spairani, R., et al., 2019. The synergy between radiographic and macroscopic observation of skeletal lesions on dry bone. Int. J. Leg. Med. https://doi.org/10.1007/s00414-019-02122-0.

periosteal reactions are aggressive types associated with malignancy (Bloom et al., 1987; Miller, 2008).

Mixed metastases present both osteolytic and osteoblastic components and manifest as a cortical osteolytic lesion surrounded by a sclerotic area on X-rays (Figs. 6.16–6.18) (Theriault and Theriault, 2012).

Most metastases to bone are osteolytic (75%), while 15% are osteoblastic and 10% are mixed. They are usually multifocal although solitary metastases may appear (Ortner, 2003). Certain solid tumors may show a predilection: the carcinomas of the kidney, lung and thyroid are predominantly osteolytic, prostate metastases are predominantly osteoblastic and

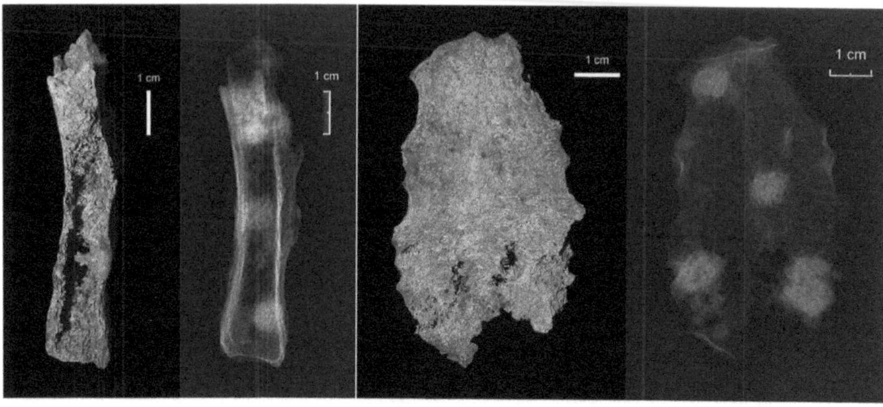

Figure 6.10 Macroscopic and radiographic images of the sternal body (left-to-right lateral view, right anterior view) with spongiosclerotic lesions appearing as radiodense areas on radiographs (osteoblastic metastases). Skeleton #422 of the CAL Milano Cemetery Skeletal Collection with a clinical diagnosis of bladder carcinoma. Reproduced with permission from Biehler-Gomez, L., Tritella, S., Martino, F., Campobasso, C.P., Franchi, A., Spairani, R., et al., 2019. The synergy between radiographic and macroscopic observation of skeletal lesions on dry bone. Int. J. Leg. Med. https://doi.org/10.1007/s00414-019-02122-0.

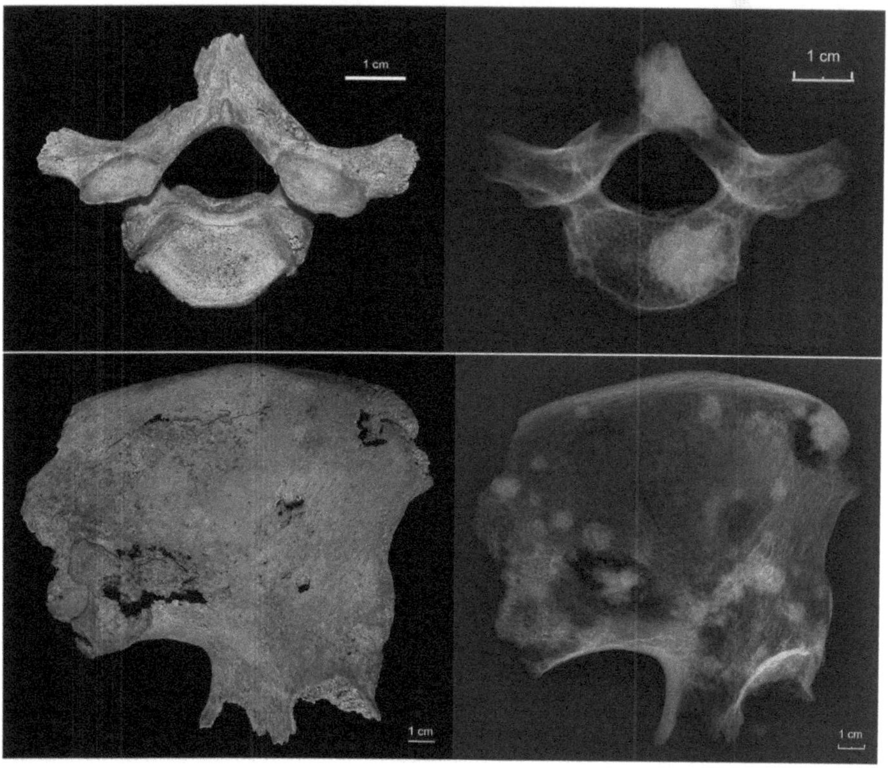

Figure 6.11 Macroscopic and radiographic images of a thoracic vertebra (superior view, top) and left ilium (anterior view, bottom) with spongiosclerotic lesions appearing as radiodense areas on radiographs (osteoblastic metastases). Skeleton #422 of the CAL Milano Cemetery Skeletal Collection with a clinical diagnosis of bladder carcinoma. Reproduced with permission from Biehler-Gomez, L., Tritella, S., Martino, F., Campobasso, C.P., Franchi, A., Spairani, R., et al., 2019. The synergy between radiographic and macroscopic observation of skeletal lesions on dry bone. Int. J. Leg. Med. https://doi.org/10.1007/s00414-019-02122-0.

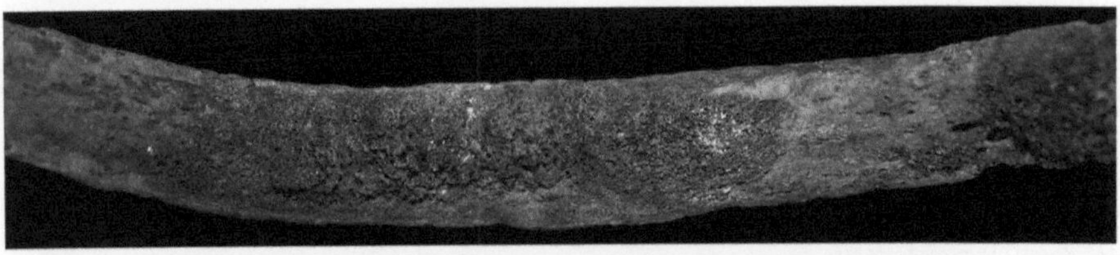

Figure 6.12 Coarse periosteal new bone on the visceral surface of a left rib (osteoblastic metastasis). Skeleton #897 of the CAL Milano Cemetery Skeletal Collection with a clinical diagnosis of bladder carcinoma.

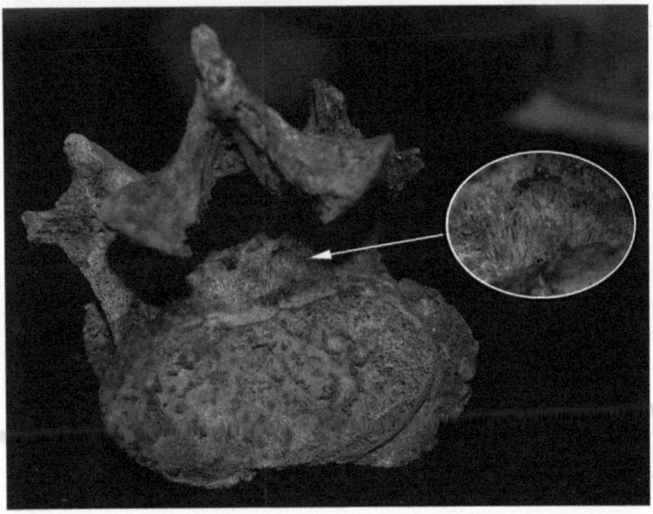

Figure 6.13 Spiculated periosteal new bone on the posterior surface of the vertebral body of L1 (osteoblastic metastasis). Skeleton #1013 of the CAL Milano Cemetery Skeletal Collection with a clinical diagnosis of prostate carcinoma.

Figure 6.14 Coarse periosteal new bone on the anterior left surface of the vertebral body of L1 (osteoblastic metastasis). Skeleton #1013 of the CAL Milano Cemetery Skeletal Collection with a clinical diagnosis of prostate carcinoma.

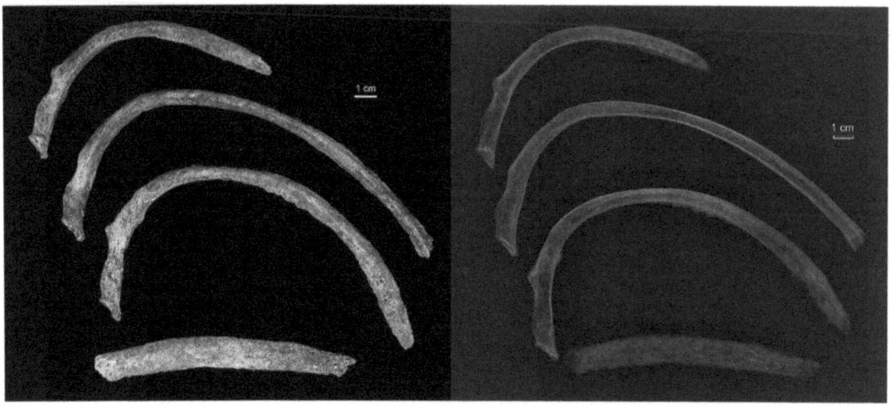

Figure 6.15 Macroscopic and radiographic images of left ribs with coarse and spiculated periosteal new bone (osteoblastic metastases). Note that the spiculated periosteal new bone is observable on X-rays (first and third ribs from the top) whereas the second rib with coarse periosteal new bone giving it a "swollen" aspect is not detected on radiography and wrongly appears normal. Skeleton #897 of the CAL Milano Cemetery Skeletal Collection with a clinical diagnosis of bladder carcinoma. Reproduced with permission from Biehler-Gomez, L., Tritella, S., Martino, F., Campobasso, C.P., Franchi, A., Spairani, R., et al., 2019. The synergy between radiographic and macroscopic observation of skeletal lesions on dry bone. Int. J. Leg. Med. https://doi.org/10.1007/s00414-019-02122-0.

Figure 6.16 Close-up view of a mixed metastasis on the left ilium: note the osteolytic lesion with denticulated margins and extensive trabecular bone resorption exposing an island of trabecular bone with spongiosclerosis. Skeleton #422 of the CAL Milano Cemetery Skeletal Collection with a clinical diagnosis of bladder carcinoma.

breast cancer exhibits most commonly mixed metastases (Aufderheide and Rodríguez-Martín, 1998; Brothwell, 2008; Lipton and Vigorita, 2016; Ortner, 2003; Randall, 2015; Waldron, 2008). These mixed metastases in breast cancer may be the result of osteoblastic or sclerotic reaction as an

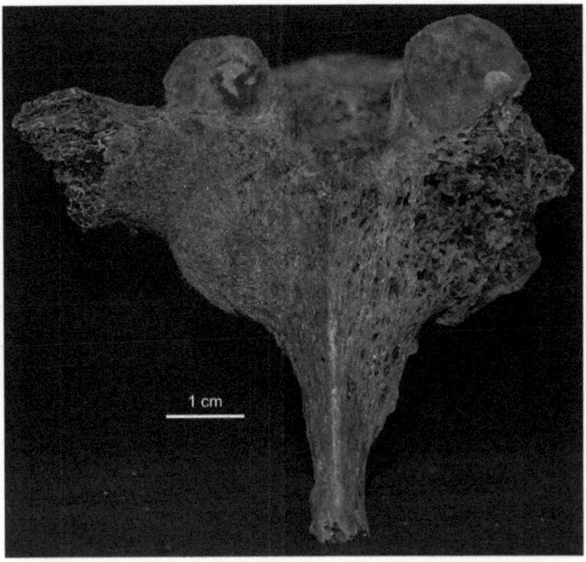

Figure 6.17 Posterior view of the fourth thoracic vertebra showing on the right lamina an osteolytic lesion and on the left lamina, a thin and coarse layer of periosteal new bone (osteoblastic metastasis). Skeletons #897 of the CAL Milano Cemetery Skeletal Collection with clinical diagnoses of bladder carcinoma.

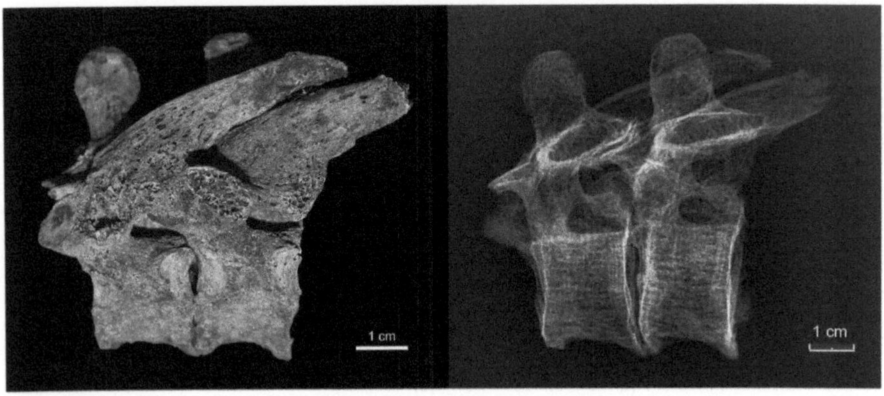

Figure 6.18 Macroscopic and radiographic images of the fifth and sixth thoracic vertebrae showing macroscopically an osteolytic lesion exposing spongiosclerosis and associated with surrounding coarse periosteal new bone (mixed metastasis); however, no lesion is detectable on the radiograph. Skeleton #897 of the CAL Milano Cemetery Skeletal Collection with a clinical diagnosis of bladder carcinoma. Reproduced with permission from Biehler-Gomez, L., Tritella, S., Martino, F., Campobasso, C.P., Franchi, A., Spairani, R., et al., 2019. The synergy between radiographic and macroscopic observation of skeletal lesions on dry bone. Int. J. Leg. Med. https://doi.org/10.1007/s00414-019-02122-0.

attempt at bone repair surrounding osteolytic metastases in a predominantly lytic carcinoma (Mundy, 2002). The primary tumor mechanisms responsible for osteolytic and/or osteoblastic metastases are based on the specific expressions of tumor factors and their selective interaction with the osteoblastic and osteoclastic cells function and activity (Guise et al., 2006, 2003, 1996).

Bone metastases can lead to skeletal-related events associated with an increased clinical morbidity and life-threatening complications. In the mid of 2000s, the frequency of an individual with metastatic cancer to experience a skeletal-related event was estimated to be every 3 – 6 months (Coleman, 2006). About two-thirds of patients with breast cancer will develop one or more skeletal-related events (Harvey and von Reyn Cream, 2007). These include severe bone pain, pathologic fractures, hypercalcemia, spinal cord compression, and other nerve compression syndromes. Bone pain and impaired mobility are noted in 65%–75% of patients with bone metastases (Vassiliou et al., 2013). Pathologic fractures are most commonly observed in osteolytic metastases affecting the cortex of weight-bearing bones. Spinal cord compression is a medical emergency associated with a poor prognosis. Hypercalcemia is a life-threatening complication resulting from the release of calcium during bone destruction (Coleman, 2006; Harvey and von Reyn Cream, 2007; Randall, 2015; Vassiliou et al., 2013). Although most of these skeletal-related events are clinical outcomes, pathologic fractures and vertebral collapse are possible to be observed on dry bones (Aufderheide and Rodríguez-Martín, 1998).

Rothschild and Rothschild (1995) demonstrated the importance of radiographic imaging of the skeleton for the observation of bone metastases, often hidden from macroscopic examination—in their study: 11 individuals were diagnosed with metastatic bone disease by visual examination compared to 33 with radiographs. However, they concede that some macroscopic lesions were not recognizable on radiography due to the 30%–50% reduction in bone density required for a metastatic lesion for being recognized on radiographs). Ragsdale et al. (2018) detailed the morphological bone changes in metastatic cancer and advocate an organized approach for the diagnosis of metastatic bone lesions, including distribution (solitary vs multifocal), character of margins, details of periosteal reactions, and remnants of mineralized matrix. Following this idea, several studies based on known collections (in particular the Terry, Hamann-Todd, Lisbon, Coimbra, and the

CAL Milano Cemetery Skeletal Collection collections) have examined bone lesions attributable to metastatic cancer (Marques et al., 2018; Rothschild et al., 1998), and studies with knowledge of the primary organ of origin of the metastatic cancer from the associated documentation have documented the distribution and aspect of bone lesions in prostate (Castoldi et al., 2017), breast (Biehler-Gomez et al., 2019b), and bladder carcinomas (Biehler-Gomez et al., 2019c), evidencing differences potentially useful for a distinction in cases without knowledge of the primary organ of origin.

The main issue in the diagnosis of metastatic cancer is the differential diagnosis with multiple myeloma or pseudopathology, which may result challenging or even indistinguishable on dry bones (Kirkpatrick et al., 2018; Ortner, 2003, p. 535). While the potential of histomorphology for malignant tumor diagnosis on dry bone is limited to the recognition of the type of metastasis (osteolytic, osteoblastic, or mixed) (De Boer et al., 2013), protein analyses of osseous lesions have permitted the identification of tumors in skeletal remains dating back as far as the Neolithic (Bona et al., 2014; Nerlich, 2018; Pérez-Martínez et al., 2016; Schultz et al., 2007).

Diagnosis and Differential Diagnosis

The diagnosis of metastatic cancer depends on several factors: the age of the skeleton, the distribution of the lesions as well as their morphology, size and nature. As already mentioned, the bone tissue can basically react in only two ways: either with bone proliferation or with bone resorption. Consequently, osteolytic and osteoblastic lesions can be evocative of multiple pathological conditions. Therefore, other criteria have become necessary to distinguish them on dry bone, including the pattern of distribution of the lesions, their shape and characteristics, and the sex and age of the individual. As previously said, cancer metastases to bone can be osteolytic (coalescing porosity or round/oval osteolytic foci of various size), osteoblastic (spongiosclerosis or periosteal reaction), or mixed (with both osteolytic and osteoblastic components). They tend to be multifocal and located primarily in the axial skeleton, the skull and proximal ends of the femora and humeri with a sparing of the bones distal to the knees and elbows. Moreover, metastatic carcinoma has a peak onset in individuals over 40 (Miller, 2008). This specific morphology, distribution and age category is suggestive of metastatic cancer (Anderson et al.,

1992; Assis and Codinha, 2010; Binder et al., 2014; Duhig et al., 1996; Luna et al., 2008; Marks and Hamilton, 2007; Marques et al., 2013; Šefčáková et al., 2001; Wasterlain et al., 2011) but a differential diagnosis must be considered.

Differential Diagnosis of Osteolytic Lesions

When the lesions are predominantly osteolytic, the most likely conditions responsible also include multiple myeloma, Langerhans cell histiocytosis, leukemia, secondary lesions to tuberculosis, fungal disease, and taphonomic alterations (in particular osteophageous insects and roots). The ability of taphonomic bone alterations to mimic pathological lesions is the reasons why pseudopathology should always be considered in the differential diagnosis of osteolytic lesions. Postdepositional damage caused by roots, termites, or beetles can mimic the superficial appearance of osteolytic lesions due to cancer metastases. However, these lesions do not extend within the bone, they appear as regular demarcated tunnels and insects do not show a preference for particular skeletal elements (Binder et al., 2014; Strouhal, 1991).

Tuberculosis is a chronic infectious disease caused by *Mycobacterium tuberculosis*. The morphology of the skeletal lesions due to tuberculosis is not specific and primarily osteolytic in nature, and thus may overlap with osteolytic bone metastases. Nonetheless, tuberculosis is a disease of young people, with rare purely osteolytic lesions. Pott's disease (i.e., tuberculous spondylitis) is the most common form of skeletal involvement in bone tuberculosis. It can present as osteolytic destruction of a vertebral body causing a collapse of the vertebra and a sharp angulation of the spine due to the preservation of the neural arches of the vertebrae. Spine lesions almost exclusively involve vertebral bodies. Deformation of the joints and ankyloses may appear. Affection of the bones of the hands and feet is frequent. Cranial lesions are rare in adults (Aufderheide and Rodríguez-Martín, 1998; Ortner, 2003).

Langerhans cells histiocytosis, originally known as Histiocytosis X (Lichenstein, 1953) represents three syndromes of unknown etiology (Letterer-Siwe disease, Hand-Schtiller-Christian disease, and eosinophilic granuloma), characterized by an abnormal proliferation and mobility of histiocytic cells. This malignant pathology can produce sharply circumscribed osteolytic lesions of 10 – 20 mm in size with no to little peripheral reaction that may appear similar to bone metastases

(Aufderheide and Rodríguez-Martín, 1998; Marks and Hamilton, 2007; Ortner, 2003). Nevertheless, the condition affects males twice as frequently as females with a frequency of 80% under 30 years and 50% under 10 (Dorfman and Czerniak, 1998), and is thus less likely to be found in mature adults.

Leukemias are a group of malignant cancers of the myeloid and lymphoid hematopoietic cells of the bone marrow. Lesions present as numerous, scattered, and diffuse superficial solitary pits (1 – 3 mm in diameter) with smooth minimally remodeled margins in non-articular areas, thus leukemia can be distinguished macroscopically from metastatic carcinoma on dry bone (Aufderheide and Rodríguez-Martín, 1998; Ortner, 2003; Rothschild et al., 1997).

Multiple myeloma is a highly malignant plasma cell tumor emanating in the blood-forming bone marrow. Both multiple myeloma and metastatic carcinoma have a peak onset in individuals over 40, causing multifocal lesions with an outward progression in the bone, most commonly in the axial skeleton, thoracic cage, skull, and proximal ends of femora and humeri (Strouhal, 1991). This considerable overlap explains why the distinction between these two diseases may be extremely challenging, if not impossible in some cases (Ortner, 2003). In spite of these difficulties, differences do exist. Multiple myeloma is purely osteolytic and affects males most commonly with a male-to-female ratio of 2:1, contrasting with the female predominance and the possible remodeling of metastatic carcinoma. In the former, foci are numerous and scattered with a regularly spheroid or round geometry, sharp edges, and smooth surrounding bone. By opposition, the latter exhibits less numerous and localized osteolytic foci, with an irregular morphology and scalloped margins. Moreover, lesions are thought to be of uniform small to medium size in multiple myeloma contrary to metastatic carcinoma, but this criterion is not sufficiently reliable alone (Rothschild et al., 1998). On radiographs, lesions due to multiple myeloma are sharply demarcated and do not present an obscure, cloudy or "moth-eaten" appearance characteristic of metastatic carcinoma (Biehler-Gomez et al., 2019d; Marks and Hamilton, 2007; Rothschild et al., 1998; Strouhal, 1993, 1991). Another element helping to distinguish multiple myeloma from metastatic carcinoma is the suggested restriction of myeloma lesions in the spine to the vertebral bodies with sparing of the posterior elements (Jacobson et al., 1958).

Fungal disease, specifically blastomycosis, may also be differentiated from bone metastases in their involvement of cortical and trabecular bone: equal in the former, more extensive in the trabecular bone for the latter (Hershkovitz et al., 1998).

Differential Diagnosis of Osteoblastic Lesions

The most common differential diagnosis on dry bone of proliferative lesions evocative of osteoblastic metastases includes Paget's disease, Ewing's sarcoma, osteosarcoma, and infectious conditions such as osteomyelitis and pulmonary tuberculosis.

Pulmonary tuberculosis is associated with a periosteal reaction on the ribs (Roberts et al., 1994) possibly confused with proliferative bone metastases, common in this skeletal area. However, rib periostitis in cases of known pulmonary tuberculosis is restricted to the internal or visceral surface of the rib, mainly on the vertebral end and shows a layer of new bone that contrasts with the exuberant "coral-like" appearance of periosteal new bone observed in metastatic bone disease (Santos and Roberts, 2006).

Osteomyelitis is a bone infection primarily involving the medullar cavity of long bones, characterized by a sequestrum (i.e., bone necrosis), surrounded by an involucrum (i.e., envelope of reactive new bone) and the presence of a draining cloaca (Ortner, 2003). These features are not present in bone metastases.

Primary bone malignancies, in particular Ewing's sarcoma and osteosarcoma, may appear similar to osteoblastic metastases. Sarcoma distant metastases are possible but considerably rarer than epithelial tumor metastases. Osteosarcoma is the most common primary bone tumor, presenting both osteolytic and osteoblastic lesions and often exhibiting the characteristic spiculated sunburst periosteal reaction. The malignancy is present in 80% of cases in individuals under 30 years of age, in males twice often as females, affecting primarily the knee but the proximal femur and humerus are other possible locations (Brothwell, 2008; Miller, 2008; Ortner, 2003; Waldron, 2008). Ewing's sarcoma is an uncommon primary tumor occurring in the femur, pelvis or tibia of adolescents and young adults under 30, males more than females. The aggressive tumor may progressively involve more bones, with both osteolytic lesions and the typical "onion-skin" appearance of periosteal reaction notable on radiographs (Biermann and Baker, 2000; Brothwell, 2008; Miller, 2008;

Waldron, 2008). The age of the individual as well as the general multiplicity of bone lesions in metastatic carcinoma may allow its distinction with these primary bone malignancies.

Paget's disease is a chronic skeletal disease due to dysregulated bone remodeling and skeletal deformity which evolves over many years for which viral and genetic pathogenic pathways have been proposed (Singer, 2016), following three stages: (1) an osteolytic stage; (2) a mixed osteolytic and sclerotic stage with a predominant osteoblastic activity; and (3) a sclerotic stage with a declining osteoblastic activity (Merczi et al., 2014; Ortner, 2003; Waldron, 2008). In the final stage, the bones become enlarged with cortical thickening due to periosteal bone deposition. The disorder typically affects the skull, lumbar spine, pelvis and proximal femur of individuals over 40 years. The best diagnostic criteria of Paget's disease is the pathognomonic mosaic pattern observable during histological examination (De Boer et al., 2013; Ortner, 2003; Waldron, 2008), allowing its distinction with bone metastases.

Primary Organ Identification

The ultimate step in the analysis of bone metastases on dry bone is the proposal of probabilistic hypotheses for the organ of origin of the cancer. Of course, a definite diagnosis of the primary tumor on dry bones is too hazardous to be affirmed. Nonetheless, distinctions in the pattern of bone involvement between primaries can sometimes allow the construction of a most probable case scenario.

As mentioned earlier, the carcinomas of the prostate, breast, thyroid, and lung are the most common to metastasize to bone, with a frequency of 65% to 80% of cases for the first two primaries. Prostate cancer most commonly involves the vertebrae (in particular, the lumbar spine), pelvis, ribs, long bones (especially the femur), skull, and sternum (Lipton and Vigorita, 2016; Prates et al., 2011). Contrary to the majority of carcinomas, prostate bone metastases are predominantly osteoblastic with proliferative bone reaction and osteosclerosis. In fact, osteoblastic metastases are so typical in prostate cancer that, at least up to 1990s, authors could say: "all patients with prostate carcinoma will develop osteoblastic bone metastases if they live long enough" (Mundy, 1997). However, an osteolytic component remains; mixed metastases may be observed and osteolytic ones are scarce (Lipton and Vigorita, 2016). Spiculated or "sunburst" periosteal reactions are a rare occurrence in metastatic carcinoma but known to prostatic cancer (Bloom et al., 1987; Castoldi et al., 2017; Waldron, 2008, 1997). Therefore, the high occurrence of prostatic bone metastases, male sex, the typical axial skeletal distribution and the specific morphology of the lesions with osteoblastic predominance makes the diagnosis of prostate cancer very likely (Baraybar and Shimada, 1993; de la Rúa et al., 1995; Mays et al., 1996; Merczi et al., 2014; Prates et al., 2011; Schultz et al., 2007; Tkocz and Bierring, 1984; Wakely et al., 1995).

Breast carcinoma is the most common cancer diagnosed in women, the leading cause of cancer-related deaths in female sex, and the first cause of death in women between 40 and 59 years (Randall, 2015; Siegel et al., 2018). While breast cancer metastases to bone are predominantly osteolytic, most metastases are actually mixed (Aufderheide and Rodríguez-Martín, 1998; Randall, 2015; Rosenthal, 1997). The most common location affected are the vertebrae and pelvis, followed by the skull, ribs, femur, and humerus (Allison et al., 1980; Lipton and Vigorita, 2016; Randall, 2015; Waldron, 2008). Male breast cancer does occur but represents less than 1% of all breast cancer cases (Anderson et al., 2010). Given the propensity of breast cancer metastases to bone, a mixed pattern of bone metastases primarily in the axial skeleton of a female individual over 40 years of age is highly suggestive of a breast metastatic carcinoma (Allison et al., 1980; Melikian, 2006; Merczi et al., 2014; Smith, 2002; Strouhal, 1993). Nonetheless, and despite this high likelihood, it does not exclude other carcinomas as the primary disease and a definite diagnosis cannot be achieved from the sole macroscopic observation of dry bone. Similarly, a case of osteolytic bone metastases distinct from multiple myeloma found on a male individual, especially if the ribs are particularly affected, may be suggestive of a case of malignant carcinoma of the lung (Grupe, 1988). But again, this combination of factors does not strictly exclude other carcinomas as possible primary organs of origin.

Consequently, the diagnosis of the primary site of disease on dry bone can only be narrowed down to the most probable case scenario, based on the sex and age of the individual, the skeletal distribution of the metastases and the morphology of the lesions; but in the end, "the final decision has to be made on probabilistic grounds" (Waldron, 2008). However, further research on pathological biomarkers (Pérez-Martínez et al., 2016) may facilitate a definitive diagnosis of the disease and could permit the identification of the primary organ of origin.

References

Allison, M.J., Gerszten, E., Munizaga, J., Santoro, C., 1980. Metastatic tumor of bone in a Tiahuanaco female. Bull. N. Y. Acad. Med. 56, 581–587.

Anderson, T., Wakely, J., Carter, A., 1992. Medieval example of metastatic carcinoma: A dry bone, radiological, and SEM study. Am. J. Phys. Anthr. 89, 309–323. Available from: https://doi.org/10.1002/ajpa.1330890305.

Anderson, W.F., Jatoi, I., Tse, J., Rosenberg, P.S., 2010. Male breast cancer: a population-based comparison with female breast cancer. J. Clin. Oncol. 28, 232–239. Available from: https://doi.org/10.1200/JCO.2009.23.8162.

Assis, S., Codinha, S., 2010. Metastatic carcinoma in a 14th–19th century skeleton from Constância (Portugal). Int. J. Osteoarchaeol. 20, 603–620. Available from: https://doi.org/10.1002/oa.1084.

Aufderheide, A.C., Rodríguez-Martín, C., 1998. The Cambridge Encyclopedia of Human Paleopathology. Cambridge University Press, Cambridge, United Kingdom.

Baraybar, J.P., Shimada, I., 1993. A possible case of metastatic carcinoma in a middle Sican burial from Batán Grande, Perú. Int. J. Osteoarchaeol. 3, 129–135. Available from: https://doi.org/10.1002/oa.1390030210.

Biehler-Gomez, L., Giordano, G., Cattaneo, C., 2019a. Multiple myeloma bone lesions in skeletal remains: report of two known cases from the 20th century CAL Milano Cemetery Skeletal Collection. Int. J. Osteoarchaeol. 101–107. https://doi.org/10.1002/oa.2721.

Biehler-Gomez, L., Giordano, G., Cattaneo, C., 2019b. The appearance of breast cancer metastases on dry bone: Implications for forensic anthropology. J. Forensic Leg. Med. 61, 5–12. Available from: https://doi.org/10.1016/j.jflm.2018.10.007.

Biehler-Gomez, L., Giordano, G., Cattaneo, C., 2019c. The overlooked primary: bladder cancer metastases on dry bone. A study of the 20th century CAL Milano Cemetery Skeletal Collection. Int. J. Paleopathol. 24, 130–140. Available from: https://doi.org/10.1016/j.ijpp.2018.10.005.

Biehler-Gomez, L., Tritella, S., Martino, F., Campobasso, C.P., Franchi, A., Spairani, R., et al., 2019d. The synergy between radiographic and macroscopic observation of skeletal lesions on dry bone. Int. J. Leg. Med. https://doi.org/10.1007/s00414-019-02122-0

Biermann, J.S., Baker, L.H., 2000. Sarcomas of Soft Tissue and Bone. In: Humes, H.D., DuPont, H.L., Gardner, L.B., Griffin, J.W., Harris, E.D., Hazzard, W.R., King, T.E., Loriaux, D.L., Nabel, E.G., Todd, R.F., Traber, P.G. (Eds.), Kelley's Textbook of Internal Medicine. Lippincott Williams & Wilkins, Philadelphia, PA, pp. 1648–1653.

Binder, M., Roberts, C.A., Spencer, N., Antoine, D., Cartwright, C., 2014. On the antiquity of cancer: evidence for metastatic carcinoma in a young man from ancient Nubia (c. 1200BC). PLoS One 9, 1–11. Available from: https://doi.org/10.1371/journal.pone.0090924.

Bladé, J., Rosiñol, L., 2007. Complications of multiple myeloma. Hematol. Oncol. Clin. North. Am. 21, 1231–1246. Available from: https://doi.org/10.1016/j.hoc.2007.08.006.

Bloom, R.A., Libson, E., Husband, J.E., Stoker, D.J., 1987. The periosteal sunburst reaction to bone metastases. A literature review and report of 20 additional cases. Skelet. Radiol. 16, 629–634.

Bona, A., Papai, Z., Maasz, G., Toth, G.A., Jambor, E., Schmidt, J., et al., 2014. Mass spectrometric identification of ancient proteins as potential molecular biomarkers for a 2000-year-old osteogenic sarcoma. PLoS One 9. https://doi.org/10.1371/journal.pone.0087215

Brothwell, D., 2008. Tumor and tumor-like processes. In: Pinhasi, R., Mays, S. (Eds.), Advances in Human Palaeopathology. John Wiley & Sons, Chichester, England, pp. 253–281.

Brothwell, D., 2012. Tumors: problems of differential diagnosis in paleopathology. In: Grauer, A.L. (Ed.), A Companion to Paleopathology. Wiley-Blackwell, Oxford, pp. 420–433.

Bussard, K.M., Gay, C.V., Mastro, A.M., 2008. The bone microenvironment in metastasis; what is special about bone? Cancer Metastasis Rev. 27, 41–55. Available from: https://doi.org/10.1007/s10555-007-9109-4.

Campanacci, M., 1999. Osteoid osteoma. In: Bone and Soft Tissue Tumors. Springer, pp. 391–414.

Capasso, L.L., 2005. Antiquity of cancer. Int. J. Cancer 113, 2–13. Available from: https://doi.org/10.1002/ijc.20610.

Castoldi, E., Cappella, A., Gibelli, D., Sforza, C., Cattaneo, C., 2017. The difficult task of diagnosing prostate cancer metastases on dry bone. J. Forensic Sci. https://doi.org/10.1111/1556-4029.13617.

Cattaneo, C., Gelsthorpe, K., Phillips, P., Waldron, T., Booth, J.R., Sokol, R.J., 1994. Immunological diagnosis of multiple myeloma in a medieval bone. Int. J. Osteoarchaeol. 4, 1–2. Available from: https://doi.org/10.1002/oa.1390040102.

Chell, J., Fernandes, J.A., Bell, M.J., 2001. The orthopaedic presentation of acute leukaemia in childhood. Ann. R. Coll. Surg. Engl. 83, 186–189.

Chew, F.S., 2012. Skeletal Radiology: the Bare Bones, 3rd ed. Lippincott Williams & Wilkins, Philadelphia, PA.

Chhem, R.K., Brothwell, D., 2008. Paleoradiology: Imaging Mummies and Fossils. Springer, Berlin (Germany).

Coleman, R.E., 1997. Skeletal complications of malignancy. Cancer 80, 1588–1594. https://doi.org/10.1002/(SICI)1097-0142(19971015)80:8 + < 1588: AID-CNCR9 > 3.0.CO;2-G.

Coleman, R.E., 2001. Metastatic bone disease: clinical features, pathophysiology and treatment strategies. Cancer Treat. Rev. 27, 165–176. Available from: https://doi.org/10.1053/ctrv.2000.0210.

Coleman, R.E., 2006. Clinical features of metastatic bone disease and risk of skeletal morbidity. Clin. Cancer Res. 12, 6243.

David, A.R., Zimmerman, M.R., 2010. Cancer: an old disease, a new disease or something in between? Nat. Rev. Cancer 10, 728. Available from: https://doi.org/10.1038/nrc2914.

De Boer, H.H., Van der Merwe, A.E., Maat, G.J.R., 2013. The diagnostic value of microscopy in dry bone palaeopathology: a review. Int. J. Paleopathol. 3, 113–121. Available from: https://doi.org/10.1016/j.ijpp.2013.03.004.

de la Rúa, C., Baraybar, J.P., Etxeberria, F., 1995. Neolithic case of metastasizing carcinoma: multiple approaches to differential diagnosis. Int. J. Osteoarchaeol. 5, 254–264. Available from: https://doi.org/10.1002/oa.1390050304.

Delgado, J., Martinez, L.M., Sa, T.T., Gonza, G., Sánchez, T.T., Ramirez, A., et al., 2005. Lung cancer pathogenesis associated with wood smoke exposure. Chest 128, 124–131. Available from: https://doi.org/10.1378/chest.128.1.124.

DeVita, V.T., Chu, E., 2008. A history of cancer chemotherapy. Cancer Res. 68, 8643.

Dorfman, H.D., Czerniak, B., 1998. Bone tumors. Mosby.

Duhig, C., Strouhal, E., Němečková, A., 1996. Case of a secondary carcinoma of Anglo-Saxon period from Edix Hill, Barrington, Cambridgeshire, England. J. Paleopathol. 8, 25–32.

Edwards, C.M., Zhuang, J., Mundy, G.R., 2008. The pathogenesis of the bone disease of multiple myeloma. Bone 42, 1007–1013. Available from: https://doi.org/10.1016/j.bone.2008.01.027.

Emadi, A., Law, J., 2018. Overview of Leukemia - Merck Manual for Health Professionals [WWW Document]. Available from: <https://www.merckmanuals.com/professional/hematology-and-oncology/leukemias/overview-of-leukemia>

Faraji, F., Eissenberg, J.C., 2013. Seed and soil: a conceptual framework of metastasis for clinicians. Mo. Med. 110, 302–308.

Fidler, I.J., 1989. Origin and biology of cancer metastasis. Cytometry 10, 673–680. Available from: https://doi.org/10.1002/cyto.990100602.

Galasko, C.S.B., 1986. Skeletal metastases. Clin. Orthop. Relat. Res. 210, 18–30.

Greenspan, A., 1993. Benign bone-forming lesions: osteoma, osteoid osteoma, and osteoblastoma. Skelet. Radiol. 22, 485–500.

Gruber, R., 2012. Reader's digest of the pathophysiology of bone metastases. Wien. Medizinische Wochenschr. 162, 370–373. Available from: https://doi.org/10.1007/s10354-012-0110-3.

Grupe, G., 1988. Metastasizing carcinoma in a medieval skeleton: Differential diagnosis and etiology. Am. J. Phys. Anthr. 75, 369–374. Available from: https://doi.org/10.1002/ajpa.1330750308.

Guise, T.A., 2002. The vicious cycle of bone metastases. J. Musculoskelet. Neuronal Interact. 2, 570–572.

Guise, T.A., Mohammad, K.S., Clines, G., Stebbins, E.G., Wong, D.H., Higgins, L.S., et al., 2006. Basic mechanisms responsible for osteolytic and osteoblastic bone metastases. Clin. Cancer Res. 12, 6213–6216.

Guise, T.A., Yin, J.J., Mohammad, K.S., 2003. Role of endothelin-1 in osteoblastic bone metastases. Cancer 97, 779–784. Available from: https://doi.org/10.1002/cncr.11129.

Guise, T.A., Yin, J.J., Taylor, S.D., Kumagai, Y., Dallas, M., Boyce, B.F., et al., 1996. Evidence for a causal role of parathyroid hormone-related protein in the pathogenesis of human breast cancer-mediated osteolysis. J. Clin. Invest. 98, 1544–1549. Available from: https://doi.org/10.1172/JCI118947.

Gupta, G.P., Massagué, J., 2006. Cancer metastasis: building a framework. Cell 127, 679–695. Available from: https://doi.org/10.1016/j.cell.2006.11.001.

Harvey, H.A., von Reyn Cream, L., 2007. Biology of bone metastases: causes and consequences. Clin. Breast Cancer 7, S7–S13. Available from: https://doi.org/10.3816/CBC.2007.s.001.

Hershkovitz, I., Rothschild, B.M., Dutour, O., Greenwald, C.M., 1998. Clues to recognition of fungal origin of lytic skeletal lesions. Am. J. Phys. Anthropol. 106, 47–60. https://doi.org/10.1002/(SICI)1096-8644(199805)106:1<47::AID-AJPA4>3.0.CO;2-A.

Isidro, A., Seiler, R., Seco, M., 2019. Leukemia in ancient Egypt: earliest case and state-of-the-art techniques for diagnosing generalized osteolytic lesions. Int. J. Osteoarchaeol. 29, 273–280. Available from: https://doi.org/10.1002/oa.2736.

Jacobson, H.G., Poppel, M.H., Shapiro, J.H., Grossberger, S., 1958. The vertebral pedicle sign: a roentgen finding to differentiate metastatic carcinoma from multiple myeloma. Am. J. Roentgenol. Radium Ther. Nucl. Med. 80, 817–821.

Joyce, M.J., 2012. Metastatic Bone Tumors - Merck Manual for Health Professionals [WWW Document]. Available from: <https://www.merckmanuals.com/professional/musculoskeletal-and-connective-tissue-disorders/tumors-of-bones-and-joints/metastatic-bone-tumors>

Kirkpatrick, C.L., Campbell, R.A., Hunt, K.J., 2018. Paleo-oncology: taking stock and moving forward. Int. J. Paleopathol. 21, 3–11. Available from: https://doi.org/10.1016/j.ijpp.2018.02.001.

Klaus, H.D., 2016. A probable case of acute childhood leukemia: skeletal involvement, differential diagnosis, and the bioarchaeology of cancer in South America. Int. J. Osteoarchaeol. 26, 348–358. Available from: https://doi.org/10.1002/oa.2411.

Kumar, S.K., Rajkumar, V., Kyle, R.A., Van Duin, M., Sonneveld, P., Mateos, M.V., et al., 2017. Multiple myeloma. Nat. Rev. Dis. Prim. 3, 1–20. Available from: https://doi.org/10.1038/nrdp.2017.46.

Lichenstein, L., 1953. Histiocytosis X; integration of eosinophilic granuloma of bone, Letterer-Siwe disease, and Schuller-Christian disease as related manifestations of a single nosologic entity. AMA. Arch. Pathol. 56, 84–102.

Lipton, J.F., Vigorita, V.J., 2016. Metastatic bone disease. In: Vigorita, V.J., Ghelman, B., Mintz, D. (Eds.), Orthopaedic Pathology. Lippincott Williams & Wilkin, Philadelphia, pp. 594–619.

Lowenberg, B., Downing, J.R., Burnett, A., 1999. Acute myeloid leukemia. N. Engl. J. Med. 341, 1051–1062. Available from: https://doi.org/10.1056/NEJM199909303411407.

Luna, L.H., Aranda, C.M., Bosio, L.A., Beron, M.A., 2008. A case of multiple metastasis in Late Holocene hunter-gatherers from the Argentine Pampean region. Int. J. Osteoarchaeol. 18, 492–506. Available from: https://doi.org/10.1002/oa.950.

Marks, M.K., Hamilton, M.D., 2007. Metastatic carcinoma: palaeopathology and differential diagnosis. Int. J. Osteoarchaeol. 17, 217–234. Available from: https://doi.org/10.1002/oa.874.

Marques, C., Matos, V., Costa, T., Zink, A., Cunha, E., 2018. Absence of evidence or evidence of absence? A discussion on paleoepidemiology of neoplasms with contributions from two Portuguese human skeletal reference collections (19th–20th century). Int. J. Paleopathol. 21, 83–95. Available from: https://doi.org/10.1016/j.ijpp.2017.03.005.

Marques, C., Santos, A.L., Cunha, E., 2013. Better a broader diagnosis than a misdiagnosis: the study of a neoplastic condition in a male individual who died in Early 20th Century (Coimbra, Portugal). Int. J. Osteoarchaeol. 23, 664–675. Available from: https://doi.org/10.1002/oa.1294.

Mastro, A.M., Gay, C.V., Welch, D.R., 2003. The skeleton as a unique environment for breast cancer cells. Clin. Exp. Metastasis 20, 275–284. Available from: https://doi.org/10.1023/A:1022995403081.

Mays, S., Strouhal, E., Vyhnánek, L., Němečková, A., 1996. A case of metastatic carcinoma of medieval date from Wharram Percy, England. J. Paleopathol. 8, 33–42.

Melikian, M., 2006. A case of metastatic carcinoma from 18th century London. Int. J. Osteoarchaeol. 16, 138–144. Available from: https://doi.org/10.1002/oa.813.

Merczi, M., Marcsik, A., Bernert, Z., Józsa, L., Buczkó, K., Lassányi, G., et al., 2014. Skeletal metastatic carcinomas from the Roman Period (1st to 5th Century AD) in Hungary. Pathobiology 81, 100–111.

Miler, S.F., Thomas, C.Y., Shiozawa, Y., 2017. Molecular involvement of the bone marrow microenvironment in bone metastasis. Introduction to Cancer Metastasis. Academic Press, pp. 263–276. Available from: https://doi.org/10.1016/B978-0-12-804003-4.00014-1.

Miller, T.T., 2008. Bone tumors and tumorlike conditions: analysis with conventional radiography. Radiology 246, 662–674. Available from: https://doi.org/10.1148/radiol.2463061038.

Mostoufi-Moab, S., Halton, J., 2014. Bone morbidity in childhood leukemia: Epidemiology, mechanisms, diagnosis, and treatment. Curr. Osteoporos. Rep. 12, 300–312. Available from: https://doi.org/10.1007/s11914-014-0222-3.

Mundy, G.R., 1997. Mechanisms of bone metastasis. Cancer 80, 1546–1556. https://doi.org/10.1002/(SICI)1097-0142(19971015)80:8 + < 1546::AID-CNCR4 > 3.0.CO;2-I.

Mundy, G.R., 2002. Metastasis: metastasis to bone: causes, consequences and therapeutic opportunities. Nat. Rev. Cancer 2, 584–593.

National Cancer Institute, 2017. Cancer Statistics [WWW Document]. Available from: <https://www.cancer.gov/about-cancer/understanding/statistics>

Nerlich, A.G., 2018. Molecular paleopathology and paleo-oncology–State of the art, potentials, limitations and perspectives. Int. J. Paleopathol. 21, 77–82. Available from: https://doi.org/10.1016/j.ijpp.2017.02.004.

Nerlich, A.G., Rohrbach, H., Bachmeier, B., Zink, A., 2006. Malignant tumors in two ancient populations: an approach to historical tumor epidemiology. Oncol. Rep. 16, 197–202.

O'Sullivan, G.J., Carty, F.L., Cronin, C.G., 2015. Imaging of bone metastasis: an update. World J. Radiol. 7, 202–211. Available from: https://doi.org/10.4329/wjr.v7.i8.202.

Ortner, D.J., 2003. Identification of Pathological Conditions in Human Skeletal Remains, 3rd ed. Smithsonian Institution Press, New York.

Paget, S., 1889. The distribution of secondary growths in cancer of the breast. Lancet 133, 571–573. Available from: https://doi.org/10.1016/S0140-6736(00)49915-0.

Pérez-Martínez, C., Prieto-Bonete, G., Pérez-Cárceles, M.D., Luna, A., 2016. Usefulness of protein analysis for detecting pathologies in bone remains. Forensic Sci. Int. 258, 68–73. Available from: https://doi.org/10.1016/j.forsciint.2015.11.009.

Prates, C., Sousa, S., Oliveira, C., Ikram, S., 2011. Prostate metastatic bone cancer in an Egyptian Ptolemaic mummy, a proposed radiological diagnosis. Int. J. Paleopathol. 1, 98–103. Available from: https://doi.org/10.1016/j.ijpp.2011.09.002.

Preston, S.H., 1995. Human mortality throughout history and prehistory. The State of Humanity. Blackwell, Oxford, pp. 30–36.

Ragsdale, B.D., Campbell, R.A., Kirkpatrick, C.L., 2018. Neoplasm or not? General principles of morphologic analysis of dry bone specimens. Int. J. Paleopathol. 21, 27–40. Available from: https://doi.org/10.1016/j.ijpp.2017.02.002.

Randall, R.L., 2015. Metastatic Bone Disease: An Integrated Approach to Patient Care. Springer.

Retief, F.P., Cilliers, L., 2011. Breast cancer in antiquity Ancient concept of tumours Breast cancer : historical overview. South. Afr. Med. J. 101, 513–515.

Riccio, I., Marcarelli, M., Del Regno, N., Fusco, C., Di Martino, M., Savarese, R., et al., 2013. Musculoskeletal Problems in Pediatric Acute Leukemia. J. Pediatr. Orthop. B 22.

Riccomi, G., Fornaciari, G., Giuffra, V., 2019. Multiple myeloma in paleopathology: a critical review. Int. J. Paleopathol. 24, 201–212. Available from: https://doi.org/10.1016/j.ijpp.2018.12.001.

Roberts, C.A., Lucy, D., Manchester, K., 1994. Inflammatory lesions of ribs: An analysis of the Terry Collection. Am. J. Phys. Anthropol. 95, 169–182. Available from: https://doi.org/10.1002/ajpa.1330950205.

Roberts, C.A., Manchester, K., 2007. The Archaeology of Disease, 3rd ed. Cornell University Press, Ithaca, New York.

Roodman, G.D., 2004. Mechanisms of bone metastasis. N. Engl. J. Med. 350, 1655–1664. Available from: https://doi.org/10.1056/NEJMra030831.

Rosenthal, D.I., 1997. Radiologic diagnosis of bone metastases. Cancer 80, 1595–1607. https://doi.org/10.1002/(SICI)1097-0142(19971015)80:8 + <1595::AID-CNCR10>3.0.CO;2-V.

Rothschild, B.M., Hershkovitz, I., Dutour, O., 1998. Clues potentially distinguishing lytic lesions of multiple myeloma from those of metastatic carcinoma. Am. J. Phys. Anthropol. 105, 241–250. https://doi.org/10.1002/(SICI)1096-8644(199802)105:2<241::AID-AJPA10>3.0.CO;2-0.

Rothschild, B.M., Hershkovitz, I., Dutour, O., Latimer, B.M., Rothschild, C., Jellema, L.M., 1997. Recognition of leukemia in skeletal remains: Report and comparison of two cases. Am. J. Phys. Anthropol. 102, 481–496. https://doi.org/10.1002/(SICI)1096-8644(199704)102:4<481::AID-AJPA5>3.0.CO;2-V.

Rothschild, B.M., Rothschild, C., 1995. Comparison of radiologic and gross examination for detection of cancer in defleshed skeletons. Am. J. Phys. Anthr. 96, 357–363. Available from: https://doi.org/10.1002/ajpa.1330960404.

Rothschild, B.M., Ruhli, F., Rothschild, C., 2002. Skeletal clues apparently distinguishing Waldenstrom's macroglobulinemia from multiple myeloma and leukemia. Am. J. Hum. Biol. 14, 532–537. Available from: https://doi.org/10.1002/ajhb.10077.

Rybak, L.D., Rosenthal, D.I., 2001. Radiological imaging for the diagnosis of bone metastases. Q. J. Nucl. Med. 45, 53–64.

Santos, A.L., Roberts, C.A., 2006. Anatomy of a serial killer: Differential diagnosis of tuberculosis based on rib lesions of adult individuals from the Coimbra identified skeletal collection, Portugal. Am. J. Phys. Anthropol. 130, 38–49. Available from: https://doi.org/10.1002/ajpa.20160.

Sawyers, C.L., 1999. Chronic myeloid leukemia. N. Engl. J. Med. 340, 1330–1340. Available from: https://doi.org/10.1056/NEJM199904293401706.

Schultz, M., Parzinger, H., Posdnjakov, D.V., Chikisheva, T.A., Schmidt-Schultz, T.H., 2007. Oldest known case of metastasizing prostate carcinoma diagnosed in the skeleton of a 2,700-year-old Scythian king from Arzhan (Siberia, Russia). Int. J. Cancer 121, 2591–2595. Available from: https://doi.org/10.1002/ijc.23073.

Šefčáková, A., Strouhal, E., Němečková, A., Thurzo, M., Staššíková-Štukovská, D., 2001. Case of metastatic carcinoma from end of the 8th–Early 9th century Slovakia. Am. J. Phys. Anthropol. 116, 216–229. Available from: https://doi.org/10.1002/ajpa.1117.

Siegel, R.L., Miller, K.D., Jemal, A., 2018. Cancer statistics, 2018. CA. Cancer J. Clin. 68, 7–30. Available from: https://doi.org/10.3322/caac.21442.

Singer, F., 2016. Paget's disease of bone, in: Endotext [Internet]. MDText. com, Inc.

Smith, M.O., 2002. A probable case of metastatic carcinoma from the late prehistoric eastern Tennessee River Valley. Int. J. Osteoarchaeol. 12, 235–247. Available from: https://doi.org/10.1002/oa.618.

Steeg, P.S., 2006. Tumor metastasis: mechanistic insights and clinical challenges. Nat. Med. 12, 895. Available from: https://doi.org/10.1038/nm1469.

Strouhal, E., 1991. Myeloma multiplex versus osteolytic metastatic carcinoma: differential diagnosis in dry bones. Int. J. Osteoarchaeol. 1, 219–224. Available from: https://doi.org/10.1002/oa.1390010314.

Strouhal, E., 1993. A case of metastatic carcinoma from Christian Sayala (Egyptian Nubia). Anthropol. Anz. 51, 97–115.

Strouhal, E., Němečková, A., 2009. History and palaeopathology of malignant tumours. Anthropol 47, 289–294.

Strouhal, E., Vhynáek, L., Horáčková, L., Bnesová, L., Nemečková, A., 1996. Two unusual benign tumours in skulls from the Ossuary at Křtiny (Czech Republic). Int. J. Osteoarchaeol. 6, 289–299. https://doi.org/10.1002/(SICI)1099-1212(199606)6:3 < 289::AID-OA272 > 3.0.CO;2-R.

Talmadge, J.E., Fidler, I.J., 2010. AACR centennial series: the biology of cancer metastasis: historical perspective. Cancer Res. 70, 5649–5669. Available from: https://doi.org/10.1158/0008-5472.can-10-1040.

Theriault, R.L., Theriault, R.L., 2012. Biology of bone metastases. Cancer Control. 19, 92–101.

Tkocz, I., Bierring, F., 1984. A medieval case of metastasizing carcinoma with multiple osteosclerotic bone lesions. Am. J. Phys. Anthr. 65, 373–380. Available from: https://doi.org/10.1002/ajpa.1330650406.

Vassiliou, V., Chow, E., Kardamakis, D., 2013. Bone metastases: a translational and clinical approach. Springer Science & Business Media.

Vilar, J., Lezana, A.H., Pedrosa, C.S., 1979. Spiculated periosteal reaction in metastatic lesions of bone. Skelet. Radiol. 3, 230–233. Available from: https://doi.org/10.1007/BF00360941.

Vincent Rajkumar, S., 2009. Multiple myeloma. Curr. Probl. Cancer 33, 7–64. Available from: https://doi.org/10.1016/j.currproblcancer.2009.01.001.

Wakely, J., Anderson, T., Carter, A., 1995. A multidisciplinarian case study of prostatic(?) carcinoma from Mediaeval Canterbury. J. Archaeol. Sci. 22, 469–477. Available from: https://doi.org/10.1006/jasc.1995.0046.

Waldron, T., 1997. A nineteenth-century case of carcinoma of the prostate, with a note on the early history of the disease. Int. J. Osteoarchaeol. 7, 241–247. https://doi.org/10.1002/(SICI)1099-1212(199705)7:3 < 241::AID-OA354 > 3.0.CO;2-2.

Waldron, T., 2008. Palaeopathology. Cambridge University Press, Cambridge, United Kingdom.

Wasterlain, S.N., Ascenso, B.F., Silva, A.M., 2011. Skeletal metastatic carcinoma: A case from 15th–20th century Coimbra. Portugal. Int. J. Osteoarchaeol. 21, 336–346. Available from: https://doi.org/10.1002/oa.1130.

Weinstein, I.B., Case, K., 2008. The history of cancer research: Introducing an AACR centennial series. Cancer Res. 68, 6861–6862. Available from: https://doi.org/10.1158/0008-5472.CAN-08-2827.

Wells, C., 1963. Ancient egyptian pathology. J. Laryngol. Otol. 77, 261–265. Available from: https://doi.org/10.1017/S0022215100060606.

World Health Organization, 2017. Cancer World Health Organization Statistics [WWW Document].

CHAPTER 7

Calcified Residues of Soft Tissue Disease

Lucie Biehler-Gomez, Emanuela Maderna and Cristina Cattaneo
LABANOF, Department of Biomedical Sciences for Health, University of Milan, Milan, Italy

The Importance of Non-Skeletal Material

It is important to remember that in the forensic anthropology practice, the analysis of skeletal remains is not limited to the examination of bones, but also includes biological remains they may be associated with. Indeed, the skeleton is not the only material useful for anthropological analyses. While forensic anthropologists are mindful of the recovery of any man-made element that may be useful in a forensic setting (e.g., clothing, weapons, jewelry, etc.), the associated and near-by soil and dirt may also contain elements of forensic value; for instance, small bones (such as phalanges, sesamoid bones, auditory ossicles, and hyoid bone), unfused epiphyses, nails, hair, teeth but also biological calcifications, and products of diseases (Fig. 7.1).

The recovery of this non-skeletal material can provide substantial additional information to the construction of the biological profile, as these elements may permit further anthropological analyses (e.g., small bones, unfused epiphyses and teeth for age-at-death and sex estimations as well as the estimation of the minimum number of individuals), serve for specific analyses (such as DNA or toxicological analyses, e.g., hair and human nails) and be indicators of advanced age (e.g., ossified cartilage) or products of pathological conditions (e.g., atherosclerotic calcification, gallstones, pleural plaques, etc.). Nonetheless, and prior to their identification, a careful and meticulous sieving of the soil and dirt associated to the skeleton is necessary for the recovery of these small and insidious elements. This may seem obvious, but it is a time-consuming exercise easy to skip. However, time and effort should be dedicated to this important step. You would be surprised at the quantity of material you can retrieve through a meticulous recovery (Box 7.1).

Interpreting Bone Lesions and Pathology for Forensic Practice. DOI: https://doi.org/10.1016/B978-0-323-85162-6.00007-6

Figure 7.1 Assembled material associated to a random skeleton of the CAL Milano Cemetery Skeletal Collection. It is important to carefully sieve the soil associated to the skeletal remains as many elements of anthropological and forensic value may be found. For instance, on this photograph, four atherosclerotic calcifications as well as a fragment of ossified costal cartilage may be seen.

Physiological Ossifications or Calcification: Ossified Cartilage

Costal cartilage allows the junction of the osseous part of the ribs to the sternum while providing a necessary degree of flexibility to the thorax for respiratory functions, movements and bending as well as shock absorption. Thyroid cartilage (from the Greek word "shield") is constituted of two laminae; it forms the main part of the anterior wall of the larynx and protects the vocal cords. Cricoid cartilage (from the Greek "ring-shaped") located inferiorly to the thyroid cartilage in the laryngeal structure, forms a ring around the trachea and functions as a site of attachment for muscles playing a role in phonation. With increasing age, these types of hyaline cartilage undergo changes in their microstructure including calcification and ossification. These changes are normal and gradual alterations associated with aging. The onset of cartilage mineralization is estimated in the second to third decade of life while ossification starts around 25 years of age and lamellar tissue is observed in individuals over 30 years (Kampen et al., 1995; Rejtarova et al., 2009).

Contrary to intramembranous ossification where bone is directly laid down in mesenchymal connective tissue, cartilage acts as a precursor for bone formation in endochondral ossification (Kusafuka et al.,

Box 7.1 How to Recover Non-skeletal Material: A Needle in a Haystack

On the scene, be mindful to collect the soil associated to the skeleton and not just the bones. Use a sieve with metal wires and small openings to sift the soil samples. It is important to sift small quantities of soil to make sure you are not missing anything. By filling the sieve with too much soil, it will not sift through the wires and you will not be able to see anything, thus defeating the purpose of the sieving. If you have large quantities of soil to go through, this make take time, but better to do it once slowly than going too fast and having to do it all over again. Be careful to separate the sieved and to-be-sieved piles of soil. Use tweezers to separate and pick elements and place them in Eppendorf or somewhere you do not risk losing them. When you are done, you may wish to clean the recovered elements to better identify them. We recommend using a small paintbrush with soft bristles. Try to remove the dirt without using water first, it is often enough to remove dirt. If you really need to, you can humidify the paintbrush with water but be careful not to damage the element. Wet biological material has a tendency to bend and break more easily. Finally, let the material dry before observation and always document it prior to processing it for destructive analyses.

2001). The mechanisms responsible for cartilage ossification are not well-understood. Histological studies have demonstrated that cartilage does indeed ossify, and that there is evidence of both perichondral and endochondral ossifications (King, 1939; Rejtarova et al., 2009). Cartilage cells experience stages of proliferation and differentiation that ultimately culminate in the mineralization of the matrix and chondrocyte hypertrophy (i.e., the cartilage becomes calcified in the hypertrophic zone) and activation of the cells' osteogenic capability (i.e., start of the ossification process). Hypertrophic chondrocytes lay down collagen type X, release matrix vesicles including alkaline phosphatase and induce vascular invasion. While matrix vesicles mediate cartilage calcification, both collagen type X and alkaline phosphatase are essential for the ossification process (Amizuka, 2012; Bahrami et al., 2001; Rejtarova et al., 2009). Kusafuka et al. (2001) described tracheal cartilage ossification process as different from endochondral ossification given that "lamellar bone tissue was directly adhered to the degraded cartilage matrix." Consequently, tracheal and costal ossifications are both physiological processes related to aging but regulated by different mechanisms and cellular pathways.

Different patterns of ossification exist depending on the ribs. Costal cartilage ossification is initiated with degenerative changes in the central area of the cartilage, but first rib cartilage ossification is a physiological process starting in the border and involving the center of the cartilage last (Rejtarova et al., 2009). Moreover, the patterns and extent of costal cartilage ossification have been studied for their potential use for sex, age, and ancestry estimations. Indeed, a study by Rejtovará and colleagues on 1044 chest and abdominal radiographs reports an association of peripheral ossification of rib cartilage with male sex with a 99.6% of probability and central ossification in women with 100% probability (Rejtarova et al., 2004). However, population affinity estimations based on costal ossification gave contradictory results and the techniques for determination of age and sex have not been considered suitable for forensic or anthropological practice (Barchilon et al., 1996). In the thyroid cartilage, the ossification pattern typically starts symmetrically at the base of the inferior horns and spreads along the posterior and inferior borders, and although the process of ossification is not always symmetrical, it tends to be bilateral. In addition, ossification process of the thyroid cartilage is similar in males and females in the early stages, but females tend to rarely show complete ossification. Correlations between thyroid cartilage ossification and population affinity are largely unexplored. Ossification of the cricoid cartilage generally occurs last in the laryngeal structure, after that of the thyroid cartilage. It begins at the superior border of the lamina and gradually spreads inferiorly and anteriorly, typically in bilateral pattern. Nonetheless, methods based on thyroid and cricoid cartilage ossification are not accurate enough to be used for age estimation in forensic settings. At best, trends of ossification of the laryngeal structure may only be used to differentiate broad age groups, such as juveniles, young adults, and middle-aged adults (Dang-Tran et al., 2010; Garvin, 2008; Ng et al., 2018).

Histologically, in ossifying costal cartilage, it is possible to observe a biphasic pattern composed of chondrocytes and osteons separated by a transitional zone, in which hypertrophic chondrocytes lost proteoglycans in their matrix and accumulated hydroxyapatite crystals that progressively formed lamellar bone tissue (Fig. 7.2). Polarized light permits the observation of mature bone formation adjacent to the cartilaginous tissue (Kampen et al., 1995; Rejtarova et al., 2009). In non-decalcified sections, the cellular details of the cartilaginous and bone components may be noted, namely chondrocytes and osteon islands (Fig. 7.3). By opposition, the cell nuclei are lost in the decalcified sections, but the zone of progressive ossification can be more clearly observed, as decalcified sections are typically thinner than undecalcified ones.

This histomorphological description is quite distinctive from other material that may be found among skeletal remains (Table 7.1). Bone is the exception, but the presence of chondrocytes clearly indicates a cartilaginous nature of the material under study.

The sections presented here were taken from cadaver-derived samples (with a postmortem interval inferior to three days) and skeletons from the CAL Milano Cemetery Skeletal Collection, buried for at least 20 years before exhumation. As you can notice, both cadaver and cemeterial samples provided similar histological pictures. This parallel indicates that regardless of the postmortem interval, the characteristic features of ossifying cartilage may be observed, even after 20 years of burial. This is particularly valuable for the identification of fragmented

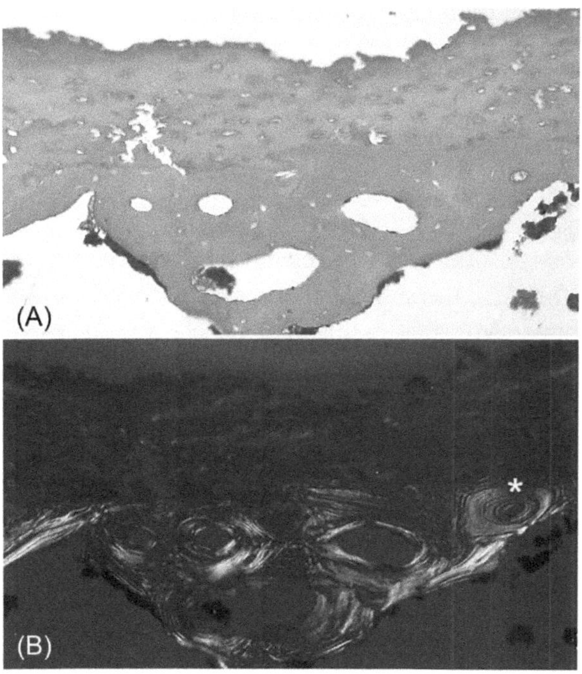

Figure 7.2 Decalcified histological sections of ossifying costal cartilage from a skeleton of the CAL Milano Cemetery Skeletal Collection. (A) unpolarized light; (B) polarized light, note the osteon (*). Magnification ×10.

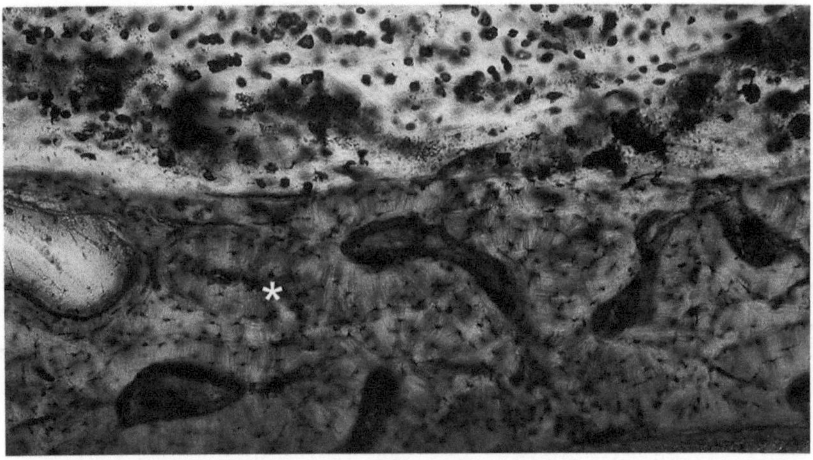

Figure 7.3 Undecalcified histological section of ossifying costal cartilage from a skeleton of the CAL Milano Cemetery Skeletal Collection. Note the osteon (*). Magnification ×10.

structures found in association with skeletal remains, as ossified costal cartilage may be recognized and identified after a long postmortem interval and may thus be distinguished macroscopically and microscopically from other non-skeletal elements that may be found in association with skeletal remains.

Traumatic Calcifications: Heterotopic Ossification

Heterotopic ossification (derived from Greek "other place") refers to a bone formation outside of the skeletal system. This osseous formation may occur in the skin, the subcutaneous tissue, muscles or in fibrous tissue adjacent to joints. Myositis ossificans, the commonly used term for the condition, is in fact a misnomer—it implies an initial inflammatory process and a specific muscle involvement, whereas heterotopic ossification encompasses larger clinical manifestations. Although the etiology of the condition is unknown, the pathogenesis of the heterotopic ossification starts with an inciting event, typically a localized trauma (identified in about 60%–75% of cases, in the remaining cases the trauma may have gone unnoticed such as microtrauma or repetitive mechanical stress). An influx of inflammatory cells migrates to the site of injury and sends a signal activating the differentiation of mesenchymal cells into osteoblasts and chondroblasts in a permissive environment, conducive to the production of heterotopic bone. Histologically, this heterotopic bone formed via intramembranous and endochondral pathways is indistinguishable from callus formation of a

Table 7.1 Differential diagnosis of non-skeletal material.

		Macroscopic features	Microscopic features	References
Human bone		Cortical and trabecular structures of the bone tissue	Organized structures in Haversian systems (central canal enclosed by cylindrical lamellae)	Hillier and Bell (2007)
Plastic		Synthetic aspect	Polymers (repeated units) organized in lamellae and spherulites in flow or Maltese cross patterns	Sawyer et al. (2008)
Ossified cartilage		Thick brown structure, flat or multilobular, similar to bone	Biphasic pattern with chondrocytes and osteons separated by a transition zone	Kampen et al. (1995); Rejtarova et al. (2009)
Biological calcifications	Heterotopic ossification	Irregular shape with a smooth outer cortex of variable size	Well circumscribed, with a surrounding fibrous pseudocapsule and thick-walled blood vessels; woven bone with prominent osteoblastic cell lining is characteristic; advanced lesions resemble bone	DiMaio and Francis (2001); Meyers et al. (2019)
	Leiomyoma	Ovoid mass with a smooth irregular surface	Smooth muscle cells with varying amounts of fibrous connective tissue	Baud and Kramar (1991); Murase et al. (1999)
	Ovarian cyst	Round mass with possible vascular impressions	Cyst wall made up of a laminated membrane lined by germinal epithelium producing scoleces with hooklets	Komar and Buikstra (2003); Özdemir et al. (2015)
	Mesenteric cyst	Relatively small ovoid mass	Lined with a single layer of columnar or cuboidal epithelial cells with microvilli and desmosomes; contains inflammatory and fibrin-hemorrhagic materials	Komar and Buikstra (2003); Özdemir et al. (2015); Pinotti et al. (2018)
	Calcified lymph node	Ovoid mass with numerous perforations, eggshell appearance	Fibrillar structure	Baud and Kramar (1991); Komar and Buikstra (2003)
	Hydatid cyst	Ovoid and hollow concretion irregular externally and smooth internally	Bilayered and surrounded by fibroblasts, mononuclear cells, eosinophils and multinucleated giant cells	Baud and Kramar, 1991; Fatnassi et al. (2017)
	Biological stones	Round, oval, multilobular or polyedric shape with a smooth, porous or	Laminar concentric rings of organized matrix with an orderly layered deposition of minerals	Abboud (2008); Biehler-Gomez et al. (2019a); Steinbock (1990b, 1990a); Stoller et al. (1994)

(Continued)

Table 7.1 (Continued)

		Macroscopic features	Microscopic features	References
		rough texture. Various colors and sizes.		
	Aortic valve calcification	Small nodules of calcification	Different grading of aortic valve calcification and structural damage in the fibrosa, spongiosa, and ventricularis layers	Demer and Tintut (2008); Mosch et al. (2017)
	Phlebolith	Small round mass	Calcified thrombus with a concentric pattern of mineralization, surrounded by granulation tissue and small capillaries under a hyaline layer	Armentano et al. (2012); Gouvêa Lima et al. (2015); Nagaraja et al. (2016); Saha et al. (2015)
	Tunica media calcification	Long and thin cylindrical calcifications (non-lumen obstructive)	At early stage, irregular deposits within the media; later stage calcifications may distort the media layer junctions and undergo osseous metaplasia resulting in true bony trabeculae	Biehler-Gomez et al. (2019a); Lanzer et al. (2014)
	Tunica intima calcification	Convex-concave plaques with a stratified structure and a pale yellow to brown coloration	Stratified layers of fibrous tissue with « ghosts » of macrophages foam cells, lipid cholesterol cleft and calcification core	Ababneh et al. (2014); Biehler-Gomez et al. (2018b), (2018a); Stary et al. (1995)
	Pleural plaque	Thin and flat plaques of various dimensions with a yellowish color	Acellular tissue, parallel bands of avascular and hyaline collagen with sporadic spindle-shaped fibroblasts	Hourihane et al. (1966); Roberts (1971)
	Calcified ovary	Ovoid mass with possible vascular impressions	Either a fine-sand-like calcification pattern located in the necrotic material within cystic structures, or a solid and laminar calcification pattern located in the wall or the septum	Komar and Buikstra (2003); Okada et al. (2005); Russel (1979); Wen et al. (2018)
	Psammoma body	Grain of sand size	Concentric lamellated and calcified structures	Das (2009); Komar and Buikstra (2003); Özdemir et al. (2015)
Botanic elements		Roots, stems, seeds and leaves	Unique features such as stomata, vein patterns and trichome shapes	Coyle et al. (2014)
Geological stones		Solid and hard mass	Inorganic mineral compounds with a closed-packed crystal structure and no cellular organization	Craig et al. (1994)

healing fracture. It is constituted of woven bone gradually replaced by mature lamellar bone, at which point the heterotopic process cannot be differentiated from normal skeletal tissue. The condition typically occurs in young adults (about the second to third decade of life), although it may affect individuals of all ages, and is more common in males (male-to-female ratio of 3:2). Contributing factors include hypercalcemia, tissue hypoxia, prolonged immobilization or mobility after a prolonged immobilization as well as bone-forming conditions such as ankylosing spondylitis, osteoarthritis, and DISH.

Five clinical settings have been described: (1) genetic heterotopic ossification: due to fibrodysplasia ossificans progressiva and progressive osseous heteroplasia, which are excessively rare conditions inducing a progressive spontaneous soft-tissue ossification; (2) post-traumatic heterotopic ossification, occurring secondary to a localized traumatic tissue injury, fracture or dislocation (up to 30% of patients with a dislocation); (3) neurogenic heterotopic ossification: following a head or spinal cord trauma (up to 50% of patients with a spinal cord trauma) or a long coma; (4) post-surgical heterotopic ossification, secondary to an orthopedic surgery (up to 40% of patients with a total hip arthroplasty); and (5) in hands and feet, subsequent to a high-energy trauma. In severe traumatic amputations, heterotopic ossification is seen in over 90% of patients. In addition, the extra-skeletal bone formation can occur in severe burns (about 20% of patients with third degree burns). The bone formation may involve any location in the body although it is more common in sites susceptible to trauma such as the elbow, thigh, pelvis, shoulder, head and neck as well as the fingers. Clinical symptoms include localized pain, tenderness, swelling, with complications ranging from a decreased range of motion to nerve or blood vessel impingement. On radiographs, the lesion is seen as a well-demarcated radiodense mass with a calcified outline referred to as "eggshell calcification." In advanced cases, heterotopic ossification may lead to the ankylosis of the joint. The main differential diagnosis of the condition is osteosarcoma but the latter lacks bone "maturation", the characteristic feature of heterotopic ossification (Bossche and Vanderstraeten, 2005; McCarthy and Sundaram, 2005; Meyers et al., 2019).

Neoplastic Calcifications

A leiomyoma is a benign tumor of smooth muscle. Although it may be found in any organ, it is most common in the uterus (also known as uterine fibroids), esophagus and small bowel. On gross examination, leiomyomata appear as spherical or lobular masses with necrotic centers and a smooth but irregular external surface. On decalcified sections, a fibrillar texture may be observed (Baud and Kramar, 1991; Cole et al., 2015).

Ovarian cysts are fluid-filled cysts that may be non-neoplastic (i.e., follicle cysts, corpus luteum cysts and endometriotic cysts), benign neoplastic (e.g., endometriomas and dermoid cysts) or rarely, malignant neoplastic (e.g., serous cystadenocarcinoma) (Khan et al., 2009). Non-neoplastic ovarian cysts are typically less than 5 cm in diameter and may show vascular impressions. Dermoid cysts may occur in various locations such as the brain, face, scrotum, pharynx, vagina, and ovary. They are teratomas, a type of germ cell tumor that may contain several different types of tissue. Thus macroscopically, they appear as masses of various shape and size (typically over 6 cm diameter), with a usually thin outer calcification, containing hair, teeth or bone (Armentano et al., 2012; Komar and Buikstra, 2003; Waters-Rist et al., 2014).

Mesenteric cysts are uncommon tumors occurring in the mesentery (i.e., a double fold of peritoneal tissue that attaches and maintains the small intestine and large intestine to the posterior abdominal wall) of the gastrointestinal tract. They are relatively small and ovoid masses that may clinically be either benign or malignant.

Infectious Calcifications

Calcified lymph nodes are a common occurrence in tuberculosis infection, although they may also be seen in metastatic cancer, sarcoidosis, rheumatoid arthritis, systemic sclerosis and fungal infections. The nodes most commonly involved are the submandibular lymph nodes as well as the superficial and deep cervical lymph nodes (Gunduz et al., 2014). Tuberculosis may also cause calcified pleura and calcified granulomas in the lungs. Macroscopically, calcified lymph nodes are small (less than 2–3 cm in diameter) ovoid masses with numerous perforations and nodules surrounded by a thin fibrous capsule (less than 2 mm thick) in an "eggshell" appearance. Histologically, they show a fibrillar structure (Baud and Kramar, 1991; Waters-Rist et al., 2014).

Hydatidosis is a parasitic infection caused by tapeworm of the *Echinococcus granulosus* species. Hydatid disease is endemic in South America, Central Asia, and the Mediterranean basin. Human's infection is accidental and results from an egg ingestion. Cysts are mainly found in the liver and lungs; they may contain daughter cysts, grow about 1 cm per year and may reach a size ranging 1–20 cm in diameter. On gross examination, hydatid cysts are hollow ovoid concretions with a smooth internal surface and an irregular external surface. Although often univesicular, they may be multichambered if they present daughter cysts. In thin sections, collagen fibers may be seen as well as mononuclear cells, eosinophils and multinucleated giant cells (Baud and Kramar, 1991; Fatnassi et al., 2017; Vicidomini et al., 2007; Waters-Rist et al., 2014).

Biological Stones

Stones can be divided into two categories: gallstones (cholelithiasis) and urinary stones (urolithiasis), which include stones from the bladder, kidneys and/or ureter (Kim et al., 2003; Knoll, 2010). These biological stones result from bacterial infections and/or secondary to alterations in the composition of the gallbladder bile or urine (Carey, 1993; Coe et al., 1992; Johnston and Kaplan, 1993; Knoll, 2010; Knoll et al., 2011).

Stones can be classified by composition, morphology, anatomical location or original formation site. Urinary stones include calcium oxalate, calcium phosphate, uric acid, struvite, and cystine stones. The incidence of primary bladder stones (cystolithiasis) has substantially decreased over the past three decades, whereas that of renal stones (nephrolithiasis) simultaneously increased due to genetic, dietary and environmental factors. Gallstones are typically classified based on their major component: cholesterol stones rich in cholesterol, as opposed to pigment stones rich in calcium bilirubinate, phosphate, and carbonate, later subdivided into black and brown pigment stones. Cholelithiasis is more common in females whereas urolithiasis is most commonly seen in males, typically in adults and the elderly (Abboud, 2008; Kim et al., 2003; Moe, 2006; Womack et al., 1963).

Morphological features of the cross-sectional surface of stones (including the presence of crystals or an amorphous structure, radiating, and/or concentric/laminated layers) can reflect their chemical composition and permit their recognition and classification. The macroscopic and microscopic study of these biological stones based on preserved collections of extracted stones from clinical cases or well-preserved cadavers during autopsies (Biehler-Gomez et al., 2019; Kim et al., 2003; Steinbock, 1990a,

1990b; Womack et al., 1963) as well as their chemical analysis (Abboud, 2008; Ashok et al., 2003; Athanasiadou et al., 2013; Chandran et al., 2007; Gault and Chafe, 2000) permits the documentation of known biological stones. By comparison with some reference differential diagnoses of soft tissue calcifications (Baud and Kramar, 1991; Komar and Buikstra, 2003), these known data allowed for the diagnosis of biological stones in skeletonized cases (Anderson, 2001; Giuffra et al., 2008; Jaskowiec et al., 2017; Özdemir et al., 2015).

Biological stones are a common occurrence in modern populations and yet, they are rarely found in skeletonized cases. Indeed, in dry bone, without mummification of tissues or the recovery of stones *in situ* near the location of the gallbladder, ureter or kidney, it is difficult to recognize them and identify them with certainty.

Stones can appear macroscopically in large range of shapes, sizes and colors (Fig. 7.4, Table 7.1). They may assume a round, oval, multilobular, or even polygonal shape, with sizes ranging from a few millimeters to several centimeters in diameter. The texture of the external surface can be smooth, porous, or rough, with a large array of coloration varying from grey, shades of white and red, yellow, brown, black to even green. This variation may be explained by the fact that the external color of stones can change after drying (Kim et al., 2003). Histological observations reflect their cross-sectional morphology: different patterns can be observed, namely radiating, concentric or laminated, and amorphous structures (Figs. 7.5 and 7.6). The first two structures can appear combined (i.e., in two distinct layers) or mixed (i.e., superimposed). Typically, when crystals are present, they appear either clustered in the center of the stone or covering the entire surface of the section (Biehler-Gomez et al., 2019; Kim et al., 2003; Steinbock, 1990a,b).

Vascular Calcifications

Aortic valve leaflets, through systole and diastole mechanisms, allow the blood to flow in the right direction and prevent regurgitation (i.e., retrograde flow). The calcification of aortic valves is an active and multifactorial process manifesting as calcified nodules in the aortic valve leaflets and impairing leaflet flexibility. Aortic valve calcification can lead to aortic valve stenosis, a condition present in 2%–7% of the population over 65 years of age (Stewart et al., 1997; Towler, 2008).

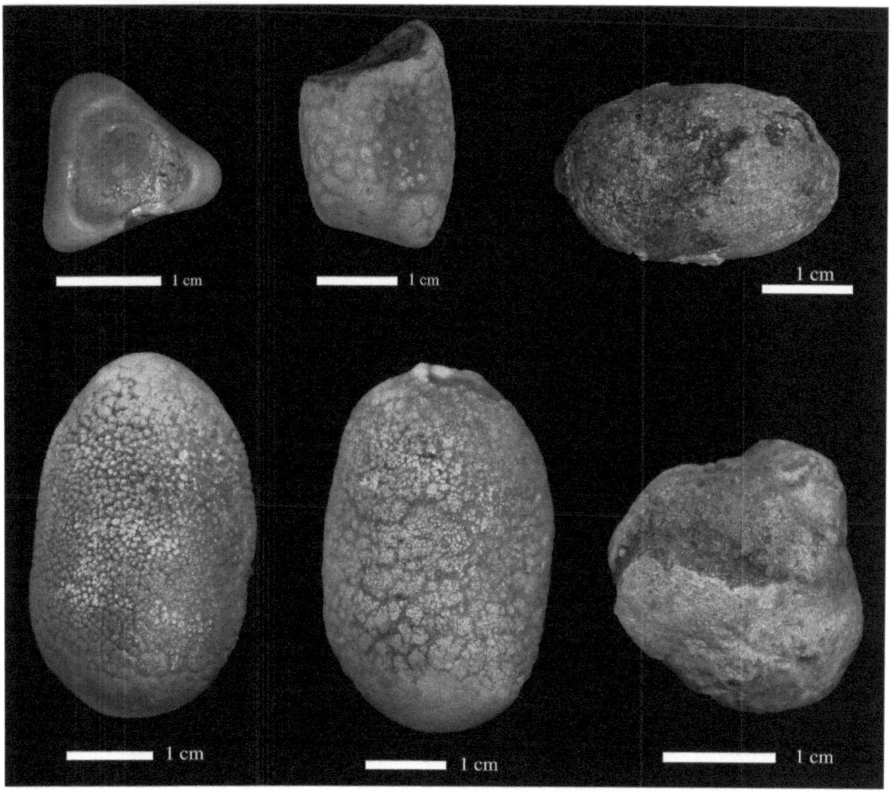

Figure 7.4 Gallstones extracted from well-preserved cadavers during autopsies at the medico-legal institute of Milan in accordance with mortuary regulations and "aged" by maceration. Note the varying external morphology of gallstones. Reproduced with permission from Biehler-Gomez, L., Maderna, E., Brescia, G., Cappella, A., Rizzi, A., Cattaneo, C., 2019. "Aged" autopsy gallstones simulating dry bone context: A morphological, histological and SEM-EDS analysis. Int. J. Paleopathol. 24, 60–65. https://doi.org/10.1016/j.ijpp.2018.09.004.

Phleboliths (meaning "vein stones") are calcified thrombi within blood vessels (in other words, calcifications of blood clots). They may be caused by a vessel injury (in the intima layer) or a stagnation of the blood flow. Phleboliths are constituted of calcium carbonate and phosphate salts and develop progressively resulting in a characteristic concentric ring or onion-like structure. They are small masses and may appear radiolucent in the center (which allows their distinction from urolithiasis when found in the abdomen) or radiodense on radiographs (Gouvêa Lima et al., 2015; Mandel and Perrino, 2010; Nagaraja et al., 2016).

Medial artery calcification, also known as "Mönckeberg's mediasclerosis" or "Mönckeberg's mediacalcinosis" (Mönckeberg, 1903) originates in the muscle layer or tunica media of the artery. Medial artery

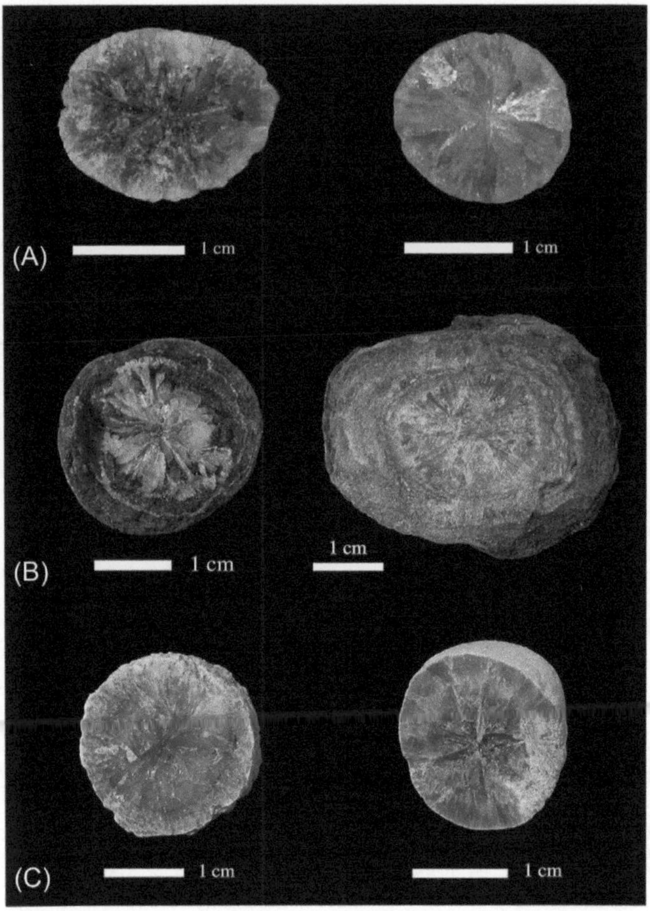

Figure 7.5 Cholesterol gallstones (cut surfaces). (A) pure cholesterol stones, note the radiating pattern from the center; (B) combination cholesterol stones, note the two distinct layers with a center of cholesterol and the external crown of pigment; (C) mixed cholesterol stones, note the superposition of the radiating and concentric patterns. Reproduced with permission from Biehler-Gomez, L., Maderna, E., Brescia, G., Cappella, A., Rizzi, A., Cattaneo, C., 2019. "Aged" autopsy gallstones simulating dry bone context: A morphological, histological and SEM-EDS analysis. Int. J. Paleopathol. 24, 60–65. https://doi.org/10.1016/j.ijpp.2018.09.004.

calcification is more commonly encountered in the abdominal aorta, aortic arch, popliteal and peroneal arteries as well as the tibial and femoral arteries and leads to increased arterial wall stiffness as well as reduced compliance of the vessel (Mönckeberg, 1903). The condition is associated to type II diabetes mellitus, chronic kidney disease, increased lower extremity amputation, and cardiovascular morbidity and mortality. On gross examination, medial artery calcifications can be seen as circumferential and contiguous calcifications (in other

Figure 7.6 Undecalcified histological sections of gallstones. Magnification ×*4. Left: note the cholesterol crystals deposited in a disorganized fashion; middle: central aspect with a radial structure and the periphery organized in concentric layers with varying coloration; right: superposition of radial and concentric layers over the entire surface of the section.* Reproduced with permission from Biehler-Gomez, L., Maderna, E., Brescia, G., Cappella, A., Rizzi, A., Cattaneo, C., 2019. "Aged" autopsy gallstones simulating dry bone context: A morphological, histological and SEM-EDS analysis. Int. J. Paleopathol. 24, 60–65. https://doi.org/10.1016/j.ijpp.2018.09.004.

words, long cylinders) and do not obstruct the lumen of the artery (Fig. 7.7). Despite the fragility of their structure, they may be recovered in clothing of forensic cases (Fig. 7.8).

Intimal artery calcification or atherosclerosis is a progressive, chronic, pro-inflammatory, and fibroproliferative condition responsible for plaque formation in the intima layer of the walls of large and medium-sized arteries (Falk, 2006; Lusis, 2000). With time, the lesion calcifies in a process akin to bone formation (Falk, 2006; Glass and Witztum, 2001; Libby, 2003; Lusis, 2000). Luminal narrowing, thickening of an arterial wall, and atheromatous findings may be visualized through ultrasonography, x-ray angiography, angioscopy, computed tomography, thermal imaging, and best of all, magnetic resonance imaging (Fayad and Fuster, 2001).

As these artery calcifications are the direct product of the vascular conditions, their recovery and identification can constitute "surrogate markers" for their diagnosis (Doherty et al., 2003). Interestingly in forensic sciences, their calcified properties enable them to survive the decomposition processes. Indeed, although intimal and medial artery calcifications are conditions of soft tissues, evidence of the disease may be found in skeletonized remains. Subirana-Domènech et al. (2012) reported the finding of a long cylindrical calcification in the clothing of a forensic case and raised the problem of their macroscopic recognition given the lack of literature on dry bone. Later, Binder and Roberts (2014) demonstrated the presence of atherosclerosis at least 3000 years ago from the recovery of atherosclerotic calcifications associated to skeletal remains buried in Amara West, Sudan (1300 – 1800

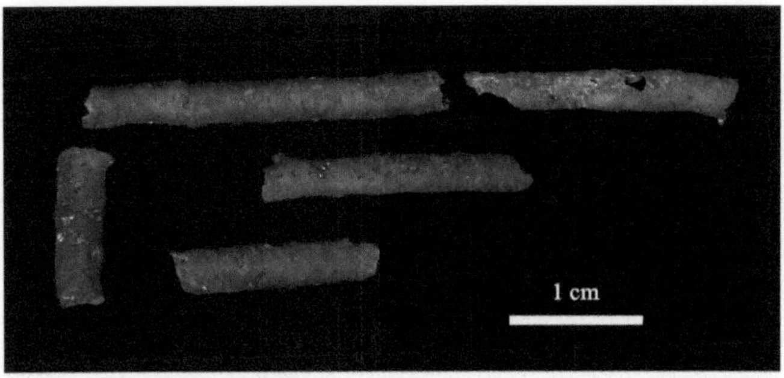

Figure 7.7 Medial artery calcifications collected in the tights of skeleton #298 of the CAL Milano Cemetery Skeletal Collection with a clinical diagnosis of coronaropathy. Reproduced with permission from Biehler-Gomez, L., Cappella, A., Castoldi, E., Martrille, L., Cattaneo, C., 2018. Survival of Atherosclerotic Calcifications in Skeletonized Material: Forensic and Pathological Implications. J. Forensic Sci. 63, 386–394. https://doi.org/10.1111/1556-4029.13592.

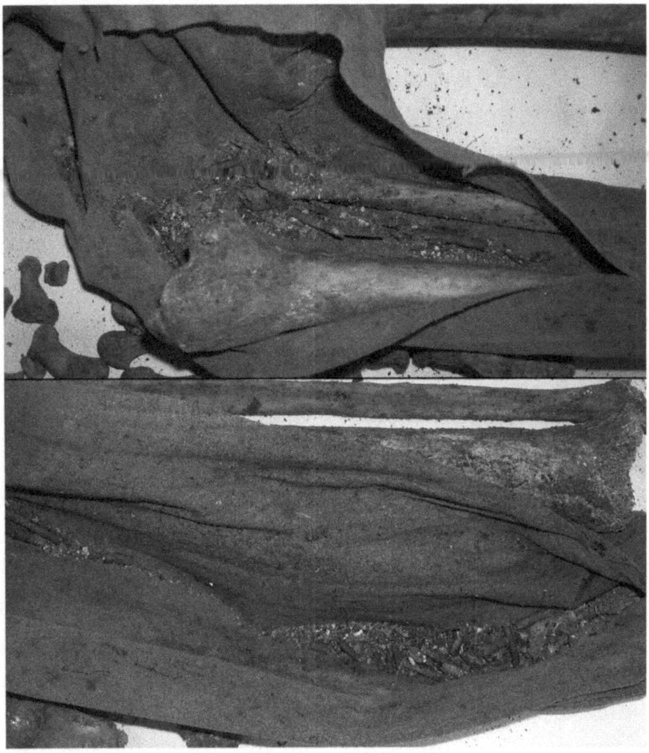

Figure 7.8 In situ *finding of medial artery calcifications in the tights of skeleton #298 of the CAL Milano Cemetery Skeletal Collection.* Reproduced with permission from Biehler-Gomez, L., Cappella, A., Castoldi, E., Martrille, L., Cattaneo, C., 2018. Survival of Atherosclerotic Calcifications in Skeletonized Material: Forensic and Pathological Implications. J. Forensic Sci. 63, 386–394. https://doi.org/10.1111/1556-4029.13592.

BCE). Biehler-Gomez et al. (2018a) performed a study on 24 skeletal remains of the CAL Milano Cemetery Skeletal Collection (including 12 individuals who died of a vasculopathy) and found a total of 205 medial artery calcifications in tights and socks and 293 intimal artery calcifications identified by comparison with atherosclerotic calcifications from autopsy cases (gold standard), demonstrating the possibility to find and identify these fragile markers of disease if sufficient care is given to their recovery.

As a result, atherosclerotic calcifications are pale yellow to brown convex-concave plaques constituted of superimposed layers (Fig. 7.9). They possess a smooth concave luminal surface modeled by the continuous passage of the blood flow and a stratified convex surface caused by a successive calcification process over time from the tunica media of the artery (Biehler-Gomez et al., 2018b) (Fig. 7.10). Histological thin sections show a concentric layered structure consistent with the pathological etiology of atherosclerotic plaques and literature description of soft tissue samples (Ababneh et al., 2014; Stary et al., 1995; van Engelen et al., 2013; Virmani et al., 2000). In particular, decalcified section permit the observation of the arterial layers surrounding a lipid-rich tissue with calcified core and cholesterol crystals; the lipid cholesterol cleft and foaming macrophages remain as "ghosts" or imprints in the structure of the plaques (Fig. 7.11). Medial artery calcifications can be distinguished from calcifications of the tunica intima as the characteristic histological features of the latter (i.e., calcium phosphate crystals in cholesterol-rich lesions and "ghosts" of macrophages foam cells) are absent in the pathogenesis of the former (Yoshida et al., 2011).

As Aufderheide and Rodríguez-Martín (1998, p. 79) suggest: "Awareness of these lesions' appearance combined with careful excavation can be expected to identify these conditions much more regularly in the future." However, evidence of arterial calcifications in dry bone remains rarely reported (Binder and Roberts, 2014; Subirana-Domènech et al., 2012).

Other Biological Calcifications

In the literature, pleural plaques are described as ivory-like, discrete, raised, irregularly shaped, and sharply circumscribed lesions of varying

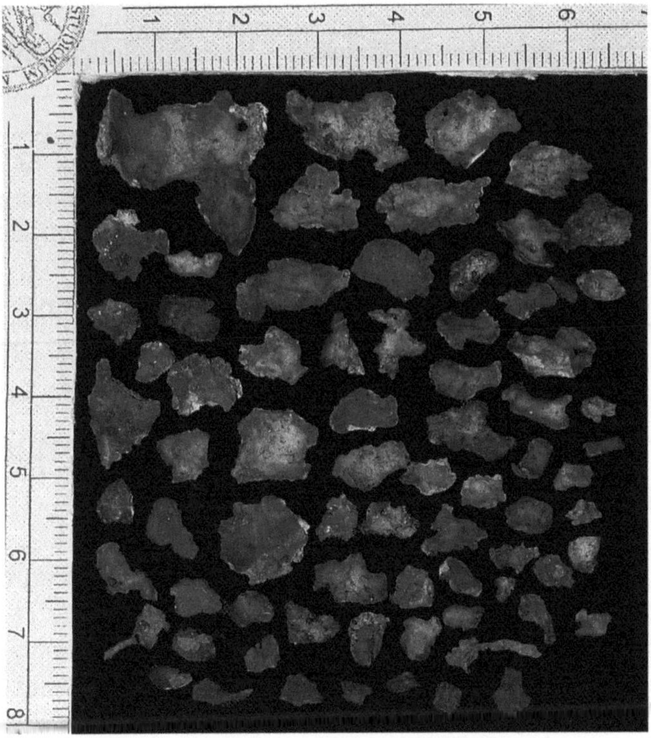

Figure 7.9 Intimal artery calcifications found in skeleton #403 of the CAL Milano Cemetery Skeletal Collection with a clinical diagnosis of arterial hypertension.

size and smooth or coarse texture, generally localized on the parietal pleura of the lateral chest wall, diaphragm or mediastinum (Clarke et al., 2006; Gevenois et al., 1998; Hourihane et al., 1966; Roberts, 1971). They are non-cancerous, most often asymptomatic lesions that do not require treatment but they are associated with a higher risk of pleural mesothelioma, pulmonary fibrosis, and lung cancer (Hillerdal, 1994). The accepted consensus in the scientific community is that pleural plaques are specific indicators of long term asbestos exposure (after a latency of about 20–30 years), especially if bilateral (Clarke et al., 2006; Gevenois et al., 1998). Indeed, scientific studies have shown an existing relation between the increased number of asbestos bodies in the lungs and the probability to develop pleural plaques (Roberts, 1971). However, the presence of pleural plaques does not categorically prove a past asbestos exposure as other factors may cause their formation. In particular, pulmonary tuberculosis and trauma (e.g., rib fractures and hemothorax) may lead to pleural plaques, typically

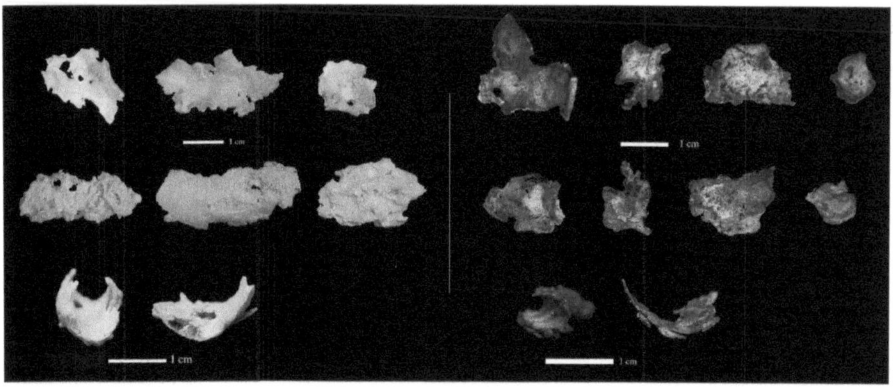

Figure 7.10 Morphology of atherosclerotic calcifications. Left: plaques extracted from well-preserved cadavers during autopsies at the medico-legal institute of Milan in accordance with mortuary regulations and macerated for several weeks; right: plaques found among the skeletal remains of individuals from the CAL Milano Cemetery Skeletal Collection. Top row: luminal view, note the smooth internal surface for the lumen of the artery; middle row: external view, note the superimposed layers of calcifications that give the stratified structure to the plaque; bottom row: transverse view, note the convex-concave shape of the plaques. Reproduced with permission from Biehler-Gomez, L., Maderna, E., Brescia, G., Caruso, V., Rizzi, A., Cattaneo, C., 2018. Distinguishing atherosclerotic calcifications in dry bone: implications for forensic identification. J. Forensic Sci. 64, 839–844. https://doi.org/10.1111/1556-4029.13948.

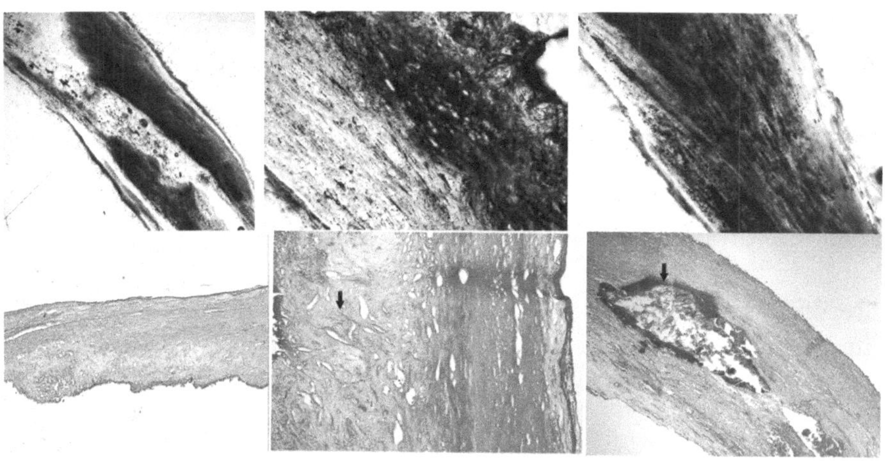

Figure 7.11 Histological sections illustrating the stratified structure of atherosclerotic calcifications (top row: undecalcified sections, bottom row: decalcified sections stained in Hematoxylin and Eosin) with "ghosts" elements (black arrow, bottom middle) and calcification core (black arrow, bottom right). Magnification ×1 (left), ×4 (middle), ×10 (right). Reproduced with permission from Biehler-Gomez, L., Maderna, E., Brescia, G., Caruso, V., Rizzi, A., Cattaneo, C., 2018. Distinguishing atherosclerotic calcifications in dry bone: implications for forensic identification. J. Forensic Sci. 64, 839–844. https://doi.org/10.1111/1556-4029.13948.

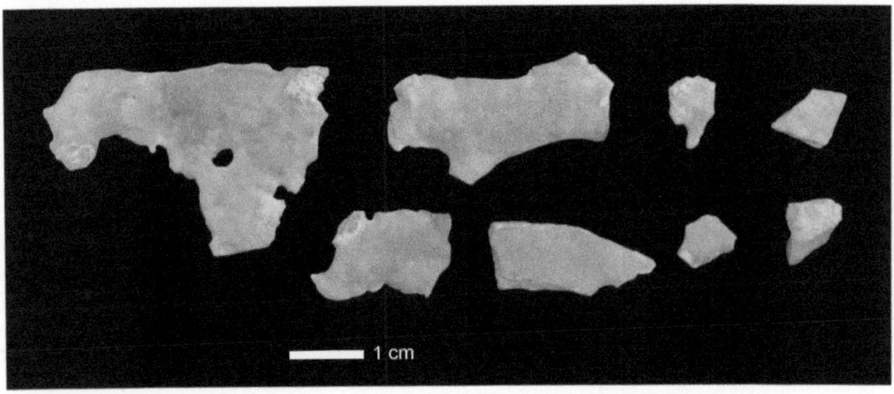

Figure 7.12 Calcifications recovered from a macerated pleural plaque extracted from a well-preserved cadaver during autopsy at the medico-legal institute of Milan, in accordance with mortuary regulations.

Figure 7.13 Undecalcified thin section of a pleural plaque showing mineralized matrix, magnification × 10.

unilaterally. Ankylosing spondylitis (two cases), calcifying fibrous pseudotumor, and scleroderma (one case each) are medical conditions that have been described in cases with pleural plaques and fibers exposure. In particular erionite (i.e., a rare naturally occurring zeolite), silicates, and man-made vitreous fibers have been found in epidemiological studies to be related to higher incidence of pleural plaques (Anton, 1967; Clarke et al., 2006).

Pleural plaques appear macroscopically as thin and flat plaques of various sizes with a yellowish color. Histological decalcification allows the observation of the microscopic structure that constitutes the non-mineralized matrix of the plaque—pleural plaques are generally acellular, formed of laminated dense bands of avascular and hyaline collagen, deposited parallel to the surface of the plaque. The only detectable cellular component is the presence of sporadic spindle-shaped fibroblasts. In addition, asbestos bodies may be seen. The demarcation between the plaque and the pleura is clearly identifiable. Below the plaque, adipose tissue with vascular structures and an important population of lymphocytes and plasma cells can be noted.

The thin sections presented here (Figs. 7.12–7.14) come from two pleural plaques (bilateral calcification—one pleural plaque was harder than the other, indicating advanced calcification) collected in situ during the autopsy of an unidentified male over 65 years of age at the medico-legal institute of Milan, who died at the hospital following a cerebral stroke and a terminal pulmonary edema.

Ovarian calcification is a dystrophic mechanism that may be found in tumors (e.g., mature teratoma and mucinous cystadenoma). Two types may be distinguished: psammomatous, characterized by the presence of psammoma bodies (which may be indicative of an ovarian tumor), and non-psammomatous. Psammoma bodies are small (size of

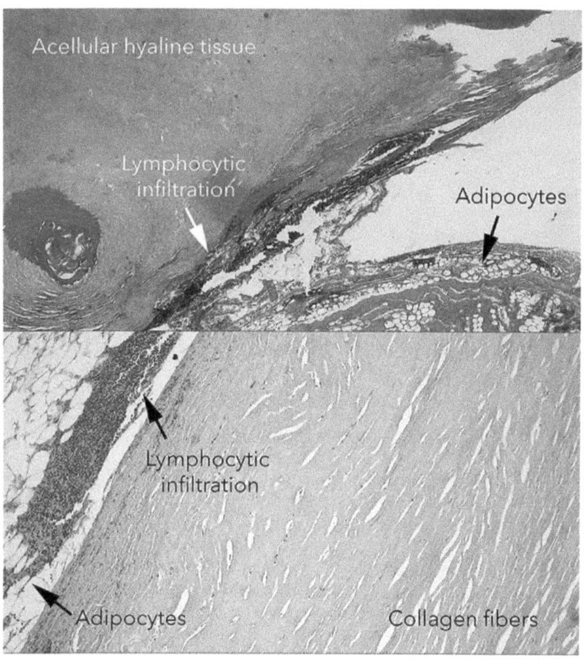

Figure 7.14 Decalcified thin sections of both pleural plaques (top: harder plaque) showing mineralized matrix, magnification × 10.

a grain of sand) dystrophic calcifications with a lamellated concentric structure. Thus, psammomatous ovarian calcifications present an onion-like appearance due to the concentric lamination, whereas non-psammomatous calcifications are irregular, dense and non-laminated. On gross observation, calcified ovaries are small (1.5 – 4 cm in diameter), ovoid and amorphous masses with vascular impressions (Das, 2009; Komar and Buikstra, 2003; Okada et al., 2005; Russel, 1979; Waters-Rist et al., 2014; Wen et al., 2018).

References

Ababneh, B., Rejjal, L., Pokharel, Y., Nambi, V., Wang, X., Tung, C.-H., et al., 2014. Distribution of calcification in carotid endarterectomy tissues: comparison of micro-computed tomography imaging with histology. Vasc. Med. 19, 343–350. Available from: https://doi.org/10.1177/1358863X14549270.

Abboud, I.A., 2008. Mineralogy and chemistry of urinary stones: patients from North Jordan. Environ. Geochem. Health 30, 445–463. Available from: https://doi.org/10.1007/s10653-007-9128-7.

Amizuka, N., 2012. Histology of epiphyseal cartilage calcification and endochondral ossification. Front. Biosci. E4, 2085. Available from: https://doi.org/10.2741/526.

Anderson, T., 2001. A recently discovered mediaeval bladder stone from Norwich, with a review of British archaeological bladder stones and documentary evidence for their treatment. BJU Int. 88, 351–354. Available from: https://doi.org/10.1046/j.1464-410X.2001.02298.x.

Anton, H.C., 1967. Multiple pleural plaques. Br. J. Radiol. 40, 685–690. Available from: https://doi.org/10.1259/0007-1285-40-477-685.

Armentano, N., Subirana, M., Isidro, A., Escala, O., Malgosa, A., 2012. An ovarian teratoma of late Roman age. Int. J. Paleopathol. 2, 236–239. Available from: https://doi.org/10.1016/j.ijpp.2012.11.003.

Ashok, M., Rautray, T.R., Nayak, P.K., Vijayan, V., Jayanthi, V., Narayana Kalkura, S., 2003. Energy dispersive X-ray fluorescence analysis of gallstones. J. Radioanal. Nucl. Chem. 257, 333–335. Available from: https://doi.org/10.1023/A:1024735930031.

Athanasiadou, D., Godelitsas, A., Sokaras, D., Karydas, A.-G., Dotsika, E., Potamitis, C., et al., 2013. New insights into the chemical and isotopic composition of human-body biominerals. I: cholesterol gallstones from England and Greece. J. Trace Elem. Med. Biol. 27, 79–84. Available from: https://doi.org/10.1016/j.jtemb.2012.08.004.

Aufderheide, A.C., Rodríguez-Martín, C., 1998. The Cambridge Encyclopedia of Human Paleopathology. Cambridge University Press, Cambridge, United Kingdom.

Bahrami, S., Plate, U., Dreier, R., DuChesne, A., Willital, G.H., Bruckner, P., 2001. Endochondral ossification of costal cartilage is arrested after chondrocytes have reached hypertrophic stage of late differentiation. Matrix Biol. 19, 707–715.

Barchilon, V., Hershkovitz, I., Rothschild, B.M., Wish-Baratz, S., Latimer, B.M., Jellema, L.M., et al., 1996. Factors affecting the rate and pattern of the first costal cartilage ossification. Am. J. Forensic Med. Pathol. 17, 239–247. Available from: https://doi.org/10.1097/00000433-199609000-00012.

Baud, C.-A., Kramar, C., 1991. Soft tissue calcifications in paleopathology. In: Ortner, D.J., Aufderheide, A.C. (Eds.), Human Paleopathology: Current Syntheses and Future Options. Smithsonian Institution Press, Washington, DC, pp. 257–260.

Biehler-Gomez, L., Cappella, A., Castoldi, E., Martrille, L., Cattaneo, C., 2018a. Survival of atherosclerotic calcifications in skeletonized material: forensic and pathological implications. J. Forensic Sci. 63, 386–394. Available from: https://doi.org/10.1111/1556-4029.13592.

Biehler-Gomez, L., Maderna, E., Brescia, G., Cappella, A., Rizzi, A., Cattaneo, C., 2019. "Aged" autopsy gallstones simulating dry bone context: a morphological, histological and SEM-EDS analysis. Int. J. Paleopathol. 24, 60–65. Available from: https://doi.org/10.1016/j.ijpp.2018.09.004.

Biehler-Gomez, L., Maderna, E., Brescia, G., Caruso, V., Rizzi, A., Cattaneo, C., 2018b. Distinguishing atherosclerotic calcifications in dry bone: implications for forensic identification. J. Forensic Sci. 64, 839–844. Available from: https://doi.org/10.1111/1556-4029.13948.

Binder, M., Roberts, C.A., 2014. Calcified structures associated with human skeletal remains: possible atherosclerosis affecting the population buried at Amara West, Sudan. (1300–800 BC). Int. J. Paleopathol. 6, 20–29. Available from: https://doi.org/10.1016/j.ijpp.2014.03.003.

Bossche, L. Vanden, Vanderstraeten, G., 2005. Heterotopic ossification: a review. J. Rehabil. Med. 37, 129–136. Available from: https://doi.org/10.1080/16501970510027628.

Carey, M.C., 1993. Pathogenesis of gallstones. Am. J. Surg. 165, 410–419. Available from: https://doi.org/10.1016/S0002-9610(05)80932-8.

Chandran, P., Kuchhal, N.K., Garg, P., Pundir, C.S., 2007. An extended chemical analysis of gallstone. Indian. J. Clin. Biochem. 22, 145–150. Available from: https://doi.org/10.1007/BF02913334.

Clarke, C.C., Mowat, F.S., Kelsh, M.A., Roberts, M.A., 2006. Pleural plaques: a review of diagnostic issues and possible nonasbestos factors. Arch. Environ. Occup. Health 61, 183–192. Available from: https://doi.org/10.3200/AEOH.61.4.183-192.

Coe, F.L., Parks, J.H., Asplin, J.R., 1992. The pathogenesis and treatment of kidney stones. N. Engl. J. Med. 327, 1141–1152. Available from: https://doi.org/10.1056/NEJM199210153271607.

Cole, G., Rando, C., Sibun, L., Waldron, T., 2015. Case report: a giant calcified uterus, likely due to benign leiomyoma. Int. J. Paleopathol. 10, 51–57. Available from: https://doi.org/10.1016/j.ijpp.2015.05.003.

Coyle, H.M., Lee, H., Palmbach, T., 2014. Forensic botany: plants as evidence in criminal cases and as agents of bioterrorism. In: Forensic DNA Applications. CRC Press, pp. 394–411.

Craig, J.R., Vaughan, D.J., Hagni, R.D., 1994. Ore Microscopy and Ore Petrography, 2nd edn. John Wiley & Sons, New York, USA.

Dang-Tran, K., Dedouit, F., Joffre, F., Rougé, D., Rousseau, H., Telmon, N., 2010. Thyroid cartilage ossification and multislice computed tomography examination: a useful tool for age assessment? J. Forensic Sci. 55, 677–683.

Das, D.K., 2009. Psammoma body: a product of dystrophic calcification or of a biologically active process that aims at limiting the growth and spread of tumor? Timely Rev. 37, 534–541. Available from: https://doi.org/10.1002/dc.

Demer, L.L., Tintut, Y., 2008. Vascular calcification: pathobiology of a multifaceted disease. Circulation 117, 2938–2948. Available from: https://doi.org/10.1161/circulationaha.107.743161.

DiMaio, V.J.M., Francis, J.R., 2001. Heterotopic ossification in unidentified skeletal remains. Am. J. Forensic Med. Pathol. 22, 160–164.

Doherty, T.M., Asotra, K., Fitzpatrick, L.A., Qiao, J.-H., Wilkin, D.J., Detrano, R.C., et al., 2003. Calcification in atherosclerosis: Bone biology and chronic inflammation at the arterial crossroads. Proc. Natl. Acad. Sci. U. S. A. 100, 11201–11206. Available from: https://doi.org/10.1073/pnas.1932554100.

Falk, E., 2006. Pathogenesis of atherosclerosis. J. Am. Coll. Cardiol. 47, C7–C12. Available from: https://doi.org/10.1016/j.jacc.2005.09.068.

Fatnassi, R., Turki, E., Majdoub, W., Hammami, S., Hajji, M., 2017. Primary ovarian hydatid cyst: a case report and review of literature. Insights Reprod. Med. 1, 5.

Fayad, Z.A., Fuster, V., 2001. Clinical imaging of the high-risk or vulnerable atherosclerotic plaque. Circ. Res. 89, 305–316. Available from: https://doi.org/10.1161/hh1601.095596.

Garvin, H.M., 2008. Ossification of laryngeal structures as indicators of age. J. Forensic Sci. 53, 1023–1027. Available from: https://doi.org/10.1111/j.1556-4029.2008.00793.x.

Gault, M.H., Chafe, L., 2000. Relationship of frequency, age, sex, stone weight and composition in 15,624 stones: comparison of results for 1980 to 1983 and 1995 to 1998. J. Urol. 164, 302–307. Available from: https://doi.org/10.1016/S0022-5347(05)67345-4.

Gevenois, P.A., de Maertelaer, V., Madani, A., Winant, C., Sergent, G., De Vuyst, P., 1998. Asbestosis, pleural plaques and diffuse pleural thickening: three distinct benign responses to asbestos exposure. Eur. Respir. J. 11, 1021.

Giuffra, V., Costantini, L., Costantini Biasini, L., Caramella, D., Fornaciari, G., 2008. Giant bladder stone in a natural mummy of the early 19th century. Urology 72, 780–781. Available from: https://doi.org/10.1016/j.urology.2008.04.031.

Glass, C.K., Witztum, J.L., 2001. Atherosclerosis: the road ahead. Cell 104, 503–516. Available from: https://doi.org/10.1016/S0092-8674(01)00238-0.

Gouvêa Lima, G., de, M., Moraes, R.M., Cavalcante, A.S.R., Carvalho, Y.R., Anbinder, A.L., 2015. An isolated phlebolith on the lip: an unusual case and review of the literature. Case Rep. Pathol. 2015. Available from: https://doi.org/10.1155/2015/507840.

Gunduz, K., Canitezer, G., Avsever, H., 2014. Tuberculous lymph node calcification detected on routine panoramic radiography: an unusual case. J. Oral. Maxillofac. Radiol. 2, 61–63. Available from: https://doi.org/10.4103/2321-3841.138650.

Hillerdal, G., 1994. Pleural plaques and risk for bronchial carcinoma and mesothelioma. Chest 105, 144–150. Available from: https://doi.org/10.1378/chest.105.1.144.

Hillier, M.L., Bell, L.S., 2007. Differentiating human bone from animal bone: a review of histological methods. J. Forensic Sci. 52, 249–263.

Hourihane, D.O., Lessof, L., Richardson, P.C., 1966. Hyaline and calcified pleural plaques as an index of exposure to asbestos. Br. Med. J. 1, 1069–1074.

Jaskowiec, T.C., Grauer, A.L., Lee, M., Rajnic, S., 2017. No stone unturned: the presence of kidney stones in a skeleton from 19th century Peoria, Illinois. Int. J. Paleopathol. 19, 18–23. Available from: https://doi.org/10.1016/j.ijpp.2017.08.004.

Johnston, D.E., Kaplan, M.M., 1993. Pathogenesis and treatment of gallstones. N. Engl. J. Med. 328, 412–421. Available from: https://doi.org/10.1056/NEJM199302113280608.

Kampen, W.U., Ciaassen, H., Kirsch, T., 1995. Mineralization and osteogenesis in the human first rib cartilage. Ann. Anat. 177, 171–177. Available from: https://doi.org/10.1016/S0940-9602(11)80069-5.

Khan, N., Afroz, N., Aqil, B., Khan, T., Ahmad, I., 2009. Neoplastic and nonneoplastic ovarian masses: diagnosis on cytology. J. Cytol. 26, 129–133. Available from: https://doi.org/10.4103/0970-9371.62180.

Kim, I.S., Myung, S.J., Lee, S.S., Lee, S.K., Kim, M.H., 2003. Classification and nomenclature of gallstones revisited. Yonsei Med. J. 44, 561–570. Available from: https://doi.org/10.3349/ymj.2003.44.4.561.

King, J.B., 1939. Calcification of the costal cartilages. Br. J. Radiol. 12, 2–12. Available from: https://doi.org/10.1259/0007-1285-12-133-2.

Knoll, T., 2010. Epidemiology, pathogenesis, and pathophysiology of urolithiasis. Eur. Urol. Suppl. 9, 802–806. Available from: https://doi.org/10.1016/j.eursup.2010.11.006.

Knoll, T., Schubert, A.B., Fahlenkamp, D., Leusmann, D.B., Wendt-Nordahl, G., Schubert, G., 2011. Urolithiasis through the ages: data on more than 200,000 urinary stone analyses. J. Urol. 185, 1304–1311. Available from: https://doi.org/10.1016/j.juro.2010.11.073.

Komar, D.A., Buikstra, J.E., 2003. Differential diagnosis of a prehistoric biological object from the Koster (Illinois) Site. Int. J. Osteoarchaeol. 13, 157–164. Available from: https://doi.org/10.1002/oa.670.

Kusafuka, K., Yamaguchi, A., Kayano, T., Takemura, T., 2001. Ossification of tracheal cartilage in aged humans: a histological and immunohistochemical analysis. J. Bone Miner. Metab. 19, 168–174.

Lanzer, P., Boehm, M., Sorribas, V., Thiriet, M., Janzen, J., Zeller, T., et al., 2014. Medial vascular calcification revisited: Review and perspectives. Eur. Heart J. 35, 1515–1525. Available from: https://doi.org/10.1093/eurheartj/ehu163.

Libby, P., 2003. Vascular biology of atherosclerosis: overview and state of the art. Am. J. Cardiol. 91, 3–6. Available from: https://doi.org/10.1016/S0002-9149(02)03143-0.

Lusis, A.J., 2000. Atherosclerosis. Nature 407, 233–241.

Mandel, L., Perrino, M.A., 2010. Phleboliths and the vascular maxillofacial lesion. J. Oral. Maxillofac. Surg. 68, 1973–1976. Available from: https://doi.org/10.1016/j.joms.2010.04.002.

McCarthy, E.F., Sundaram, M., 2005. Heterotopic ossification: a review. Skelet. Radiol. 34, 609–619. Available from: https://doi.org/10.1007/s00256-005-0958-z.

Meyers, C., Lisiecki, J., Miller, S., Levin, A., Fayad, L., Ding, C., et al., 2019. Heterotopic ossification: a comprehensive review. JBMR Plus 3, e10172. Available from: https://doi.org/10.1002/jbm4.10172.

Moe, O.W., 2006. Kidney stones: pathophysiology and medical management. Lancet 367, 333–344. Available from: https://doi.org/10.1016/S0140-6736(06)68071-9.

Mönckeberg, J.G., 1903. Über die reine Mediaverkalkung der Extremitätenarterien und ihr Verhalten zur Arteriosklerose. Virchows Arch. Pathol. Anat. Physiol. Klin. Med. 171, 141–167.

Mosch, J., Gleissner, C.A., Body, S., Aikawa, E., 2017. Histopathological assessment of calcification and inflammation of calcific aortic valves from patients with and without diabetes mellitus. Histol. Histopathol. 32, 293.

Murase, E., Siegelman, E.S., Outwater, E.K., Perez-Jaffe, L.A., Tureck, R.W., 1999. Uterine leiomyomas: histopathologic features, MR imaging findings, differential diagnosis, and treatment. Radiographics 19, 1179–1197.

Nagaraja, A., Kumar, N., Kumar, B., Naik, R., Sangineedi, Y., 2016. A solitary phlebolith in the buccal mucosa: report of a rare entity and clinicopathologic correlation. J. Contemp. Dent. Pr. 17, 706–710.

Ng, S.J.K., Lee, J.K.T., Thian, Y.L., 2018. Cricoid ridge ossification mimicking ingested fish bone on plain radiography: prevalence in Singapore. Singap. Med. J. 59, 356–359. Available from: https://doi.org/10.11622/smedj.2017117.

Okada, S., Ohaki, Y., Inoue, K., Kawamura, T., Hayashi, T., Kato, T., et al., 2005. Calcifications in mucinous and serous cystic ovarian tumors. J. Nippon. Med. Sch. 72, 29–33.

Özdemir, K., Akyol, A.A., Erdal, Y.S., 2015. A Case of Ancient Bladder Stones from Oluz Höyük, Amasya, Turkey. Int. J. Osteoarchaeol. 25, 827–837. Available from: https://doi.org/10.1002/oa.2349.

Pinotti, E., Ceresoli, M., Montuori, M., Sandini, M., Trovato, A., Cereda, M., et al., 2018. Huge abdominal cystic mass: A diagnostic dilemma. Open J. Clin. Med. Case Reports 4, 1492.

Rejtarova, O., Hejna, P., Soukup, T., Kuchar, M., 2009. Age and sexually dimorphic changes in costal cartilages. A preliminary microscopic study. Forensic Sci. Int. 193, 72–78. Available from: https://doi.org/10.1016/j.forsciint.2009.09.009.

Rejtarova, O., Slizova, D., Smoranc, P., Rejtar, P., Bukac, J., 2004. Costal cartilages--a clue for determination of sex. Biomed. Pap. Med. Fac. Univ. Palacky. Olomouc. Czech. Repub. 148, 241–243.

Roberts, G.H., 1971. The pathology of parietal pleural plaques. J. Clin. Pathol. 24, 348–353.

Russel, P., 1979. The pathological assessment of ovarian neoplasms: I. Introduction to the common '"epithelial"' tumors and analysis of benign '"epithelial"' tumors. Pathology 11, 5–26.

Stary, H.C., Chandler, A.B., Dinsmore, R.E., Fuster, V., Glagov, S., Insull, W., et al., 1995. A definition of advanced types of atherosclerotic lesions and a histological classification of atherosclerosis. A Rep. Comm. Vascular Lesions of the Council on Arteriosclerosis, American Heart Association. 92, 1355–1374. Available from: https://doi.org/10.1161/01.cir.92.5.1355.

Saha, A., Mohapatra, M., Patra, S., Saha, K., 2015. Phlebolith in arteriovenous malformation in buccal fat pad masquerading sialolith: A rare case report. Contemp. Clin. Dent. 6, 254.

Sawyer, L., Grubb, D.T., Meyers, G.F., 2008. Polymer Microscopy, 3rd edn. Springer Science & Business Media.

Steinbock, R.T., 1990a. Studies in ancient calcified soft tissues and organic concretions. II: urolithiasis (renal and urinary bladder stone disease). J. Paleopathol. 3, 39–59.

Steinbock, R.T., 1990b. Studies in ancient calcified soft tissues and organic concretions. III: gallstones (Cholelithiasis). J. Paleopathol. 3, 95–106.

Stewart, B.F., Siscovick, D., Lind, B.K., Gardin, J.M., Gottdiener, J.S., Smith, V.E., et al., 1997. Clinical factors associated with calcific aortic valve disease. J. Am. Coll. Cardiol. 29, 630–634.

Stoller, M., Gupta, M., Bolton, D., Irbyiii, P.B., 1994. Clinical correlates of the gross, radiographic, and histologic features of urinary matrix calculi. J. Endourol. 8, 335–340.

Subirana-Domènech, M., Borondo-Alcázar, J.C., Armentano-Oller, N., Font Valsecchi, G., Galtés Vicente, I., Castellà-García, J., 2012. Arteriosclerosis in paleopathology. Are macroscopic findings well known? Int. J. Paleopathol. 2, 246–248. Available from: https://doi.org/10.1016/j.ijpp.2012.10.001.

Towler, D.A., 2008. Vascular calcification: a perspective on an imminent disease epidemic. IBMS Bonekey 5, 41–58.

van Engelen, A., Niessen, W.J., Klein, S., Groen, H.C., van Gaalen, K., Verhagen, H.J., et al., 2013. Automated segmentation of atherosclerotic histology based on pattern classification. J. Pathol. Inf. 4, S3. Available from: https://doi.org/10.4103/2153-3539.109844.

Vicidomini, S., Cancrini, G., Gabrielli, S., Naspetti, R., Bartoloni, A., 2007. Muscular cystic hydatidosis: case report. BMC Infect. Dis. 7, 1–5. Available from: https://doi.org/10.1186/1471-2334-7-23.

Virmani, R., Kolodgie, F.D., Burke, A.P., Farb, A., Schwartz, S.M., 2000. Lessons from sudden coronary death: a comprehensive morphological classification scheme for atherosclerotic lesions. Arterioscler. Thromb. Vasc. Biol. 20, 1262–1275.

Waters-Rist, A.L., Faccia, K., Lieverse, A., Bazaliiskii, V.I., Katzenberg, M.A., Losey, R.J., 2014. Multicomponent analyses of a hydatid cyst from an Early Neolithic hunter-fisher-gatherer from Lake Baikal, Siberia. J. Archaeol. Sci. 50, 51–62. Available from: https://doi.org/10.1016/j.jas.2014.06.015.

Wen, J., Zhao, Z., Huang, L., Li, L., Li, J., Zeng, Y., et al., 2018. Switch of the ovarian cancer cell to a calcifying phenotype in the calcification of ovarian cancer. J. Cancer 9, 1006.

Womack, N.A., Zeppa, R., Irvin, G.L., 1963. The anatomy of gallstones. Ann. Surg. 157, 670–686.

Yoshida, H., Yokoyama, K., Yaginuma, T., Ohkido, I., Yamamoto, H., Utsunomiya, Y., et al., 2011. Difference in coronary artery intima and media calcification in autopsied patients with chronic kidney disease. Clin. Nephrol. 75, 1–7.

CHAPTER 8

Trauma

Annalisa Capella[1], Debora Mazzarelli[1], Carmelo Messina[2] and Cristina Cattaneo[1]
[1]LABANOF, Department of Biomedical Sciences for Health, University of Milan, Milan, Italy,
[2]Diagnostic and Interventional Radiology, IRCCS Istituto Ortopedico Galeazzi, Milan, Italy

Pathology is usually divided into two categories: natural and traumatic. Up to now, we have dealt with natural pathology affecting bone. In this chapter, we will focus on trauma, and mainly bone fractures and as we will see, trauma—in its antemortem and perimortem forms—is crucial for two forensic aspects: identification and determining the manner and cause of death. As this book deals with bone pathology, more relevance will be given in this chapter to antemortem trauma (i.e., callus formation). However, perimortem trauma will also be discussed.

The term "injury" or "wound" refers to a damage to any part of the body (i.e., tissue and organs) caused by the application of a mechanical insult. Indeed, when the intensity of an applied force exceeds the tissue capability to absorb or adapt to that specific stress, an injury will be the direct consequence. The effective damage depends on the nature of the tissue as well as the type of mechanical insult (Knight, 1996).

In anthropology as in forensic pathology, the term "trauma" indicates a physical injury or wound to the living bone tissue caused by an external stress that can be either accidental or intentional. The correct identification and interpretation of skeletal lesions and traumata is of the utmost importance for providing key clues in the comprehension of the manner and cause of death, which is why it is a mandatory step in the forensic analysis of skeletal remains (Cunha and Cattaneo, 2006).

The analysis of traumatic bone injuries encompasses the evaluation of the position, morphology, and all significant characteristics of the injuries, the interpretation of the nature of the trauma (whenever

Interpreting Bone Lesions and Pathology for Forensic Practice. DOI: https://doi.org/10.1016/B978-0-323-85162-6.00008-8

possible), and the identification of the probable weapons involved (if any have been used) (Hart, 2005; Reichs, 1998; Sauer, 1998). The resulting trauma pattern will contribute to the interpretation of the events that occurred around the time of death and to the determination of the cause of death (Semeraro et al., 2012). In addition, traumatic bone injuries should be distinguished from environmental and taphonomic alterations which can often hinder trauma analysis (Galloway and Zephro, 2005; Reichs, 1998).

Timing of Bone Fractures

The identification of skeletal lesions and the interpretation of their time of production (i.e., whether the event that caused the injury occurred before, around or after the time of death) is nearly always the starting point of trauma analysis. Injuries to bone are typically classified as "*antemortem*", "*perimortem*", or "*postmortem*". This analysis is crucial and must be applied to all types of lesions, including fractures in blunt force injuries, cutmarks or stab wounds in sharp force injury, and gunshot wounds.

"*Antemortem*" lesions are injuries that occurred during life; in other words, the individual was alive when the trauma occurred and survived for some time. This survival time was enough for the person to start a bone healing response in order to resolve the bone damage caused by the injury.

"*Perimortem*" lesions are injuries that occurred near the time of death of the individual—in this case, the individual could had been alive or not. If the trauma occurred shortly before death, the survival time was not long enough for the bone to respond by activating the healing process, at least in terms of visible healing signs on bone. After the time of death, the bone tissue maintains its chemical, structural, and physical properties, in particular elasticity, similarly to living bone (except for the biological ability to actively restore the tissue). Therefore, the bone tissue mechanical properties in a cadaver are similar to those of a living individual. In a perimortem fracture, only the presence of vital signs of hemorrhaging will be able to classify it as "just before death".

Finally, "*postmortem*" lesions are injuries that have been surely produced after death. In this situation, and regardless of the length of time after death, the bone tissue lost its elastic properties resulting in a very different pattern of fracture from the one occurring on a fresh bone, even if caused by the same trauma.

The specific classification based on these three types of skeletal trauma (i.e., *antemortem*, *perimortem*, and *postmortem*), is typical for dry bone. In contrast, forensic pathology, which deals also with soft tissue, discriminates only between *antemortem* and *postmortem* wounds because of the presence of biomarkers of inflammation. Occasionally, even on dry bone, residues of such "biological materials" (e.g., in skin, muscles, and blood, which are degraded due to decomposition) can still be observed either macro- or microscopically and can function as additional interpretative tools for a better understanding of the timing of the injury.

Distinguishing Perimortem and Postmortem Trauma

Distinguishing between *postmortem* and *perimortem* lesions in skeletal remains may be particularly complex. While it is possible to exclude a lesion as *antemortem* from the lack of visible healing signs, it is more difficult to define a traumatic lesion as surely *perimortem*. Indeed, many factors may affect the interpretation of lesions as *perimortem* or *postmortem*, including taphonomic and environmental conditions, the time elapsed since death (i.e., postmortem interval), the type of bone tissue involved in the trauma and *postmortem* changes (Ortner, 2003; Sauer, 1998). Typical postmortem lesions are those caused by environmental factors, such as surface erosions, sun bleaching, carnivore tooth marks, weathering (among others), and by accidental events produced by soil pressure (for buried remains), human activity, transport, and fortuitous trauma (Ubelaker, 1997). By opposition, any injury directly associated with the manner of death or the handling of the remains in an early postmortem period may be considered as *perimortem* (Sauer, 1998). According to Wieberg and Wescott (2008), and arguably so, the term *perimortem* seems to be ineffective in a forensic context since it refers to a temporal period instead of a physical condition (i.e., fresh or dry). However, questions such as how long characteristics of *perimortem* fractures persist after death remain unanswered in the literature. Therefore, it is unclear what "around the time of death" exactly means in terms of both time and expected skeletal modifications. Nonetheless, *perimortem* injuries and *postmortem* changes to bone are potentially discernible (Ortner, 2003).

Fracture morphology is the most indicative aspect useful for their distinction—*perimortem* and *postmortem* lesions exhibit major morphological differences because the trauma occurred in different types of bone which are called respectively "fresh" and "dry" bone. Depending on the moisture content of the bone tissue and the quantity of collagen matrix (which gives flexibility to the bone tissue), a "green fracture" is the result of a trauma in a fresh bone tissue (same properties of strength, elasticity and flexibility as in a living tissue), while a "dry fracture" occurs on dry bone. Once the bone tissue starts losing its original components (such as collagen matrix, fat, water, and liquids), its own properties will change profoundly and invariably—the tissue becomes gradually "dry," with a significant loss of flexibility and resistance to subsequent stress (Harkess et al., 1996; Johnson, 1985). Thus, depending on its quality, the bone will behave differently to an applied stress resulting in a dissimilar morphological pattern of fracture. However, the properties of bone tissue can also exhibit characteristics intermediate between "fresh" and "dry" bones, hence causing a fracture morphology more difficult to interpret.

The properties of the bone tissue are not only influenced by the passing of time since death but also by the cumulative effects related to the decomposition process, taphonomic events, and environmental factors that occurred over time (Calce and Rogers, 2007; Moraitis et al., 2009; Sauer, 1998; Ubelaker, 1991; Wieberg and Wescott, 2008).

The general morphology of the fracture, its outline as well as the angle, roughness, and color of the fracture margins are features that may help the differentiation between *perimortem* and *postmortem* lesions (Table 8.1) (Karr and Outram, 2015, 2012; LaCroix, 2013; Ubelaker and Adams, 1995; Wheatley, 2008; Wieberg and Wescott, 2008).

Table 8.1 Morphological comparison between fresh and dry bone features.

Features	Fresh bone characteristics	Dry bone characteristics
Outline	Radial pattern circling diaphysis	Perpendicular/horizontal fracture surface
Surface	Smooth	Rough
Fracture angle	Obtuse and acute angles	Right angles
Color surface	Homogeneous color with external bone	Heterogeneous color with external bone
Other	Loading point present	Loading point absent
Other	Fracture front never crosscut epiphyseal ends	Fracture front can crosscut epiphyseal ends

Adapted from Johnson, E., 1985. Current developments in bone technology. In: Schiffer, M.B. (Ed.), Advances in Archaeological Method and Theory. Elsevier, pp. 157–235; Wieberg, D.A.M., Wescott, D.J., 2008. Estimating the timing of long bone fractures: correlation between the postmortem interval, bone moisture content, and blunt force trauma fracture characteristics. J. Forensic Sci. 53, 1028–1034.

In general, the breaking pattern of a lesion in fresh bone (i.e., green fracture) is more complex than one in dry bone—concentric, circular, and spiral fractures are usually typical of green fractures. Nevertheless, this is not a strict rule as some authors have described these patterns in dry bones (Ubelaker and Adams, 1995). Conversely, dry bone fractures are characterized by the presence of several small fragments, brittle flaking or shattering, and multiple surface cracking (Maples, 1998). Angle and color are additional discriminating features—dry fractures usually show irregular to jagged edges, which are often lighter in color than the darkened adjacent bone and exhibit breakage at nearly right angles relative to the longitudinal axe of bones with almost flat ends, as shown in Fig. 8.1. On the opposite, smooth, often beveled, sharp fracture edges with sporadic sharp projections, and obtuse or acute fracture angles are associated with *perimortem* trauma (Fig. 8.1). Furthermore, green fractures are characterized by smooth fractures edges of the same color as the adjacent bone

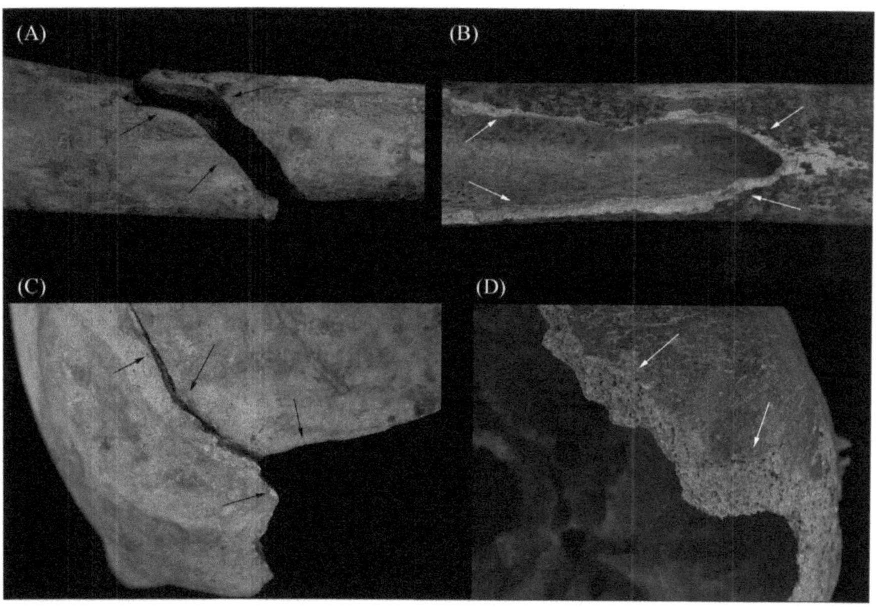

Figure 8.1 Examples of post-mortem and perimortem fractures: (A) perimortem fracture (green fracture) to a femur diaphysis; (B) postmortem breakage to a dry human femur (white arrows); (C) perimortem skull fracture (green fracture) to a frontal bone indicated by the black arrows; (D) postmortem skull breakage to a dry human frontal bone (white arrows). The perimortem fractures exhibit bevelled, sharp and smooth edges together with acute and obtuse fracture angles and homogeneous margins color which are all strong indicators suggesting a perimortem trauma. In contrast, the post-mortem fractures exhibit irregular and jagged fracture edges and are lighter in color than the darker adjacent tissue.

(Bonnichsen, 1979; Morlan, 1984; Quatrehomme and Alunni, 2013; Ubelaker and Adams, 1995; Villa and Mahieu, 1991; Wieberg and Wescott, 2008). Indeed, color staining is caused by decomposition fluids, blood, soil, dirty water, leaf stains, and organic matter. Thus, if the color is homogenous between the fracture margins and the external bone layer, the fracture could be considered *perimortem* as both fracture margins and adjacent bone have been exposed for the same time to the staining materials. Alternatively, *postmortem* fracture margins will appear in a lighter color than the adjacent external layer because they were exposed after decomposition. However, the coloration of fracture edges should be used with caution in the distinction between *perimortem* and *postmortem* trauma given its very variable nature, highly dependent upon the depositional environment (Cappella et al., 2014; Moraitis et al., 2009; Wieberg and Wescott, 2008).

Antemortem Trauma

In trauma analysis, the lesions defined as "*antemortem*" have all occurred before death. But why is it so important to time lesions with respect to death? And once a lesion is determined as antemortem, can the anthropologist or pathologist provide additional information concerning its specific dating?

Antemortem trauma in forensics is of paramount importance: it can reveal precious information about the person providing clues for the biological profile and identification (e.g., establishing that the person broke a finger weeks, months or years before dying). Moreover, it can also provide fundamental data for interpretation of the manner of death, revealing maltreatments, abuses, and torture that a person was subjected to during days, weeks, or months before death (e.g., in cases of imprisonment).

As a result of trauma, the living bone tissue will respond by activating the healing process which includes a well-known series of events that normally occur in succession (Cruess and Dumont, 1975; Ortner, 2003); some can be seen in skeletonized remains through gross macroscopic analysis. Other healing bone tissue events, especially the ones occurring in the very earliest bone response phases, can instead be recognizable only through a microscopic and radiological analysis. This will lead to the estimation of the posttraumatic survival time (PTST), thus providing an interval of the time elapsed since the trauma occurred and the death ensued. But before entering these issues, let us see how bone heals.

Bone Healing Process

Bone is a living material exposed during life to mechanical stresses that challenge its structural integrity and which the tissue resolves through its remodeling process. When stress load exceeds the bone's strength, fracture of the bone tissue, and tearing of associated soft tissues (muscle, tendons, ligaments, bone marrow etc.) occurs, but the bone tissue can repair itself, regardless of the cause and type of damage. Once a bone is broken, strength and stability have to be restored quickly to allow it to maintain its biomechanical integrity. As a consequence, the bone tissue will activate an auto-orchestrated biological healing process which follows a specific regenerative cascade including the participation of numerous cells and signaling molecules (Cappella and Cattaneo, 2019; Einhorn, 1998).

Regardless of the type of injury, the fracture exhibits two or more broken parts, called fragments, in case of complete fractures or just a gap between the partial separation of fragments in incomplete fractures.

Fracture healing can ensue through either direct or indirect ossification. Direct fracture healing, also known as primary healing, is typical in cases of anatomic reduction of fracture fragments which is reached by internal fixation or decreased interfragmentary strain. Primary or direct healing refers to a direct attempt of the tissue to form new Haversian systems through the action of discrete remodeling units (the so-called "cutting cones") (McKibbin, 1978). In this process, a discrete periosteal reaction may be seen but no bone callus is formed. The cells forming the new tissue, the osteoblasts, differentiate from osteoprogenitor cells migrated and derived from the vascular endothelial and the perivascular mesenchymal cells (Einhorn, 1998; McKibbin, 1978). The direct formation of new bone and the restoration of the tissue without forming any granulation/cartilaginous tissue will be the final result.

By opposition, the indirect or secondary healing is the most common process in fracture healing. Newly formed tissue develops in and around the site of the fracture in order to merge the two fractured extremities with a tissue bridge, the so-called callus. The callus is the characteristic feature of the indirect healing process and the result of the combination of the two different types of ossifications: intramembranous and endochondral (Einhorn, 1998). Here, periosteal activity plays a key role—osteoprogenitor and undifferentiated mesenchymal cells residing in the periosteum (i.e., the outermost bone layer) migrate to the fracture site for callus formation where the intramembranous ossification has already started to directly form new bone (i.e., without first forming cartilage). The bone marrow also contributes to the early stages of callus formation, specifically when endothelial cells differentiate into polymorphic cells expressing osteoblastic phenotype (Brighton and Hunt, 1991). Essentially, the recruitment, proliferation, and differentiation of the mesenchymal cells are typical phases of endochondral ossification leading to the initial formation of a cartilage tissue, its calcification and its replacement with bone tissue. In secondary healing, the formation of the early callus, called "soft callus" as it is not yet constituted of bone tissue, is fundamental as it stabilizes temporarily the fracture fragments. Over time, the cartilage constituting the "soft callus" is replaced by bone, forming a "hard callus." Its formation is provided by the cooperation of multiple tissues—mainly, the periosteum adjacent to the fracture site, but also the numerous surrounding external soft tissues such as muscles and vessels (Dimitriou et al., 2005).

The healing process, although still not fully understood, may be divided in six well-discernible stages and three principal phases (Aubin et al., 1993; Dimitriou et al., 2005; Doblaré et al., 2004), as shown in Fig. 8.2:

1. initial formation of a hematoma and inflammation (inflammatory/reactive phase);
2. subsequent angiogenesis and formation of a granuloma/cartilage (initial reparative phase);
3. cartilage calcification (progressive reparative phase);
4. cartilage removal (progressive reparative phase);
5. immature bone formation (final reparative phase);
6. bone remodeling replacing the woven bone tissue with lamellar bone (remodeling phase).

Essentially, the secondary healing process consists in an initial inflammatory phase, a subsequent reparative phase (with first a fibrocartilaginous callus formation that later evolves in a woven bony

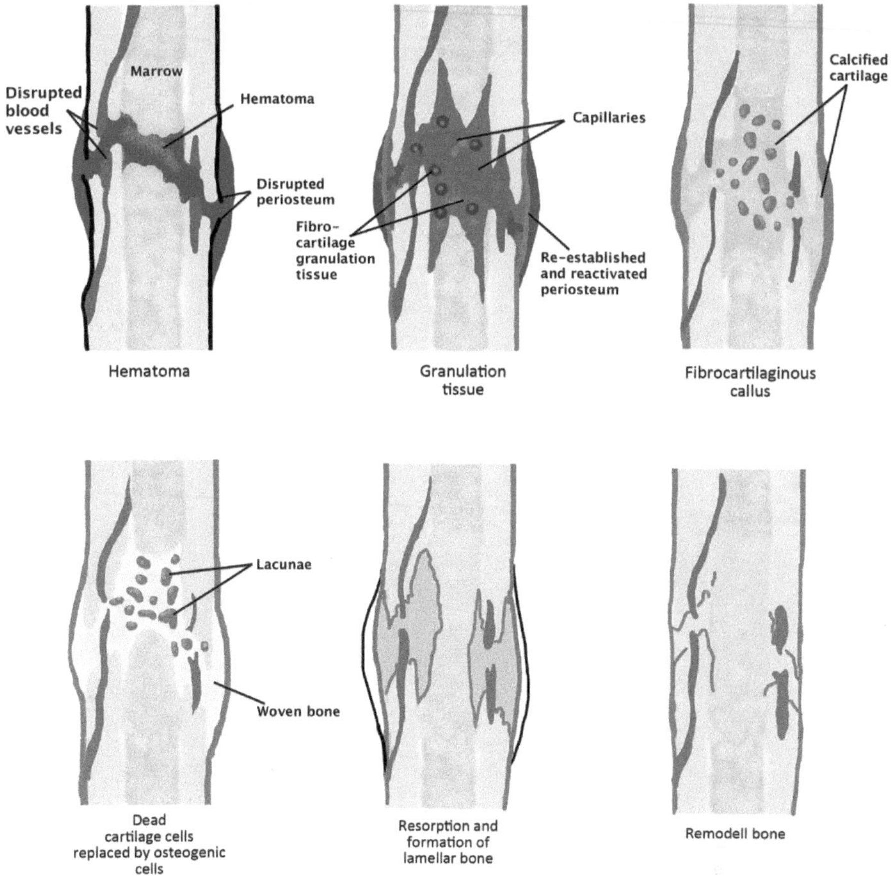

Figure 8.2 Schematic drawing of the six phases that represent the bone healing process following a trauma.

callus), and a final remodeling phase restoring the normal bone architecture (Fig. 8.3).

In the initial inflammatory phase, blood pools into the fracture area due to the disruption of vessels and coagulates, forming a hematoma (Collins, 1966; Frost, 1989). Indeed, the fracture causes the disruption of the entire bone tissue (i.e., matrix and cells), the surrounding soft tissues (i.e., periosteum, bone marrow, muscles, etc.) and the vascular system (i.e., blood vessels). The extravasation of blood into the fractured area is accumulated within the bone tissue and the adjacent areas, specifically the trabecular bone and the medullary canal, between the fractured bone fragments (inside the fracture line), among the bone marrow and beneath the periosteum and muscle tissue in the

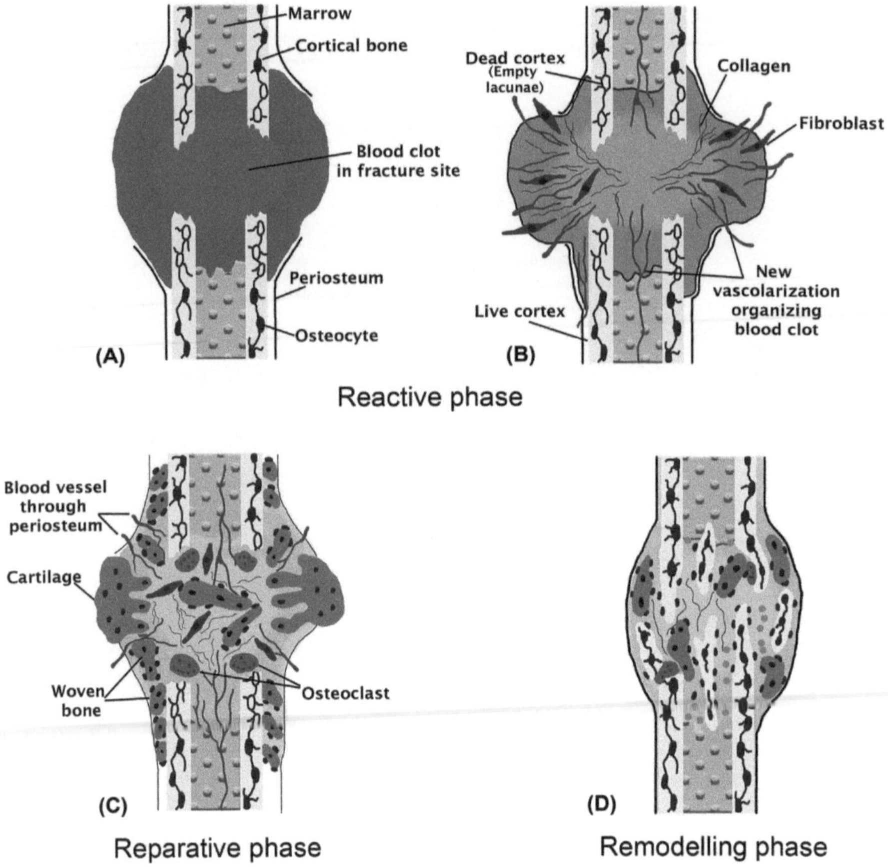

Figure 8.3 Schematic drawing of the three phases that represent the bone healing process following a trauma: (A) and (B) represent the inflammatory/reactive phase, while (C) and (D) represent respectively the reparative and the remodeling phases. (A) Soon after the fracture, blood vessels are constricted and disrupted, releasing blood cells within and around the gap where the hematoma will be formed. (B) Cells within the blood clot and the hematoma start to degenerate and die but fibroblasts survive, replicate and form new collagen fibers constituting new the granulation tissue and carrying on the reactive phase. (C) Cells of periosteum replicate and transform in chondroblasts and osteoblasts which respectively will form new cartilage and woven bone. These two new tissues grow in volume and unite together to form the callus structure. Once the new tissue has grown it will be slowly replaced by the lamellar bone tissue trough mineralization, vascularization and osteoblastic activity that forms at first the trabecular bone. (D) The new trabecular bone is replaced by compact bone where necessary, through the osteoclast and osteoblast activity which is performed by the BMUs. This phase will lead to a continuous remodeling process until a final shape which closely replicate the original shape and strength.

fracture proximity (Cappella and Cattaneo, 2019; Cattaneo et al., 2017). Within the first 24/48 h, the hemorrhage progresses into a hematoma which includes neutrophils and macrophages migrated into the fracture line, in addition to numerous bone marrow cells, erythrocytes and platelets derived from the injured vessels and marrow spaces (Ozaki et al., 2000; Schmidt-Bleek et al., 2009). Coagulation ensues which is fundamental for limiting further hemorrhaging by acting as a hemostatic plug. This inflammatory phase peaks at 48 h after the trauma and ceases about 1 week later (Einhorn, 1998; Marenzana and Arnett, 2013; Marsell and Einhorn, 2011; Phillips, 2005). The inflammatory response is critical for bone healing: signaling molecules (e.g., cytokines and growth factors) mediate the rapid recruitment of inflammatory cells (e.g., mesenchymal stem cells (MSCs)), the stimulation of angiogenesis, and the persistence of the inflammation which induces the formation and differentiation of osteoblasts and osteoclasts (Cho et al., 2006; Kon et al., 2001; Lee and Lorenzo, 2006; Marsell and Einhorn, 2011; Sfeir et al., 2005; Yang et al., 2007). Simultaneously, the necrotic bone (i.e., dead bone tissue), which results from the separation of bone cells from the connected—and now disrupted—vascular system, is resorbed by osteoclasts and osteocytes no longer have a proper nutritional connection. The resorption of the necrotic bone by osteoclasts may not immediately occur after the fracture but may be seen following the acute inflammatory phases (Collins, 1966).

Afterwards, fibroblasts and supporting cells differentiated from osteoprogenitor cells start producing a soft fibrous granulation tissue (i.e., granuloma) (Fig. 8.2). The granuloma is formed at each fracture end by extending into the hematoma. During this reparative phase, osteoblasts produce woven bone, osteoclasts resorb the necrotic tissue, progenitor cells continuously generate new osteoblasts, macrophages eat away the hematoma, and fibroblasts extend their activity by producing the new intercellular material. In addition, new blood vessels are formed into the fracture line from the surrounding soft tissues through a process called angiogenesis which will restore the vascular system (Cappella and Cattaneo, 2019; Frost, 1989; Hendrix, 2002).

The formation of the primary callus across the fracture represents the next stage in the healing process and once complete it will provide temporary biomechanical stability to the bone. The primary callus is initially formed by chondrocytes. This cartilaginous callus is not yet calcified and still slightly soft, hence its name "soft callus." At this stage, it is possible to distinguish different parts of the callus—the intermediate or sealing callus, which lies in between the two fracture ends; the endosteal callus, which is the part of the callus that merges the open marrow spaces; and the periosteal callus, which is the most visible and outer part of the callus forming the bridge that attaches the fracture fragments around and outside the fracture site. There are no structural distinctions between these three types of calluses (which are distinguished only conceptually). The intermediate callus is created from the granulation tissue via the deposition of the osteoid by osteoblasts into the fibrous connective tissue, where both become ossified with an orientation following that of the fibrous matrix. The endosteal callus is formed into the fracture line by osteoblasts derived from the endosteum. The periosteal callus is produced by osteoblasts differentiated from the periosteum and presents its characteristic bulging shape observable macroscopically (Frost, 1989). Thus, the cartilaginous callus is gradually resorbed and replaced by immature bone (i.e., woven bone) (Table 8.2).

Subsequently, basic multicellular units (BMUs) operated by osteoclasts that remove the pre-existing tissue and osteoblasts that lay down new bone in its stead, remodel the primary bone callus (i.e., woven bone) into a secondary and more stable callus (i.e., lamellar bone) (Frost, 1989) (Figs. 8.4 and 8.5). The BMUs operate the replacement of woven bone with a more organized lamellar bone—the granulation tissue becomes calcified cartilage that is first resorbed and then substituted by woven bone but once the latter has been formed the BMUs will remove it and then replace it with new lamellar bone.

Once the healing process is understood, one has to think about estimating the PTST for an *antemortem* trauma, which can be grossly estimated macroscopically in case of visible and recognizable signs on the outer bone surface or can be evaluated more precisely through a radiological and microscopical analysis. Among these two analyses, one can detect some of the earliest phases (not visible macroscopically) but also the signs pertaining both to the endosteal and the intermediate callus of the reparative phase. The next paragraph will show the potential and limits of dating fractures and the possible advantages of using microscopic and radiological techniques for reaching the most reliable and accurate time interval possible.

A critical aspect is the possibility to detect early signs of vital reaction in bone fractures indicating survival and allowing us to switch the diagnosis of a lesion from *perimortem* to *antemortem*. In particular, histology may detect the presence of signs or biomarkers indicative of a biological response (e.g., hemorrhage or hematoma). This peculiar aspect will be treated in the last part of the chapter.

Table 8.2 Main fracture repair events in adults.

Reactive—inflammation phase
Disruption of vascular supply Hemorrhage Hematoma formation Hypoxic and acidic environment Necrosis of bone at the fracture area (endosteal and periosteal) and at the fracture fragments Disruption of osteons, lacunae and bone marrow spaces (releasing enzymes) Removal of dead tissue (clot) by macrophages Re-established and reactivated periosteum Activation of fibroblasts and osteoprogenitor in order to start the bone reparative process Osteoclast activation leads to osteolytic activity at fracture borders Granulation tissue formation
Reparative Phase (Soft and hard callus)
Proliferation of osteoblasts in periosteum Fibroblasts, chondroblasts and osteoblasts activity forms external callus and soft tissue collar Development of internal callus Proliferation of osteoclasts and migration of macrophages to continue removal of tissue Conversion of external and internal callus to woven (immature) bone Increased vascularity and cellularity Firm union woven bone
Remodeling phase
Gradual conversion of fibrous bone to lamellar bone by BMUs (external surface, endosteum, and medullary cavity)
Adapted from Heppenstall, R.B., 1980. Fracture healing. In: Heppenstall, R.B. (Ed.), Fracture Treatment and Healing. Saunders, Philadelphia, PA, pp. 35–64; Boyd, D.C., 2018. The anatomical basis for fracture repair: Recognition of the healing continuum and its forensic applications to investigations of pediatric and elderly abuse. Forensic Anthropol. Theor. Framew. Sci. Basis 149–200.

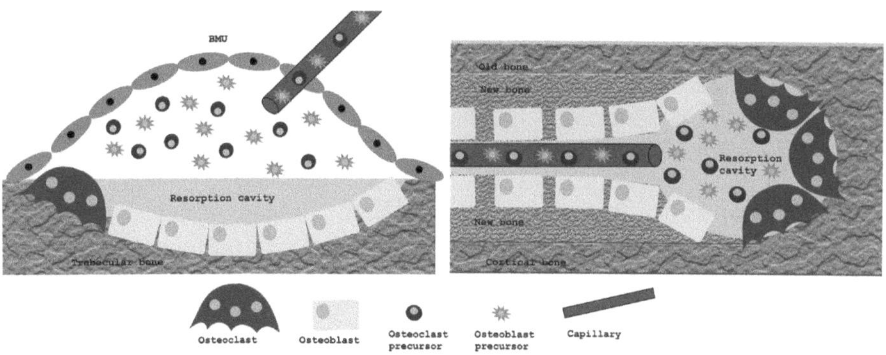

Figure 8.4 Schematic representation of a BMU and associated remodeling stage in cortical bone (left image) and trabecular one (right image). The remodeling canopy in trabecular bone is covered by the underneath bone lining cells.

Dating Fractures and Calluses

In *antemortem* lesions, the estimation of the amount of time elapsed between the traumatic event and the death (the so-called PTST or post-traumatic interval) is very challenging although often of extreme value

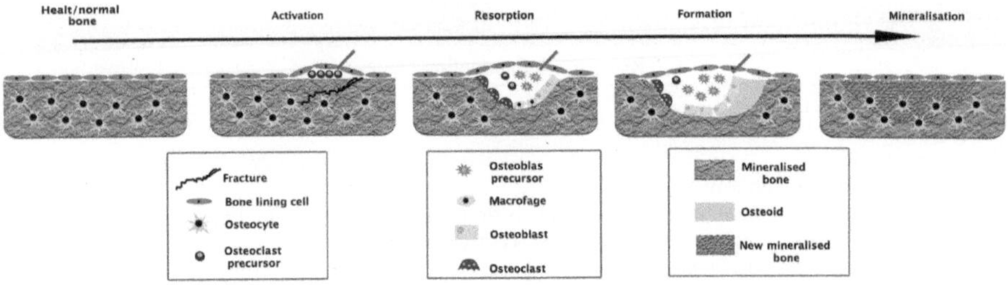

Figure 8.5 A pictorial listing the main stages of the remodeling phase where different cells are involved to form the diverse types of tissue that will be progressively replaced by mineralized bone (all process involving the BMUs). This process is always ongoing in the bones of adults and is the same as in the last phase of bone fracture repair, where the morphological and functional properties of bone have to be restored.

(Cappella et al., 2019). For instance, it can have implications in legal proceedings, including reconstructing the chain of events leading to death; corroborating witness testimonies; adding precious data to the biological profile of a unknown cadaver; and establishing a sequence when multiple traumas are found in an individual as in cases of torture and maltreatment (Cappella et al., 2019, 2013). In these terms, dating fractures and bone calluses consists substantially in estimating the PTST based on the bone tissue healing response, which follows the aforementioned developmental sequence and whose speed, however, depends on a multitude of variables: the type of fracture, the type of bone affected, and the age, sex, and health status of the individual are factors that can influence the rapidity of healing. Thus, the estimation of the PTST on the basis of the visible fracture healing response is problematic as it generally results in large time ranges and may at times have a very limited informative potential (Cappella et al., 2019).

Macroscopically, the evaluation of the healing process is limited to the recognition of the main stages. In fact, the early phases usually do not leave macroscopic signs on the bones because they mostly consist of cellular and molecular activities as well as changes in the inner tissue not visible through gross examination, unless some periosteal activity around the fracture margins already started. When no bone signs are visible macroscopically (Fig. 8.6), we should still talk of *perimortem* lesions but mention that from a microscopic (and even radiological, although less accurate at this stage on skeletonized remains) standpoint, the presence of specific biomarkers (e.g., cells, molecules, tissue activities) indicative of a "vital" reaction may be detected thus demonstrating the *antemortem* timing of the lesion.

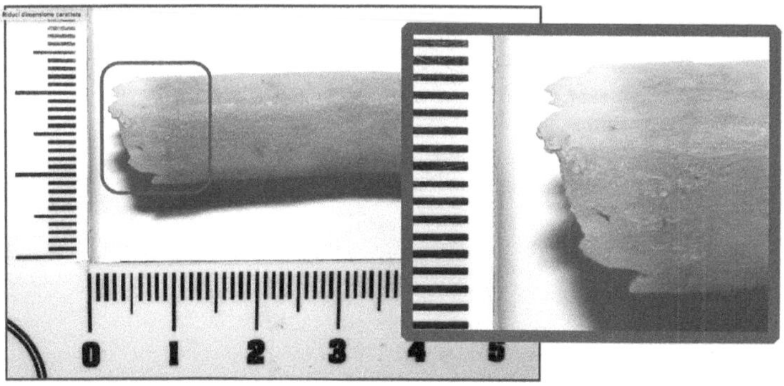

Figure 8.6 Nine-day-old rib fracture of an adult male. The observable macroscopic features around the fracture margins are consistent with a perimortem *fracture, occurred around the time of death. In this case, it is suggested to perform a histological analysis in order to look for microscopic features which may enable to switch the diagnosis from* perimortem *to* antemortem, *and possibly provide a more precise and reliable PTST.*

By opposition, the reparative phase is well visible and detectable in skeletonized remains. This phase begins 7–14 days after the trauma and can last for several weeks. During this time, the bone develops cartilage and granular tissue which is substituted by woven bone in and around the fracture site before becoming new lamellar bone (soft and hard calluses). At this point, it is possible to observe a soft "collar" at the broken ends as well as the presence of semi-rigid tissue bridging the two ends (Fig. 8.7) which indicates an *antemortem* trauma. Specifically, this type of callus is formed between 14 and 30/40 days after the trauma (if not more) and is highly variable with age, sex and health status (Fig. 8.7).

Once the remodeling phase starts to replace the hard callus with the final lamellar bone, the bulging shape gradually disappears (Fig. 8.8), and the bone reassumes its original structure (Fig. 8.9), although, sometimes, a bulge may remain (De Boer et al., 2015, 2013; Maat, 2008). However, it is difficult to reliably date this healing phase which varies depending on the subject (i.e., sex, age, and population affinity), trauma (i.e., type, severity, location, and cause), its treatment and local biomechanical factors. Thus, only the minimum PTST can be estimated, namely at least over 2–3 months. Undoubtedly, this is the most temporally broad and unpredictable aspect of bone healing. In addition, there is a considerable overlap in the majority of the healing features discussed: the processes of bone deposition and resorption are in fact coupled together along with much of the healing process, making it difficult to determine discrete stages or phases and so the most plausible PTST (Boyd, 2018).

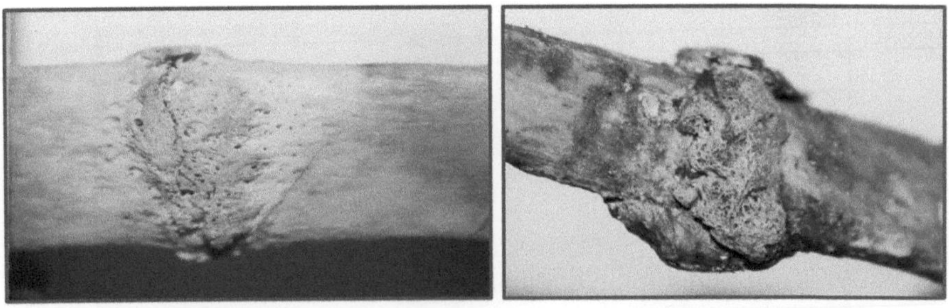

Figure 8.7 Left: 28-day-old rib fracture of an adult male. The callus is well visible with ongoing tissue conversion (resorption of the fibrocartilage in favor of woven bone deposition, that is, mineralization). The fracture line is still perceivable in the outer surfaces between the two fracture extremities. Right: 42-day-old rib fracture of an adult male. This callus shows similar characteristics but with a more bulging shape and a complex and irregular bridge merging the two fracture extremities. The fracture line is not well detectable from the outer surface: this can be due to its definitive merging, at least on the outside bone surface. But internally (i.e., in the inner endosteal tissue) the fracture line could still be separated and/or filled with fibrocartilage tissue (which may be verified through radiological examination or histological analysis).

Light microscopy can substantially improve PTST determination, or at least its minimum value—it can readily assess the subtle physiological changes within the healing continuum, which may not be evident radiographically or macroscopically. A method combining histology and radiology, or "compound" method, has been proposed based on a healing timetable (De Boer et al., 2015) linking specific radiological and histological features with PTSTs (Maat and Huls, 2010; Maat, 2008). Although it can be useful for estimating the PTST, and in particular the minimum PTST (Cappella et al., 2019), this method is however not devoid of limits.

The method consists in the identification of specific microscopic features of the healing process. For instance, histologically, after 4 days, the fracture margins can appear smooth instead of frayed with the first Howship's lacunae (i.e., the cavities where the osteoclasts resorb the bone, also called resorption bays). These findings in the absence of any macroscopic sign of healing, permit to change the timing of the trauma from *perimortem* to *antemortem*, and the dating of the *antemortem* trauma can be estimated.

Even when a callus is visible macroscopically, histological and radiological analyses can provide specific information for dating of the trauma. Indeed, the formation of the periosteal and endosteal callus start respectively 7 and 10 days after the trauma whereas osteoporotic activity of the cortex is found 12 days after the event. Light

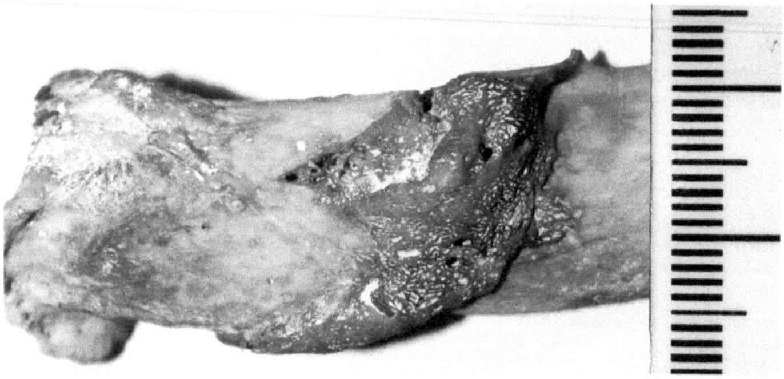

Figure 8.8 72-day-old rib fracture of an adult male. The callus is well visible with a bulging shape, even if almost completely replaced by lamellar bone (mineralized bone).

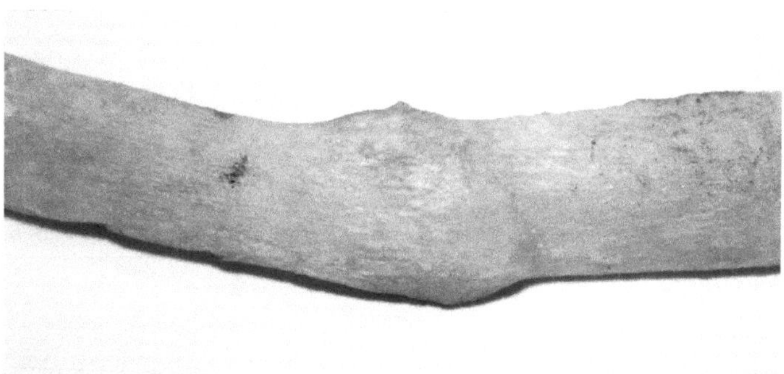

Figure 8.9 Two-year-old rib fracture of an adult female. The callus is well visible, even if the bulging shape of the prior callus has started to remodel into the original shape of the bone. Nonetheless, it is possible that, at this point, the callus already reached its final shape of remodeling and that the bulge may always remain. No precise information about the PTST can be given in this case: the trauma was definitive healed and can be dated at least 6 months to 1 year before death, but a shorter or longer period cannot be excluded.

microscopy also permits the recognition of the transitions of fibrocartilaginous to woven bone calluses as well as woven to lamellar bone calluses (the latter starting 14 days after the trauma with cutting and closing cones). Successively, the endosteal callus becomes indistinguishable from cancellous bone in the marrow cavity after 17 days and the periosteal callus attaches to the cortex after 6 weeks (Table 8.3). Figs. 8.10–8.13 show several microscopic characteristics linked to Table 8.3 that help predict the PTST.

If on the one hand, histology can help dating early stages of fracture healing, on the other hand, radiological analysis may be useful for the

Table 8.3 Healing timetable summarizing the overall histological features detectable in dry bone with related posttraumatic survival time.

General histological healing features	Posttraumatic survival time
Lesion margins with frayed bone lamellae	From start
First Howship's lacunae near the margins of the lesion	After 4 days
Smoothening of the lesion margins	After 4 days
Initial periosteal callus formation separated from the cortex and distant to the fracture margins	After 7 days
Clearly visible endosteal callus formation	After 10 days
Osteoporotic appearance of the cortex	After 12 days
Beginning of replacement of fibrocartilage and primary woven bone with lamellar bone.	After 14 days
Increase of cortical cutting and closing cones orientated towards the lesion	After 14 days
Clearly visible periosteal callus	After 15 days
Endosteal callus becomes indistinguishable from the cancellous bone in the marrow cavity	After 17 days
Union by bridging of the cortical bone discontinuity at first by primary woven bone and then by lamellar bone	After 21 days
Periosteal callus firmly attached to the cortex (becoming inseparable)	After 6 weeks
Quiescent appearance indicating subsided healing (after adequate immobilization)	After 1 year

Adapted from De Boer, H.H., Van Der Merwe, A.E., Maat, G.J.R., 2013. Survival time after fracture or amputation in a 19th Century mining population at Kimberley, South Africa. In: The South African Archaeological Bulletin Goodwin Series. JSTOR, pp. 52–60; Cappella, A., de Boer, H.H., Cammilli, P., De Angelis, D., Messina, C., Sconfienza, L.M., et al., 2019. Histologic and radiological analysis on bone fractures: estimation of posttraumatic survival time in skeletal trauma. Forensic Sci. Int. 302, 109909.

dating of fractures with advanced healing and healed lesions, as summarized in Table 8.4. Yet, the limited number of healing features visible in X-ray images makes this type of analysis often not sufficiently reliable for PTST estimations in forensic cases (Fig. 8.14). However, computed tomography (CT), and in particular Cone-Beam CT, may be used for the detection of the features of the last healing phases (including the fracture line, the inner organization of the different layers of the callus, and the degree of mineralization around the fracture line and inside the callus as visible in Fig. 8.15). However, because of the lack of healing time models (i.e., *antemortem* fractures and calluses of known ages) based on these specific features, they do not yet have a correlation with PTSTs in known samples (Cappella et al., 2013).

Currently, no pathological or skeletal collection possesses enough *antemortem* trauma samples with known PTSTs to fit a theoretical and statistical model capable of predicting PTST from score values. The collection of larger known samples for comparison could permit a more objective healing assessment based on realist time ranges of fracture healing, increasing the reliability of PTST estimation. Of course, given the continuous and overlapping nature of the healing process

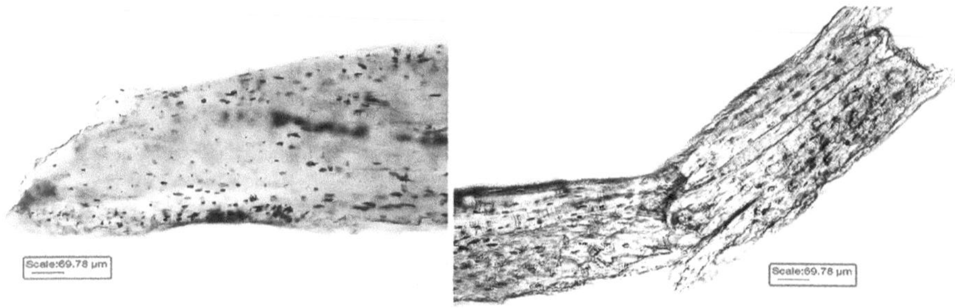

Figure 8.10 Undecalcified sections of a 9-day-old rib fracture from an adult male. (100× magnification). Both images show a fracture extremity characterized by smooth lamellae margins, a feature linked to a minimum PTST of 4 days. This feature is only detectable histologically.

Figure 8.11 Undecalcified sections of a 9-day-old rib fracture from an adult male. (200× magnification). The arrows indicate numerous Howship's lacunae near the fracture line indicating a resorption by osteoclasts (at this stage, the necrotic tissue must be removed to be replaced by a temporary tissue of fibrocartilage or woven bone) and may set the minimum PTST at around 7 days after the trauma.

phases, we should keep in mind that it may never be possible to provide exact dates or stages to *antemortem* traumas (Boyd, 2018).

Perimortem Fractures: Traces of Vital Reaction or "Vitality"

So far, this chapter has briefly discussed all the aspects concerning the interpretation and dating of dry bone *antemortem* trauma—we have seen that chances to grossly estimate PTST exist, in particular if the analysis is supported by histology and radiology. Nonetheless, an issue which still presents different solutions concerns switching from *perimortem* to *antemortem* (in a strictly pathological sense) when not enough time has gone by for even the earliest microscopic callus formation to have begun, and when only hours or a day have gone by between fracture production and

Figure 8.12 Undecalcified sections of a 28-day-old rib fracture from an adult male. (25× magnification). The arrows indicate the periosteal (larger arrow) and endosteal (narrow arrow) fibrous bone formation.

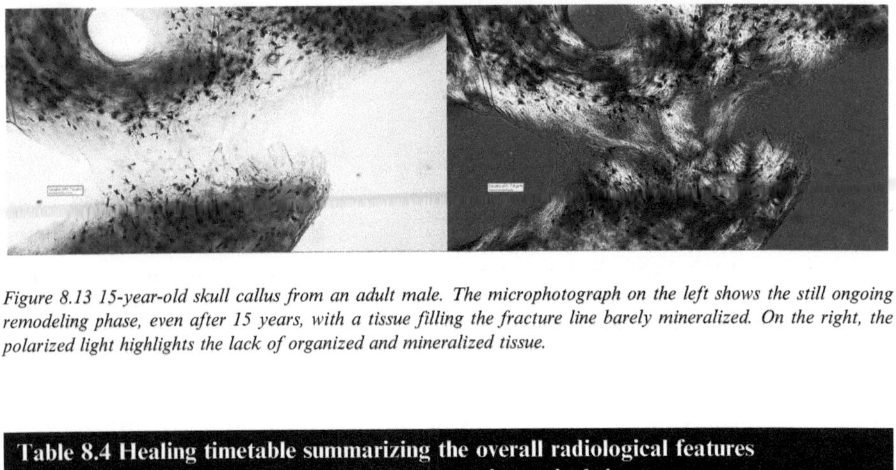

Figure 8.13 15-year-old skull callus from an adult male. The microphotograph on the left shows the still ongoing remodeling phase, even after 15 years, with a tissue filling the fracture line barely mineralized. On the right, the polarized light highlights the lack of organized and mineralized tissue.

Table 8.4 Healing timetable summarizing the overall radiological features detectable in dry bone with related posttraumatic survival time.

General radiological healing features	Posttraumatic survival time
Clearly visible endosteal callus formation	After 10 days
Osteoporotic appearance of the cortex	After 12 days
Clearly visible periosteal callus	After 15 days
Endosteal callus becomes indistinguishable from the cancellous bone in the marrow cavity	After 17 days
Union by bridging of the cortical bone discontinuity	After 21 days
Periosteal callus firmly attached to the cortex (becoming inseparable)	After 6 weeks
Smoothening of the periosteal callus outline	After 2 months

Adapted from De Boer, H.H., Van Der Merwe, A.E., Maat, G.J.R., 2013. Survival time after fracture or amputation in a 19th Century mining population at Kimberley, South Africa. In: The South African Archaeological Bulletin Goodwin Series. JSTOR, pp. 52–60; Cappella, A., de Boer, H.H., Cammilli, P., De Angelis, D., Messina, C., Sconfienza, L.M., et al., 2019. Histologic and radiological analysis on bone fractures: estimation of posttraumatic survival time in skeletal trauma. Forensic Sci. Int. 302, 109909.

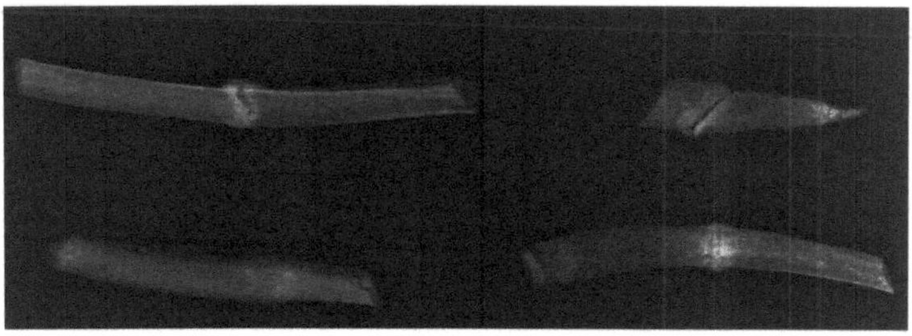

Figure 8.14 X-ray images of four different calluses: the upper left picture depicts a 90-day-old callus, the lower left a 2-year-old callus, the upper right image represents a 20-day-old callus and the lower right a 28-day-old one. In all calluses except for the 2-year-old one it is possible to verify the presence of the fracture lines.

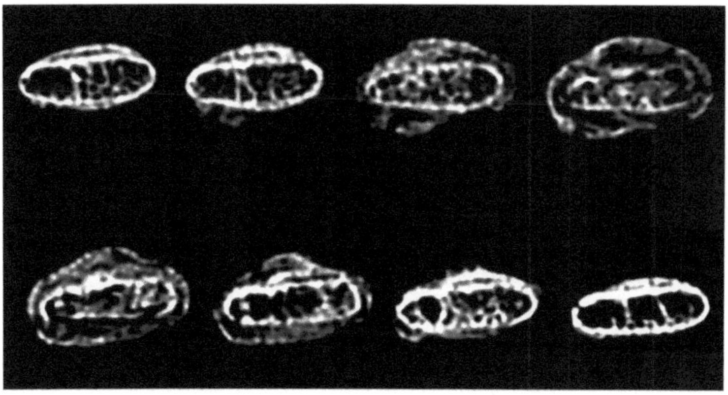

Figure 8.15 Cone-Beam CT image showing the inner organization of a 28-day-old rib callus in eight sequential sections on the transversal plane. The image allows the detection of the different stages of mineralization of the inner structure, which would not be perceived on conventional radiographs and with difficult at this precision in histological sections, due to both practice and execution problems.

death. Overcoming the impossibility of determining whether a fracture was caused after death or a few hours before death would represent a great success in anthropology, if it were possible to adapt histopathological methods to dry or almost dry bone in order to look for residues of the soft tissue inflammatory reaction on bone margins. In cases of fresh cadavers or putrefied corpses, where anthropologists work in collaboration with forensic pathologists for the analysis of bone trauma, methods performed by pathologists (e.g., histochemical and histological techniques) can be adopted to interpret vitality traces. These techniques are able to perceive vital reactions that characterize the first fracture healing signs. Indeed, traces of hemorrhaging, markers of inflammation (Cappella et al., 2015a; Cappella and Cattaneo, 2019; Cattaneo et al., 2010; Cattaneo and Cappella, 2017) and early osteoclastic/osteoblastic activity

(Cappella et al., 2013; Cappella and Cattaneo, 2019; De Boer et al., 2015; Maat, 2008) are "soft tissue" signs that can allow anthropologists to define a trauma as *antemortem* instead of having to resort to a non-specific *perimortem* diagnosis. It is, however, very difficult to find such soft tissue components in dry bone. Nonetheless, when visible, the presence of accumulated erythrocytes and bone marrow within the fractured trabecular bone or a hematoma adherent to the margins within the fracture gap, testifies of short survival times, as shown in Fig. 8.16.

Hemorrhaging in the fracture area is characterized by agglutinated or dispersed red blood cells within the fatty cell structures of the bone marrow damaged by the trauma. The findings of erythrocytes without their typical biconcave morphology, degraded in loci and associated with hemosiderin indicate an old hemorrhage (i.e., hours or days old). Similarly, the migration of cell populations occurs during the following acute inflammatory response (Cappella and Cattaneo, 2019). Another sign of vitality consists in the detection of necrotic tissue debris around the fracture site and the fractured trabeculae. If detected in fractures, these signs confirm the vitality of the lesion in the early stages of healing (i.e., within the first 48–72 hours).

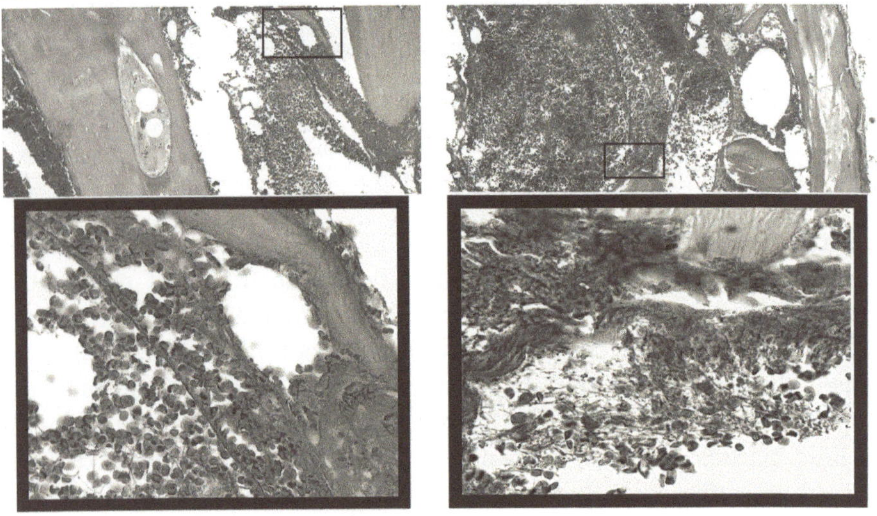

Figure 8.16 Decalcified bone sections, Hematoxylin-Eosin staining, 100× magnification. Both pictures show a massive blood extravasation within the trabecula bone of a vertebra (left) and a rib (right) in an adult male with a little survive (few minutes). In both fractures, signs of vital reaction (hemorrhaging and hematoma) are well detectable: in some areas the hematoma is already formed (agglutination of erythrocytes) while in others as in the boxes (400× magnification) the erythrocytes maintained their morphology and are not yet agglutinated but dispersed. Such evidence suggests a recent hemorrhaging and hematoma with any traces of inflammation reaction.

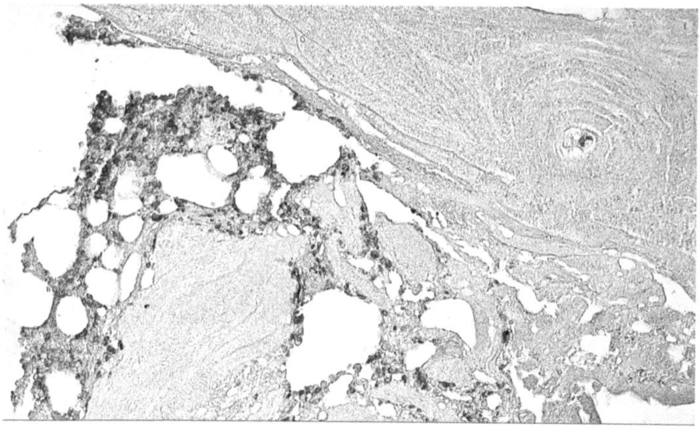

Figure 8.17 Decalcified bone section, immunohistochemistry (antihuman Glycophorin-A staining), 200 × magnification. Traces of hematoma/clot in a skull fracture found in a quasi-skeletonized cadaver indicating a short survival (adult individual survived for about 30 h). The small dark-colored areas are membrane proteins/residues of red blood cells which in putrefied remains usually do not exhibit their morphology anymore because of the decomposition process. In case of putrefied cadavers, this kind of analysis allows to detect traces of agglutinated or disperse erythrocytes which are not more detectable with a standard histological staining as Hematoxylin-Eosin. In this case, immunohistochemistry aided to detect traces of vitality and confirm the survival of this individual.

However, little research has been carried out in order to investigate the persistence of vital signs or biomarkers within skeletal material from different taphonomic contexts. In particular, studies have focused on the morphological changes of red blood cells during the decomposition process (which may be often misinterpreted as something different, e.g., pollen) (Cappella et al., 2015b), and the persistence of microscopic residues of soft tissues in bone fractures of decomposed and skeletonized human remains (Fig. 8.17). So far, results proved a good survival of these biomarkers to taphonomic processes and that blood cells inside the fracture gap can persist over months and sometimes years (Cappella et al., 2015a; Cattaneo et al., 2010). However, these studies only focused on few experimental conditions and different taphonomic conditions should be tested in order to prove its potential in the field of anthropology, and hopefully create the foundation of a new approach in the interpretation of *perimortem* traumas in human remains; the following two cases illustrate how this can be done.

Case 1

In the spring of 2010, the skeleton of a woman was found in the woods near Como (Italy), next to a dump (Fig. 8.18A). The cranium was

Figure 8.18 (A) Skeleton found next to a dump in the wood near Como during the spring of 2010; (B) pieces of a sink (indicated by the arrow) found around the fractured cranium.

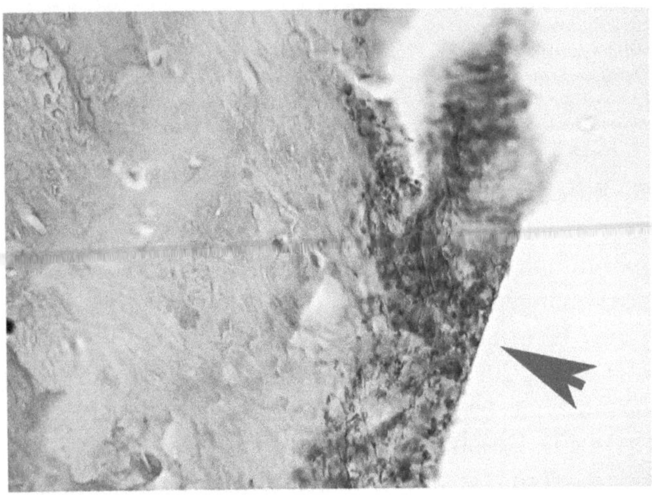

Figure 8.19 Decalcified bone section; antihuman Glycophorin-A staining; 400 × magnification. The parietal fracture margins are positive for signs of vital reaction tested by immunohistochemistry. The fracture margin exhibits traces of a clot formation (dark-colored and indicated by the arrow) which suggests evidence of survival.

severely fractured. Macroscopically, the lesions could only be classified as perimortem and may have been caused by someone dumping a sink (in Fig. 8.18B, one can see pieces of the sink around the cranium) or could have been related to the actual cause of death (i.e., blunt trauma to the head). Although the remains corresponded to almost dry bones, the margins of a fracture on the parietal were tested with immunohistochemical methods for signs of vital inflammatory reaction (Cattaneo et al., 2010). Fig. 8.19 represents an apparent clot formation (in dark) on the fractured margin, suggestive of a vital reaction. If more research is performed, in the next few years this kind of result can provide clear evidence of antemortem trauma.

Case 2

In the winter of 2008, a skeleton was found chained to a wall in a cellar of an abandoned building in Saronno (Italy). A witness confessed that the young man had been beaten, brought to the cellar, chained, and held hostage as retaliation towards the group of drug smugglers he was a member of. The witness said that the man had been kept alive for a month and then stabbed to death. The magistrate was therefore very interested in verifying whether there were signs of the first beating. Indeed, the supraspinous portion of the left scapula was broken, but new woven bone could be seen "gluing" the fragments of bone, visible as the darker brown more porous bone (arrow in Fig. 8.20). The macroscopic characteristics of the woven bone are consistent with a 3–4-week-old callus. This is an example of how bone traumatic pathology can be used to establish beatings or maltreatment.

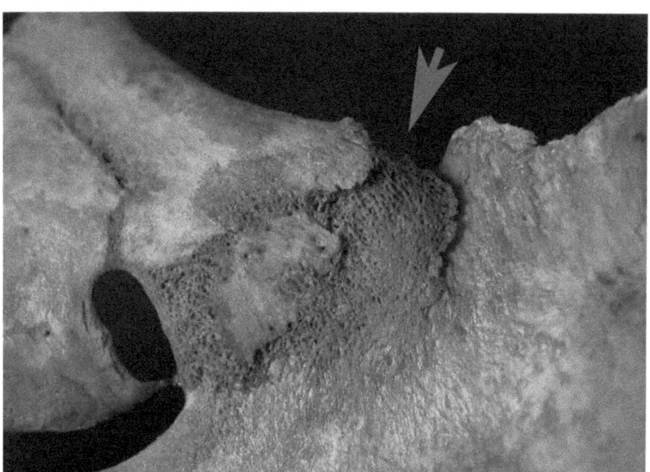

Figure 8.20 Broken left scapula with woven bone (arrow). The macroscopic characteristics suggest a callus of 3–4 weeks.

The next chapter will show how useful the pathology of fracture healing can be for building the biological profile or even for positive identification.

References

Aubin, J.E., Turksen, K., Heersche, J.N.M., 1993. Osteoblastic cell lineage. In: Noda, M. (Ed.), Cellular and Molecular Biology of Bone. Elsevier, pp. 1–45.

Bonnichsen, R., 1979. Pleistocene Bone Technology in the Beringian Refugium. Mercury Series, Archaeological Survey of Canada. Pap. No. 89.

Boyd, D.C., 2018. The anatomical basis for fracture repair: Recognition of the healing continuum and its forensic applications to investigations of pediatric and elderly abuse. Forensic Anthropol. Theor. Framew. Sci. Basis 149–200.

Brighton, C.T., Hunt, R.M., 1991. Early histological and ultrastructural changes in medullary fracture callus. JBJS 73, 832–847.

Calce, S.E., Rogers, T.L., 2007. Taphonomic changes to blunt force trauma: a preliminary study. J. Forensic Sci. 52, 519–527. Available from: https://doi.org/10.1111/j.1556-4029.2007.00405.x.

Cappella, A., Amadasi, A., Gaudio, D., Gibelli, D., Borgonovo, S., Di Giancamillo, M., et al., 2013. The application of cone-beam CT in the aging of bone calluses: a new perspective? Int. J. Leg. Med. 127, 1139–1144.

Cappella, A., Amadasi, A., Castoldi, E., Mazzarelli, D., Gaudio, D., Cattaneo, C., 2014. The difficult task of assessing perimortem and postmortem fractures on the skeleton: a blind text on 210 fractures of known origin. J. Forensic Sci. 59, 1598–1601. Available from: https://doi.org/10.1111/1556-4029.12539.

Cappella, A., Bertoglio, B., Castoldi, E., Maderna, E., Di Giancamillo, A., Domeneghini, C., et al., 2015a. The taphonomy of blood components in decomposing bone and its relevance to physical anthropology. Am. J. Phys. Anthropol. 158, 636–645.

Cappella, A., Stefanelli, S., Caccianiga, M., Rizzi, A., Bertoglio, B., Sforza, C., et al., 2015b. Blood or spores? A cautionary note on interpreting cellular debris on human skeletal remains. Int. J. Leg. Med. 129, 919–926.

Cappella, A., Cattaneo, C., 2019. Exiting the limbo of perimortem trauma: A brief review of microscopic markers of hemorrhaging and early healing signs in bone. Forensic Sci. Int. 302, 109856.

Cappella, A., de Boer, H.H., Cammilli, P., De Angelis, D., Messina, C., Sconfienza, L.M., et al., 2019. Histologic and radiological analysis on bone fractures: estimation of posttraumatic survival time in skeletal trauma. Forensic Sci. Int. 302, 109909.

Cattaneo, C., Andreola, S., Marinelli, E., Poppa, P., Porta, D., Grandi, M., 2010. The detection of microscopic markers of hemorrhaging and wound age on dry bone: a pilot study. Am. J. Forensic Med. Pathol. 31, 22–26.

Cattaneo, C., Cappella, A., 2017. Distinguishing between peri-and post-mortem trauma on bone. In: Schotsmans, E.M.J., Marquez-Grant, N., Forbes, S.L. (Eds.), Taphonomy of Human Remains: Forensic Analysis of the Dead and the Depositional Environment. Wiley Online Library, pp. 352–368.

Cattaneo, C., Cappella, A., Cunha, E., 2017. Post mortem anthropology and trauma analysis, in: Ferrara, S.D. (Ed.), P5 Medicine and Justice. Springer, pp. 166–179.

Cho, H.H., Kyoung, K.M., Seo, M.J., Kim, Y.J., Bae, Y.C., Jung, J.S., 2006. Overexpression of CXCR4 increases migration and proliferation of human adipose tissue stromal cells. Stem Cell Dev. 15, 853–864.

Collins, D.H., 1966. Pathology of Bone. Butterworths, London, UK.

Cruess, R.L., Dumont, J., 1975. Healing of bone, tendon and ligament. Fractures. Lippincott Williams & Wilkins, Philadelphia, PA, pp. 91–97.

Cunha, E., Cattaneo, C., 2006. Forensic anthropology and forensic pathology. In: Schmitt, A., Cunha, E., Pinheiro, J. (Eds.), Forensic Anthropology and Medicine. Springer, Totowa, New Jersey, pp. 39–53.

De Boer, H.H., Van Der Merwe, A.E., Maat, G.J.R., 2013. Survival time after fracture or amputation in a 19th Century mining population at Kimberley, South Africa. In: The South African Archaeological Bulletin Goodwin Series. JSTOR, pp. 52–60.

De Boer, H.H., Van der Merwe, A.E., Hammer, S., Steyn, M., Maat, G.J.R., 2015. Assessing post-traumatic time interval in human dry bone. Int. J. Osteoarchaeol. 25, 98–109.

Dimitriou, R., Tsiridis, E., Giannoudis, P.V., 2005. Current concepts of molecular aspects of bone healing. Injury 36, 1392–1404.

Doblaré, M., Garcıa, J.M., Gómez, M.J., 2004. Modelling bone tissue fracture and healing: a review. Eng. Fract. Mech. 71, 1809–1840.

Einhorn, T.A., 1998. The cell and molecular biology of fracture healing. Clin. Orthop. Relat. Res. 355, S7–S21.

Frost, H.M., 1989. The biology of fracture healing: an overview for clinicians. Part II. Clin. Orthop. Relat. Res. 248, 294–309.

Galloway, A., Zephro, L., 2005. Skeletal trauma analysis of the lower extremity. In: Rich, J., Dean, D. E. (Eds.), Forensic Medicine of the Lower Extremity. Springer, Totowa, New Jersey, pp. 253–277.

Harkess, J.W., Ramsey, W.C., Harkess, J.W., 1996. Principles of fractures and dislocations in adults. In: Rockwood, C.A., Green, D.P. (Eds.), Rockwood's and Green's Fractures in Adults. Lippincott Williams & Wilkins, Philadelphia, PA, pp. 3–210.

Hart, G.O., 2005. Fracture pattern interpretation in the skull: differentiating blunt force from ballistics trauma using concentric fractures. J. Forensic Sci. 50, JFS2004219-6.

Hendrix, R.W., 2002. Fracture healing. In: Rogers, L.F. (Ed.), Radiology of Skeletal Trauma. Churchill Livingstone, pp. 203–230.

Heppenstall, R.B., 1980. Fracture healing. In: Heppenstall, R. B., (Ed), Fracture Treatment and Healing. Saunders, Philadelphia, PA, pp. 35–64.

Johnson, E., 1985. Current developments in bone technology. In: Schiffer, M.B. (Ed.), Advances in Archaeological Method and Theory. Elsevier, pp. 157–235.

Karr, L.P., Outram, A.K., 2012. Tracking changes in bone fracture morphology over time: environment, taphonomy, and the archaeological record. J. Archaeol. Sci. 39, 555–559.

Karr, L.P., Outram, A.K., 2015. Bone degradation and environment: understanding, assessing and conducting archaeological experiments using modern animal bones. Int. J. Osteoarchaeol. 25, 201–212.

Knight, B., 1996. Forensic Pathology, 2nd ed. Arnold, London, UK.

Kon, T., Cho, T., Aizawa, T., Yamazaki, M., Nooh, N., Graves, D., et al., 2001. Expression of osteoprotegerin, receptor activator of NF-κB ligand (osteoprotegerin ligand) and related proinflammatory cytokines during fracture healing. J. Bone Miner. Res. 16, 1004–1014.

LaCroix, M.N., 2013. A study of the impact of weathering upon the minmal force required to fracture bone. Unpublished MS thesis.

Lee, S.-K., Lorenzo, J., 2006. Cytokines regulating osteoclast formation and function. Curr. Opin. Rheumatol. 18, 411–418.

Maat, G., Huls, N., 2010. Histological fracture dating of fresh and dried bone tissue. In: Bilo, R. A.C., Robben, S.G.F., van Rijn, R.R. (Eds.), Forensic Aspects of Pediatric Fractures: Differentiating Accidental Trauma from Child Abuse. Springer, Berlin (Germany), pp. 194–201.

Maat, G.J.R., 2008. Case study 5.3: dating of fractures in human dry bone tissue—the Berisha case. In: Kimmerle, E., Baraybar, J.P. (Eds.), Skeletal Trauma: Identification of Injuries Resulting from Human Rights Abuse and Armed Conflict. CRC Press, Boca Raton, FL, pp. 245–254.

Maples, W.R., 1998. Trauma analysis by the forensic anthropologist. In: Reichs, K.J. (Ed.), Forensic Osteology: Advances in the Identification of Human Remains. Charles C. Thomas, Springfield, IL.

Marenzana, M., Arnett, T.R., 2013. The key role of the blood supply to bone. Bone Res. 1, 203–215.

Marsell, R., Einhorn, T.A., 2011. The biology of fracture healing. Injury 42, 551–555.

McKibbin, B., 1978. The biology of fracture healing in long bones. J. Bone Jt. Surg. Br. 60, 150–162.

Moraitis, K., Eliopoulos, C., Spiliopoulou, C., 2009. Fracture characteristics of perimortem trauma in skeletal material. Internet J. Biol. Anthropol. 3, 585.

Morlan, R.E., 1984. Toward the definition of criteria for the recognition of artificial bone alterations. Quat. Res. 22, 160–171.

Ortner, D.J., 2003. Identification of Pathological Conditions in Human Skeletal Remains, 3rd ed. Smithsonian Institution Press, New York.

Ozaki, A., Tsunoda, M., Kinoshita, S., Saura, R., 2000. Role of fracture hematoma and periosteum during fracture healing in rats: interaction of fracture hematoma and the periosteum in the initial step of the healing process. J. Orthop. Sci. 5, 64–70.

Phillips, A.M., 2005. Overview of the fracture healing cascade. Injury 36, S5–S7.

Quatrehomme, G., Alunni, V., 2013. Bone trauma. In: Siegel, J.A., Sauko, P.J., Houck, M.M. (Eds.), Encyclopaedia of Forensic Sciences. Academic Press, pp. 89–96.

Reichs, K.J., 1998. Forensic Osteology: Advances in the Identification of Human Remains, 2nd ed. Charles C. Thomas, Springfield, IL.

Sauer, N.J., 1998. The timing of injuries and manner of death: distinguishing among antemortem, perimortem and postmortem trauma. In: Reichs, K.J. (Ed.), Forensic Osteology: Advances in the Identification of Human Remains. Charles C. Thomas, Springfield, IL, pp. 321–331.

Schmidt-Bleek, K., Schell, H., Kolar, P., Pfaff, M., Perka, C., Buttgereit, F., et al., 2009. Cellular composition of the initial fracture hematoma compared to a muscle hematoma: a study in sheep. J. Orthop. Res. 27, 1147–1151.

Semeraro, D., Passalacqua, N.V., Symes, S., Gilson, T., 2012. Patterns of trauma induced by motorboat and ferry propellers as illustrated by three known cases from Rhode Island. J. Forensic Sci. 57, 1625–1629.

Sfeir, C., Ho, L., Doll, B.A., Azari, K., Hollinger, J.O., 2005. Fracture repair. Bone Regeneration and Repair. Springer, pp. 21–44.

Ubelaker, D.H., 1997. Taphonomic applications in forensic anthropology. In: Sorg, M.H., Haglund, W.D. (Eds.), Forensic Taphonomy: The Postmortem Fate of Human Remains. CRC press, Boca Raton, FL, pp. 77–90.

Ubelaker, D.H., 1991. Perimortem and postmortem modification of human bone. Lessons from forensic anthropology. Anthropol 171–174.

Ubelaker, D.H., Adams, B.J., 1995. Differentiation of perimortem and postmortem trauma using taphonomic indicators. J. Forensic Sci. 40, 509–512.

Villa, P., Mahieu, E., 1991. Breakage patterns of human long bones. J. Hum. Evol. 21, 27–48.

Wheatley, B.P., 2008. Perimortem or postmortem bone fractures? An experimental study of fracture patterns in deer femora. J. Forensic Sci. 53, 69–72.

Wieberg, D.A.M., Wescott, D.J., 2008. Estimating the timing of long bone fractures: correlation between the postmortem interval, bone moisture content, and blunt force trauma fracture characteristics. J. Forensic Sci. 53, 1028–1034.

Yang, X., Ricciardi, B.F., Hernandez-Soria, A., Shi, Y., Camacho, N.P., Bostrom, M.P.G., 2007. Callus mineralization and maturation are delayed during fracture healing in interleukin-6 knockout mice. Bone 41, 928–936.

CHAPTER 9

Biological Profile and Personal Identification

Debora Mazzarelli, Danilo De Angelis, Daniele Gibelli, Pasquale Poppa, Davide Porta, Lucie Biehler-Gomez and Cristina Cattaneo
LABANOF, Department of Biomedical Sciences for Health, University of Milan, Milan, Italy

Personal identification is an essential process both ethically, to bring closure to the families and avoid the trauma of ambiguous loss, to return the remains of the deceased to their loved ones, and juridically and administratively for civil, criminal, and insurance purposes. The study of bone disease is inherently related to identity. All bone diseases and prosthetic devices related to disease are useful for identification; even trauma and the signs of healing and degeneration that ensue. Most forensic scientists immediately associate trauma to the analysis of cause of death, but actually, trauma and its consequences, even in badly burnt material (Cappella et al., 2019; De Angelis et al., 2017), are fundamental in the process of identification. We will not dwell on all morphological methods of anthropological identification for which we recommend the indications of FASE (Forensic Anthropology Society of Europe) (De Boer et al., 2020; De Angelis et al., 2020) but we will develop in this chapter those which have to do with bone disease, from degenerative disease to tuberculosis.

In fact, osteology and the study of bone disease can provide general and specific information on the skeleton of the deceased. This is fundamental in implementing the biological profile, and first of all for what is known as "general identification." In addition, bone traits and morphology can be pivotal in personal identification as markers of individuality, although they are still too rarely considered in forensic practice. As such, bone morphology can be used in the same manner as fingerprints or odontological characteristics, through the assessment of topographical and morphological concordance of the same features between antemortem and postmortem images and the expression of the probability that two persons may share it. Therefore, as bone disease

Interpreting Bone Lesions and Pathology for Forensic Practice. DOI: https://doi.org/10.1016/B978-0-323-85162-6.00009-X

can significantly and uniquely change bone morphology, it is a crucial and potent tool for identification.

Bone Disease for the Biological Profile

Generally, in forensic anthropology, the biological profile is understood in its most narrow sense as the estimation of sex, age-at-death, population affinity, stature, and other variables useful for describing a possible "identikit" of that person from his or her bones. Hence bone disease can complement this biological profile by providing additional information on the life or death of the individual. But how exactly can this information help in a forensic setting?

In the same manner as facial reconstruction, which is a biological yet artistic reproduction of the face of a deceased from anthropological data based on anatomical principles, bone disease can add useful details regarding the individual to the biological profile. Indeed, a facial reconstruction is just a possible representation of the likely appearance of the individual and constitutes a non-specific information that may orient the search for a matching missing person. Physical details such as a crooked nose, marked facial asymmetry, or large lips are not identifying features, but they can narrow down the list of possible candidates for an identification. Using the same approach, the interpretation of bone disease can provide additional useful pieces in the puzzle that is forensic identification. The information acquired for the interpretation of bone lesions and bone disease provides clues that may be used to reduce the likely possibilities in a missing persons' list for the identification of unknown decedents. A correct interpretation of bone lesions can indicate potential symptoms and disabilities that the individual may have suffered from. For instance, osteomyelitis may induce local pain, skin manifestations (i.e., ulcers, tissue swelling), limping during walking (if a lower limb was affected) and reduced joint mobility. The morphological characteristics of the lesion can provide details about the severity, extent, degree of healing and temporality of the lesion (e.g., woven bone vs lamellar bone). Through the analysis of lesions, it is possible to reliably infer whether they occurred recently or had the time to remodel, their etiology and pathogenesis, their impact on the joints and nearby tissues, clinical manifestations as well as musculoskeletal implications. This quantity of information, although not definite because the interpretation of bone disease should always be considered in the larger perspective of differential diagnosis, can complement the biological profile in forensic practice and narrow down a list of missing individuals for forensic identification. In addition, if the individual was suffering from a pathological condition and its associated clinical manifestations, he may have sought medical help. Similarly, the presence of a medical device indicates a surgical intervention. Relevant medical institutions may possess records (with antemortem imaging) that may be used for identification comparison. Thus, the recording of bone disease in the biological profile may provide insight as to where to look for further information regarding the individual and for data useful for personal identification.

The following are a series of case studies where pathology became crucial for the reconstruction of the biological profile.

Case 1

Searches for a victim of organized crime in 2018 in the outskirts of Milano led to the finding of a buried body under the cement floor of a cellar. Anthropological analysis immediately pointed to a young male with previous nasal trauma.

Both nasal bones showed signs of bone remodeling with the formation of a bone callus. The lesion had smooth rounded margins which suggested that it had reached complete healing (Fig. 9.1).

Regarding the dating of the lesion, the indications in the literature allowed a general judgment on the basis of the morphological changes found: a fracture without complications tends to heal in a period of time between 4 weeks and 3 months (Blau and Ubelaker, 2009). But fracture repair, as mentioned, depends on multiple factors, such as age or pathological conditions so it is always best to maintain large margins of time.

In this specific case, the bone apposition had smooth margins and although it was still distinguishable from the remaining bone tissue, its appearance suggested a completely remodeled callus. It was also possible to assume that the original fracture dated back to at least one or two years before death. These are the type of indications to give investigating authorities when asking them to search at emergency wards or clinics.

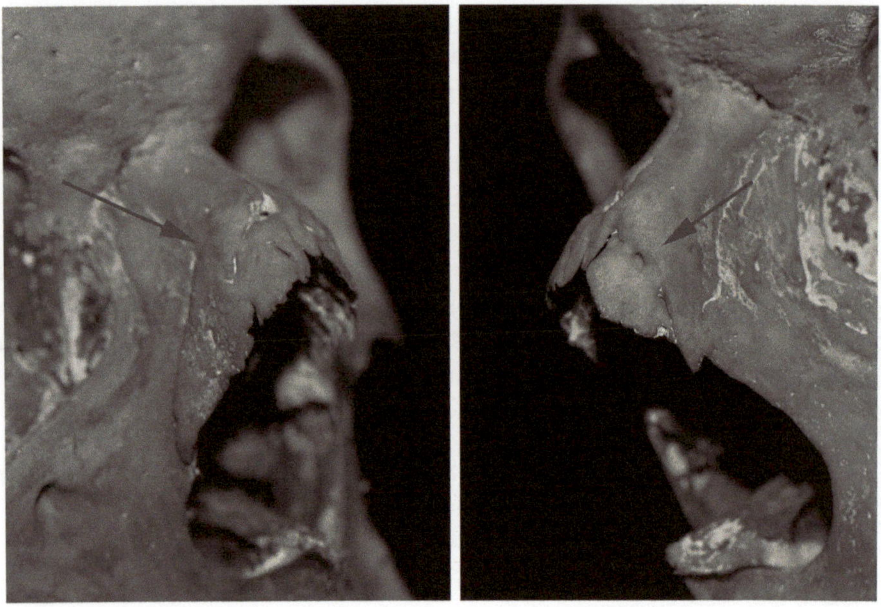

Figure 9.1 Bone callus found on the nasal bones. Arrows indicate the callus where the original fracture was.

Furthermore, at the distal epiphysis of the right tibia and fibula, two areas of bone neoformation were highlighted, with smooth contours and remodeled margins suggesting a previous fracture at the right ankle (Fig. 9.2).

An adduction fracture of the foot severe enough to cause the injury of both the fibular and tibial malleolus could explain the calluses observed (McGuigan, 2011). Nevertheless, this would not have caused a permanent visible limb; perhaps only occasional pain in the ankle.

The appearance of the lesions described (i.e., nasal bones and right ankle) argued in favor of antemortem lesions which occurred at least one to two years before death. In particular, with respect to the injury at the right ankle, it undoubtedly caused pain and disability at the time of the accident that may have required the patient to be admitted to an emergency room. It is possible to hypothesize that the subject was hospitalized and underwent a diagnostic investigation such as a radiographic test.

This led to a suspicion of identity among missing persons in the criminal environment. An examination of the antemortem documentation of

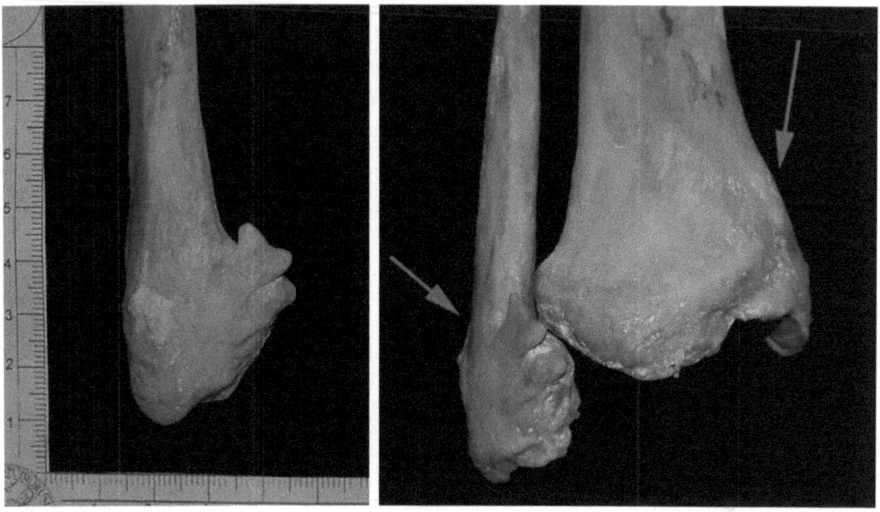

Figure 9.2 Remodeled antemortem fractures (arrow). To the left, the distal extremity of the fibula and to the right, tibia and fibula in anatomical position.

the suspected identity revealed that around 20 years before his death, he had an accident causing a bimalleolar fracture in his right ankle. In addition, the victim's family reported a fracture to the nose, never treated surgically, that occurred two years before his disappearance. However, no antemortem radiological data was available. Positive identification was therefore achieved through dental clinical documentation.

Case 2

In 2010, two scuba divers found a human cranium with some soft tissue at the bottom of Lake Lecco in Lombardy. After cleaning and upon anthropological examination the following was found: in the area between the greater wing of the right sphenoid bone and the right parietal bone, an irregular discontinuation about 72 mm long could be seen, progressing superiorly and antero-posteriorly (Fig. 9.3) the lesion was superficial and presented rounded margins with signs of bone remodeling.

On the left parietal near the sagittal suture there were two rounded button-like areas of new bone formation, in relief, with a smooth surface, and a diameter of 0.5 cm, compatible with the diagnosis of osteoma (Fig. 9.4A); at the base of the cranium, *tuberculum precondilare*, a non-metric trait, 0.8 cm in diameter (Fig. 9.4B).

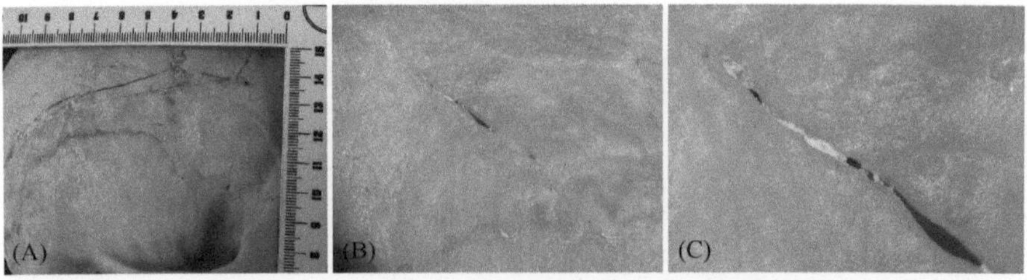

Figure 9.3 (A) Discontinuation of the right parietal consistent with an old fracture. The arrows indicate the areas where the lesion is thicker; (B,C) Stereomicroscopic view of the point indicated by the top arrow starting from the bottom upwards at different optical magnifications (6× and 10×); margins of the discontinuation are rounded and smooth.

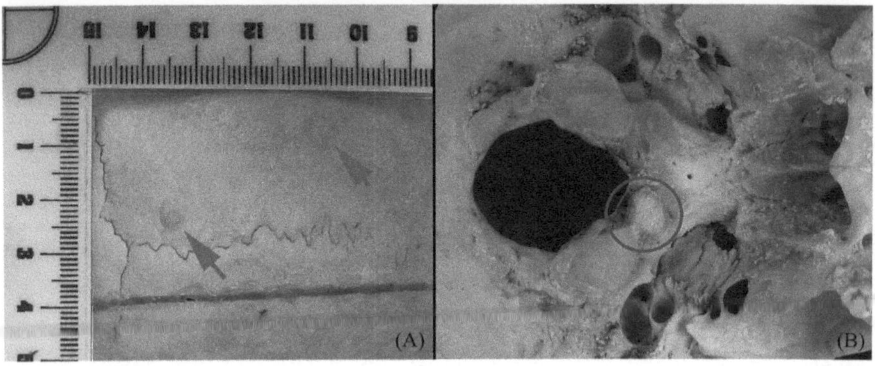

Figure 9.4 (A) osteoma left parietal. (B) tuberculum precondilare.

Even dental elements provided some sort of pathological information. In correspondence of the collar of 47 and 48 and on the mesial surface of 48, dental restorations in glass ionomer cement were noted (Fig. 9.5A). This kind of material is rarely used in Italy to treat dental cavities. Furthermore, mandibular canines showed discrete enamel hypoplasia. (Fig. 9.5B).

The head belonged to a young African woman who had been dismembered. She had a probable history of drug addiction (the bones resulted positive for cocaine), probably with a poor upbringing yet she had been well taken care of for she could allow herself to apply means of caries prevention such as these resin fillings. Furthermore, sometime before death she had succumbed to some sort of serious cranial trauma with fractures. All this information accompanied the craniofacial reconstruction on the news, local papers and LABANOF website, but the woman still remains unidentified (Fig. 9.6).

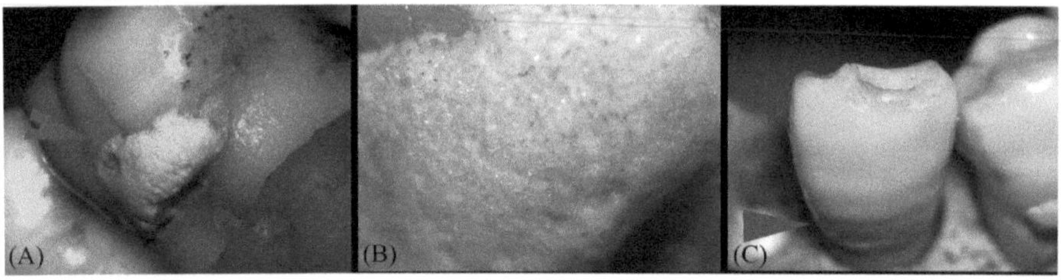

Figure 9.5 (A) White resin restorations; (B) in microscopy 10×; (C) linear hypoplasia.

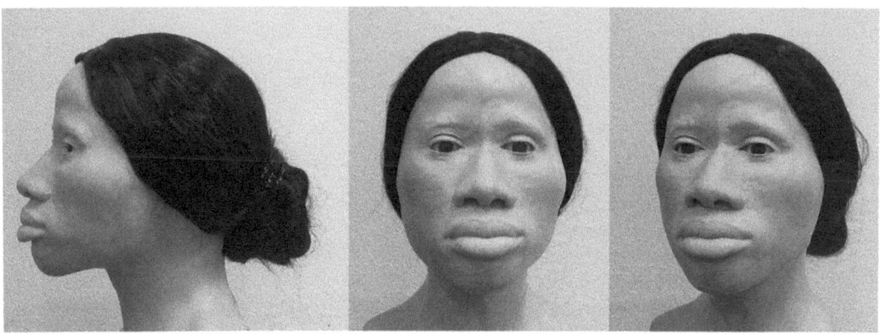

Figure 9.6 Craniofacial reconstruction which accompanied the biological profile given to media and investigating authorities: African female, 20–30 years of age, severe head trauma (possible accident?) at least one year before her remains were found; some preventive dental work, possible cocaine user.

Case 3

In 2019, the skeletonized body of a middle-aged woman was found in a power plant. Total body radiographic examination was performed. This examination is especially intended to highlight any outcome from antemortem trauma or from surgery. It was possible to verify the presence of an intramedullary screw in the first metatarsal of the left foot (Fig. 9.7).

Contrary to popular belief, screws or prosthetic devices do not always bear registration numbers on them. However, orthopedic surgeons can provide indications for the biological profile. In fact, this was most likely the outcome of a surgery performed in order to correct the bone malformation of hallux valgus (bunions).

Case 4

In the summer of 2017, in the woods near Milano, skeletal remains were found at the foot of a tree.

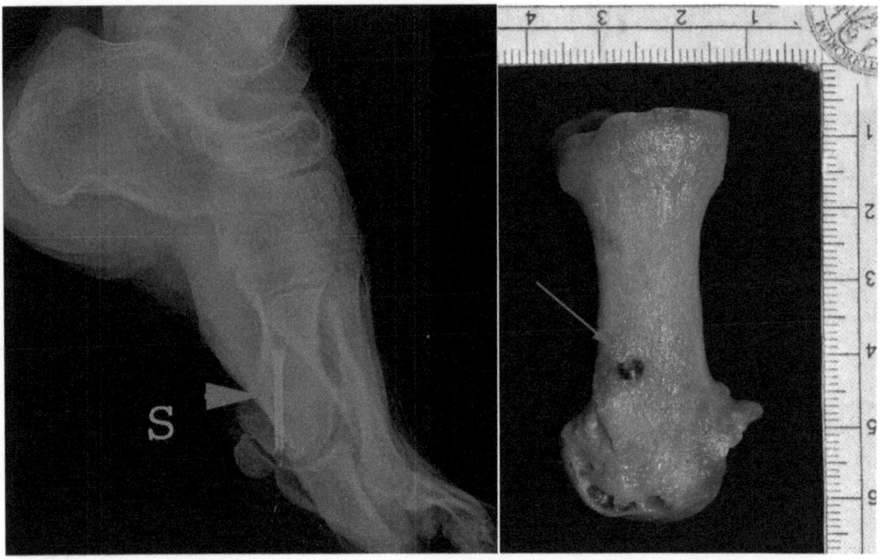

Figure 9.7 The arrow indicates the screw both in the X-ray and in the cleaned bone. Courtesy Dr. G. Merelli, Università degli Studi di Milano.

The anthropological examination highlighted several non-metric traits, also known as anatomical variants, which in some cases are hereditary, and as such indicative of the existence of kinship within a certain group (Buikstra and Ubelaker, 1994).

Photographic and graphic documentation of the dental elements was also reported (Fig. 9.8).

Three bridges could be noted in the superior arch:

1. Gold resin bridge involving the dental elements 12, 11, 21, 22; the pillars of the bridge being 11 and 22. A longitudinal fracture could be seen on 11, which occupied (inferiorly to superiorly) two-thirds of the crown. Dental element 22 showed a loss of about a third of the resin surface.
2. Gold resin bridge on the superior right arch, which involved the dental elements 14, 15, 16 and 17, and where 17 and 15 were the pillars of the bridge itself.
3. Gold resin bridge on the superior left arch, which involved elements 25 and 26, and where 26 was the pillar of the bridge and had no resin cover.

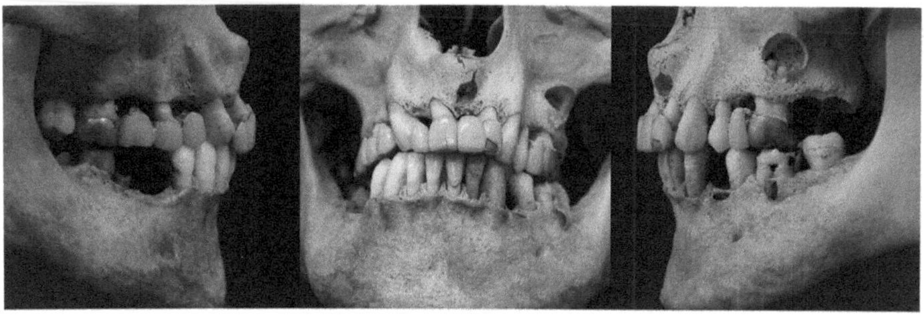

Figure 9.8 Norma lateralis *and* norma frontalis *of the maxillary and mandibular bones.*

We also observed:

- an expanding maxillary cystic lesion at the alveolus of the dental element 21, superiorly and posteriorly;
- a periapical osteolytic area in correspondence with the dental element 26;
- at the dental element 34, which was lost antemortem, a circular bone resorption area of 0.5 cm in diameter;
- at the tooth element 36, on the buccal surface, oval-shaped inter-radicular bone resorption area and greater longitudinal diameter of 0.4 cm.

Dental restorative traits were important for the biological profile because they may be related to the country where they were performed and to the socio-economic status of the missing person. Overall, the skeletal remains did not present traumatic or pathological elements of relevance; instead, mainly signs related to repeated functional stresses or due to minor antemortem trauma were observed, which affected several skeletal areas.

In the fourth, fifth, and sixth cervical vertebrae, we could see a bipartite transverse foramen. This trait is genetically determined (Fig. 9.9A). The right clavicle showed an osteolytic lesion medio-inferiorly. This sign is to be considered as a costal syndesmosis (Fig. 9.9B). Generally, this type of injury results from the application of stress to the shoulder girdle, in particular lifting of weights with the shoulders "bent" forward (Capasso et al., 1999). The fifth lumbar vertebra showing a non-union of the arch (at the level of the lamina) with the vertebral body was observed. This condition is defined as lumbar spondylolysis (Fig. 9.9C).

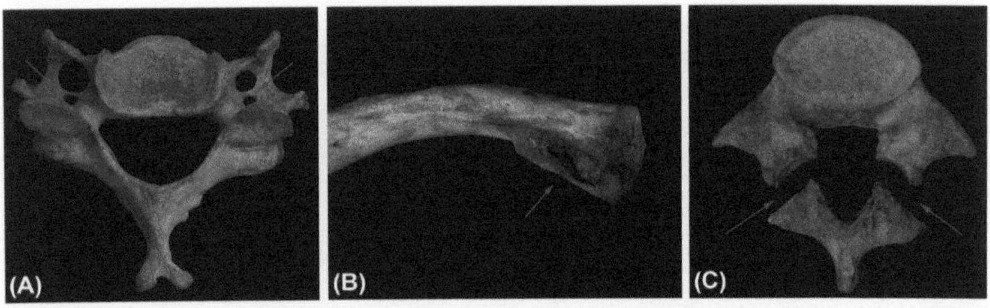

Figure 9.9 (A) Cervical vertebrae, with bipartite transverse foramina; (B) right clavicle showing a lytic lesion medio-inferiorly; (C) fifth lumbar vertebra showing non-union of the arch.

Spondylolysis can be due to stress fractures, as a result of repeated trauma to the bone, or may be hereditary. Spondylolysis of the fifth lumbar vertebra can also be a consequence of functional stresses to which the inferior spine can be easily subjected, especially during locomotion (Waldron, 2008).

Scars of two minor traumatic events on the frontal bone (left eyebrow arch and left frontal draft) could be noted (Fig. 9.10), as well as on the left hamate (Fig. 9.11A), right fifth metacarpal (Fig. 9.11B), sternal ends of the sixth and seventh ribs bilaterally (Fig. 9.12B) and the coccyx (Fig. 9.12C). The observed bone calluses had smooth margins thus corresponding to completely remodeled fractures dating back to at least one or two years before death.

Therefore, along with dental work not very frequent in Italy, the skeleton showed evidence of a young man with probable mechanical stress related to trauma to his back and hands, possibly occupational. This information led the authorities to select among the missing persons a young man from Romania who had worked from a very young age as a builder and had several accidents. He had disappeared from Milano in 2014. Positive identification was then obtained through forensic odontology.

Bone Disease for Personal Identification

Personal identification in forensic anthropology consists in restoring an identity to unknown skeletal remains beyond reasonable doubt. Information relating to the potential identity is referred to as antemortem data, whereas postmortem data pertain to the unidentified skeletal remains under examination. The two sets of data are examined,

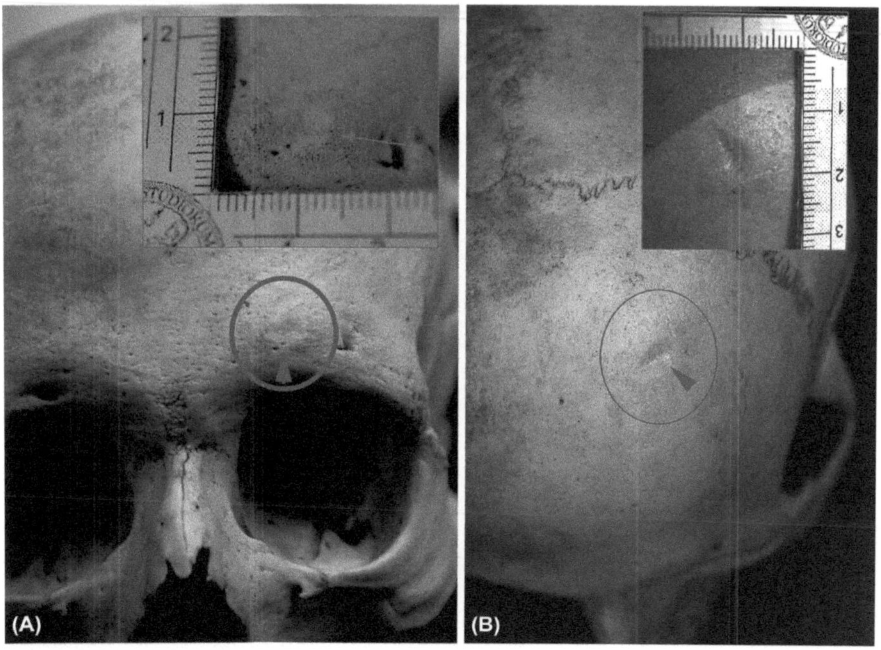

Figure 9.10 (A) Middle third of the supraorbital arch showing a slight depression of the external table, roughly oval in shape with a larger transverse diameter of about 0.8 cm and a smaller, longitudinal diameter of 0.5 cm (1 mm deep); (B) Left side of the frontal bone showing a depression on the external table. This depression, roughly triangular in shape with an antero-medial apex and 0.8 cm long, had a maximum depth of 1 mm and was characterized by smooth and remodeled margins.

searching for consistencies and inconsistencies that may either support or refute the hypothesis that they originated from a single person. Through the comparison and matching of antemortem and postmortem data, it is possible to link a presumed identity to skeletal remains, if the scientific methods used are sound enough and provide sufficient evidence.

According to Interpol's Disaster Victim Identification guide, the primary and most reliable methods of identification include the comparisons of antemortem and postmortem dental records, antemortem and postmortem fingerprints, and postmortem DNA profiles with reference samples. However, so-called primary methods cannot always be used in forensic settings: postmortem data may be lacking or damaged (i.e., at times DNA is highly susceptible to contamination and degradation, teeth may be partially or completely absent and fingerprints are decomposed in skeletonized individuals), and antemortem data may not be available. They also mention that unique serial numbers

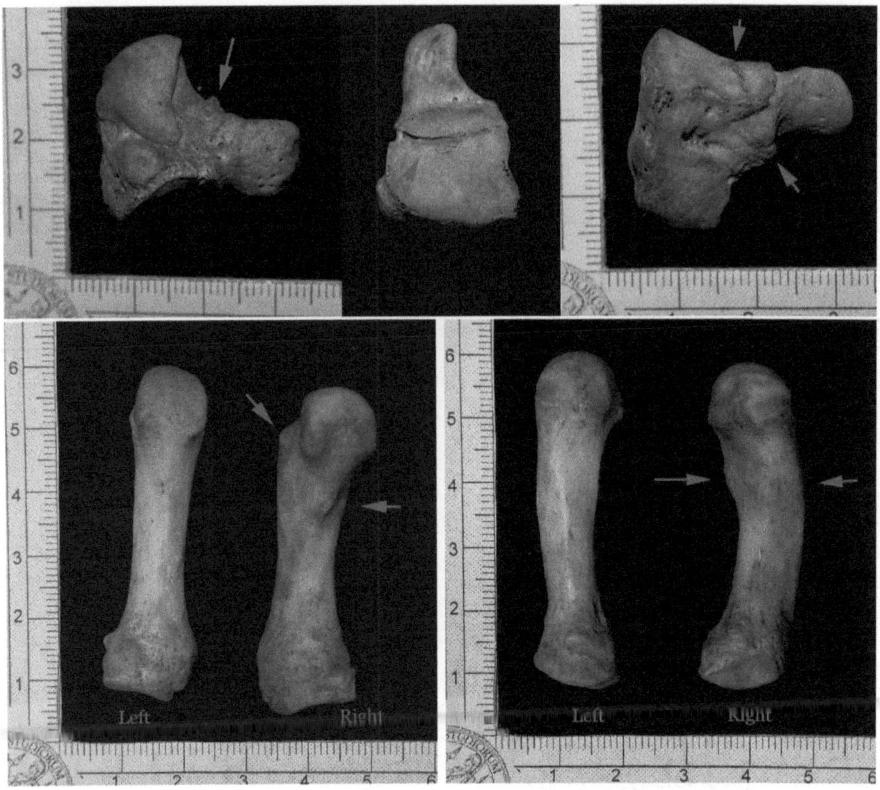

Figure 9.11 Top: left hamate showing signs of bone remodeling with thickening of the bone tissue; bottom: palmar (left) and medial (right) views of the fifth metacarpals showing thickening of the bone tissue at the distal end of the shaft, with an abnormal curvature of the shaft. This anomaly may have been caused by a traumatic event during life.

from medical implants (such as prostheses) can constitute a reliable mean of identification. The ICRC's recommendations in *Forensic Identification of Human Remains* add "other identifiers such as unique physical and medical traits" to the previous list and FASE (Forensic Anthropology Society of Europe) reinstate the goodness of anthropological and osteological markers (De Boer et al., 2020).

Morphological bone features are particular physical traits of the skeleton. Their singular morphological details, due to inter-individual variation, can make them unique features useful for personal identification through the comparison of antemortem and postmortem images (typically medical imaging such as radiography, computed tomography (CT), multi-detector computed tomography (MDCT), and magnetic

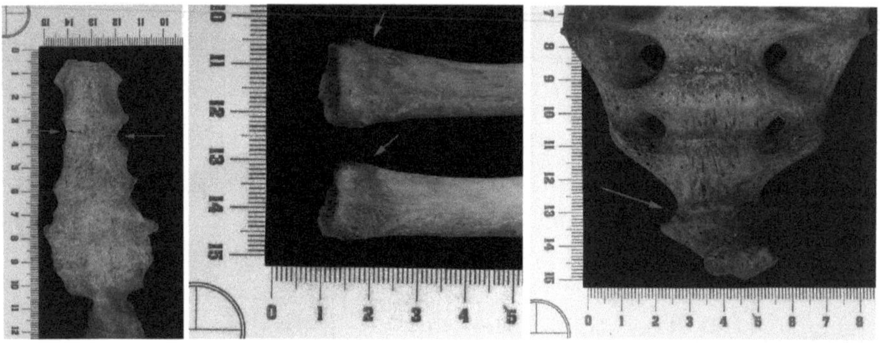

Figure 9.12 Left: incomplete fusion of the first and second sternal portions of the body (arrows). This condition could have been caused by functional stress or due to a failure to fuse the ossification centers during growth; middle: sternal ends of the sixth and seventh bilateral ribs showing signs of bone remodeling with thickening of the body. These signs were the consequence of a reparative process that affected the bone following an antemortem trauma; right: coccyx fused to the sacrum and orientated to the left, showing a strong asymmetry. This condition could be related to a mild traumatic event that led to the fusion of the coccyx with the sacrum. Photo and case courtesy Dr. Barbara Ciprandi.

resonance imaging (MRI)). They can be divided in three main categories (De Angelis et al., 2020):

- therapeutic features such as prostheses, internal fixations and other structures that may be inserted in soft tissues,
- pathological features such as bone calluses, caries, osteomas and bone lesions,
- anatomical features, namely the shape and morphology of skeletal and dental structures as well as anatomical variants.

Previous studies have demonstrated the utility of morphological bone features for personal identification: these include the morphological variation of bone shape and anatomical variants (Brogdon, 2011; De Angelis et al., 2016, 2012; Koot et al., 2005; Kuharić et al., 2011; Mann, 1998; Stephan et al., 2014; Valenzuela, 1997; Verna et al., 2013), frontal sinuses (Patil et al., 2012; Quatrehomme et al., 1996), pathological bone changes (specifically, osteophytes, exostoses, and fractures) (Jablonski and Shum, 1989; Komar and Lathrop, 2006; Scott et al., 2010; Silva et al., 2014; Wilcher, 2008), and dental morphology (De Angelis et al., 2007), as well as the presence of medical devices (De Angelis et al., 2017; Fleischman, 2015; Matoso et al., 2013; Pushparani et al., 2012; Wilson et al., 2011).

Virtually, any bone may be used for identification; however, the reliability of the individuality increases with the multiplication of the number of anatomical, therapeutic or pathological features considered. Breaking it down per anatomical area, here are some of the features that you can use for personal identification (Ciaffi et al., 2011; De Angelis et al., 2020):

- *Head*—the most relevant structure useful for identification in the head is the morphological assessment of frontal sinuses given their high variability in size and shape as well as their individuality. In fact, even homozygotic twins have different frontal sinuses (Pfaeffli et al., 2007). The remaining paranasal sinuses also constitute individualizing structures although their use is less common and standardized than for frontal sinuses;
- *Trunk*—the high availability of thoracic medical imaging and the multiplicity of observable features in the thorax make it an area highly valuable for forensic identification, in particular with the anatomical features of the clavicles, ribs and vertebrae (Kuehn et al., 2002; Valenzuela, 1997);
- *Limbs*—hand radiographs (Koot et al., 2005), clavicles (Stephan et al., 2014), and bone trabecular patterns (Kahana and Hiss, 1994; Mann, 1998) are morphological evaluations useful for identification.

However, for morphological features to constitute a valuable identifier, they must be stable over time (Kahana et al., 2002). This is particularly important for bone disease, as pathological bone lesions may show signs of healing and resolve with medical treatments, or they may worsen if left untreated, leaving in any case bone manifestations that, if not for personal identification, may be useful for the construction of the biological profile. Consequently, in order to limit the potential of evolution over time of the aspect of bone lesions, antemortem medical images must have been taken close to the time of death to be relevant for forensic identification.

Despite the application of personal identification to forensic anthropology, a standardized method for the expression of the results has not yet been defined (De Angelis et al., 2020). For instance, some authors have argued that one to four concordant features (Fischman, 1985), or points of concordance in two different skeletal areas (Kuehn et al., 2002) are needed to reach an identification, or even that expert opinion alone is sufficient (Rogers and Allard, 2004).

Over the past two decades, forensic anthropologists have been faced with a new challenge in court—the need for statistical quantification.

This is due in part to the impressively specific probabilities supplied by DNA identifications. Indeed, explaining the likelihood of a matching through a mathematical value permits both judges and juries to clearly understand the weight of the evidence. Now, standard errors of estimates (when applicable) must be implemented in expert reports and statistical values are increasingly demanded to clarify phrases such as "beyond any reasonable doubt." Statistical frameworks, such as the Bayesian approach, may be applied to forensic identification: likelihood ratios, when properly formulated, can accurately reflect the strength of the putative identification (Steadman et al., 2006). Indeed, a statistical evaluation of the strength of the antemortem/postmortem matching for positive identification can provide quantifiable evidence of the probability of identity and of the reliability of the method. Up until now, methods for identification using morphological bone features are mainly based on a number of points of correspondence between antemortem and postmortem images. However, the Bayesian approach may answer the question of the likelihood that another person may express the exact same morphological bone features as the presumed identity. So far, studies performed in this sense are rare (Christensen, 2005; Watamaniuk and Rogers, 2010). While the statistical approach is promising and will most certainly constitute a requirement in forensic anthropology in the future, further research is still needed to standardize the approach for its application to morphological bone features. In particular, two limitations can be raised: (1) the selection of the reference sample in the population at large to compute the posterior odds and (2) the subjectivity in the interpretation of the likelihood ratio, in other words, the lack of threshold for the statistical value to be considered enough for a positive identification.

The following are a series of cases which will be used as examples of how bone pathology may be used to identify through comparative bone analysis. Of course, for all these cases, DNA, dental or fingerprint identification was not possible.

Case 1

In April 2010, in the north of Italy, the remains of a partly skeletonized woman were found in a ditch in the countryside. Nearby a purse with some identification documents inside were present. This led to a possible identity: a middle-aged woman who had disappeared 8 months before. She had fallen several years before her death, with multiple fractures to the hip bones. Antemortem radiological documentation was recovered.

The anthropological analysis revealed a biological profile (i.e., sex, age-at-death, population affinity, stature) in full agreement with the suspected identity, as well as additional descriptors. Superimpositions were performed to confirm these observations and reach a positive identification. Specifically, the sacrum and right innominate, both characterized by the presence of bone calluses as a result of a previous trauma, were compared to antemortem imaging of the suspected identity and permitted the identification of the individual. Profiles of osseous anomalies were superimposed (Figs. 9.13 and 9.14).

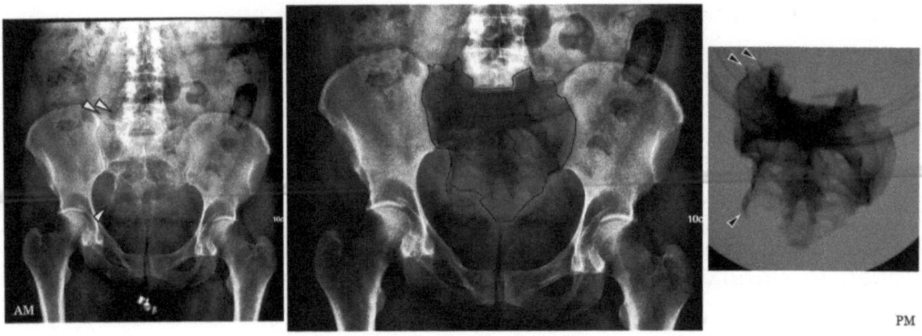

Figure 9.13 Comparison of the radiographic image of the sacrum performed on the corpse (arrows, right image) and the abdominal antemortem radiograph of the suspected identity (arrows, left image); the result of the superimposition is shown with a black contour in the image in the center. AM, antemortem; PM, postmortem.

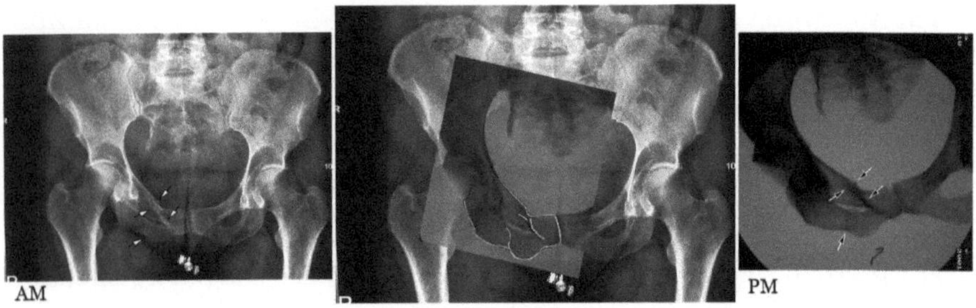

Figure 9.14 Comparison of the radiographic image of the right innominate performed on the corpse (right image) and the abdominal antemortem radiograph of the suspected identity (left image); the result of the superimposition is shown in the image in the center. One can notice several bone spicules (arrows) due to remodeling which perfectly superimpose.

Case 2

After years of searching, the body of a young man victim of a murder was found buried in the woods outside of Milano. Investigations and a witness had already led to a possible identity. In the present case, dental superimposition was also performed to achieve identification, but for the purpose of this chapter we wish to show how small changes in shape in the hand phalanges and metacarpals after a small accident (compression) to the hand can, when all bones are perfectly recovered, identified and sided, and when adequate antemortem information is acquired, lead to identification.

In this specific case, antemortem radiographs of the right had been taken following a trauma several years before. Virtual 3D models of the metacarpals from the recovered body were acquired by means of a precision laser scanner "5 Series CMF MARELLI" for superimposition.

To compare the antemortem and postmortem images, it is necessary to orient them in the same angle, so as to not produce different bi-dimensional projection of the 3D model (i.e., images) that could alter the comparison of the morphological elements useful for identification purposes. This method, applied in other fields of forensic anthropology for the superposition and comparison of morphological data (De Angelis et al., 2009), provides us with a 3D model of the anatomical structures analyzed, useful for reducing the possible alterations induced by an incorrect orientation of the skeletal elements.

The 3D models can be rotated and oriented in space while maintaining the proportions of the bone, in order to obtain the same position as the bones visible on the antemortem radiograph. The correct positioning of the bone elements allows a morphological and dimensional evaluation resulting in either correspondence or exclusion.

The following images show the phases of overlap between the radiographic image and the virtual model of the second and fifth metacarpals of the right hand (Figs. 9.15 and 9.16).

In the image below, the red arrows indicate some of the anatomical features that show a full correspondence between the postmortem 3D model and the antemortem radiograph (Fig. 9.17).

In addition, from the observation of the radiograph antemortem, it is possible to notice the presence of a unique contour in the

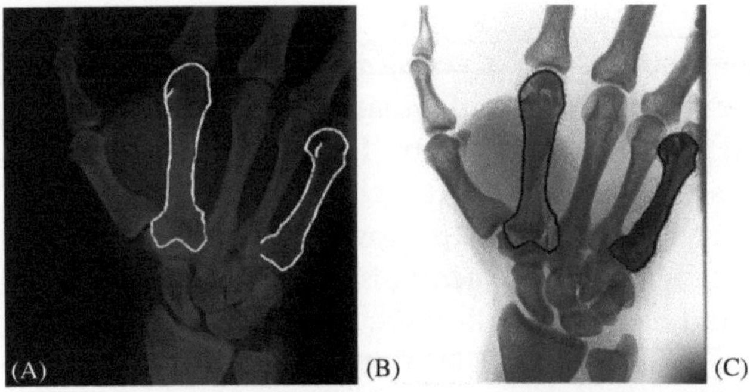

Figure 9.15 (A) the contour of the second and fifth metacarpals is traced on the X-ray (indicated with a white color); (B) following multiple adjustments, the correct orientation of the 3D models of the two metacarpals is obtained, the 3D models of the two metacarpals are made transparent and the outline of the two 3D models indicated in black is drawn; (C) the radiograph is removed leaving the two contours in comparison. Total correspondence is appreciated.

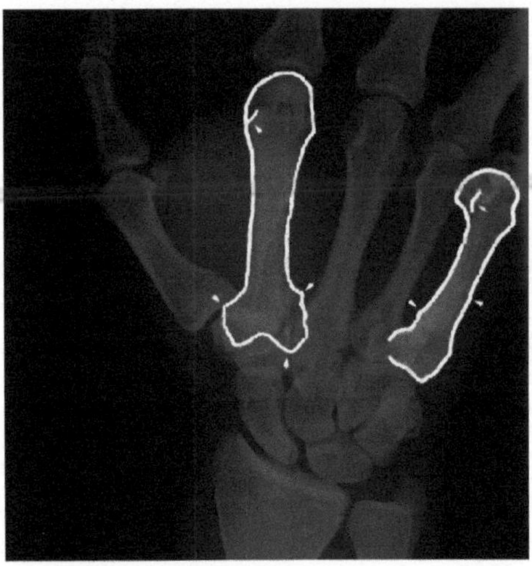

Figure 9.16 Superimposition of the postmortem 3D models (in a transparent color and with a white contour) on the antemortem radiographs with some of the corresponding anatomical features indicated with the arrows.

morphology of the proximal phalanx of the second finger. Based on the second proximal phalanx, it was possible to make a further comparison between the antemortem radiograph and the postmortem material, specifically an X-ray and a photograph of the bone. At this point, the comparisons were possible (Fig. 9.17).

Ultimately, both the dimensional and anatomical characteristics of the bones examined (proximal phalanx of the second finger as well as

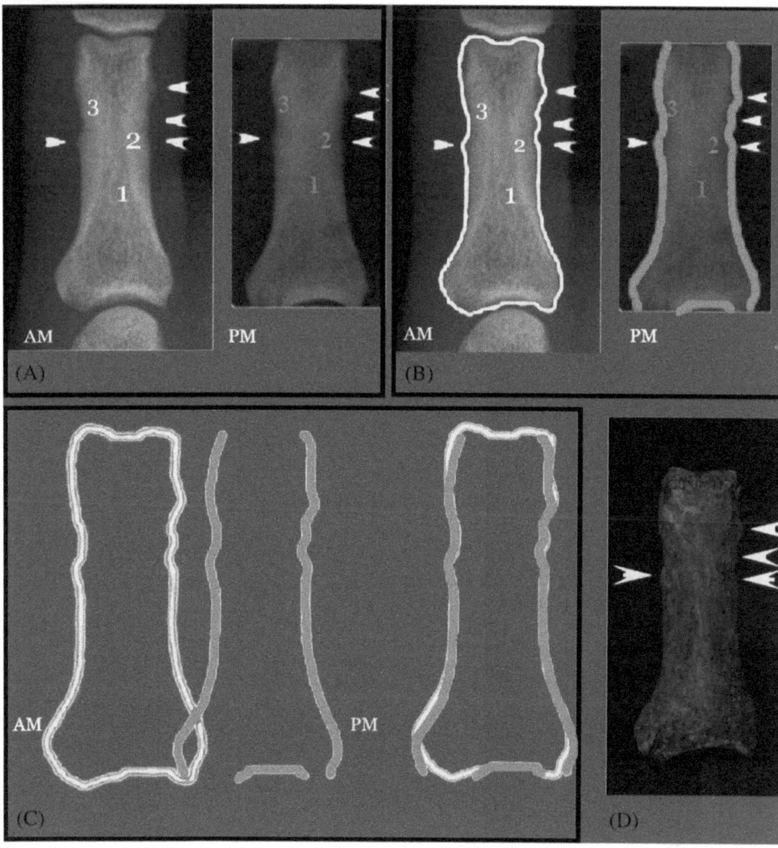

Figure 9.17 (A) Antemortem (left) and postmortem (right) radiographs of the second proximal phalanx (B) showing the characteristics of the outline (traced contour and arrows) and the trabeculation (indicated with numbers) coinciding in both images (A–B); (C) Antemortem (left) and postmortem (right) comparison of the contour of the bone and their superimposition in the center; (D) On the right, the photograph of the phalanx (dorsal view) with the morphological characteristics of the contour are indicated with arrows.

second and fifth metacarpals of the right hand) demonstrated a full correspondence between the antemortem documentation and the postmortem images of the skeletal remains of the right hand, allowing for a positive identification of the individual.

Case 3

In 2016, a skeletonized individual was found 250 m away from the Hospital of Nancy, France. A hospital identification band was present around the right radius and the suspected identity corresponded to an individual reported missing from the hospital two years prior (Martrille et al., 2020). Obviously, the presence of this hospital identification band provided a strong case for the positive identification of the skeletal remains discovered, but it would be a mistake to stop there and consider the case closed. Further analyses are necessary for a reliable assessment of positive identification as personal objects (such as ID cards and passports) can be given to another person and thus not represent the identity of the person in its possession. The individual was formally identified through the comparison of dental records, but other elements may have been used for positive identification and will be presented here, specifically, bone disease.

Based on the anthropological examination of the remains, several pathological lesions were described. In particular, two osteolytic lesions of 15 and 23 mm of diameter were noted on the endocranial surface of the left parietal bone with an external progression (Fig. 9.18). The smaller lesion perforated the external table and created a 27 mm wide ectocranial depression with bone remodeling. In the vertebral column, an extensive osteolytic destruction was reported on the vertebral body of the 6th thoracic vertebra while preserving the neural

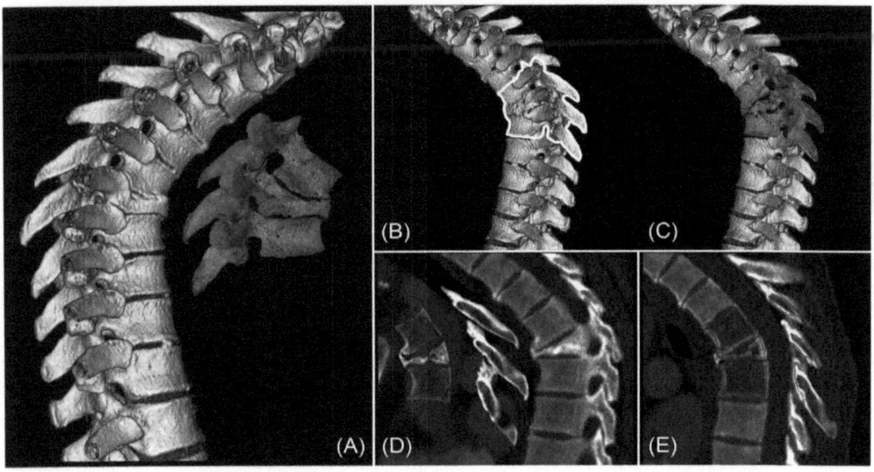

Figure 9.18 Comparison and superposition of the antemortem and postmortem images of the vertebral lesion. (A) comparison of the postmortem photograph of T5–T7 and the antemortem 3D reconstruction of the vertebral column (right lateral view); (B) superposition of the contour of T5–T7 from the postmortem photograph of the bones (white outline) on the antemortem 3D reconstruction of the vertebral column (left lateral view); (C) superposition of the postmortem photograph of T5–T7 on the antemortem 3D reconstruction of the vertebral column (left lateral view); (D) comparison of the postmortem CT image of T5–T7 and the antemortem CT image of the vertebral column; (E) superposition of the postmortem CT image of T5–T7 and the antemortem CT image of the vertebral column; note that the sagittal sections used in (D) and (E) are different. Reproduced with permission from Martrille, L., De Angelis, D., Blum, A., Gauchotte, G., Cattaneo, C., Biehler-Gomez, L., 2020. The potential of bone disease for personal identification: a case of tuberculosis. Int. J. Leg. Med. 1–6. https://doi.org/10.1007/s00414-020-02348-3.

arch, resulting in a deformation at the level of T5–T7 typical of "Pott's disease" (Fig. 9.19). Moreover, a right partial sacroiliac ankylosis (i.e., a partial fusion of the right sacroiliac articulation) was evidenced as well as an osteolytic lesion of 5 mm of diameter on the anterior right ala of the sacrum (Fig. 9.20). The most probable diagnosis accounting for these lesions was determined as tuberculosis by confrontation with the clinical and dry bone literature.

Because the missing person suffered from multiple infections (HIV infection for 14 years, AIDS stage, diffuse large B cell lymphoma,

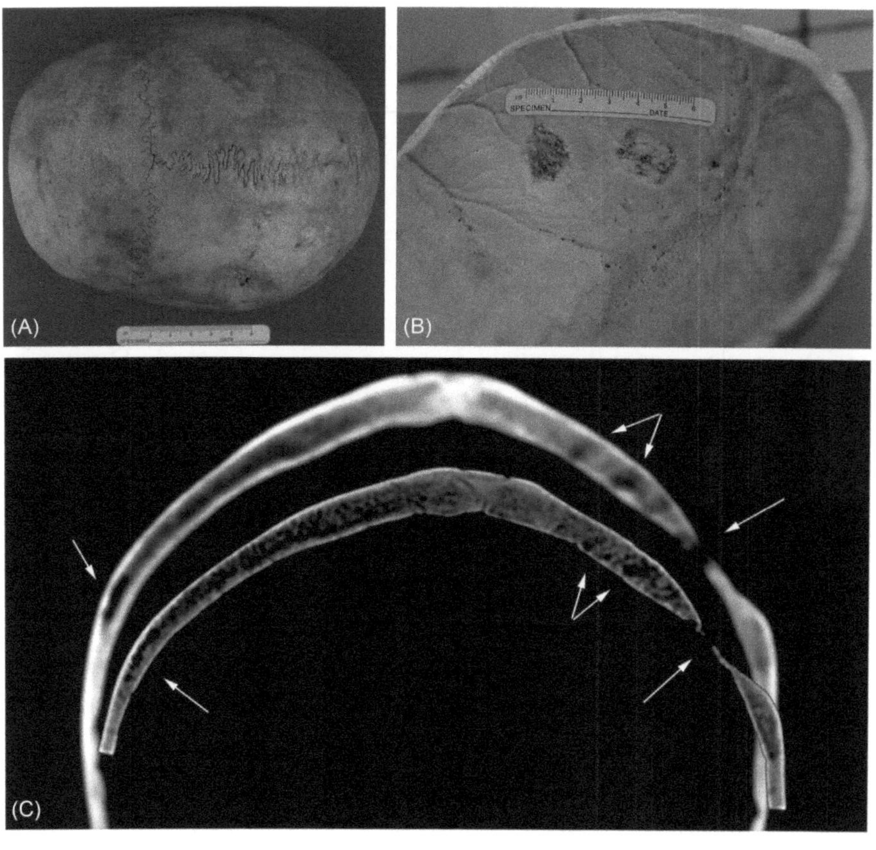

Figure 9.19 Comparison and superposition of the antemortem and postmortem images of the cranial lesions. (A) superior view of the calvarium showing an osteolytic lesion on the left parietal bone; (B) endocranial view of the calvarium showing the osteolytic lesions; (C) comparison of the antemortem (top) and postmortem (bottom) coronal CT sections; the osteolytic lesions are indicated by the white arrows. Reproduced with permission from Martrille, L., De Angelis, D., Blum, A., Gauchotte, G., Cattaneo, C., Biehler-Gomez, L., 2020. The potential of bone disease for personal identification: a case of tuberculosis. Int. J. Leg. Med. 1–6. https://doi.org/10.1007/s00414-020-02348-3.

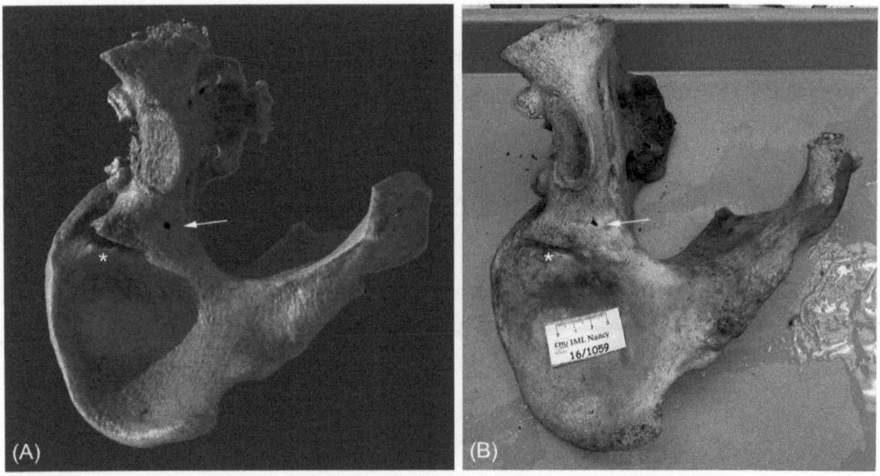

Figure 9.20 Antemortem and postmortem comparison of the morphological characteristics of the lesions on the sacrum and right innominate. (A) antemortem 3D reconstruction; (B) postmortem photograph realized during the autopsy of the remains; note the osteolytic lesion on the right ala of the sacrum (white arrow) and the partial right sacroiliac ankylosis (white asterisk). Reproduced with permission from Martrille, L., De Angelis, D., Blum, A., Gauchotte, G., Cattaneo, C., Biehler-Gomez, L., 2020. The potential of bone disease for personal identification: a case of tuberculosis. Int. J. Leg. Med. 1–6. https://doi.org/10.1007/s00414-020-02348-3.

Pneumocystis pneumonia, and multiple relapses of cerebral toxoplasmosis), regular control medical imaging was performed. During his last hospitalization, a cranial, thoracic, abdominal, and pelvic CT-scan was realized and available.

CT-scanning and 3D reconstructions with volume rendering technique were performed on the cranial vault and pathological vertebrae and oriented as in the antemortem imaging for comparison and superimposition. Based on the date of the declared disappearance of the suspected identity and the location of recovery of the remains, the most probable estimation of the time elapsed between the date of the antemortem imaging and the time of death was 7 months.

As a result of the comparison and superimposition of the antemortem (i.e., CT scans and 3D reconstructions) and postmortem (i.e. photographs and CT scans), images of the same bone lesions in the vertebrae, pelvis, and cranium, anatomical and pathological correspondence of the lesions were evidenced on the skeleton and on the bones, including character of the lesion (osteolytic and/or osteoblastic features), and morphological characteristics (anatomical details of the bones and pathological features of the lesions) (Figs. 9.18–9.20). In fact, several points of correspondence were highlighted (Martrille et al., 2020):

- *Vertebrae*—the shape and anatomical characteristics of the vertebral bodies and spinous processes and the outline of the pathological changes at the level of T5–T7 (i.e., destruction of the vertebral body of the sixth thoracic vertebra, compression fracture due to the normal pressure applied by the superior vertebra on the weakened sixth thoracic vertebra creating a kyphosis at T5–T7);
- *Cranial vault*—the anatomical contour of the cranial vault, the outline of the osteolytic bone changes in the cranium and the exact same location of the osteolytic lesions on the cranium;
- *Pelvis*—the shape and anatomical characteristics of the right innominate bone and sacrum, the shape, contour and pathological features of the sacral osteolytic lesion and of the partial right sacroiliac fusion.

Consequently, the correspondence of the pathological morphological features and anatomical characteristics of the bones between the antemortem and postmortem images and the absence of any point of disagreement permits a positive identification of the individual and presents the same evidentiary value as dental records or other primary identifiers.

This last case is an excellent example of how tuberculous lesions, in absence of antemortem information, could have led to a very precise biological profile of a young man with tuberculosis: Pott's disease and the cranial lesion leave very few doubts which eventually could be confirmed by biomolecular analyses.

References

Blau, S., Ubelaker, D.H., 2009. Handbook of forensic anthropology and archaeology. Left Coast Press, Walnut Creek, CA.

Brogdon, B.G., 2011. Radiological identification of individual remains. Forensic Radiology. CRC Press, Boca Raton, pp. 149–187.

Buikstra, J.E., Ubelaker, D.H., 1994. Standards for Data Collection from Human Skeletal Remains. Arkansas Archaeological Survey Report Number 44, Fayetteville, Arkansas.

Capasso, L., Kennedy, K.A.R., Wilczak, C.A., 1999. Atlas of Occupational Markers on Human Remains. Edigrafital.

Cappella, A., Gibelli, D., Obertová, Z., Cummaudo, M., Castoldi, E., De Angelis, D., et al., 2019. The Utility of Skeletal and Surgical Features for the Personal Identification Process: A Pilot Study. J. Forensic Sci. 64, 1796–1802.

Christensen, A.M., 2005. Testing the reliability of frontal sinuses in positive identification. J. Forensic Sci. P, JFS2004145-5.

Ciaffi, R., Gibelli, D., Cattaneo, C. (Eds.), 2011. Radiologia forense ed identifi cazione personale dei cadaveri: revisione della letteratura. Radiol. Medica 116, 960–968. Available from: https://doi.org/10.1007/s11547-011-0677-6.

De Angelis, D., Cattaneo, C., Grandi, M., 2007. Dental superimposition: a pilot study for standardising the method. Int. J. Leg. Med. 121, 501–506. Available from: https://doi.org/10.1007/s00414-007-0198-y.

De Angelis, D., Collini, F., Muccino, E., Cappella, A., Sguazza, E., Mazzucchi, A., et al., 2017. Analysis of metallic medical devices after cremation: the importance in identification. Sci. Justice 57, 128–135.

De Angelis, D., Gibelli, D., Palazzo, E., Sconfienza, L., Obertova, Z., Cattaneo, C., 2016. Skeletal idiopathic osteosclerosis helps to perform personal identification of unknown decedents: A novel contribution from anatomical variants through CT scan. Sci. Justice 56, 260–263. Available from: https://doi.org/10.1016/j.scijus.2016.03.003.

De Angelis, D., Messina, C., Sconfienza, L., Sardanelli, F., Cattaneo, C., Gibelli, D., 2020. Forensic Radiology and Identification. In: Lo Re, G., Argo, A., Midiri, M., Cattaneo, C. (Eds.), Radiology in Forensic Medicine. Springer, pp. 63–85.

De Angelis, D., Riboli, F., Gibelli, D., Cappella, A., Cattaneo, C., 2012. Palatal rugae as an individualising marker: Reliability for forensic odontology and personal identification. Sci. Justice 52, 181–184. Available from: https://doi.org/10.1016/j.scijus.2011.09.002.

De Angelis, D., Sala, R., Cantatore, A., Grandi, M., Cattaneo, C., 2009. A new computer-assisted technique to aid personal identification. Int. J. Leg. Med. 123, 351–356.

De Boer, H.H., Obertová, Z., Cunha, E., Adalian, P., Baccino, E., Fracasso, T., et al., 2020. Strengthening the role of forensic anthropology in personal identification: Position statement by the Board of the Forensic Anthropology Society of Europe (FASE). Forensic Sci. Int. 315, 110456.

Fischman, S.L., 1985. The use of medical and dental radiographs in identification. Int. Dent. J. 35, 301–306.

Fleischman, J.M., 2015. Radiographic identification using midline medical sternotomy wires. J. Forensic Sci. 60, S3–S10.

Jablonski, N.G., Shum, B.S.F., 1989. Identification of unknown human remains by comparison of antemortem and postmortem radiographs. Forensic Sci. Int. 42, 221–230.

Kahana, T., Goldin, L., Hiss, J., 2002. Personal identification based on radiographic vertebral features. Am. J. Forensic Med. Pathol. 23, 36–41.

Kahana, T., Hiss, J., 1994. Positive identification by means of trabecular bone pattern comparison. J. Forensic Sci. 39, 1325–1330.

Komar, D., Lathrop, S., 2006. Frequencies of Morphological Characteristics in Two Contemporary Forensic Collections: Implications for Identification*. J. Forensic Sci. 51, 974–978. Available from: https://doi.org/10.1111/j.1556-4029.2006.00210.x.

Koot, M.G., Sauer, N.J., Fenton, T.W., 2005. Radiographic human identification using bones of the hand: a validation study. J. Forensic Sci. 50, JFS2004229-6.

Kuehn, C.M., Taylor, K.M., Mann, F.A., Wilson, A.J., Harruff, R.C., 2002. Validation of Chest X-ray Comparisonsfor Unknown Decedent Identification. J. Forensic Sci. 47, 1–5.

Kuharić, J., Kovacic, N., Marusic, P., Marusic, A., Petrovecki, V., 2011. Positive Identification by a Skull with Multiple Epigenetic Traits and Abnormal Structure of the Neurocranium, Viscerocranium, and the Skeleton*. J. Forensic Sci. 56, 788–793. Available from: https://doi.org/10.1111/j.1556-4029.2011.01718.x.

Mann, R.W., 1998. Use of bone trabeculae to establish positive identification. Forensic Sci. Int. 98, 91–99. Available from: https://doi.org/10.1016/S0379-0738(98)00138-8.

Martrille, L., De Angelis, D., Blum, A., Gauchotte, G., Cattaneo, C., Biehler-Gomez, L., 2020. The potential of bone disease for personal identification: a case of tuberculosis. Int. J. Leg. Med. 1–6. Available from: https://doi.org/10.1007/s00414-020-02348-3.

Matoso, R.I., de Novaes Benedicto, E., de Lima, S.H.R., Prado, F.B., Daruge, E., Júnior, E.D., 2013. Positive identification of a burned body using an implanted orthopedic plate. Forensic Sci. Int. 229, 168–e1.

McGuigan, F.X., 2011. Skeletal Trauma. In: Wiesel, S.W., Delahay, J.N. (Eds.), Essentials of Orthopedic Surgery. Springer, New York, USA, pp. 35–73.

Patil, N., Karjodkar, F.R., Sontakke, S., Sansare, K., Salvi, R., 2012. Uniqueness of radiographic patterns of the frontal sinus for personal identification. Imaging Sci. Dent. 42, 213–217.

Pfaeffli, M., Vock, P., Dirnhofer, R., Braun, M., Bolliger, S.A., Thali, M.J., 2007. Post-mortem radiological CT identification based on classical ante-mortem X-ray examinations. Forensic Sci. Int. 171, 111–117.

Pushparani, C., Ravichandran, C.P., Sivakumari, K., 2012. Radiography superimposition in personal identification-a case study involving surgical implants. J. Forensic Res. 3.

Quatrehomme, G., Fronty, P., Sapanet, M., Grévin, G., Bailet, P., Ollier, A., 1996. Identification by frontal sinus pattern in forensic anthropology. Forensic Sci. Int. 83, 147–153. Available from: https://doi.org/10.1016/S0379-0738(96)02033-6.

Rogers, T.L., Allard, T.T., 2004. Expert testimony and positive identification of human remains through cranial suture patterns. J. Forensic Sci. 49, 1–5.

Scott, A.L., Congram, D., Sweet, D., Fonseca, S., Skinner, M., 2010. Anthropological and radiographic comparison of antemortem surgical records for identification of skeletal remains. J. Forensic Sci. 55, 241–244.

Silva, R.F., Franco, A., Mendes, S.D.S.C., Picoli, F.F., de Azevedo Marinho, D.E., 2014. Human identification through the patella—Report of two cases. Forensic Sci. Int. 238, e11–e14. Available from: https://doi.org/10.1016/j.forsciint.2014.02.025.

Steadman, D.W., Adams, B.J., Konigsberg, L.W., 2006. Statistical basis for positive identification in forensic anthropology. Am. J. Phys. Anthropol. 131, 15–26. Available from: https://doi.org/10.1002/ajpa.20393.

Stephan, C.N., Amidan, B., Trease, H., Guyomarc'h, P., Pulsipher, T., Byrd, J.E., 2014. Morphometric comparison of clavicle outlines from 3D bone scans and 2D chest radiographs: a shortlisting tool to assist radiographic identification of human skeletons. J. Forensic Sci. 59, 306–313.

Valenzuela, A., 1997. Radiographic Comparison of the Lumbar Spine for Positive Identification of Human Remains: A Case Report. Am. J. Forensic Med. Pathol. 18.

Verna, E., Piercecchi-Marti, M., Chaumoitre, K., Bartoli, C., Leonetti, G., Adalian, P., 2013. Discrete traits of the sternum and ribs: a useful contribution to identification in forensic anthropology and medicine. J. Forensic Sci. 58, 571–577.

Waldron, T., 2008. Palaeopathology. Cambridge University Press, Cambridge, United Kingdom.

Watamaniuk, L., Rogers, T., 2010. Positive personal identification of human remains based on thoracic vertebralmargin morphology. J. Forensic Sci. 55, 1162–1170. Available from: https://doi.org/10.1111/j.1556-4029.2010.01447.x.

Wilcher, G., 2008. The use of multiple exostoses in the identification of incinerated human remains. Med. Sci. Law 48, 82–86.

Wilson, R.J., Bethard, J.D., DiGangi, E.A., 2011. The use of orthopedic surgical devices for forensic identification. J. Forensic Sci. 56, 460–469.

CHAPTER 10

The Challenge of Taphonomic Alterations

Lucie Biehler-Gomez, Mirko Mattia and Cristina Cattaneo
LABANOF, Department of Biomedical Sciences for Health, University of Milan, Milan, Italy

Taphonomy is the multidisciplinary study of changes affecting biological remains (and in particular here, human skeletal remains) from the time of death to their recovery. Thus, taphonomic alterations encompass the effects of decomposition, damage from the soil (e.g., acidity, humidity), weather (i.e., if exposed to the surface), water (i.e., in an aquatic environment), fauna (e.g., carnivore activity, insects and displacement), and flora (e.g., root impressions, breakage and displacement) as well as archaeological excavation or forensic recovery (e.g., shovel or trowel bone breakage, missed small bones) to the skeletal remains. Effects on bones include color changes, microscopic alterations, macroscopic physical damage (such as cracking, erosion, and bone consumption), and loss of skeletal elements through dispersal away from the location of initial body deposition (Pokines and Symes, 2014). Contrary to anthropological analyses that give information directly on the individual, taphonomy permits the understanding and reconstruction of the events that affected the body and the environment that surrounded it—specifically, the information derived from taphonomic observations and analyses can inform on the depositional contexts of the remains, their absolute duration and provide a relative timing of events from the time of the death to that of recovery (Pokines and Symes, 2014). Taphonomy is thus of considerable value in a forensic setting. However, taphonomic alterations present substantial challenges to the interpretation of bone disease.

Taphonomic Alterations of Bone Disease

Unfortunately, taphonomic alterations also imply a degradation of skeletal remains. This degradation may be both quantitative (i.e., state of completeness of the remains) and qualitative (i.e., state of preservation of the remains) and may range from microscopic alterations invisible to

Interpreting Bone Lesions and Pathology for Forensic Practice. DOI: https://doi.org/10.1016/B978-0-323-85162-6.00010-6

the naked eye in a fully complete skeleton to substantial bone loss resulting in brittle bones in a largely incomplete skeleton. Taphonomic effects on skeletal remains are a major factor influencing anthropological analyses as they can impact bone recovery and the preservation of anatomical landmarks and structures useful for anthropological estimations. This is as true for the estimations of sex, age-at-death, stature, and population affinity as for the study of bone disease.

All anthropologists know that the interpretation and diagnosis of bone disease is based on the location, distribution, and morphology of bone lesions. The impossibility to examine one of these criteria hampers a diagnosis and considerably widens the differential diagnosis. Taphonomic factors can affect any of these criteria. By altering the quality of the bone or causing bone breakage, the location of the lesion may be misinterpreted. Similarly, the loss of some bones may prevent a correct understanding of the etiology responsible for the observed bone lesions. In addition to location and distribution, postmortem processes may also alter the morphology of bone lesions. Bone disease and taphonomic processes can both cause bone erosions; however, they may be morphologically and microscopically distinguished—in particular, changes in the color of the bone and irregular or broken margins are characteristics of postmortem processes causing bone loss (Figs. 10.1 and 10.2). Nonetheless, a pathologic lesion may be present on a bone, but after death, taphonomic alterations may modify the morphological characteristics of the lesion, making it appear taphonomic and preventing its recognition as disease (Figs. 10.3–10.5).

An example is perhaps easier to understand. We know that bone lesions in rheumatoid arthritis are typically erosive, numerous, bilateral, symmetric, articular, and/or para-articular and involve primarily the small bones of the hands and wrist and can later spread to more distant joints. Let us assume that you have the skeleton of an adult with bilateral and symmetric articular erosive bone changes in the scaphoid (i.e., a carpal bone). The skeleton is complete apart from the remaining hand bones and most bones of the feet. This is not unusual as these small bones are often lost due to taphonomic processes. Can you say that this is a case of rheumatoid arthritis? Not really, because as you know, you need hands and/or wrists to make a reliable diagnosis and one hand bone is not enough. You can (and should) include it in the differential diagnosis alongside

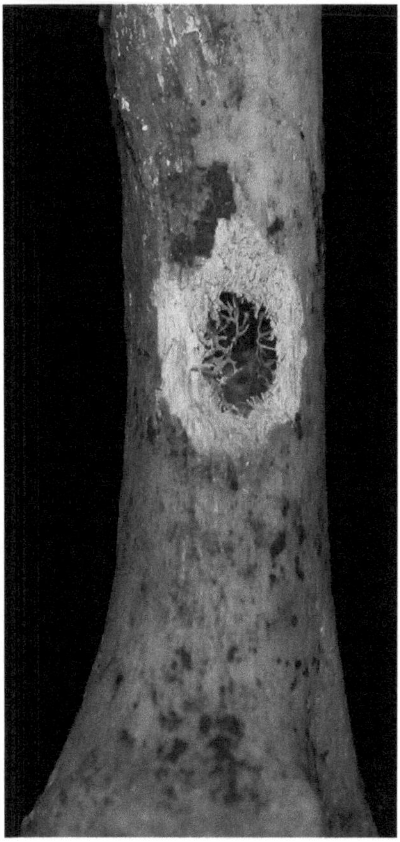

Figure 10.1 Typical taphonomic osseous lesion: the margins of the lesions are irregular, show flaking, and exhibit a white coloration distinct from the color of the bone cortex. Skeleton #1080 of the CAL Milano Cemetery Skeletal Collection.

osteoarthrosis, but you do not have enough to say more: osteoarthrosis is more likely based on your evidence but rheumatoid arthritis, especially if the individual is a female over 30 years, is a possibility. Now, imagine you have that same skeleton, but with the bones of the hands present. However, the cortical layer of the bones is eroded, the bones show cracking, the heads of the phalanges, and metacarpals are damaged if not lost and most bones are broken. How can you recognize bone lesions and identify their pattern of distribution in this context? With great difficulty—if that individual had bone lesions due to rheumatoid arthritis when he died, the anthropological diagnosis might result particularly challenging considering the taphonomic state of preservation of the remains.

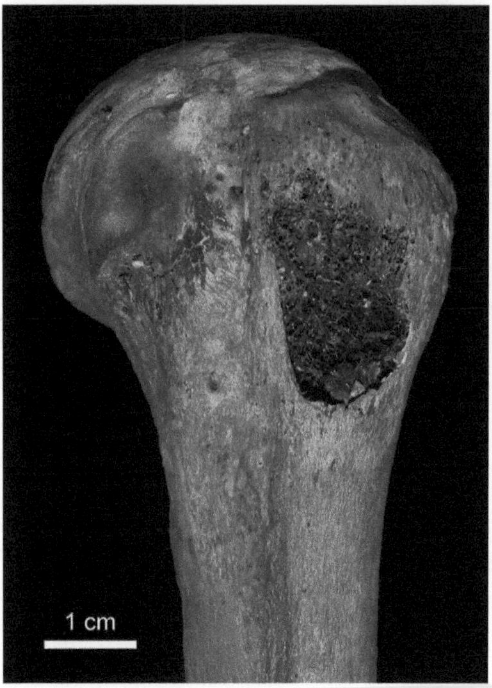

Figure 10.2 Taphonomic alteration on bone: note the irregularity and flaking of the margins both of the bone cortex and trabecular bone. Skeleton #1091 of the CAL Milano Cemetery Skeletal Collection.

Figure 10.3 Osteolytic metastasis on a left ilium (medial view, auricular surface on the right) altered by taphonomic factors: the white deposition inside the lesion may give the impression of a taphonomic alteration when this is in fact an osteolytic metastasis and the alteration occurred postmortem. Skeleton #10 of the CAL Milano Cemetery Skeletal Collection with a clinical diagnosis of liver metastatic carcinoma.

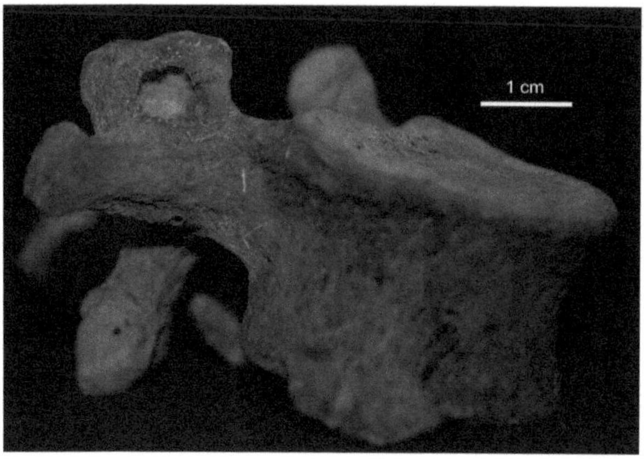

Figure 10.4 Osteolytic metastasis on the neural arch of the first lumbar vertebra altered by taphonomic factors: the white deposition inside the lesion may give the impression of a taphonomic alteration when this is in fact an osteolytic metastasis and the alteration occurred postmortem. Skeleton #10 of the CAL Milano Cemetery Skeletal Collection with a clinical diagnosis of liver metastatic carcinoma.

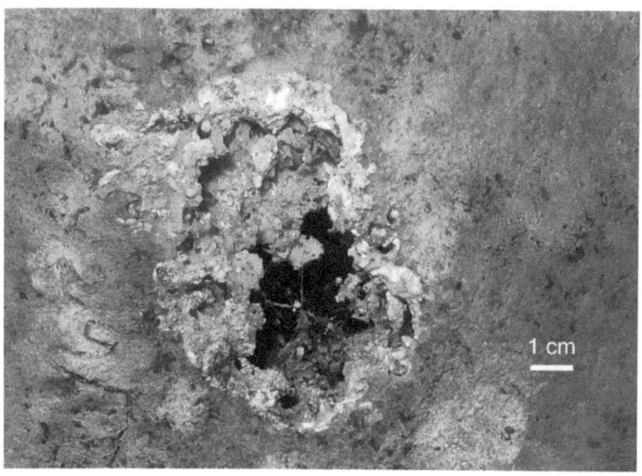

Figure 10.5 Osteolytic metastasis on the occipital bone altered by taphonomic factors: the denticulated margins of the lesion and the extensive trabecular bone resorption are suggestive of an osteolytic metastasis, but the reader might be confused by the white deposition on the margins and dirt in the lesion. This is an example of postmortem alterations on a pathological lesion. Skeleton #912 of the CAL Milano Cemetery Skeletal Collection with a clinical diagnosis of breast carcinoma.

Thus, taphonomic processes may render pathologic bone lesions unrecognizable and may prevent the identification of bone lesions. Absence of evidence is not evidence of absence; in other words, you can only interpret what you see. You may see only one osteolytic lesion but remember that taphonomic factors may have caused the loss of skeletal elements or areas with bone lesions and altered the morphology of other lesions making it look like there was no lesion in the first place. In this aspect, taphonomic alterations challenge bone pathology by losing evidence of bone disease; however, they can also fake pathological osseous lesions.

Taphonomic Lesions Mimicking Disease

Taphonomic alterations may mimic pathological bone lesions, confusing the reader. The study and recognition of these lesions that resemble the effects of a disease but are not actually caused by one is referred to as pseudopathology in bone pathology.

For instance, weathering may cause cracking, flaking, and in more advanced cases, removal of the external layers of the bone (Behrensmeyer, 1978). Carnivore alterations on skeletal elements includes grooves, scalloped edges, when teeth have penetrated the bone cortex, and puncture marks, described as shallow circular to oval lesions with small cortex fragments oriented perpendicularly to the bone surface and pressed into the interior (Milner and Smith, 1989). Insects, and in particular dermestid beetles and termites, may also present morphological similarities to osteolytic lesions. Dermestid beetles cause characteristic ovoid shaped pits of regular size and smooth delimited margins (Corron et al., 2017; Huchet et al., 2011). Derry (1911) first described the damage done to bones by termites making holes with "white, gnawed edges." Termites have been seen to favor skulls, creating pits, perforations and tunneling, associated with star-shaped marks, parallel striations, and etched bone surface (Backwell et al., 2012; Huchet et al., 2011). Fungi and algae can cause small holes, cavities, and tunnel-like canals in the compact bone during their growth (Ortner, 2003, pp. 79–80). Postmortem damage produced by termites or beetles can mimic the superficial appearance of osteolytic lesions due to cancer metastases. Similarly, the tunnels created by fungi and algae can converge into larger destructive lesions which may resemble osteoporosis or metastatic tumor lesions on x-rays (Ortner, 2003, pp. 79–80). Nonetheless, and by opposition to pathological processes, taphonomic lesions do not extend within the bone, they have a regular shape, are well-demarcated and do not manifest a preference for specific skeletal areas (Binder et al., 2014; Strouhal, 1991). Plant roots can leave groovy impressions on bones during growth; in the ectocranial and endocranial surfaces in particular, these may be confused with vascular impressions and may simulate the labyrinthine irregular small grooves on a coarse bed of inflammatory processes of the scalp and the attached bone (e.g., non-specific infection, treponemal diseases) (Ortner, 2003, pp. 79–80).

Just like recognizing complete and partial bones is a skill acquired through practice, the identification of bone lesions needs experience. However, some lesions can pose difficulties, especially when the remains are poorly preserved, and occasionally, they cannot be differentiated by macroscopic or radiological analysis, even for experts in the field with the most experience. In these situations, microscopic techniques (Schultz, 2001) may prove their taphonomic origin and distinguish between postmortem or pathological changes through characteristics such as Howship's lacunae on bone surfaces (indicating an osteoclastic activity) and the aspect of edges of resorptive bone lesions, where osteoclasts have eaten away the bone. Postdepositional processes may also mimic proliferative bone lesions, appearing similar as thickened new bone deposition on the bone cortex originating as result of a periosteal reaction. Thin section examined through light microscopy can permit the observation of aggregated crystals formed during diagenesis (Ortner, 2003, pp. 79–80).

Consequently, the damage caused by postmortem factors can be falsely interpreted as products of disease. This is why "pseudopathology" (i.e., taphonomic lesions mimicking disease) should always be considered and excluded first when interpreting bone lesions. When macroscopic (through color and margin changes) or radiological examinations are not sufficient for their distinction, microscopic observation may determine or exclude their postmortem origin.

Taphonomic Paradox: Supporting Bone Pathology

Taphonomic alterations entail irreversible bone degradation and potentially the destruction of evidence of bone disease. Logically, if you study bone disease, taphonomic activity will be your best enemy—it will always be on your mind, you will hope not to see too much of it but once it is there, you will try to understand it and make sure it does not make any more damage than it already has. However, sometimes taphonomic alterations may actually help the interpretation of bone disease.

Postmortem changes damage bones and cause bone breakage. On the bright side, bone breakage allows us to see where we normally cannot see—the internal structure of the bone. Of course, radiographs are usually the technique to do just that. Macroscopic analysis of bones is generally limited to the external surface of bones, but we know that radiographs allow the detection of many bone lesions hidden from gross examination (Biehler-Gomez et al., 2019; Rothschild and Rothschild, 1995). However, radiographs are not systematically performed, and in bioarchaeology, they are carried out when suggestive lesions are noted on bones (such as bone lesions or trauma). Yes, postmortem factors damage bones but they can, on rare occasions, allow us to see bone lesions that could have remained undetected. In particular, spongiosclerosis (i.e., trabecular thickening with the deposition of new bone in the existing trabeculae) is a clear finding on radiographs, visible as an area of sclerosis (i.e., radiodense area) but an uncommon one through gross examination as it is located in the trabecular bone, concealed by the bone cortex from naked eye observation. Bone breakage permits the observation of the spongy structure of the bone and the potential finding of spongiosclerosis (Figs. 10.6 and 10.7). However, this is a subtle and tricky lesion, difficult to find and to recognize, especially for an untrained eye. Therefore, broken pieces of bone should be carefully

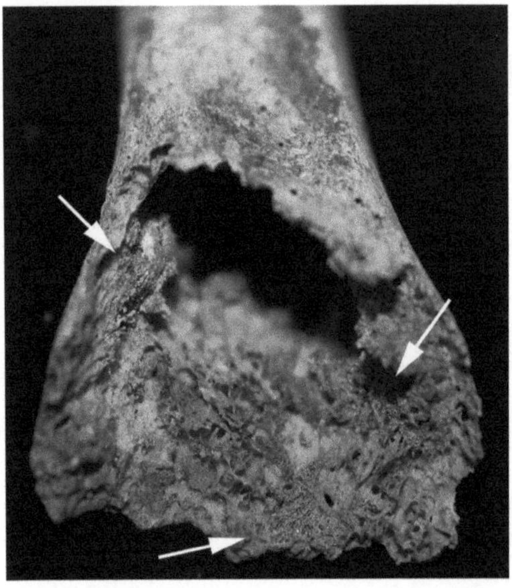

Figure 10.6 Broken humerus (postmortem) evidencing areas of spongiosclerosis (white arrows). Skeleton #422 of the CAL Milano Cemetery Skeletal Collection with a clinical diagnosis of bladder carcinoma.

Figure 10.7 Fragment of the sacrum (broken postmortem) evidencing a spongiosclerotic metastasis (i.e., new bone "coating" the existing trabecular bone). Skeleton #422 of the CAL Milano Cemetery Skeletal Collection with a clinical diagnosis of bladder carcinoma.

examined as particular bone lesions may be exposed by taphonomic alterations.

A final word should be said on the taphonomy of prosthetic devices. The metal and synthetic nature of prostheses or medical devices can be severely altered by taphonomic alterations, and particularly by fire. Pacemakers can turn into unrecognizable burnt wires difficult to distinguish from metal from a car or a house, and dentures can melt into anonymity. An interesting review of these effects can be found in De Angelis et al. (2017).

References

De Angelis, D., Collini, F., Muccino, E., Cappella, A., Sguazza, E., Mazzucchi, A., et al., 2017. Analysis of metallic medical devices after cremation: the importance in identification. Sci. Justice 57, 128–135.

Backwell, L.R., Parkinson, A.H., Roberts, E.M., D'Errico, F., Huchet, J.-B., 2012. Criteria for identifying bone modification by termites in the fossil record. Palaeogeogr. Palaeoclimatol. Palaeoecol. 337–338, 72–87. Available from: https://doi.org/10.1016/J.PALAEO.2012.03.032.

Behrensmeyer, A.K., 1978. Taphonomic and ecologic information from bone weathering. Paleobiology 4, 150–162. https://doi.org/DOI: 10.1017/S0094837300005820.

Biehler-Gomez, L., Tritella, S., Martino, F., Campobasso, C.P., Franchi, A., Spairani, R., et al., 2019. The synergy between radiographic and macroscopic observation of skeletal lesions on dry bone. Int. J. Leg. Med. https://doi.org/10.1007/s00414-019-02122-0

Binder, M., Roberts, C.A., Spencer, N., Antoine, D., Cartwright, C., 2014. On the antiquity of cancer: evidence for metastatic carcinoma in a young man from ancient Nubia (c. 1200bc). PLoS One 9, 1–11. Available from: https://doi.org/10.1371/journal.pone.0090924.

Corron, L., Huchet, J.-B., Santos, F., Dutour, O., 2017. Using classifications to identify pathological and taphonomic modifications on ancient bones: do "taphognomonic" criteria exist? BMSAP 29, 1–18. Available from: https://doi.org/10.1007/s13219-016-0176-3.

Derry, D.E., 1911. Damage done to skulls and bones by termites. Nature 86, 245.

Huchet, J.-B., Deverly, D., Gutierrez, B., Chauchat, C., 2011. Taphonomic evidence of a human skeleton gnawed by termites in a Moche-civilisation grave at Huaca de la Luna, Peru. Int. J. Osteoarchaeol. 21, 92–102. Available from: https://doi.org/10.1002/oa.1110.

Milner, G.R., Smith, V.G., 1989. Carnivore alteration of human bone from a late prehistoric site in illinois. Am. J. Phys. Anthropol. 79, 43–49. Available from: https://doi.org/10.1002/ajpa.1330790105.

Ortner, D.J., 2003. Identification of Pathological Conditions in Human Skeletal Remains, 3rd ed. Smithsonian Institution Press, New York.

Pokines, J., Symes, S.A., 2014. Manual of Forensic Taphonomy. CRC Press, Boca Raton, FL.

Rothschild, B.M., Rothschild, C., 1995. Comparison of radiologic and gross examination for detection of cancer in defleshed skeletons. Am. J. Phys. Anthr. 96, 357–363. Available from: https://doi.org/10.1002/ajpa.1330960404.

Schultz, M., 2001. Paleohistopathology of bone: a new approach to the study of ancient diseases. Am. J. Phys. Anthropol. 116, 106–147. Available from: https://doi.org/10.1002/ajpa.10024.

Strouhal, E., 1991. Myeloma multiplex versus osteolytic metastatic carcinoma: Differential diagnosis in dry bones. Int. J. Osteoarchaeol. 1, 219–224. Available from: https://doi.org/10.1002/oa.1390010314.

CHAPTER 11

Conclusions and the Future of Bone Pathology

Lucie Biehler-Gomez[1], Gaia Giordano[1], Domenico Di Candia[2] and Cristina Cattaneo[1]
[1]LABANOF, Department of Biomedical Sciences for Health, University of Milan, Milan, Italy, [2]Section of Legal Medicine, Department of Biomedical Sciences for Health, University of Milan, Milan, Italy

We have already mentioned in most chapters how research is focusing and hopefully will continue to strive toward new methods of implementing the understanding of disease manifestations on bone through microscopy, DNA analysis, and proteomics. In this final chapter, we wish to conclude our survey with a brief discussion concerning a discipline which is slowly making its way through dry bone in forensic settings: toxicology. Drugs are closely related to disease—whether they are the cause of it or whether they are taken to contrast it. Toxicology is fundamental for providing details on the drug history of a skeleton and therefore for building the biological profile—although the same cannot and must not be said concerning cause and manner of death.

In some forensic cases, when the body is extremely decomposed and the identity of the person is unknown, further investigations are necessary to implement the biological profile of the individual. These include toxicological analyses, but typical matrices may not be available. Bones, hair, and nails (frequent companions of dry bone), however, may be found after a long postmortem interval depending on taphonomic conditions and be subjected to forensic toxicological analyses (Orfanidis et al., 2018).

Indeed, after heavy metals exposure or the intake of exogenous substances (such as drugs), the bone tissue can store some of the toxicological deposits in a detoxification effort, thus removing a percentage from the bloodstream and reducing their toxicological effects on the other tissues. As the serum concentrations of the toxicological substances decrease, the bone tissue will gradually excrete the stored substances into the bloodstream for their degradation by the body. This

Interpreting Bone Lesions and Pathology for Forensic Practice. DOI: https://doi.org/10.1016/B978-0-323-85162-6.00011-8

detoxification process implies that a fraction of toxicological substances remains trapped inside the bone matrix after exposure and has thus the potential to be detected in bones (Premkumar, 2011; Saladin, 2018). In hair samples, drugs and other exogenous substances can enter and be stored in the hair shaft through at least three mechanisms: absorption from the external environment, from sweat and sebum, or from the deposition in the growing hair shaft, collecting substances from the blood (Kintz, 2004). Nails can incorporate xenobiotics in various ways, including deposition into the root of the growing nail via the blood flow in the nail matrix, incorporation via the nail bed during growth from the lunula to the beginning of the free margin (Palmeri et al., 2000), and potentially through diffusion from biological fluids such as sweat, sebum and saliva (Cappelle et al., 2014).

Detection of Drugs

Together with osteological and pathological analyses of bone remains, toxicological analyses on bones, hair and nails may be performed in order to add further information to the biological profile of the unknown individual. Indeed, toxicological investigations on bones, hair, and nails can permit the detection of drugs of abuse and drugs under medical prescription.

While analyses on bone samples demonstrate an exposure to exogenous substances at some point during life, hair and nails analyses can permit a precise determination of the time of intake prior to death (usually months or even years) (Wilson, 2005). Indeed, the hair shaft has a constant growth rate per month (estimated to about 0.6–1.4 cm/month) that can allow the estimation of the time of the drug assumption (Kintz, 2004). Additionally, nail grow at an average rate of 3.0 mm/month for fingernails and 1.0 mm/month for toenails, with a regeneration time of 3-5 months for fingernails and 8-16 months for toenails (Cappelle et al., 2014).

Drug analyses are not only important in forensic contexts but may also be useful in cases with very long postmortem intervals, as in historical or ancient settings. In fact, such investigations can help the identification of diseases: by evaluating the pathological signs left on bones by diseases and performing toxicological analyses, a disease could be reassociated to a possible medical treatment, corroborating and implementing historical sources (Kepa et al., 2012; Rasmussen et al., 2008). For instance, Kepa et al. (2012) found mercury in bone samples and thus concluded that the detection of mercury may help in the diagnosis of syphilis.

Fortunately, nowadays other drugs are used to treat diseases, and studies have shown that these drugs can be detected in bones immediately after death (Fernandez-Lopez et al., 2019; Horak and Jenkins, 2005; McGrath and Jenkins, 2009; Orfanidis et al., 2018; Raikos et al., 2001; Vardakou et al., 2014), after 1 year (Raikos et al., 2001) or even 7.5 years (Grellner and Glenewinkel, 1997).

There is a paucity of toxicological research in human bone samples from skeletonized remains (Watterson, 2006). The authors have performed toxicological analyses to search drugs in the skeletal remains of the CAL Milano Cemetery Skeletal Collection with a postmortem interval over 23 years. The associated documentation of the individuals selected for the study mentioned either acute intoxication due to psychoactive drugs or drug addiction. Sampling was performed in three sites: cranium, ribs, and vertebrae. In six out of seven individuals of the study sample, drugs were detected and included benzodiazepines (i.e., delorazepam, diazepam, nordiazepam, and lorazepam), benzoylecgonine (i.e., the metabolite of cocaine), buprenorphine, methadone, THCCOOH (i.e., the metabolite of tetrahydrocannabinol (THC)), and methylenedioxyamphetamine (MDA). With the positive results obtained, the suitability of the bone matrix for toxicological analyses after over 23 years of postmortem interval was confirmed. Moreover, an application of the results obtained was the reassociation of the antemortem data to the drugs detected with the analyses. For example, "drug addiction," mentioned in two cases, could be confirmed as methadone was detected in both cases and THCCOOH in one. Indeed, methadone is used to treat opioid addiction and THCCOOH is the metabolite of THC, the active principle of cannabis, another drug of abuse. In the remaining four cases, in which the associated documentation specified "acute intoxication due to psychoactive drugs" (two cases), "suspected overdose" (one case), and "benzodiazepine poisoning" (two cases), the antemortem data could be either directly verified (diazepam, a benzodiazepine, was found in the cases of "benzodiazepine poisoning"); or, when no specific drugs were reported in the antemortem data, toxicological analyses permitted to specify which ones had been taken at some point during life: diazepam, nordiazepam, delorazepam, which are benzodiazepines, MDA (i.e., an amphetamine), buprenorphine (i.e., a derivative opioid), and benzoylecgonine (i.e., the metabolite of cocaine).

Detection of Heavy Metals

In a similar approach, performing toxicological qualitative and quantitative analyses of heavy metals on bones, hair, and nails can provide information about exposure to heavy metals, whether environmental or industrial. In fact, determining exposure to heavy metals can be essential to reconstruct the hypothesis of a chronic intoxication caused by heavy metals, either due to environmental pollution or exposure in the work setting (such as agricultural or industrial works) (Di Candia et al., 2020; López-Costas et al., 2020).

Toxicological analyses of heavy metals can also be useful in the reconstruction of the evolution of atmospheric pollution through time, often related to specific historical events and even health, through the analyses of diet and diseases. The evolution of atmospheric pollution and the reciprocal interaction between the global environment and human activity can be investigated through the analyses of isotopic ratio of heavy metals. Indeed, with the data from natural archives (such as peats, lakes, snow, and ice), a trend of the environmental concentrations of heavy metals throughout time can be developed. Moreover, López-Costas et al. (2020) suggested that human bones can be used as an environmental archive of past atmospheric metal pollution, in which bone samples follow the same trend of heavy metals pollution as natural archives. In addition, the analysis of heavy metals trends can permit the investigation of the migration of individuals from a region with higher geologic background to another or the comparison between individuals who live in zones with different levels of atmospheric pollution (López-Costas et al., 2020).

The pollution of the atmosphere was influenced, over the centuries, by cadmium (Cd), mercury (Hg), and lead (Pb), as a consequence of human activities (Norton, 2007). In fact, studies have shown that lead, copper, iron, and cadmium exposures due to mining and smelting activity can be detected in skeletal remains (Grattan et al., 2002; López-Costas et al., 2020; Martínez-García et al., 2005). The quantification of cadmium remains uncommon due to the low environmental concentration and the substantial mobility of the metal. Instead, mercury and lead are relatively immobile and can record the historic trends of atmospheric deposition to evaluate negative effects on the ecosystem and human health (Norton, 2007).

Surely in the next decades toxicology will add more and more potential to the extrapolation of disease and therapy from dry bone.

Future Perspectives

The future of the study of bone disease lies in interdisciplinarity. To perform reliable diagnoses of disease on dry bone, we need to implement our knowledge on the natural variation of bone manifestations for each condition involving the skeletal system (or causing calcifications that may survive decomposition), to understand their correlation with ancestry, age, and sex, and to integrate comorbidity to our analysis (a concept still largely ignored in bone pathology). This cannot be done just by comparison with the clinical literature and based on archaeological specimens. Our horizons need to be expanded.

Known collections, established throughout the world, can present the idiosyncratic variation of disease manifestations and are a phenomenal resource that can constitute a game-changer in the study of bone disease. Microscopy, and in particular light microscopy, from immunohistochemistry, which may in the future be applicable to dry bone, to scanning electron microscopy, can provide specific information on the etiology of lesions, which is why knowledge of cellular mechanisms in bone disease is essential for bone pathology. Biomolecular techniques, including DNA analysis and proteomics, have the potential to confirm or refute diagnoses, even if no skeletal lesion is macroscopically apparent. Advanced imaging techniques, such as radiology, computed tomography, and 3D reconstructions, can improve our understanding of bone lesions, their starting point, and extension. Toxicology can detect a large range of interesting molecules such as drugs, pesticides, contaminants, and heavy metals. The finding of these substances is useful for reconstructing the lifestyle, drug history, and health of an individual, thus implementing the biological profile. Hence, the potential for examining bone pathology is expanding and will in the next decades surely increase our capacity of adding to the biological profile of skeletons from the near and recent past.

References

Cappelle, D., Yegles, M., Neels, H., van Nuijs, A.L.N., De Doncker, M., Maudens, K., et al., 2014. Nail analysis for the detection of drugs of abuse and pharmaceuticals: a review. Forensic Toxicol. 33, 12–36.

Di Candia, D., Biehler-Gomez, L., Giordano, G., Cattaneo, C., 2020. A case of thallium intoxication by walking in a field. Forensic Sci. Int. Rep. 2, 100102. Available from: http://doi.org/10.1016/j.fsir.2020.100102.

Fernandez-Lopez, L., Luna-Maldonado, A., Falcon, M., Mastrobattista, L., Navarro-Zaragoza, J., Mancini, R., 2019. Development and validation of a gas chromatography–mass spectrometry method for opiates and cocaine in human bone. J. Pharm. Biomed. Anal. 164, 636–641. Available from: https://doi.org/10.1016/j.jpba.2018.11.015.

Grattan, J., Huxley, S., Karaki, A., Toland, H., Gilbertson, D., Pyatt, B., et al., 2002. "Death ... more desirable than life"? The human skeletal record and toxicological implications of ancient copper mining and smelting in Wadi Faynan, southwestern Jordan. Toxicol. Ind. Health 18, 297–307. Available from: https://doi.org/10.1191/0748233702th153oa.

Grellner, W., Glenewinkel, F., 1997. Exhumations: synopsis of morphological and toxicological findings in relation to the postmortem interval: survey on a 20-year period and review of the literature. Forensic Sci. Int. 90, 139–159. Available from: https://doi.org/10.1016/S0379-0738(97)00154-0.

Horak, E.L., Jenkins, A.J., 2005. Postmortem tissue distribution of olanzapine and citalopram in a drug intoxication. J. Forensic Sci. 50, 1–3. Available from: https://doi.org/10.1520/jfs2004067.

Kepa, M., Kozłowski, T., Szostek, K., Drozd, A., Walas, S., Mrowiec, H., et al., 2012. Analysis of mercury levels in historical bone material from syphilitic subjects - pilot studies (short report). Anthropol. Anz. 69, 367–377. Available from: https://doi.org/10.1127/0003-5548/2012/0163.

Kintz, P., 2004. Value of hair analysis in postmortem toxicology. Forensic Sci. Int. 142, 127–134. Available from: https://doi.org/10.1016/j.forsciint.2004.02.027.

López-Costas, O., Kylander, M., Mattielli, N., Álvarez-Fernández, N., Pérez-Rodríguez, M., Mighall, T., et al., 2020. Human bones tell the story of atmospheric mercury and lead exposure at the edge of Roman World. Sci. Total. Environ. 710, 136319. Available from: https://doi.org/10.1016/j.scitotenv.2019.136319.

Martínez-García, M.J., Moreno, J.M., Moreno-Clavel, J., Vergara, N., García-Sánchez, A., Guillamón, A., et al., 2005. Heavy metals in human bones in different historical epochs. Sci. Total. Environ. 348, 51–72. Available from: https://doi.org/10.1016/j.scitotenv.2004.12.075.

McGrath, K.K., Jenkins, A.J., 2009. Detection of drugs of forensic importance in postmortem bone. Am. J. Forensic Med. Pathol. 30, 40–44. Available from: https://doi.org/10.1097/PAF.0b013e31818738c9.

Norton, S.A., 2007. Atmospheric metal pollutants-archives, methods, and history. Water, Air, Soil. Pollut. Focus. 7, 93–98. Available from: https://doi.org/10.1007/s11267-006-9089-3.

Orfanidis, A., Gika, H., Mastrogianni, O., Krokos, A., Theodoridis, G., Zaggelidou, E., et al., 2018. Determination of drugs of abuse and pharmaceuticals in skeletal tissue by UHPLC–MS/MS. Forensic Sci. Int. 290, 137–145. Available from: https://doi.org/10.1016/j.forsciint.2018.07.004.

Palmeri, A., Pichini, S., Pacifici, R., Zuccaro, P., Lopez, A., 2000. Drugs in nails. Physiology, pharmacokinetics and forensic toxicology. Clin. Pharmacokinet. 38, 95–110.

Premkumar, S., 2011. Biology of bone and cartilage. Textbook of Craniofacial Growth. Jaypee Brothers Medical Publisher (P) Ltd, New Delhi, pp. 1–4.

Raikos, N., Tsoukali, H., Njau, S.N., 2001. Determination of opiates in postmortem bone and bone marrow. Forensic Sci. Int. 123, 140–141. Available from: https://doi.org/10.1016/S0379-0738(01)00529-1.

Rasmussen, K.L., Boldsen, J.L., Kristensen, H.K., Skytte, L., Hansen, K.L., Mølholm, L., et al., 2008. Mercury levels in Danish Medieval human bones. J. Archaeol. Sci. 35, 2295–2306. Available from: https://doi.org/10.1016/j.jas.2008.03.003.

Saladin, S., 2018. Bone tissue. Anatomy & Physiology: The Unity of Form and Function. McGraw-Hill, pp. 218–219.

Vardakou, I., Athanaselis, S., Pistos, C., Papadodima, S., Spiliopoulou, C., Moraitis, K., 2014. The clavicle bone as an alternative matrix in forensic toxicological analysis. J. Forensic Leg. Med. 22, 7–9. Available from: https://doi.org/10.1016/j.jflm.2013.11.012.

Watterson, J., 2006. Challenges in forensic toxicology of skeletonised human remains. Analyst 131, 961–965. Available from: https://doi.org/10.1039/b609130j.

Wilson, A.S., 2005. Hair as a bioresource in Archaeological Study. In: Tobin, D.J. (Ed.), Hair in Toxicology: An Important Bio-Monitor. RSC Publishing, Northampton, pp. 321–336.

INDEX

Note: Page numbers followed by "*f*," "*t*," and "*b*" refer to figures, tables, and boxes, respectively.

FSC
www.fsc.org
MIX
Papier | Fördert
gute Waldnutzung
FSC® C083411

Kolibri 360 GmbH
Ferdinand-Jühlke-Straße 7
99095 Erfurt, Deutschland
produktsicherheit@kolibri360.de